D1598097

# The Educational Legacy of Woodrow Wilson

# The Educational Legacy of Woodrow Wilson

## *From College to Nation*

Edited by James Axtell

University of Virginia Press *Charlottesville and London*

University of Virginia Press

Printed in the United States of America on acid-free paper

First published 2012

9 8 7 6 5 4 3 2 1

LIBRARY OF CONGRESS CATALOGING-IN-PUBLICATION DATA
The educational legacy of Woodrow Wilson : from college to nation /
edited by James Axtell.
p. cm.
Includes bibliographical references and index.
ISBN 978-0-8139-3194-4 (cloth : alk. paper) — ISBN 978-0-8139-3211-8 (e-book)
1. Wilson, Woodrow, 1856-1924—Political and social views. 2. Princeton University—Presidents—Biography. 3. Presidents—United States—Biography. I. Axtell, James.
E767.1.E35 2012
973.91′3092—dc23

2011021732

*Frontispiece:* Woodrow Wilson walking to his last Princeton commencement as president of the university in 1910. The following year he assumed the governorship of New Jersey and in 1913 the presidency of the United States. (Princeton University Library)

We must reëxamine the college, reconceive it, reorganize it. It is the root of our intellectual life as a nation.

—WOODROW WILSON

# Contents

# Acknowledgments

Since Gutenberg, the making of books has been a collective enterprise, and this one is no exception. It began with the close collaboration of John Milton Cooper Jr., who proposed a conference, initially at the Woodrow Wilson Presidential Library in Staunton, Virginia, to focus on Wilson's educational ideas and legacy. But John and I soon decided that Princeton University was a more appropriate and accessible setting. After we selected the nine principals, we chose three experts to discuss "Woodrow Wilson in Princeton Today." W. Barksdale Maynard, Edward Tenner, and Princeton Archivist Daniel J. Linke each made memorable and spirited contributions to the conference proceedings.

The conference at Princeton on October 16–17, 2009, would not have been possible without the generous and cheerful assistance of four people. Before she left for the State Department, Anne-Marie Slaughter, then dean of the Woodrow Wilson School of Public and International Affairs, agreed to host and underwrite our gathering in beautiful Robertson Hall, designed by the architect Minoru Yamasaki. Professor Stanley Katz was instrumental in making our case to her. Karyn Olsen, the school's manager of communications, handsomely designed all of our ads and publicity. And Professor Katz's ace assistant, Mindy Weinberg, managed every detail of planning and execution with consummate grace and efficiency. We are sincerely grateful to them all.

The conference was and the resulting book is equally beholden, as are all students of Wilson, to Arthur Link's 69-volume *Papers of Woodrow Wilson,* published by Princeton University Press. This model of documentary editing not only inspired our collective researches but also made our work much easier and extremely pleasant.

By the same token, we are grateful to Princeton for other courtesies. President Shirley Tilghman opened the conference with an articulate and heartfelt appreciation of Wilson's impact on the university she now leads. The frontispiece photograph of her historic predecessor was provided by the University Archives, Department of Rare Books and Special Collections, Princeton University Library. I am personally grateful to the Princeton Department of History and to Associate Dean of the College Peter Quimby for allowing me to teach a graduate seminar and a freshman seminar on the history of Princeton during the semester the conference was held.

Finally, we would have no book had editor Richard Holway, the University of Virginia Press, and two anonymous readers not believed in its scholarly merit. That Woodrow Wilson was born just down the road in Staunton and attended UVA's law school makes its publication in Charlottesville all the more appropriate and satisfying. We are also grateful for the careful editing, design, and production of the book provided by the Press, just as we are to Nadine Zimmerli for technical assistance in the manuscript's preparation and to Jacqueline Kinghorn Brown for eagle-eyed copyediting.

# The Educational Legacy of Woodrow Wilson

# Introduction

James Axtell

Woodrow Wilson needs no introduction. As the twenty-eighth president of the United States, his is a household name, and his top-ten, often top-seven, ranking by historians and political scientists is well established. But he is also the object of much misunderstanding and sharply divided opinion. A highly effective leader and agent of change, he also possessed a complex personality, sporadically affected by ill health, that was often hard to read or to love. Scholars have endlessly scoured and dissected his political career as governor of New Jersey (1911–13) and president of the United States (1913–21), but the general public often draws a blank when asked to cite his accomplishments. In polls he places well down the list of great American leaders, even though his progressive legislation, foreign policies, and handling of the First World War and subsequent peace paved the way for Franklin Delano Roosevelt, who consistently ranks as one of the top three presidents in both scholarly and public polls.

Less well known is the fact that Wilson was one of the most influential educators of his time, one whose influence is still seen and felt in American higher education. Before he entered politics, he was one of the country's leading political scientists and historians. A Ph.D. from Johns Hopkins University (1886), he was elected president of both the American Political Science Association (1910) and, in retirement, the American Historical Association (1924). Somewhat better known is his association with Princeton University, where he was usually voted the most popular professor by the students between 1890 and 1902 and which he profoundly transformed as its president between 1902 and 1910. Yet his long academic career, including a year and a half of legal study at the University of Virginia (1879–80) and teaching stints at Bryn Mawr College (1885–88) and Wesleyan University (1888–90), has always been overshadowed by his comparatively brief occupation of the White House, even though his unlikely and rapid rise from professor to U.S. president was unprecedented and remains unique.

The disparity of attention to Wilson's two careers is measured by the 4,216 items in a comprehensive but admittedly incomplete Wilson bibliography of publications to 1994.[1] Of the 3,900 books and articles about Wilson, roughly 7 percent were devoted to his formative years and educational career (80 percent of his 67 years) and 93 percent covered in exhausting detail his political career, just 20 percent of his life. Since 1994, the proportions of published attention to Wilson have remained the same, reinforced in large measure by the completion that year of, and allocation of space in, Arthur S. Link's monumental edition of *The Papers of Woodrow Wilson;* 22 of 69 volumes cover his life to 1910. Indeed, Wilson himself urged later generations not to lavish too much attention on his political career. Just weeks before his death, he told Raymond Fosdick, a former student and an officer of the Rockefeller Foundation's General Education Board, that he realized "his contribution to his generation—if he had made any—was in connection not so much with his political work as with his activities as a teacher and college administrator."[2]

The time seems right to honor that plea. Three recent books began to redress the imbalance by addressing Wilson's academic career anew and its connection with his subsequent public life: W. Barksdale Maynard's feisty *Woodrow Wilson: Princeton to the Presidency* (2008), my *The Making of Princeton University: From Woodrow Wilson to the Present* (2006), and John Milton Cooper Jr.'s magnum opus, *Woodrow Wilson: A Biography* (2009). These books prompted John Cooper and me to invite some of the best junior and senior scholars in the field to gather in Princeton to reconsider Wilson's educational legacy, not only at Princeton but nationally as well. Through the good offices of Professor Stanley N. Katz, the Woodrow Wilson School of Public Policy and International Affairs at Princeton generously sponsored and hosted the conference in Minoru Yamasaki's soaring Robertson Hall in October 2009.

A Woodrow Wilson Presidential Library conference on race and democracy in Staunton, Virginia, Wilson's birthplace, and a conference held at the Woodrow Wilson International Center for Scholars in Washington, D.C., on the 150th anniversary of Wilson's birth resulted in noteworthy published reappraisals of Wilson.[3] We decided to follow suit and asked each contributor to first write a substantial scholarly essay for a book and then to reduce its essence for oral presentation at the conference. For the most part, we did not assign our authors specific topics, though we counted on their known interests and expertise to provide broad coverage and scholarly surprises. On both counts they exceeded all our expectations.

The resulting book examines the central role that Wilson played in the evolution of American higher education at a critical turning point in its maturation. While he was influenced by his experiences at Johns Hopkins, the University of Virginia, Bryn Mawr, and Wesleyan, Princeton gave him a national platform. He used it to make American educators rethink the direction of higher education and to raise the standard over a new kind of institution, a self-conscious blend of liberal arts college and research university. The first four essays treat the Wilsonian remodeling and elevation of Princeton to national prominence as the leading "liberal university." They address the steady and coherent evolution of Wilson's educational philosophy and policies and his contemporary reputation as the most innovative, quotable, and newsworthy American college president in the first quarter—perhaps the first half—of the twentieth century.

In my opening essay, I argue that Wilson not only led Princeton through major reforms to full university status but also led the presidents of Harvard and Yale in resisting contemporary trends toward vocationalism, bigness, and scientific-technological research, by asserting the signal importance of residential undergraduate education, personalized teaching, the liberal arts and sciences, and higher education for national service broadly conceived. He was the architect of Princeton's enduring educational philosophy of selective excellence, modest size, curricular coherence, limited professional education, and social-academic coordination, which all of his successors—to a man and woman—have honored.[4] Thereafter, Princeton served as a model, as it still does today, of a great but atypical American research university.

In the second essay, Adam Nelson plots a subtle but important shift in Wilson's thinking about the need for Princeton (and other universities) to broaden their notion of education "in" and "for the nation's service." Wilson regarded liberal education as a form of statesmanship for American democracy. But after America's seizure of Puerto Rico, Guam, and the Philippines from Spain in 1898, he increasingly called upon higher education to produce graduates with aptitudes for global leadership. This shift was marked by tension between his firm belief that a nation could best be characterized and known not by specialized, technical, "universalistic" science, but by its particular history and literature. This led him to reject German university influences, but to emphasize that American higher education had to be more international in scope and competitive quality, by cultivating an "international statesmanship of mind" through the liberal arts and sciences.

In the third essay, John Thelin demonstrates that Princeton, despite its relatively small size, income, and faculty, merited its membership in the Association of American Universities. The AAU was the elite club of fifteen major universities that had been formed in 1900 to raise and somewhat standardize the quality of American universities in order to earn the respect of, and the admission of their graduates to, Europe's best universities. Among the founding giants and leaders of these American institutions, such as Charles W. Eliot of Harvard, William Rainey Harper of Chicago, and Benjamin Ide Wheeler of California, Wilson was an equal who, like them, exercised political as well as educational clout, drew on new sources of philanthropy, and consciously used publicity to fuel his institution's rise.

Among Wilson's rhetorical devices was the invocation of Oxford and Cambridge to support his initiatives. Bruce Leslie's essay analyzes the sources and manifestations of the fin de siècle Anglophilia that permeated Princeton and increasingly gave it its distinct look and feel. Both Wilson and his eventual rival, classicist Andrew Fleming West, dean of the new Graduate School, were incurably romantic fans of Oxford and Cambridge's Tudor Gothic architecture and sought to translate it to Princeton's growing campus. Both also sought to borrow certain academic features from "Oxbridge," such as tutorials, residential quadrangles, and honors programs. Each chose selectively, and in their later battle over locating the residential Graduate College both invoked Oxbridge. In calculating the significance of Anglophilia in Wilson's educational beliefs, Leslie examines the quality of Wilson's understanding and suggests that his use of an Oxbridge model shifted as American higher education and Princeton matured.

In her essay, Victoria Bissell Brown analyzes Wilson's attitudes toward women and their higher education. In the first decade of the twentieth century, when 60 percent of American colleges and universities were coeducational and women comprised 40 percent of all college enrollments, Wilson remained adamantly opposed to coeducation, although he had no objection to higher education for his three daughters and other women in single-sex institutions. Education was perfectly acceptable for women as long as it served men's interests and protected male dominance. His artistic wife, Ellen, with whom he was passionately in love, concurred with her "romantic, androcentric, conservative" partner, as Brown puts it. Their three early years at all-female Bryn Mawr, under the daunting deanship of M. Carey Thomas, did much to solidify their views. Their next two years at technically coeducational Wesleyan University (only 15 of its 200 students were women) made them even more eager to return to Princeton's all-male campus. There Wilson could champion the humanities, particularly literature, without fear of having them "feminized." Attitudes such as these colored his whole adult life, including its political phase, even after he was persuaded to support the enfranchisement of women.

The last three essays are devoted to the seamless nexus between Wilson's educational ideas and experience and his political thinking and policies. John Cooper reverses the usual trajectory of analysis by arguing that Wilson's early interest in politics and his outstanding career as a political scientist informed his *educational* career, particularly as president of Princeton. Wilson was an expert in public administration, or *practical* politics, and a keen student of congressional and parliamentary government. When he became president of Princeton, he saw himself as a "prime minister" who operated through "common counsel" (*informed* discussion) with his trustee (and decanal) cabinet, faculty backbenchers, and alumni constituents; students were not yet a political force to be reckoned with. After his predecessor's stonewalling laxity, Wilson sought to exercise firm leadership by taking from the trustees control of faculty hiring, development, organization, and firing, and then leading the revitalized faculty in major reforms of the curriculum and bringing control of the autonomous Graduate School under presidential authority. He was stymied in his reforms only after four years of brilliant success by overconfidence and a possible stroke that rendered him at times impatient and imperious. Overall, his academic experience, informed as it was by a deep study of politics and his sometimes bruising experience of academic infighting, was excellent training for his subsequent political career

Mark Nemec argues that Wilson ranks high on the list of major-university presidents who forged strong university-state connections in the late nineteenth and early twentieth centuries. Wilson's eloquence ("persuasion inspired by Conviction") served best to legitimate the conception of American universities in service to the national *state*, not just the government. Because higher-educational institutions structure ideas and define expertise, the presidents of the Association of American Universities in particular regarded their institutions as extensions of the state, in lieu of a single national university. They sought not only to train graduates for government service and to apply learned expertise to national problems but also to produce a national intelligentsia, the equivalent of a secular "church." The United States, they believed, must lead the world in industry, arts, politics, and, not least, higher education. In times of war, universities were expected to play an even more direct role by training both students, as the Student Army Training Corps did, and military personnel, as the Princeton faculty did, in Mr. Wilson's War.

In the final essay, Trygve Throntveit carefully analyzes Wilson's own education for domestic and international politics. In practicing on the public stage the active mode of leadership he had fashioned at Princeton, Wilson continued to be guided by several principles. As an inductive historian, he knew that human affairs were contingent, not determined; local; motivated more by practicality and self-interest than by doctrine; morally relative; constantly in motion but slow to change. He regarded the state, like the university, as "organic," efficiently integrated and the product of self-government and informed public discussion. As always, he regarded political leaders, including political parties, as educators, who divined the will of the people but also educated them in the need for progressive change. Wilsonian Princeton was reformed to produce (white, male) leaders for national service, but they would be selected through meritocratic, egalitarian criteria consonant with American democratic principles. He carried these political precepts from Princeton to the White House with scarcely any amendment, except what experience, that hard teacher, dictated.

To end this book, Stan Katz, historian and longtime professor at the Woodrow Wilson School, looks at Wilson not in hindsight but in a spirited prognostication of what the former president might now think of his alma mater after a century of change and growth. Since it is impossible to read minds, even one as fully documented as Wilson's, with complete clarity or objectivity, we are treated to some of Stan's personal predilections along the way. This is all to the good because he knows Princeton well and has had an affectionate but clear-eyed engagement with the town and university since 1978. Many of his essays and blogs for the *Chronicle of Higher Education* have taken Princeton to task for not living up to Wilson's and its own ideals. Thus Stan's thoughts end this historical treatment of Wilson's educational thinking and policies with the useful reminder that, although his legacy has been rich and surprisingly enduring, he could not dictate the future direction his own university would take under different leaders, however respectful they were of his seminal role.

NOTES

1. John M. Mulder, Ernest M. White, and Ethel S. White, comp., *Woodrow Wilson: A Bibliography* (Westport, Conn.: Greenwood Press, 1997).

2. See James Axtell, "The Bad Dream: Woodrow Wilson on Princeton—After Princeton," *Princeton University Library Chronicle*, 69:3 (Spring 2008), 400–36 at 433–34.

3. John Milton Cooper Jr. and Thomas J. Knock, eds., *Jefferson, Lincoln, and Wilson: The American Dilemma of Race and Democracy* (Charlottesville: University of Virginia Press, 2010); Cooper, ed., *Reconsidering Woodrow Wilson: Progressivism, Internationalism, War, and Peace* (Washington, D.C.: Woodrow Wilson Center Press and Baltimore: Johns Hopkins University Press, 2008).

4. In opening the conference, President Shirley Tilghman emphasized that she particularly admired Wilson's emphasis on making Princeton a serious intellectual place renowned for preprofessional liberal arts and sciences and being "vertically integrated" from freshman to president, partly through the use of residential campus housing, including four-year colleges or "quads" envisioned by Wilson.

# The Educational Vision of Woodrow Wilson

James Axtell

Before being elected governor of New Jersey and president of the United States, Woodrow Wilson was indisputably the most eloquent, influential, and perhaps controversial American university president in the first quarter—and arguably the first half—of the twentieth century. In leading Princeton to full university status and prominence between 1902 and 1910, he produced large numbers of polished and often witty speeches and writings on academic reform that generated as much national news and serious rethinking on other campuses as they did amazement and, eventually, alarm on his own. The boldness of his leadership and the imaginative consistency of his thinking made him the spokesman for liberal arts colleges and universities that sought to buck the era's trends toward unplanned growth, curricular chaos, extracurricular excess, and myopic vocationalism. For all their historical importance, those same qualities make him a surprisingly relevant guide for our own perplexed thinking about the goals and policies of higher education.

When Wilson became president of Princeton in 1902, he had been thinking about higher education for a long time. As a graduate student of politics and history at Johns Hopkins in the early 1880s, he scoffed at the new institution's genuflections before the altar of German "research" and complained about the aridity and factualism of his professors' teaching and scholarship. In his first appointment at nascent Bryn Mawr, he lamented his (female) students' passivity in lecture classes and his (mostly male) associates' tepid interest in his favorite subjects, politics and government. After a short breather at still small, congenially masculine, though officially coed Wesleyan, he returned in 1890 to Princeton, his more "cultured" and "progressive" alma mater.[1] There he helped forge the college's soon-proclaimed identity as a university and sang, mostly sotto voce, in the growing chorus of opposition to its feckless leader and stunted academic development.

By 1897 at the latest, a year after delivering the keynote address at the new university's sesquicentennial celebrations, he had substantially outlined what he would do if he were, as he said, "the autocrat of Princeton."[2] When unexpectedly he acquired the presidency and a mandate for change from the trustees five years later, he launched reforms of the faculty, the curriculum, teaching, and college life in an attempt to elevate Princeton's reputation from one of the best American colleges to the best university "of its kind."[3]

During Wilson's eight years at the Princeton helm, he thought hard, wrote copiously, and spoke frequently about Princeton's problems and opportunities, as well as about politics, current affairs, culture, literature, religion, and history. By his final commencement in 1910, he had given at least 57 talks to alumni groups and 180 public lectures. He had also published 17 articles (3 more remained in a drawer) and a book. Extensive newspaper coverage of his public and even intramural appearances drew additional attention to his bold thinking and campus controversies.[4] By the summer of 1910, the *New York Times* had mentioned Wilson in articles, editorials, or book advertisements 190 times; in 90 of these, his or Princeton's name featured in the headline. Eleven of the articles, many of the lectures, and virtually all of the alumni talks were devoted to higher education, but not narrowly so. Although many addressed Princeton topics for Princeton audiences, others were aimed at listeners and issues at other institutions. Still others took wing from Princeton concerns but then rose to prescriptive heights over a host of academic ailments widely shared.

When Wilson's analytical frame of mind turned local questions into broad answers, wide media attention to his often striking ideas and uncommon eloquence and wit gave his prescriptions—for what a later Princeton dean called the "liberal university"—greater exposure than the analyses of any other presidential spokesman in his day.[5] At a time when the "Big Three"—Harvard, Yale, and Princeton—were renewing their leases on the top spots in academic prestige and Columbia was making a conscious bid for national attention, Wilson's three closest presidential contemporaries—Arthur Twining Hadley of Yale, A. Lawrence Lowell of Harvard, and Nicholas Murray Butler of Columbia—could not rival his command of both the literate public's and the academy's attention. Even during much longer terms, none of the three faced—or created—high-stakes controversies on their campuses the way Wilson did, in part because none of them sought to effect reforms as major as his or as quickly.

Wilson was able to generate news in part because Princeton had further to go to become a university of *any* kind. Simply changing its name four years before it even had a graduate school was not enough to convince skeptics that it had changed its collegiate stripes. And admission to founding membership in the elite Association of American Universities in 1900 was bestowed more as recognition of Princeton's long social pedigree and academic *promise* than of achieved university status.[6] By contrast, Charles W. Eliot had decisively moved Harvard to that level well before the turn of the century, though some of its developments needed attention or curbing by the time Lowell, Wilson's friend and admirer, succeeded Eliot in 1909.[7] Columbia under Seth Low had also grown willy-nilly to fit the emerging American pattern of professional- and graduate-school dominance, faculty emphasis on research, curricular incoherence, and inattention to undergraduate education; Butler's ascendance in 1902 did little to stop or ameliorate it.[8] At least Yale, in a condition similar to Columbia's, after Timothy Dwight's conservative management had the good sense to appoint political economist Arthur Twining Hadley as his successor late in 1899. Adroitly and gradually, Hadley instituted policies and procedures that capitalized on Yale's considerable assets, seeking, in general, to make a "better, not bigger Yale" to serve as a truly "national university"—goals that complemented those being pursued simultaneously in Princeton.[9]

The differential magnitude of the challenges that Wilson and his peers faced, and the tenor and tenacity of their respective responses, dictated the amount of serious ink and attention they received nationally. During his 44-year tenure, the entrepreneurial and self-promoting Nicholas Murray Butler commanded more copy, particularly in New York papers, and published more words than Wilson, but he had less of importance to say and he said it much less well. In the same eight-year span as Wilson's, Butler was mentioned in 303 articles in the *New York Times,* mostly in connection with the reform of football, the Carnegie Foundation for the Advancement of Teaching (which he chaired), personal honors, travel, and social appearances; attention to higher educational issues beyond Columbia was conspicuously rare. Although Butler edited the *Educational Review* for nearly three decades and published numerous articles in popular and professional publications, Laurence Veysey has concluded that "no other prominent academic executive said less of significance or conviction about what either the college or the university should be. Butler simply was not a figure in the intellectual history of American higher education."[10]

The presidents of the Big Three made a much bigger impact on educational thinking than Butler did because their ideas for reform were, as Lowell assured Wilson, "very much alike" and they stood solidly against the prevailing views of the other members of the Association of American Universities, some of which were large state universities in the West and Midwest, where scientific and technological research, professional education, and bigness were the names of the game.[11] These three exact contemporaries—all born in 1856—were also friends even before they climbed into their presidential bully-pulpits and presented a united front in the (largely northeastern) cause to save the American university for liberal education and culture.[12]

Wilson had long assigned Lowell's books on government in his classes, and the two experts sparred amicably over the state of the field. When Lowell was chosen to lead Harvard, Wilson conferred on him an honorary Princeton degree and wrote warmly of anticipating future meetings in which he might often "enjoy the benefit of comparing views with you and of drawing thoughtful counsel from you." These occasions, Wilson was certain, would "draw us"—institutions and presidents—"even closer together than we have been in the past."[13] Lowell reciprocated by inviting Wilson to deliver the Phi Beta Kappa oration at the 1909 Harvard commencement (Eliot had already given him a degree) and to deliver a paper representing the Big Three's view on the importance of the preprofessional arts curriculum at the next meeting of the AAU.[14] Lowell also approved Princeton's preceptorial system in his inaugural address and by dispatching a dean to Princeton to study it, and he implicitly endorsed Wilson's prescription of residential colleges or "quads" to bridge what Lowell deemed "the chasm that has opened between college studies and college life."[15]

In the spring of 1910, as Wilson's deteriorating relations with alumni and trustees threatened to end his presidency, Lowell offered to plead Wilson's cause with anyone who might prevent what he called the looming "catastrophe for Princeton" and "a very grave misfortune for the whole cause of American college education." When Wilson was nominated for the governorship of New Jersey in September, Lowell wished him every success but rued a Wilson victory because it would remove "one of the main stays of the progressive college education" movement.[16] It did, but Lowell continued to support his friend in Wilson's national campaign in 1912 and in his fight for the League of Nations. His close adaptation of Wilson's blueprint in creating a system of concentration and distribution, tougher academic standards, tutors to guide student reading, and residential "houses" to democratize college life was perhaps his sincerest compliment to Wilson. As he told a meeting of the Association of American Colleges in 1931, Wilson was "the first college president who tried to remedy the real defect of the American college, the fact that the students in the main have not taken their education seriously."[17]

Arthur Hadley's friendship with Wilson began about the same time Lowell's did, in the late 1890s. As one of Yale's smartest and most versatile professors, Hadley had trained Yale's debating teams for their classic contests with Harvard and Princeton by analyzing "the various arguments to be developed by the opponents in the light of the personality of the debating coaches on the other team," in Princeton's case, the sui generis but readable Professor Wilson.[18] When Hadley was inaugurated in 1899, Wilson was one of four Princeton representatives at the ceremonies. Two years later, when Yale celebrated its bicentennial, Wilson—not yet a president himself—was given an honorary Litt.D. degree.[19] Four months later, Wilson and Hadley shared another platform at the installation of Johns Hopkins' new president, Ira Remsen. Both received honorary degrees: Hadley's citation spoke of him as "one of the strongest and most brilliant of this strong and brilliant company" of twenty-three honorees; former Hopkins lecturer Wilson was acknowledged as a "writer and speaker of grace and force" whom Hopkins "would gladly enroll . . . as a professor of historical and political science." The relative future weight of these two friendly rivals must have been obvious to all when "the name most cheered" all day was Wilson's. Led by a vocal row of former Hopkins students, "the applause continued unbroken for nearly five minutes" and resumed when Wilson, clearly touched, rose and bowed.[20]

When Wilson himself was inaugurated eight months later, Hadley represented Yale near the head of the procession of institutions (ordered by date of founding) and was invited to a special luncheon at Wilson's home. Although the meal was rushed in order to catch the Columbia football game, it did nothing to diminish Hadley's regard for the reliable "clearness of vision" of his "old and trusted friend."[21] As their presidencies overlapped, the first lay executives of their respective institutions seemed to be rowing in the same direction, though Yale's greater size and complexity prompted Hadley to plan more patiently for "evolution rather than revolution." Without increasing the student population, he, too, sought to raise standards in the undergraduate college, centralize administration, abolish "undemocratic" student societies, increase endowment, buck up faculty quality and rewards, build according to a coherent architectural plan, create academic departments, remodel the curriculum, tame intercollegiate sports, shore up the graduate school and science, and emphasize the university's ultimate purpose to be the liberal education of leaders for "the Service of the Nation."[22]

Not only did the "Three" presidents have similar "progressive" agendas—some of which, in light of national academic trends, might have been seen as "reactionary," a sly description of his plans that Wilson used on occasion—they wrote and spoke a good deal about them to a variety of large audiences. All published frequently, and their talks were reported more so, in their respective alumni magazines.[23] Like Wilson, Hadley and Lowell gave annual baccalaureate sermons, but, unlike Wilson, they delivered enough of them to collect and publish them in book form.[24] They, too, like Wilson, wrote lengthy annual reports, which often addressed academic problems well beyond their own campuses. All were thought sufficiently important to be printed, and indeed were sent to and read by officials at peer and aspiring institutions.[25] Taking office nearly three years before Wilson, Hadley also reached beyond the Yale campus to speak broadly on academic issues to national audiences. During his first eight years in office (comparable to Wilson's whole term), he published 23 articles in mainstream and professional periodicals.[26] Yet, for all his efforts, he merited only 20 mentions in the *New York Times* during his coterminous tenure with Wilson, who drew nearly ten times as many. Perhaps because Lowell did not assume office until Wilson had been in his presidency and the national limelight for seven eventful years, Lowell did no better during his first eight years: he, too, earned only 20 mentions in the *Times,* mostly in reference to sports reform. It may not have helped that he tended to address Harvard constituencies largely through Harvard or New England publications; such messages understandably received more generous coverage in Boston papers.[27] Apparently, after Eliot's long and newsworthy reign, it was assumed that if Harvard spoke, even in local whispers, the nation would listen.[28]

Wilson drew more press coverage and academic attention, not only because he had more progressive plans for his more conservative institution than either Hadley or Lowell, but also because he was in a bigger hurry to implement them, particularly after suffering a frightening cerebrovascular incident or stroke in 1906, only halfway through what he called his "fight for the restoration of Princeton."[29] When medical specialists deemed his condition so serious that he might have to retire to prevent further damage, he felt the urgency of the academic struggle he was in and the need to push his plans forward before it was too late.[30] The incident also breathed fire into his already winning words, which in turn provided combustible copy for his opponents among the alumni and trustees and hot news for the national press. Wilson's two friendly rivals in New Haven and Cambridge could never compete in the publicity race because he wrote—and spoke—better than both.

Hadley, the Yale- and German-trained authority on the economics of railroads, wrote clear, sensible, quite abstract, and utterly bland prose, which easily fled from memory and elicited a smile only inadvertently. The titles of his three collections of miscellaneous writings—*The Education of the American Citizen, The Moral Basis of Democracy,* and *Education and Government*—were as uninspired as most of their contents.

Because of Lowell's long career in the law, his style was as precise, logical, and informed as Hadley's, but it was sprightlier, more idiomatic, and more fluid. Lowell had some of Wilson's flair for memorable phrases, well-chosen illustrations, and witty quotations. Like Wilson, he knew how to reify his abstractions, even if he seldom equaled the passionate Princeton crusader in breathing life into them through appeals to the readers' emotions as well as their intellects.[31] At least he knew how to draw readers to his collected writings with a feisty title, *At War with Academic Traditions in America,* which Wilson might have chosen for his own favorites had he not been preoccupied with running New Jersey and then the nation.

Perhaps the best measure of Wilson's quality as an educational theorist is the surprisingly fresh relevance and durable power of his thought. As he entered the literary lists for the first time as an educator, his imagination, verbal dexterity, and passionate idealism suffused his writing and speeches with a combination of vision and vitality that won over academic recruits and large alumni gatherings with equal ease. Wilson always liked challenges, and taking Princeton to a new level of institutional excellence was as inspiring as it was daunting. Halfway through writing his inaugural address in July 1902, Wilson admitted to his wife Ellen, with some playfully false modesty, that "I never worked out the argument on liberal studies . . . before, never before having treated myself as a professional 'educator,' and so the matter is not stale but fresh and interesting. I am quite straightening out my ideas!"[32] But he knew that much had to be done to reform Princeton and that it was "impossible yet to plan it wisely all the way through." The best course, he told ally and trustee David B. Jones a month later, was to "make our general purpose distinct to ourselves, and the outline of the means by which we mean to seek its attainment, and then attack the details one at a time." The general outlines he found "forming in [his] mind with a good deal of definiteness and certainty" because, he revealed, "we have so long talked them over in a little circle in Princeton that they are easily compounded out of common counsel."[33]

Wilson was wise to plan carefully and not to rush headlong into grand new plans and policies of his own making. One reason is that he knew, from seventeen years of personal experience, that faculties jealously guarded their academic prerogatives and needed to be major players in any important changes. Another is that his philosophy matured during his eight years in office. A year after he had moved to the governor's office in Trenton, David Jones gently reminded him that "when you were elected to the presidency of Princeton you were somewhat mediaevally inclined in the cause of education," in danger of sounding like a curricular mossback. In 1900 Wilson had admitted as much to his old friend and Hopkins classmate, Frederick Jackson Turner. Expressing his suspicions of the University of Chicago's academic "fads" and undignified "hustling," Wilson confessed that "I am very old fashioned and conservative," something his sesquicentennial remarks on the excesses of science had suggested four years earlier.[34] But Jones also noted that Wilson "very soon saw that in education, as well as in politics, we had passed into another time, and that if one could not be in a conservative sense a progressive, one would have to be a reactionary."[35]

If Wilson's progress was much faster than that of some of his academic constituents, it was largely because he was quicker to recognize that America had "entered upon a new age in the development of [its] universities," and that Princeton needed to change in significant, perhaps unsettling, ways if it wanted not only to stay in the game but to take the lead in liberal academic reform as well.[36] As his tenure at Princeton was coming to an end, he told the Princeton Club of New York, whose nostalgic, club-conscious members had become some of his most vocal opponents, "The traditions of no American university fit the future development of universities in this country, Princeton not excluded. . . . We must make ourselves, therefore, conscious trustees of aspirations rather than traditions, even though we change Princeton radically and begin an utterly new tradition. . . . For other universities," he informed them, no doubt thinking—and making them think—of Lowell's Harvard and Hadley's Yale, "have seen the light as [Princeton] has seen it and have started in her direction," which he assured them was "a process of integration and growth . . . so far . . . unique in the history of education in this country." "The choice," he said, "is not whether we will form part of the procession but which part . . . the van or the rear." But, he warned, "When you have once taken up the torch of leadership you cannot lay it down without extinguishing it."[37]

Laying it down was the furthest thing from his mind when he took it up in 1902. With eager support from faculty, trustees, and alumni, he had a mandate to overcome Princeton's proud complacency and soon had a coherent plan that would involve them all in his high aspirations for the university. At the outset, he appealed to their various competitive spirits by showing how far Princeton had slipped from the top of the academic pecking order. In his first report to the trustees, and in many faculty meetings and alumni talks thereafter, he minced no words: "There was a time when Harvard, Yale, and Princeton was the list in everyone's mouth when the leading colleges of the country were spoken of; but since the greater colleges were transformed into universities Princeton had fallen out of the list. At least when academics speak; and they must be the ultimate judges. Persons who stand outside academic circles still speak of Harvard, Yale, and Princeton together," he conceded, "but those who are informed know that Princeton has not kept pace with the others in university development, and that while she has lingered, other, newer, institutions, like Columbia, the Johns Hopkins, and the University of Chicago have pressed in ahead of her." In such a situation, Wilson thought, Princeton had only two possible courses of action: "Either we may withdraw from the university competition"—which he was confident "no true Princeton man would seriously consider for a moment"—"or we must find money enough to make Princeton in fact a great university." The sum required he estimated to be $12.5 million, more than three times the current endowment.[38]

The smaller half of that awesome amount would simply level the academic playing field and meet the university's moral obligations to the public who read its catalogue. The Princeton library had too few books; the science labs were too few and under-equipped; classrooms were at a premium; the faculty was too small and underpaid. Its weakest departments—history, economics, and biology—had a total of only 9 faculty; at Harvard and Yale the same departments had 44 and 21 respectively. The larger half of Wilson's request was sought for Princeton's loftier future: to re-endow and reorganize an infant school of electrical engineering and to build from scratch a residential college for the Graduate School, a school of jurisprudence (not a conventional law school for practitioners), and a museum of natural history to anchor the biological sciences.[39]

Yet among the nuts and bolts, beakers and books, on the first list was a line item for "Fifty tutorships at $45,000 each—$2,250,000," preceded by a short diagnosis of Princeton's troubled curriculum. The root of the problem was that Princeton, like Harvard, Yale, and most other American universities, had seen "remarkable growth" in the last thirty years, "almost in spite of us," Wilson conceded, "and in ways which sometimes seem independent of our control." This resulted in "miscellaneous enlargement" rather than "systematic development," a multiplication of "uncoördinated" courses and incoherence.[40] Moreover, the dominant modes of teaching—lectures and recitations—led to student passivity or boredom, which in turn led to mental laxity, mischief, and an eager search for *extra*curricular engagement.

To Wilson's mind, all this called for "a radical change of method," a shift of emphasis from faculty *teaching* to student *learning*. Students should be expected "to get and to take, not to receive," because he was convinced, from experience and principle, that "the only study that ever does anybody any good is the study that he does for himself, and not the study that the teacher does for him."[41] This kind of learning went on routinely in science labs, but students in the "reading subjects"—philosophy, English, history, politics, economics—were denied the same opportunities for self-discovery and mastery. "University men," Wilson thought, "should be made to get up *subjects*, not lectures, for examination,—and to get them up for themselves." Exams should cover whole subjects, each prepared from "a library of books" rather than lifted from a textbook or a purchased set of lecture notes. Wilson's plan still allowed for drill work in elementary mathematics and foreign languages. However, lectures would have to be rewritten, not to convey more information, but to highlight the contours and significance of broad fields and the absorbing questions they could pose, or to model "the zest and the method of exact enquiry."[42]

To help turn the students into "reading and thinking men," Wilson proposed to add to the faculty 45–50 serious and competent young scholars as "tutors," "superintendents," "coaches," and "companions" of the juniors' and seniors' reading. In weekly meetings in their offices or homes with small groups of students, the tutors would suggest (not mandate) and discuss supplementary course reading, oral reports, and essay topics, but they would not quiz or examine, leaving those tasks to the course lecturers. The tutors would serve for no more than five years, to preserve freshness and to encourage their advancement up the professorial ladder. Securing this cadre of tutors was, he was certain, "our central and immediate need." He was also willing to wager that fifty of them "would do more to make educated men out of our students than fifty full professors . . . who did nothing but lecture to large classes."[43]

It was a bet that paid off handsomely for Princeton. With funds raised largely by a Committee of Fifty wealthy trustees and alumni, Wilson was able to hire forty-five preceptors in 1905 alone. (The new name *preceptors* came from similar coaches at the Inns of Court in London and was chosen to avoid any association with the hired tutors in American cram schools.)[44] This influx of talent had several newsworthy results. Thanks to Wilson's persuasive eloquence and charisma, it deprived twenty-five other institutions of thirty-seven of their most promising young scholars. Partly by dropping the student-faculty ratio from 12:1 to 7:1, it promoted an unusual degree of intellectual closeness between teachers and taught. This, in turn, led to a requickening of academic excitement that spilled over after class, even in table talk in the studiously unacademic eating clubs.[45] It also garnered Princeton publicity that money alone could not buy. In North America, an eyewitness recalled, "probably nothing since the founding of Johns Hopkins University had attracted such far and wide attention to things purely educational." Abroad, favorable media coverage reached as far as Africa and the Middle East. Eventually, the plan was borrowed by other colleges and universities. But, as President Hadley of Yale complained good-naturedly, none could do so immediately because "Princeton had already got all the best preceptors in the country."[46]

The advent of the unsystematic preceptorial system also brought Princeton longer-range rewards. As late as 1919, it was thought by many to have given Princeton its "greatest advantage over every other college in America."[47] It did so less because of its pedagogical novelty and bold common sense, as pronounced as those were, than because it brought to the faculty a large number of outstanding scholar-teachers whose quick promotion to full professorial status moved Princeton up several notches in academic reputation both during and long after Wilson's presidency.[48] "It was [the quality of] these new men who revolutionized Princeton," a distinguished Harvard historian and former preceptor argued in 1940, rather than the "machinery" of the system itself.[49] As even its presidential architect admitted after five years, the system had "accomplished no revolution in human nature" and left several problems to be solved.[50]

Before Wilson could augment the faculty by a third, he knew he had to reorganize it and to modernize the curriculum. These fundamental and quiet tasks were prerequisites for Princeton's more newsworthy reform efforts. That he accomplished both in less than two years, the first after a deft handling of the board of trustees, the second through full and "common counsel" with the faculty, contrasts with his later (post-stroke) reputation for stubbornness, impatience, and autocracy.

Before Wilson's advent, Princeton faculty members dealt directly with President Francis Landey Patton ("King Log"), a quick thinker and brilliant preacher but a notoriously poor administrator. His inefficient, laissez-faire style of leadership led to professorial laxity, license, and a noticeable accumulation of "deadwood" who produced neither scholarship nor effective teaching. After buying Patton out of office in June 1902, the trustees gave Wilson broad powers to whip the faculty into competitive shape. In October they "fully authorized" him to reorganize the faculty by creating "such vacancies . . . as he may deem for the best interest of the University."[51] This unpublicized power enabled Wilson in the next few years to fire several instructors and three full professors, all for inadequacies in the classroom rather than in the quality or quantity of their scholarship. These actions put teeth in Wilson's general elevation of standards for students and faculty alike. Both groups quickly noticed that the president had "put screws" to the faculty and wanted them to "get to work to improve their courses." A senior song about one of the eventual casualties intoned: "He had to make his courses hard / Or he couldn't play in Woodrow's yard."[52]

Wilson was not only given unprecedented authority by the board over faculty firing—he managed to seize it for faculty hiring. His predecessors, McCosh and Patton, had always deferred to the board's powerful curriculum committee, chaired by a prerogative-minded conservative minister, by suggesting three or four candidates and letting the trustees choose. Wilson kept only the husk of tradition by choosing his own professors, preceptors and senior stars alike, and presenting them to the board for rubber-stamping. Even the committee chair had to acquiesce when Wilson's appointments put Princeton conspicuously on the academic map and favorably in national headlines.[53]

Wilson's next move, in the fall of 1903, was to organize the 108 faculty from the hitherto separate "Academic Department" and the School of Science into eleven departments and to appoint chairmen or "heads" of each. The departments were sorted into four divisions, one of which comprised Mathematics and Science. The foundation of departments by subject matter or branches of study made possible the simultaneous creation of upper-class concentrations or majors.[54] In 1905, the departments were also given primary responsibility for filling assigned quotas of preceptors. After combing the country for candidates, the departments brought them to campus for vetting and a persuasive conversation with the president. Even in his own department, History, Politics, and Economics, Wilson let his chairmen take the lead in choosing candidates and letting colleagues go.[55]

The faculty Wilson sought to fashion had three distinguishing features. The first was its concentration on the "pure" liberal arts and sciences: mere mechanics and professional practitioners need not apply. As a true believer in the undergraduate college as the "very heart" of the "true" American university, Wilson argued at the beginning and at the end of his Princeton career that preprofessional specialization and "empiric" narrowness had no place in elite universities, certainly not in his. If they must have professional schools, they should be newly modeled to "exemplify the liberal spirit of learning" and admit no one who lacked a liberal education.[56]

Wilson's second requirement was that all faculty would be active scholars as well as keen and engaging teachers. As he reminded the audience at his inauguration, "A true university is a place of research as well as for instruction. It cannot keep alive without research." "The undergraduate," he believed, no less than the graduate student, "should have scholars for teachers." Wilson's old friend and new dean of the faculty, mathematician Henry Fine, was able to persuade him that even "clubbable" (socially winning and personable) preceptors should be proven scholars, capable—sooner than later—of moving into full professorships.[57]

The third feature of the new Wilsonian faculty is that it was a single teaching force, not bisected, as in many large universities, into separate graduate and undergraduate faculties. "We none of us believe," he said of his faculty, "that the graduate and the undergraduate work might be divided." It never was. By 1910, "a very large proportion of the courses offered to graduate students" were taught by the preceptors, just as every senior scholar taught his share of undergraduate courses.[58]

With his faculty reconfigured, Wilson moved quickly to reduce the chaos in the Patton curriculum. Calls and plans for reform had been made by faculty committees since the late 1890s, but Patton's patented foot-dragging stymied them all. In the fall of 1903, however, as the departments were being formed, Wilson as chair began to meet weekly with a new standing Committee on the Course of Study to revise and systematize the curriculum for the university of the new century. Knowing that "a wise President carries his Faculty with him in every educational reform," Wilson was careful to consult the committee on every detail and principle. He was equally solicitous of the whole faculty, which took only four nights of special meetings to pass the complex proposal unanimously the following April. The result was a resounding success. "We began a group of individuals," Wilson confessed, "and ended a *body* in common counsel."[59]

That slow, deliberate process had three important results. First, it drew the university together as an "organism" more effectively than anything else Wilson had ever seen. Second, the new curriculum so conceived, particularly after the preceptorial system was added, had a "profound influence" throughout the American academic world. Not only was it one of the earliest "reconstructions" of academic life; the Princeton faculty was regarded as the symbolic leader in adopting "definite and workable ideas" for reform in enviable concert as well. Other universities hailed its leadership, said Wilson, "not because there was anything strictly original in the ideas we adopted," but because Princeton's deliberative process and distinctive curricular product were "indispensable [models] for them all."[60]

The third result was that it taught Wilson a lifelong lesson in leadership: the need to confer with interested parties before deciding matters of importance, because the results are almost always improved. The day after passage of the new curricular plan, Wilson told his wife, "It is not, as it stands now, exactly the scheme I at the outset proposed, but it is much better." Eleven years later, while presiding over a much larger institution, he explained why. In an address to the U.S. Chamber of Commerce, U.S. President Wilson described how the curriculum committee's fourteen members had entered their deliberations all painted for war, as had its chairman, but after six months they emerged with a report "no one of us had conceived or foreseen, but with which we were all absolutely satisfied. There was not a man who had not learned in that committee more than he had ever known before about the subject, and who had not willingly revised his prepossessions; who was not proud to be a participant in a genuine piece of common counsel."[61]

The new curriculum was built on two premises. One was that the free elective system made fashionable by Harvard led to haphazard results because the student's "own inexperienced judgment is put in charge of his university training, and he is more apt to follow his whim than his judgment." Too often he avoids studies that are unfamiliar or difficult and relies too much on the advice and hearsay of fellow tyros.[62] The second premise followed from the first: "The choice that we [the faculty] make," said Wilson, "must be the chief choice, the choice the pupil makes the subordinate choice." Since even four years is too short, "we who have studied the geography of learning . . . must instruct him how in a brief space he may see most of the world, and he must choose only which one of several tours that we may map out"—which major—"he will take. . . . We must supply the synthesis and must see to it that, whatever group of studies the student selects, it shall at least represent the round whole, contain all the elements of modern knowledge, and be itself a complete circle of *general* subjects."[63] As Wilson told a critic of the new plan, "Conservative, but not illiberal, Princeton has always stood for system as against miscellany in studies." Better yet, he wrote, after sleeping on it, Princeton sought "systematic liberalization."[64]

The curriculum Wilson inherited was in need of "system" more than "liberalization" (by which Wilson meant an emphasis on the liberal arts and sciences). The main problem was in the upper-class years. In both years, the faculty allowed too many electives, which were usually unrelated, too short (two hours), superficial, too passive (lectures and cramming), and too easy. This approach led to widespread demoralization among the students and dissatisfaction among the faculty. On three occasions, Patton-era faculty committees tried to change the status quo, only to be rebuffed by King Log's stonewalling. But many of their recommendations fed the successful deliberations of Wilson's committee in 1903–1904.[65] Among them were proposals to reduce the normal course load from seven to five (four for special senior honors students), standardize courses to three credit hours, promote more small-group discussions, and add general courses in philosophy and science to the junior-year requirements.[66]

But Wilson's reforms went much further, without giving up Princeton's longstanding "preference for classical culture." To preserve the B.A. degree for those who could read Greek for admission and more of it for graduation, Princeton followed many other colleges and universities in creating a bachelor of letters (Litt.B.) degree for those who could demonstrate only Latin and French or German proficiency. The existing bachelor of science (B.S.) degree, which also did not require Greek, was reserved for students of math, science, and engineering, no longer for underprepared humanists. In a signal change from the recent past, the sciences were regarded as "indispensable parts of a liberal training" and accorded equal weight to the arts in electives and to Greek, the ne plus ultra, in freshman and sophomore requirements.[67] To equalize course rigor, candidates for all degrees were taught, and held to the same raised standards, by the same instructors.[68]

Depending on the two courses they elected in their sophomore year, students chose a departmental major for their last two years.[69] Juniors took all of the required (usually two-year-long) courses in the major subject, often another in a "cognate" subject within the same division, and a fourth outside it; the fifth course was elective, though often highly advised. Seniors took three courses from a narrow range in their major, as well as two electives. Thus, the principle of election was maintained but mostly "of substantial *subjects,* not innumerable *courses.*"[70] Wilson's favorite word to characterize this new system of "assisted election" was *elastic*: it had a well-defined shape, but also some "give" to suit the student's talents, predilections, and career goals.[71] He summed it up this way: "The freshman is to be given a preliminary schooling in university methods of thorough study; the sophomore to be put in the way of getting a view of his studies which will broaden to modern horizons; the junior to be given choice of his chief field of study without discrimination between subjects new and old; the senior to be accorded the rights of those who know at last where they stand in the domain of knowledge and wish to get a firm, final grip upon a few things."[72] The combination of required and elective, breadth and depth, gave Princeton's curriculum a look both modern for its time and surprisingly contemporary for ours.

Once the mechanics of faculty and curricular reorganization and of the preceptorial system were in place, Wilson could turn more systematically to the general, animating *principles* of his vision for Princeton's future. The more funds he asked of the alumni and the more speeches he was therefore obliged to give, the more eloquent and philosophical he could and needed to be to sell his particular dream for the university.[73] When he ran into opposition, he met it head-on and refined his arguments, in the process reaching out to wider, more public, audiences for support. As his arguments gained clarity from experience in changing circumstances and from further thought, he could better contextualize his earlier goals and efforts, gaining perspective both for contemporaries and for those of us who follow a century later.

At a time when universities increasingly looked and acted alike, Wilson argued that "the deadliest thing that could happen" would be for them to run to a standard model and "follow the same methods." "Imitation and mere reproduction" deprive institutions of their individuality and force. "Richness of power, abundance of strength," on the other hand, "come by variety, in the field of education as in every other field of endeavor."[74] For its part, Princeton never wanted to resemble any other university. To a parent who criticized some aspect of the education his son was getting at Princeton by pointing to a rival institution's methods, Wilson replied that "Princeton did not follow in the footsteps of any university, but beat her own trail as she saw fit." Even in acknowledging an honorary degree from Harvard in 1907, Wilson felt compelled to tell his hosts that "Princeton is not like Harvard, and she does not wish to be. Neither does she wish Harvard to be like Princeton."[75]

That independence earned Princeton national notice and renown. In a report to the trustees in June 1907, at the start of his campaign to install four-year residential colleges, Wilson boasted that "Princeton is the only university in the country which has found itself, which has formulated a clear ideal and deliberately set about the synthesis of plan necessary to realize it." Two years later, in a series of articles on fourteen "Great American Universities," educator-journalist Edwin Slosson backed Wilson's boast. No other universities, he wrote, could be compared with Princeton for "novelty and rapidity of transformation." In the face of widespread "uniformity and conventionality," "Princeton is steering a pretty straight course toward a port of its own choice, regardless of wind and current, perhaps even heading a trifle upstream." Rather than wild and woolly experimentation, however, "Princeton has shown its originality chiefly in going ahead and doing what others have always said ought to be done," particularly in repairing "the loss of personal relationship between instructor and student."[76] In sum, Wilson sought to realize Princeton's potential to become "the best and most distinguished institution *of its kind* in the world."[77]

Just what special kind of university that was Wilson worked hard to define during his eight years in office. For the new president, it was axiomatic that Princeton was founded and must remain "for the *Nation's* Service," not for selfish social or even solely scholastic reasons. "Princeton," he told the alumni club of Chicago, "is no longer a thing for Princeton men to please themselves with. Princeton is a thing with which Princeton men must satisfy the country." The service of *all* institutions of learning, he insisted, is "not private but public." As the nation's affairs "grow more and more complex and its interests begin to touch the ends of the earth," it needs "efficient and enlightened men. The universities of the country must take part in supplying them."[78] "My ambition," Wilson told Andrew Carnegie at the end of his first semester in office, "is to make our men reading and thinking men and to keep their thoughts upon real things, so that the University may be directly serviceable to the nation. The Scots blood that is in me makes me wish to renew the [public-service] traditions of [colonial president] John Witherspoon's day in the old place."[79]

By "directly serviceable" Wilson did not mean that Princeton should produce bookish hewers of wood and drawers of water. "The college is not for the majority who carry forward the common labour of the world, nor even for those who work at the skilled handicrafts." It is for the minority, he assured his inaugural audience, "who plan, who conceive, who superintend, who mediate between group and group and must see the wide stage as a whole." It was, in short, to produce leaders, "pilots" for "the ship of State." "Democratic nations must be served in this wise no less than those whose leaders are chosen by birth and privilege; and the college is no less democratic because it is for those who play a special part."[80]

A democratic elite, however, must be chosen "not by birth, but by ambition, by opportunity, by the compulsion of gifts of initiative." "Theoretically," Wilson admitted, "the minority that frequents the halls of the university is a self-chosen minority, chosen by reason of ambition" and cultivated talent.[81] For "the mind is a radical democrat," he famously argued, and "learning knows no differences of social caste or privilege. Genius comes into what family it pleases, and laughs at the orders of society, takes delight in humble origins, and yet will appear in palaces if it please." It was a major function of universities, therefore, "to afford open, unclogged channels for the rising of the obscure powers of a nation into observation and supremacy."[82] This meant that Princeton and other elite universities should diversify their student bodies to represent the whole nation. Although Wilson still suffered from racial and gender astigmatism, he argued that "the university should draw its students from all over the nation.[83] The more regions of the country you have represented, the safer an instrument for the service of the country is the university." Concerned about the fashionable influx of "boys from families of wealth," he was also convinced by Dean Fine that Princeton should create more opportunities for harder working, more ambitious middle-class sons, "to keep the tone of the place healthy and democratic."[84] From his own undergraduate days in the late 1870s, Wilson had held that "the great thing about our universities"—and Princeton in particular—was "their democracy. The only difference in them," he wanted to believe, despite growing evidence to the contrary, "is in achievement . . . intellectual, athletic, or social."[85]

To prepare their students for the expanding and complex new world in which they were expected to play leading roles, Wilson acknowledged that Princeton and its elite peers had a seemingly contradictory task. In giving students a rich liberal education in the arts and sciences, the university had to prepare them for a life of action and service in the noisy "real world," but optimally in a quiet, cloistered setting. "What Is a College For?" Wilson asked his audiences time and again. His answers, though variously expressed, were consistent.

"The thing that the university must do is to make men acquainted with the world intellectually, imaginatively." It should give them "the first conspectus of the mind," their intellectual orientation for the future. "Every considerable undertaking," every profession, "has come to be based on knowledge, on thoughtfulness, on the masterful handling of men and facts." The university, therefore, "must stand in the midst, where the roads of thought and knowledge interlace and cross, and, building upon some coign of vantage, command them all."[86] Even the scholar in his ivory tower "should throw his windows open to the four quarters of the world." Because the university is "a world in miniature," "more than half way to that thing which we call The World," only a liberal education can introduce students to the ongoing "mapping of the world of knowledge."[87] Not how-to or preprofessional courses, but only the pure liberal arts and sciences are "the sources whence we shall know the world in which we live,—know it in its long measurement, in its past life as well as its present,—hear its voices of passion and perceive its visions of itself."[88]

Wilson's conception of higher education was, he said, "broad enough to embrace the whole field of thought, the whole record of experience." But he emphasized that it required temporary "withdrawal from the main motives of the world's material endeavor." It was part of what he called intellectual "statesmanship" that "a certain seclusion of mind" should ideally "precede the struggle of life, . . . when no particular skill is sought, no definite occupation studied, no single aim or ambition dwelt upon, but only a general preliminary orientation of the mind." It is, he said, "a process by which the young mind is . . . laid alongside the mind of the world, as nearly as may be, and enabled to receive its strength from the nourishing mother of us all, as Ant[a]eus received his strength from contact with the round earth."[89]

For all its philosophical portability, Wilson's cloister had a very Princeton look and feel. He obviously sought to make general virtues of local realities. First, he thought the liberal university was best when privately financed. A private university like Princeton had the advantage over a state institution because it is able to preserve its "particular ideals" and characteristics from generation to generation, its goal is not "the utilitarian object loved of the tax-payer," and it is not obliged to seek "the changing favor of politicians and of the uninformed" who have a say in the running of public universities.[90] Second, as he told a somewhat startled, Columbia-heavy audience at the Brooklyn Institute of Arts and Sciences in 1902, a quiet rural setting was preferable to a noisy city one. "The gist of the university," Wilson argued, "is that it should be a community with all the wonderful advantages that that word conveys." Unless the students live and study together, they cannot get "the atmospheric advantage of the community," nor enjoy unscheduled social and intellectual contact with the faculty. If after class they "dive out into the street of a great city and become drifting and separate integral parts of urban life, they are not getting the benefit of a university. They are simply going to a day school." "You cannot go to college on a street car," he told a more sympathetic alumni audience three months later, "and know what college means." Because he believed that "the real effects of a university are wrought between the hours of 6 p.m. and 9 a.m.," he was convinced that the "compact and homogeneous" residential college was "the only proper institution."[91]

Another Princeton feature—its relatively small size—might have concerned Wilson had he wished Princeton to compete with the large public and private members of the AAU or to offer its students a plethora of specialized rather than carefully chosen general courses in the liberal arts and sciences. But he did not. With the elective system cut down to size, the curriculum did not need to map every nook and cranny of knowledge. Nor was the Princeton Graduate School so large that advanced offerings needed to engorge the course catalogue. Again, Wilson sought to capitalize on Princeton reality by telling the alumni that "we can afford to be one of the lesser universities in number if we are one of the foremost in power and quality. With good quality," he assured them, "we can be perfectly indifferent in reference to quantity." In fact, he told the Princeton Club of Philadelphia, "The *danger* to Princeton is the danger of a big, numerically big, university" because it would preclude the "close and personal contact" between teachers and learners, which was "the greatest good in education."[92]

When Wilson spoke of qualitative "power" as the proper goal for Princeton, he was uttering no presidential bromide. Throughout his tenure, he gave it specific meaning, which caused many alumni brows to furrow and many other university leaders to rethink their institutional objectives. In the chapel exercises to open his first academic year in office, he emphasized the new direction Princeton was about to take. He told the assembled faculty and especially students that "we are men in the midst of a world of men. We have put off short clothes, and the mere life of play. We are in the midst of a strenuous age" and "the world demands of us expert advice or nothing. Scholarship, he said—broad[,] luminous, thorough[,] catholic, masterful scholarship—is our chief duty and our chief glory." In the spring of 1905 he told a large gathering of western Pennsylvania alumni, to whom he was appealing for funds, that "the mere expenditure of money out of hand does not make a great university." Unlike some of the newer "money colleges," such as Chicago and Stanford, Princeton would gain notice "by genius and genius alone." On both occasions he made it clear that "scholarship" and "genius" applied equally to the faculty and the students.[93]

If there was any doubt on that score, he put it firmly to rest well before he left the presidency. After describing, to frequent applause, the campus awakening brought about by the preceptorial system and the new curriculum, Wilson told a meeting of the western alumni in 1906 that "the undergraduates have welcomed the change," hinting that their predecessors should as well. Asserting that scholarship or "education, in a country like ours, is a branch of statesmanship," he won the crowd by saying that he was “covetous for Princeton of all the glory that there is.” But he wanted them to realize that “the chief glory of a university is always intellectual glory.”[94]

By the spring of 1908, however, Wilson had clearly recognized that the new intellectual tone at Princeton was facing resistance from some familiar quarters. For the middle- and upper-class matriculants who increasingly sought college for the enjoyable life there and not the studies, the extracurriculum stood much taller than either the faculty or the library. For many eastern urban alumni, Wilson’s plans to subsume the eating clubs in a residential college system threatened their beloved recruiting and weekend stomping grounds and the anti-intellectualism they perpetuated. And surrounding the Princeton contest was the larger competition and confusion among university leaders and constituencies over the primary goals of America’s rapidly evolving universities: discipline and piety (the residue of nineteenth-century, often church-related, colleges), research (the specialized province of faculty belonging to the new academic disciplines), utility or public service (the mandate of many state institutions), and liberal culture (the cause of the eastern Big Three).[95]

Wilson sidestepped that larger context in May 1908, when he took his campaign back to the western alumni meeting in Pittsburgh and to the New England alumni in Boston. For the sake of argument, he reduced his contest to two ideals of university life, one dominant, the other “struggling for recognition.” The prevailing ideal, he said, is that a university is “a mode of life, . . . a place where young men go to get together in order to *standardize* themselves in respect to certain conceptions of life and conduct.” Unfortunately, the “intellectual processes of *individualization*” are incidental to the “college life.” The average undergraduate studies and passes exams only “to retain his connection with a delightful [way] of life.” The currently more modest ideal, but one that Wilson was confident was on the rise, was that “universities exist first, last[,] and at every turn for intellectual objects.” This he regarded as “the utter commonplace of the history of education,” but he was surprised that men congratulated him for his courage in saying it.[96]

Perhaps he was remembering his reception in March when he took his message to Hadley’s Yale. There he had expressed to a receptive audience at the annual Phi Beta Kappa dinner his incredulity that “learning is on the defensive, . . . actually on the defensive, among college men.” “Is it not time we reminded the college men of this country,” he asked rhetorically, “that they have no right to any distinctive place in any [academic] community, unless they can show it by intellectual achievement? that if a university is a place for distinction at all it must be distinguished by the conquests of the mind?" As for himself, he vowed, that was his "motto," he had "entered the field to fight for that thesis," and "for that thesis only [did he] care to fight." He went so far as to beard the Bulldog alumni in their dens (his remarks were published the following week in the Yale alumni magazine) by slyly suggesting, as he had before at Princeton, that the university award its best scholars varsity letters to recognize their major contributions to Yale. Knowing the brouhaha his suggestion would raise, he admitted that young men did need extracurricular diversions, including sports, to relieve tension and reward hard work. But his conclusion was unabated: "The object of a university is intellect; as a university its only object is intellect."[97]

In throwing his full weight behind intellectual accomplishment as the right goal for Princeton, Wilson discussed openly what other goals he was not interested in pursuing. The most popular was character-building, the chief selling point of Princeton's private feeder schools and most nineteenth-century colleges, even many that evolved into more complex universities. In his first speech to the influential New York alumni in December 1902, he must have elicited some audible harrumphing by telling the graduates of those kinds of schools that "we hear a great deal of sentimental cant nowadays about cultivating our characters. God forbid," he exclaimed, "that any man should spend his days thinking about his own character. . . . The minute you set yourselves to produce [characters] you make prigs of yourselves and render yourselves useless." "Nothing will give Princeton reputation except the achievements of men whom she creates." And character, he told them, is a "by-product," which comes, he later reminded his Yale audience, "whether you will or not, as a consequence of a life devoted to the nearest duty." In a university, that meant that "study is the object and character the result."[98]

Predictably, Wilson's notion of study was also a departure from that of his predecessors. As soon as his presidential tenure began, he heard from alumni that they were glad they had attended Princeton before his academic reforms took hold. It was what he said about the balance between work and play that gave them pause. In December 1902, he told the New York alumni that he was "not going to propose that we compel the undergraduates to work all the time"—the U.S. Constitution, he quipped, "guarantees to a man a certain amount of loafing." But he did intend to try to make them "*want* to work all the time," by showing that all subjects were "intrinsically interesting" if the students approached them from the inside, through their own inquiries and investigations.[99] After Princeton's curricular reforms and the arrival of the preceptors, the president's emphasis on serious study became only more frequent and hardnosed.

Two days after Christmas in 1907, Wilson put Indiana schoolteachers on notice that testimonials to good character, piety, and clean living would no longer secure their graduates a place in Princeton's freshman class, as they once did. Even the angel Gabriel, the president said, would not be admitted unless he passed the entrance exams. "Two or three years ago," Wilson said, "we stopped [mollycoddling applicants and students] at Princeton, and the consequence is every graduate I meet of recent years thanks his stars he graduated before that began. In a university where life smiles and is gracious, we are compelling men to shut themselves up in a room and actually study. The beauty of it," he assured the teachers, "is that when a boy once tries it he likes it" because he discovers "the zest of using his mind." The following year Wilson continued his re-education of the secondary schools with a talk at the Hotchkiss School in Connecticut, one of Princeton's (and Yale's) major feeders. He warned straightaway that at Princeton, at least, the long reign of "college life," which resembled the activities of "a very superior country club," was over. "This is not a world of play," he announced; "it is a world of work, and if you don't learn how to work in college, you have learned nothing, absolutely nothing serviceable to the world."[100]

In November 1909, Wilson took his tough new message to the public and the academy in two national magazines. Assuming that any university or college worth its salt had a curriculum like Princeton's, ordered around a few fundamental requirements, "assisted election," and culminating majors in a variety of disciplines, he argued that "the *common* discipline should come from very hard work." "The spirit of work should pervade the place—honest, diligent, painstaking work. Otherwise," he counseled, "it would certainly be no proper place of preparation for the strenuous, exacting life of America in our day."[101] Extracurricular activities, no matter how absorbing or businesslike, could not give students that vital preparation. They need a "severer . . . discipline" to fit them for "the contests and achievements of an age whose every task is conditioned upon . . . some substantial knowledge, some special insight, some trained capacity, some penetration which comes from study, not from natural readiness or mere practical experience." College "must release and quicken as many faculties of the mind as possible," but it must also put them to "the test of systematic labor. Work, definite, exacting, long continued, but not," he emphasized, "narrow or petty or merely rule of thumb, must be its law of life for those who would pass its gates and go out with its authentication."[102]

Just as Wilson wanted no make-work in the university, so he had no tolerance for "mere pedantry" in the advanced scholarship of graduate students and faculty nor unrealistic expectations for what undergraduates could accomplish. He wanted all university scholarship to be "related to the national life," directly or indirectly. "The spirit of the scholar," therefore, could not be "a spirit of pedantry," by which he meant "knowledge divorced from life, . . . knowledge so closeted, so desecrated, so stripped of the significance of life, that it is a thing apart and not connected with the vital processes in the world about us." He also realized early in his Princeton career that "no undergraduate can be made a scholar in four years." "In the graduate school," he said, "we have to make scholars." Even that was only an apprenticeship for those marked by "some largesse of Providence" in their makeup, because "the process of scholarship, so far as the real scholar is concerned, is an unending process."[103] "It takes a lifetime to be a scholar," he told the Hotchkiss students, "and most men do not manage it by the time their funeral occurs."[104]

If it was not possible for the university to give the undergraduate the true scholar's supply of "exact knowledge," it was possible—and desirable—to give him "the *spirit* of learning," the spirit that animates the scholar. In explicating what he called his whole "academic creed" in July 1909, Wilson told the Harvard Phi Beta Kappa chapter that the object of a liberal education was "not learning" per se but "discipline and enlightenment of the mind." The spirit of learning, he said, is "citizenship of the world of knowledge, but not ownership of it. Scholars are the owners of its varied plots, in severalty."[105]

Wilson characterized that spirit in slightly different ways over the course of his presidency. In his inaugural address, he spoke of the inculcation of a spirit that "is neither superficial nor pedantic, which values life more than it values the mere acquisitions of the mind." A year later in Pittsburgh, he described for the research-oriented Carnegie Institute the stimulation of the average undergraduate to "the best uses of his mind" and the imparting to him "methods of thought, impulses of investigation, habits of candid inquiry, and a knowledge of the sources of information which will make him a real master of the information which subsequent observation, reading[,] and experience will bring him."[106]

By the time he spoke at Harvard, his definition had been honed still further. "It consists," the visitor said, "in the power to distinguish good reasoning from bad" and to "digest and interpret evidence, in a habit of catholic observation and a preference for the non-partisan point of view, in an addiction to clear and logical processes of thought and yet an instinctive desire to interpret rather than to stick in the letter of the reasoning, in a taste for knowledge and a deep respect for the integrity of the human mind."[107] Although Wilson saw it as an educational "commonplace," his nuanced and implicit critique of the increasing number of universities that promoted faculty research as their primary objective, at the expense of undergraduate education, was declared by the Boston press "a new idea on the raison d'être of the university."[108] In the context of contemporary university developments, it was indeed a new idea and one of Wilson's most resonant.

Imparting the spirit of learning, Wilson insisted, was "not a method but a process," which resulted when "minds meet minds," both in and after classes. Moreover, it "requires time" and cannot be rushed.[109] To Wilson's way of thinking, it certainly took all four years, not the two or three being argued for by rivals such as Presidents Eliot of Harvard and Butler of Columbia. Eliot thought that many of his students were entering with advanced standing and could easily graduate in three years. Butler wanted to speed up the production of his many professional schools by taking students after only two years of college work and sending them out to do the world's work after a total of four years. Others argued that contemporary sophomores were as well educated as their grandfathers had been at graduation. Wilson thought all of these notions ill-conceived and based on negligible knowledge of sophomores "in the flesh." What the short-course advocates missed, he charged, was that "our sophomore is at the age of twenty no more mature than the sophomore of that previous generation was at the age of seventeen or eighteen. The sap of manhood is rising in him," quipped the president who still taught them, "but it has not yet reached his head. It is not what a man is studying that makes him a sophomore or a senior: it is the stage the college process has reached in him. A college, the American college, is not a body of studies," he reiterated. "It is a process of development. It takes, if our observation can be trusted, at least four years for the completion of that process, and all four of those years must be college years. They cannot be school years: they cannot be combined with school years. . . . The environment is of the essence of the whole effect."[110]

Wilson's belief in the sovereign effect of environment upon the educational process led in 1907 to his most daring reform of Princeton: the "social coördination" of the university. His intent, he was quick to emphasize, was not "social" per se but only the culminating, "indispensable part" of the ongoing "reorganization and revitalization of the University as an academic body, whose objects are . . . intellectual."[111] Although he acknowledged its "radical" character, he noted that it had been "taking form in my mind for many years," apparently since his inauguration, and was "the fruit of very mature consideration."[112] After the success of the preceptorial system and the planning of an impressive residential college to anchor the Graduate School, he was confident in June, when he made his initial presentation to the board, that the time was right to consolidate Princeton's national lead in university reform. In words whose cruel irony would soon emerge with defeat, he believed "there never was a time when such processes could be undertaken with less fear of serious friction or factious opposition." The "recent innovations . . . have put the whole university body in a wholesome humour of reform and have made all well-considered changes, devised and executed by frank common counsel, much easier of accomplishment." The undergraduates in particular, he asserted, were "ready to accept any thoroughgoing reform." Moreover, he warned, "other universities are likely to try this method of reintegration, but none has such materials for it or such bases of cooperative enthusiasm as we have."[113]

Wilson's overconfidence and perhaps a sense of urgency attributable to his recent stroke led him to miscalculate the timing of his presentation of the quad plan. He correctly submitted the plan to the board first, but at the end of the academic year. This allowed rumor to circulate uncontested all summer while he was in England. When classes resumed in September, he asked the assembled faculty for its opinion, without inviting their "common counsel"—he had, as usual, consulted a small circle of trusted friends and allies—or allowing a lengthy "investigation." Without the faculty's approval, Wilson thought he could not "go before the students and alumni in advocacy and explanation of his idea." After one of the greatest speeches of his life, the faculty did stand, cheer, and applaud its educational premises, but by then it was too late. The alumni, particularly the younger classes in the eastern cities that had belonged to the eating clubs, had formed such vocal opposition that, within a fortnight, even the trustees rescinded their approval of the plan when they saw its implications for the clubs.[114]

Despite his tactical mistake, Wilson's diagnosis of Princeton's socio-academic ailment was careful and astute. Many other college and university leaders accepted his well-publicized analyses of Princeton's problems as accurate pictures of their own, even if they did not share all of his premises or go as far in holding intellectual power as their institution's primary goal. His first assumption was that a university was a *community*, and a community was, in its social essence, a single *organism* whose constituent parts acted, or were supposed to act, metaphorically if not biologically, as one. Despite his own slim background in science, *organic* was his favorite adjective in discussing "our close-knit little University world." A second premise, which lay at the heart of the preceptorial plan, was that teaching was most effective in small groups. As even Wilson, a hugely popular undergraduate lecturer, admitted, "almost universal experience" showed that a teacher gets his best results by "direct, personal, intimate" interaction with his students, "not as a class but as individuals."[115] "Men must meet face to face to kindle each other." In close, companionable settings, in class or out, teachers "do not seem pedagogues but friends" and "can by the gentle *infection* of friendliness make thought a general *contagion*." Teaching of this kind, Wilson concluded, now required as its "social and indispensable environment a new social coördination."[116]

Perhaps Princeton's most serious problem calling for solution before it could claim to be a seriously intellectual place was that the *extra*curriculum needed to be tamed and subordinated to study. By the closing years of his presidency, Wilson famously said, "The peculiarity of our American universities . . . is that the sideshows have swallowed up the circus." College life organized by the students "has come to absorb [their] whole interest and attention and energy," and "those [faculty] who perform in the main tent must often whistle for their audiences."[117] This "immoderate addiction" to college life "has thrust the truest, deepest, most important objects of college work and association into the background." The undergraduates' outside interests are not only "irrelevant to study," but most are "subtly antagonistic to it" as well.[118] The problem was more serious, Wilson thought, because the extracurriculum had seduced not only the growing number of upwardly mobile students seeking "manliness," social contacts, and "the standards of true sportsmen." It had also claimed "most of the finest, most spirited, most gifted youngsters in the undergraduate body, men fit to be scholars and masters in many fields, . . . the very men the teacher most desires to get hold of and to enlist in some enterprise of the mind, . . . whose [proper] training would count for most in leadership outside of college, in the country at large, and for the promotion of every interest the nation has."[119]

In most universities, intercollegiate sports was the male undergraduates' consuming passion, but at Princeton the eating clubs posed the biggest challenge to the curriculum. Two-thirds of the upperclassmen belonged after often heart- and friendship-breaking competitions called "bicker," and thereafter enjoyed exclusive dining and party privileges in increasingly luxurious mansions on Prospect Avenue. Although the clubs were restricted to juniors and seniors, the selection process favored ready-made groups over individuals, such as prep-school cliques that formed freshman and sophomore feeder clubs. This tendency toward narrow associations offended the president's growing progressivism. He regretted the social exclusivity of the old and new monied classes and its impairment of the college's traditional democracy. He believed that "democracy is made up of unchosen experiences . . . unselected contacts." "Admission to the University must mean full membership in its community. . . . There must be no inequalities except the natural inequalities of age and experience." Moreover, the clubs were "distinctly and very seriously hostile to the spirit of study, incompatible with the principles of a true republic of letters and of learning."[120] As social arbiters, the clubs led "men in all classes [to] feel that too great absorption in study will involve a virtual disqualification for social preferment." To prove his point, Wilson noted that 41.7 percent of nonclubmen were honor students but only 9.6 percent of clubmen were. When it came to academic reform and the setting of intellectual priorities, "the clubs," he told the board, "simply happen to stand in the way."[121]

Wilson's conclusion was that "the only way in which the social life of the undergraduates can be prevented from fatally disordering, and perhaps even strangling, the academic life of the University is by the actual absorption of the social life into the academic." As a solution to Princeton's particular dilemma, he proposed to build Oxbridge-like residential colleges around or, if need be, over the eating clubs. Each college would house and feed members of all four classes, a faculty master, and a few unmarried preceptors and host other faculty fellows as well. This would bring younger students into frequent, casual, and emulative contact with older ones and involve the faculty for the first time in "university life."[122] The goal, Wilson was quick to clarify, was not to legislate or force "a marriage between knowledge and pleasure; we are simply trying to throw them a good deal together in the confidence that they will fall in love with one another." This radical but "organic" reorganization of the university through colleges, the president told the faculty in October 1907, was "nothing more or less than Professor [Andrew Fleming] West's idea of the Graduate [College] . . . adapted to the undergraduate life."[123]

That both Anglophiles thought in architectural terms of Tudor Gothic and Wilson had endorsed in principle West's published description of his dream college might seem to have secured a key faculty ally for the president's cause.[124] But appearances can be deceiving. Wilson sought to integrate the hitherto autonomously governed Graduate School into the newly coordinated university in three ways. First, he wanted to reduce the dean's authority and place it firmly under his own. Second, he wanted to add intellectual firepower to the university by adding several senior stars to recruit and teach graduate students as well as undergraduates. West had no problem with that, except that Wilson's hires proved to be intensely loyal to the president and not to the dean. And, third, Wilson wanted to locate the proposed Graduate College near the center of the campus, to serve as a visible symbol of Princeton's aspirations to the highest learning, to counter the anti-intellectualism of the clubs, and to bring advanced students into daily contact with those they were being prepared to teach. "The graduate students need humanizing," Wilson thought, perhaps remembering his own graduate isolation at Johns Hopkins, "as much as the undergraduates need sobering and inspiration; and both need to be reminded every day that learning is a part of life . . . even though it first of all be the fruit of the silent and lonely vigil."[125] West, contrarily, wanted "his" college removed from the puerile hubbub of undergraduate life and placed on an eminence overlooking the local golf course, nearly a mile from campus. This disagreement precipitated the last maneuvers in the nationally publicized "Battle of Princeton" and the defeat of Wilson's final plans for the university's academic "salvation."[126]

But those last sorry scenes did not mean the death of his plans in Princeton nor the influence of his whole design and thinking upon American education in subsequent decades.[127] Every Princeton president since Wilson has acknowledged him as the architect of Princeton's status as a major research university and perhaps the leading "liberal university" in the country. The blueprints he drew for Princeton's collegiate-university have retained their philosophical freshness and served as relevant guides to its institutional priorities for more than a century.

Perhaps the most grateful heir of Wilson's legacy was President Harold W. Dodds (1933–57), who had entered the Graduate School soon after Wilson resigned. After a decade living and writing university speeches in Prospect, Wilson's former home, Dodds discovered his predecessor's numerous writings and addresses on education. It was a "humbling experience," he admitted in 1956, the centenary of Wilson's birth, because "it revealed to me how much of what I had been saying about Princeton's aims and ambitions had been said by him so much earlier and so much better. And how I had subconsciously absorbed his ideals by a process of intellectual osmosis from the intellectual atmosphere which he had generated. And how effectively he had prepared both the scholarly and institutional foundations for what we in New Jersey call the modern Princeton was brought home to me in full strength."[128]

Dodds also testified that Wilson's "high visibility throughout the nation" enabled him to "lift . . . the sights and set new targets for all American colleges." Even when he spoke directly to Princetonians, "the whole college and university world listened. When he exposed the weaknesses of Princeton, he was exposing the prevailing maladies of all American colleges. And to the mounting unrest in educational circles of the time, he gave inspiration and direction and leadership. That so much for which our colleges and universities are striving today was implicit or explicit in his policy," Dodds concluded, "is the greatest tribute which we can pay him as an architect of educational progress."[129]

Well beyond Princeton, emulators have sought to produce their own versions—as he would have wished—of curricular coherence, preceptorial closeness, institutional synchrony, and social-academic coordination. Perhaps the best example is Harvard. As soon as he was inaugurated in 1909, President Lowell initiated a curriculum of "planned freedom" around concentration and distribution requirements (1911), reading periods and comprehensive exams (both 1914), and later a system of tutors to guide the students' reading and writing (1919).[130] By the 1930s, both Harvard and Yale had in place the beginnings of a system of residential colleges for the top three classes.[131] Many universities have followed suit as resources have allowed. In 2006, according to a "Collegiate Way" Website, 12 of the top 25 national universities in the *U.S. News & World Report* rankings and 18 other American universities "have faculty-led residential college systems that are either complete, partial, or in the works."[132] Beginning in the early 1980s, Princeton finally earned a spot on the list with a series of five colleges, crafted from existing and new buildings, for *under*classmen; one college, appropriately, was named for Wilson.[133] More recently, the university has realized Wilson's final dream more fully by building two new imposing colleges—one Gothic, the other postmodern and ecologically "green"—for all four classes and liberal quotients of graduate students and faculty fellows. A third is planned, but the eating clubs stubbornly remain, though in smaller number.[134]

Wilson's signal contributions, then, were both historic and surprisingly contemporary. At a time when America's universities were growing rapidly, adding new constituencies, and attempting to please them all, when their aims and methods were being blended and somehow reconciled to produce all-purpose institutions bearing a striking resemblance, Wilson led Princeton in spearheading the reforms of the Big Three, who stood firmly and united against the prevailing standardization. Yet his ideas and proposals, even—perhaps especially—those that failed to be realized in his own day, have shown surprising life and durability over time. They have given courage and lent clarity to leaders not only of humanly scaled liberal universities that chose to keep the undergraduate college at their core but also of liberal arts colleges that deliberately chose not to become universities. In the end, his ideas and ideals, their continuing cogency, expression, and relevance, may prove to be his greatest contribution to American higher education.

NOTES

1. Henry Wilkinson Bragdon, *Woodrow Wilson: The Academic Years* (Cambridge, Mass.: Belknap Press of Harvard University Press, 1967), 163; *The Papers of Woodrow Wilson,* ed. Arthur S. Link et al., 69 vols. (Princeton: Princeton University Press, 1966–1994), 6:623, 625 (May 5, 1890) (hereafter *PWW*).

2. Stockton Axson, *"Brother Woodrow": A Memoir of Woodrow Wilson,* ed. Arthur S. Link (Princeton: Princeton University Press, 1993), 115.

3. *PWW,* 16:453 (Sept. 16, 1906).

4. James D. Startt, *Woodrow Wilson and the Press: Prelude to the Presidency* (New York: Palgrave Macmillan, 2004), ch. 2.

5. J. Douglas Brown, "The American Liberal University," *Princeton Alumni Weekly,* May 6, 1955, 8–9; Brown, *The Liberal University: An Institutional Analysis* (New York: McGraw-Hill, 1969).

6. James Axtell, *The Making of Princeton University: From Woodrow Wilson to the Present* (Princeton: Princeton University Press, 2006), 593–95.

7. Samuel Eliot Morison, *Three Centuries of Harvard, 1636–1936* (Cambridge, Mass.: Harvard University Press, 1936), chs. 14–15, 17; Hugh Hawkins, *Between Harvard and America: The Educational Leadership of Charles W. Eliot* (New York: Oxford University Press, 1972); Henry Aaron Yeomans, *Abbott Lawrence Lowell, 1856–1943* (Cambridge, Mass.: Harvard University Press, 1948); Laurence R. Veysey, *The Emergence of the American University* (Chicago: University of Chicago Press, 1965), 87–98, 248–51.

8. Veysey, *Emergence of the American University*, 363–66, 367n90; Robert A. McCaughey, *Stand, Columbia: A History of Columbia University in the City of New York, 1754–2004* (New York: Columbia University Press, 2003), chs. 6–7; Michael Rosenthal, *Nicholas Miraculous: The Amazing Career of the Redoubtable Dr. Nicholas Murray Butler* (New York: Farrar, Straus and Giroux, 2006).

9. Morris Hadley, *Arthur Twining Hadley* (New Haven: Yale University Press, 1948), 145, 153, chs. 10, 13; Brooks Mather Kelley, *Yale: A History* (New Haven: Yale University Press, 1974), chs. 14–17; George Wilson Pierson, *Yale College: An Educational History, 1871–1921* (New Haven: Yale University Press, 1952).

10. Veysey, *Emergence of the American University*, 366. Michael Rosenthal, Butler's most recent biographer, has also concluded that "despite his impressive credentials as an educator," Butler cannot be regarded "as any sort of significant educational theorist. He left behind no body of innovative thought for the academic profession to which his name might properly be attached." Rosenthal, *Nicholas Miraculous*, 461.

11. *PWW*, 19:310 (July 14, 1909), 448 (Oct. 26, 1909). When Wilson was elected president of Princeton in June 1902, Hadley wrote to congratulate him. "Changes have been wonderfully rapid in the last few years. With you and Butler and myself in our new positions, we certainly have old friends working all together." *PWW*, 14:560 (June 10, 1902).

12. Veysey, *Emergence of the American University*, ch. 4, 252–59.

13. *PWW*, 18:622, 627 (Jan. 15, 1909), 19:254 (June 16, 1909).

14. *PWW*, 19:270 (June 26, 1909), 290 (July 3, 1909), 448 (Oct. 26, 1909).

15. *PWW*, 19:274 (June 28, 1909), 407n1, 495–96 (Nov. 12, 1909).

16. *PWW*, 20:276–77 (March 21, 1910), 21:109 (Sept. 16, 1910).

17. Yeomans, *Abbott Lawrence Lowell*, 153–55, 184–85, 188, 296, 355. In *Lawrence Lowell and His Revolution* (Cambridge, Mass.: Harvard University, 1980), former Harvard president Nathan M. Pusey was not as forthright as Lowell in acknowledging Wilson's precedence and leadership.

18. Hadley, *Arthur Twining Hadley*, 77; Axtell, *The Making of Princeton University*, 269.

19. *PWW*, 12:193–94 (Oct. 26, 1901).

20. *PWW*, 12:280–83n1 (Feb. 23, 1902).

21. *PWW*, 11:194, 560 (June 10, 1902).

22. Hadley, *Arthur Twining Hadley*, 108, 115–16, ch. 13, 272; *Dictionary of American Biography*, ed. Dumas Malone (New York, 1932), 8:77–80.

23. Hadley, for example, published 17 articles or talks on higher education in the *Yale Alumni Magazine* during his first eight years in office (comparable to Wilson's tenure) and another 31 before he retired in 1921. Hadley, *Arthur Twining Hadley*, 258–76.

24. In retirement, Lowell published *Facts and Visions: Twenty-Four Baccalaureate Ser-*

*mons,* edited by his future biographer, Henry Aaron Yeomans (Cambridge, Mass.: Harvard University Press, 1944). After only eight years in office, Hadley published a few in *Baccalaureate Addresses and Other Talks on Kindred Themes* (New York: Charles Scribner's Sons, 1907) and several more in *The Moral Basis of Democracy: Sunday Morning Talks to Students and Graduates* (New Haven: Yale University Press, 1919). But he was more comfortable with educational themes for matriculation addresses in the fall, which he tended to publish in the *Yale Alumni Magazine.* Hadley, *Arthur Twining Hadley,* 258–76.

25. Hadley, *Arthur Twining Hadley,* 125; *National Cyclopaedia of American Biography* (New York, 1944), 31:2 (q.v. Lowell, A[bbott] Lawrence); Yeomans, *Abbott Lawrence Lowell,* 497. Lowell published excerpts from twenty-three of his reports in *At War with Academic Traditions in America* (Cambridge, Mass.: Harvard University Press, 1934; reprt. Westport, Conn.: Greenwood Press, 1965), 238–352. Wilson's 1904 report (*PWW,* 15:554–69 [Dec. 8, 1904]), for example, was printed in an edition of 8,000 and distributed to alumni, other colleges, and leading preparatory schools. *PWW,* 16:3 (Feb. 18, 1905).

26. He published another twenty-seven before he retired. Hadley, *Arthur Twining Hadley,* 258–76.

27. When he collected his favorite writings in 1934, only 2 of 30 (not counting 23 annual reports) had been published outside New England. Lowell, *At War with Academic Traditions.*

28. Even in his last eight years in office (1901–1909), Eliot figured in 120 *Times* articles. He was quoted mostly on sports corruption, Harvard's need for a three-year B.A., and plans for what became the famous "Ten-Foot Shelf" of *Harvard Classics.*

29. *PWW,* 17:240–41 (July 1, 1907).

30. John M. Mulder, *Woodrow Wilson: The Years of Preparation* (Princeton: Princeton University Press, 1978), 185–86, 225; Edwin A. Weinstein, *Woodrow Wilson: A Medical and Psychological Biography* (Princeton: Princeton University Press, 1981), ch. 10; Bert Edward Park, *The Impact of Illness on World Leaders* (Philadelphia: University of Pennsylvania Press, 1986), 3–76, 331–42. For doubts about the frequency and the impact of Wilson's cerebrovascular accidents on his personality and decisions, see Robert M. Saunders, "History, Health, and Herons: The Historiography of Woodrow Wilson's Personality and Decision-Making," *Presidential Studies Quarterly,* 24:1 (Winter 1994): 57–77.

31. Lowell's slim valedictory book, *What a University President Has Learned* (New York: Macmillan, 1938), is a more thoughtful, informative, and enjoyable read than the vast majority of tomes left by the era's leading educators.

32. *PWW,* 14:27 (July 19, 1902).

33. *PWW,* 14:75 (Aug. 11, 1902).

34. *PWW,* 11:532 (April 4, 1900). Ten days after being elected president, Wilson assured the parent of a newly admitted freshman that "we are of the conservative school in education here, and I do not think we should ever get too far away from the classical model." *PWW,* 12:441 (June 19, 1902).

35. *PWW,* 23:600 (Dec. 19, 1911).

36. *PWW,* 20:347 (April 7, 1910).

37. Ibid. On March 7, 1908, Wilson told a Baltimore meeting of the Princeton Alumni Association of Maryland that "the country now says that Princeton knows what to do, and

God forbid that Princeton will ever lose that leadership. We must keep ours the leading light of the country." *PWW*, 18:11.

38. *PWW*, 14:157 (Oct. 21, 1902).

39. *PWW*, 14:156, 160 (Oct. 21, 1902).

40. *PWW*, 14:152 (Oct. 21, 1902), 175 (Oct. 25, 1902), 15:71 (Dec. 10, 1903).

41. "The College Course and Methods of Instruction," Dec. 12, 1903, in *PWW*, 15:88, 16:384 (May 4, 1906).

42. *PWW*, 14:153 (Oct. 21, 1902), 20:230 (March 11, 1910); see also 15:89–92 on the legitimate uses of lectures.

43. *PWW*, 14:154 (Oct. 21, 1902). In the fall of 1906, Wilson changed his own popular lecture course on jurisprudence to all preceptorials twice a week, partly because he was not fully recovered from a possible stroke, but mostly because "now . . . the men really read" on their own. *PWW*, 16:449–50 (Sept. 3, 1906).

44. Hardin Craig, *Woodrow Wilson at Princeton* (Norman: University of Oklahoma Press, 1960), 91.

45. Axtell, *The Making of Princeton University*, 67–68.

46. Axson, "*Brother Woodrow*," 124; *PWW*, 16:460 (Oct. 17, 1906).

47. Princeton University, *Report of the President (1919)*, 21.

48. In 1946, Dean of the Faculty Robert K. Root, one of the original preceptors, asserted that "no university in the country has ever, before or since, added to its faculty at one blow so large and so able a new recruitment. A surprisingly large proportion of them qualified for professorships, and have borne a very important part in maintaining during the past forty years the university's intellectual distinction and in administering its affairs. The group has provided Princeton University with nine chairmen of departments, four deans, and one charter trustee." Robert K. Root, "Wilson and the Preceptors," in William Starr Myers, ed., *Woodrow Wilson: Some Princeton Memories* (Princeton: Princeton University Press, 1946), 16. The last five preceptor alumni retired in 1946. "Rear Guard of 'Preceptor Guys' Retires," *Princeton Alumni Weekly*, July 19, 1946, 8–9.

49. Henry Wilkinson Bragdon, interview with Charles W. McIlwain, Jan. 2, 1940, p. 5, Woodrow Wilson Collection [WWC], Princeton University Archives [PUA], box 62, folder 11.

50. Wilson, "Five Years of the Preceptorial System," in his *Annual Report*, Jan. 1, 1910, *PWW*, 19:694; Axtell, *The Making of Princeton University*, 68–70.

51. *PWW*, 14:162, 168 (Oct. 21, 1902). Trustee and former U.S. President Grover Cleveland made the motion.

52. Axtell, *The Making of Princeton University*, 52–54; *PWW*, 14:441 (May 1, 1903); Bragdon interview with Charles Grosvenor Osgood, April 14, 1939, p. 1, WWC, PUA, box 63, folder 24. See also Myers, ed., *Woodrow Wilson: Princeton Memories*, 3, 55.

53. *PWW*, 14:486–88 (June 11, 1903), 556–57 (Sept. 1, 1903), 15:26n2 (Oct. 23, 1903); Axtell, *The Making of Princeton University*, 59–68.

54. *PWW*, 14:474 (June 5, 1903), 15:55–56 (ca. Nov. 20, 1903), 73–74 (Dec. 10, 1903), 381 (June 14, 1904).

55. Axtell, *The Making of Princeton University*, 58, 62–65.

56. *PWW*, 14:181 (Oct. 25, 1902); "Should an Antecedent Liberal Education Be Required of Students in Law, Medicine, and Theology?" 8:285–92, at 290–91 (July 26, 1893); "Position

and Importance of the Arts Course as Distinct from the Professional and Semi-Professional Courses," 19:713–27 (Jan. 5, 1910); Edwin Grant Conklin, "As a Scientist Saw Him," in Myers, ed., *Woodrow Wilson: Princeton Memories.* Harvard professor of English Louis Menand blames Harvard president Charles W. Eliot (1869–1909) for making the bachelor's degree a national prerequisite for admission to professional school and isolating the "pure" liberal arts in the undergraduate college. Wilson needed no tutelage from Cambridge on that score. Louis Menand, *The Marketplace of Ideas: Reform and Resistance in the American University* (New York: W. W. Norton, 2010), 45.

57. *PWW,* 14:152 (Oct. 21, 1902), 19:284 (July 1, 1909); Axtell, *The Making of Princeton University,* 66.

58. *PWW,* 14:158 (Oct. 21, 1902), 182 (Oct. 25, 1902), 20:231 (March 11, 1910). In January 1910, 21 graduate courses were being taught by preceptors, largely in the humanities and social sciences. But even 13 mathematicians were studying with 3 preceptors. Dean Andrew Fleming West to Dean of the College Edward Elliott, Jan. 20, 1910, Graduate School Records, West Correspondence, Princeton University Archives, Seeley G. Mudd Library, AC127, box 14, folder 1.

59. *PWW,* 12:299 (March 19, 1902), 15:264 (April 17, 1904); Axson, "*Brother Woodrow,*" 122.

60. *PWW,* 15:292, 20:339 (April 7, 1910).

61. *PWW,* 15:296 (April 26, 1904), 32:186–87 (Feb. 3, 1915). Two years earlier, Wilson told his advisor, Colonel Edward House, that "his long University training had shown him how necessary it was to confer about important matters; that he seldom went into a conference and came out with the same ideas as when he went in." *PWW,* 29:58 (Dec. 22, 1913). See also Trygve Throntveit, " 'Common Counsel': Woodrow Wilson's Pragmatic Progressivism, 1885–1913," in John Milton Cooper Jr., ed., *Reconsidering Woodrow Wilson: Progressivism, Internationalism, War, and Peace* (Washington, D.C.: Woodrow Wilson Center Press and Baltimore: Johns Hopkins University Press, 2008), ch. 2 (25–56).

62. *PWW,* 15:459 (Aug. 29, 1904).

63. *PWW,* 14:181 (Oct. 25, 1902), my emphasis. In his 1946 memoir of Wilson, professor of English J. Duncan Spaeth was "struck by his constant use of the word 'general,' as a kind of dominant motif" in his inaugural address at Princeton. J. Duncan Spaeth, "Wilson as I Knew Him and View Him Now," in Myers, ed., *Woodrow Wilson: Princeton Memories,* 78.

64. *PWW,* 15:459 (Aug. 29, 1904), 460 (Aug. 30, 1904).

65. Luther P. Eisenhart, "The Far-Seeing Wilson," in Myers, ed., *Woodrow Wilson: Princeton Memories,* 62–63.

66. *PWW,* 12:331 (April 16, 1902). See the Editorial Note on "The New Princeton Course of Study," *PWW,* 15:277–92, esp. 284–88.

67. In the 1850s, several required and a few elective sciences were offered at Princeton in the senior year, and mathematics dominated the prescribed curriculum. James Buchanan Henry and Christian Henry Scharff, *College As It Is, or, The Collegian's Manual in 1853,* ed. J. Jefferson Looney (Princeton: Princeton University Libraries, 1996), 109, 224–25, 229. By contrast, the curriculum of 1898–99 required mathematics only in the first two years and physics in the junior year; five other sciences were electives. Craig, *Woodrow Wilson at Princeton,* 74–75.

68. *PWW,* 15:252–57 (April 16, 1904), 379, 380 (June 14, 1904). Princeton dropped its Greek requirements for admission and graduation in 1919. Yale dropped Greek in 1904 and

Latin in 1931, a year after Princeton. Harvard had begun the Greek retreat in the 1880s. Frederick Rudolph, *Curriculum: A History of the American Undergraduate Course of Study since 1636* (San Francisco: Jossey-Bass, 1977), 213–14; Pierson, *Yale College*, 187.

69. The concept of majors (and minors) began in the late 1870s at Johns Hopkins, from which it spread to the Midwest, Bryn Mawr, and Stanford. In 1901, Yale began moving to a system of concentration and distribution, as did Harvard in 1910. Rudolph, *Curriculum*, 131, 227–29.

70. *PWW*, 12:328 (April 12, 1902)

71. "Princeton's New Plan of Study," *PWW*, 15:459 (ca. Aug. 29, 1904), 561, 565 (Dec. 8, 1904), 20:230 (March 11, 1910).

72. *PWW*, 15:455 (ca. Aug. 29, 1904).

73. *PWW*, 20:347 (April 7, 1910).

74. *PWW*, 15:85 (Dec. 12, 1903), 456 (Aug. 29, 1904).

75. *PWW*, 14:401–2 (March 28, 1903), 17:227 (June 26, 1907).

76. *PWW*, 17:203 (June 10, 1907); Edwin E. Slosson, *Great American Universities* (New York: Macmillan, 1910), 75–76.

77. *PWW*, 16:453 (Sept. 16, 1906), my emphasis.

78. *PWW*, 14:170 (Oct. 25, 1902), my emphasis, 20:438 (May 12, 1910). See Theodore J. Ziolkowski, "Princeton in *Whose* Service?" *Princeton Alumni Weekly*, Jan. 23, 1991, 11–16, for an astute reading of Wilson's phrase. After the Spanish-American War in 1898, Wilson put new emphasis on an international focus for higher education and renewed his faith in the liberal arts as the best way to educate young men for the nation's expanded role in the world. See the next essay in this volume, by Adam Nelson.

79. *PWW*, 14:307 (Dec. 27, 1902).

80. *PWW*, 14:176 (Oct. 25, 1902), 16:270 (Dec. 15, 1905).

81. *PWW*, 15:35 (Nov. 5, 1903), 16:270 (Dec. 15, 1905). Although Wilson had to admit that "not every man that goes out from Princeton is fit to be a leader," he did believe that every graduate was "fitted to understand and choose a leader." *PWW*, 14:486 (June 10, 1903).

82. *PWW*, 19:60 (Feb. 19, 1909), 20:160–61 (Feb. 24, 1910).

83. On Wilson's blind spots, see Gary Gerstle, "Race and Nation in the Thought and Politics of Woodrow Wilson," in Cooper, ed., *Reconsidering Woodrow Wilson*, ch. 4 (93–123). See also Victoria Bissell Brown, "Did Woodrow Wilson's Gender Politics Matter?" in Cooper, ed., ch. 5 (125–62), and her essay in this volume.

84. *PWW*, 14:299 (Dec. 19, 1902), 18:246 (April 9, 1908).

85. *PWW*, 14:285 (Dec. 12, 1902). For Wilson's growing doubts about Princeton's "democracy," see "What Is a College For?" *Scribner's Magazine*, 46 (Nov. 1909): 570–77, in *PWW*, 19:334–47.

86. *PWW*, 14:174, 184 (Oct. 25, 1902), 235 (Nov. 29, 1902), 402 (March 28, 1903).

87. *PWW*, 14:174 (Oct. 25, 1902), 402 (March 25, 1903), 18:499, 502 (Nov. 12, 1908).

88. *PWW*, 17:135–36 (May 4, 1907).

89. *PWW*, 15:40–41 (Nov. 5, 1903). In his inaugural address, "Princeton for the Nation's Service," Wilson had made the same point: "in order to learn[,] men must for a little while withdraw from action, must seek some quiet place of remove from the bustle of affairs, where their thoughts may run clear and tranquil, and the heats of business be for a time put off." *PWW*, 14:184 (Oct. 25, 1902).

90. *PWW*, 14:308 (Dec. 29, 1902), 446 (May 2, 1903).

91. *PWW*, 14:283–84 (Dec. 12, 1902), 402 (March 28, 1903); see also 14:318–19 (Jan. 3, 1903), 446 (May 2, 1903). As of December 1904, about 400 Princeton students, mostly freshmen and sophomores, lived off campus. Four years later, 345 were still not in residence, though two dormitories to hold 172 were about to be built. *PWW*, 15:567 (Dec. 8, 1904), 18:580 (Jan. 1, 1909).

92. *PWW*, 14:385 (March 8, 1903), 410 (April 15, 1903), my emphasis.

93. *PWW*, 14:132 (Sept. 18, 1902), 16:32–33 (March 19, 1905).

94. *PWW*, 16:407–8 (May 26, 1906).

95. Veysey, *Emergence of the American University*, part 1.

96. *PWW*, 18:281, 284 (May 2, 1908), 298–99 (May 15, 1908), my emphases.

97. "The Training of Intellect," *PWW*, 18:54–56 (March 18, 1908). For Wilson's suggestion that Princeton's top scholars deserve a "P," see also *PWW*, 15:284, 382 (June 14, 1904).

98. *PWW*, 14:276 (Dec. 9, 1902), 18:55 (March 18, 1908).

99. *PWW*, 14:272–73 (Dec. 9, 1902), my emphasis.

100. *PWW*, 17:581 (Dec. 27, 1907), 18:503 (Nov. 12, 1908).

101. "My Ideal of the True University," *The Delineator*, 74 (Nov. 1909): 401, 437–38, in *PWW*, 19:298, my emphasis.

102. "What Is a College For?" in *PWW*, 19:339, 345.

103. *PWW*, 14:318 (Jan. 3, 1903), 18:56 (March 18, 1908).

104. *PWW*, 18:501 (Nov. 12, 1908).

105. "The Spirit of Learning," *Harvard Graduates' Magazine*, 18 (Sept. 1909): 1–14, in *PWW*, 19:282–83, my emphasis; 19:290 (July 3, 1909).

106. *PWW*, 14:171 (Oct. 25, 1902), 15:42 (Nov. 5, 1903).

107. *PWW*, 19:283 (July 1, 1909).

108. *PWW*, 14:316.

109. *PWW*, 14:317–18 (Jan. 3, 1903).

110. *PWW*, 19:285–86 (July 1, 1909); see also 14:263–64 (Dec. 6, 1902), 16:397 (May 19, 1906). At a large meeting of Princeton alumni in New York in December 1902, the exuberant diners sang from a printed songbook a chorus verse about Wilson's position: "Now Butler at Columbia / Has cut the course in two; / He must have quite forgotten / Both the football team and crew; / But Wilson down at Princeton / Didn't stand for it a bit; / It struck him right way that it / Would graduate De Witt"—a football star in the class of '04. *PWW*, 14:289 (Dec. 13, 1902). On Eliot's views, see "Harvard Will Cling to Higher Standards," *New York Times*, Feb. 10, 1903, 8.

111. In his 1946 memoir, Dean Luther Eisenhart sought to squelch "the [still] mistaken belief that Mr. Wilson proposed his plan not as part of an *educational* program but as means of changing, if not eliminating, the Princeton club system." Eisenhart, "The Far-Seeing Wilson," in Myers, ed., *Woodrow Wilson: Princeton Memories*, 65, my emphasis. Stockton Axson also emphasized that Wilson's so-called "Quad" plan was "a purely educational reform" before Wilson's reaction to alumni opposition turned it into a fight between privilege and democracy. *"Brother Woodrow,"* 114, 128.

112. *PWW*, 14:183 (Oct. 25, 1902), 16:519 (ca. Dec. 13, 1906), 17:199, 202 (ca. June 10, 1907).

113. *PWW*, 16:525 (ca. Dec. 13, 1906), 17:176 (ca. June 6, 1907). In 1904, Charles Van Hise,

the new president of the University of Wisconsin, had proposed—not Oxbridge colleges but the more economical Midwestern equivalent—residential dormitories (of which it had only one for women and none for men), "a [dining] commons," and "a commodious and beautiful union" for the whole student body, which numbered perhaps 2,400. In the summer of 1907, Harvard men assured Wilson of their approval of his plan, saying, "If you do it, we must; and we ought all long ago to have done it." "Inaugural Address of President Charles Richard Van Hise," in *Science,* n.s. 20, no. 502 (Aug. 12, 1904); Merle Curti and Vernon Carstensen, *The University of Wisconsin, 1848–1925: A History,* 2 vols. (Madison: University of Wisconsin Press, 1949, 1974), 2:76–77, 178, 497–503; *PWW,* 17:240–41 (July 1, 1907): the editors erred in saying that *each* Wisconsin dorm was meant to have a commons and a union (241n3).

114. The fateful chronology is described in William Starr Myers, "Wilson in My Diary" and Eisenhart, "The Far-Seeing Wilson," both in Myers, ed., *Woodrow Wilson: Princeton Memories,* 47–49, 65–66, and in Craig, *Woodrow Wilson at Princeton,* 113–24. Myers was confident that, in all his reforms, Wilson "was supported in the main by a majority of both the faculty and the student body" (49). Biologist Edwin Grant Conklin thought that "the older members" of the faculty were "generally" against the quad plan, and "the younger ones for it." "As a Scientist Saw Him," in Myers, ed., *Woodrow Wilson: Princeton Memories,* 59. Duncan Spaeth, on the contrary, said that Wilson's speech "swept the faculty into all but unanimous support of his plan." "Wilson as I Knew Him," in Myers, ed., 82.

115. "The Princeton Preceptorial System," *The Independent,* 59 (Aug. 3, 1905): 239–40, in *PWW,* 14:107 (ca. June 1, 1905), 519 (ca. Dec. 13, 1906). Myers, "Wilson in My Diary," in Myers, ed., *Woodrow Wilson: Princeton Memories,* 38.

116. *PWW,* 17:180 (ca. June 6, 1907), 331 (Aug. 1, 1907), 19:285, 288 (July 1, 1909), my emphasis.

117. *PWW,* 19:57–58 (Feb. 19, 1909).

118. *PWW,* 19:279 (July 1, 1909), 344 (Aug. 18, 1909), 20:162 (Feb. 24, 1910).

119. *PWW,* 19:285, 287 (July 1, 1909), 344 (Aug. 19, 1909).

120. *PWW,* 16:522–23 (Dec. 13, 1906), 20:161, 166 (ca. Feb. 24, 1910).

121. *PWW,* 17:201 (ca. June 10, 1907), 424 (Oct. 7, 1909). Professor of English Stockton Axson, Wilson's brother-in-law, was "constantly in the house during the discussion of these matters" and "never heard Mr. Wilson at this time make any attack whatsoever upon the Princeton clubs as such. They were merely more or less of an obstacle in the way of the larger [educational] result which he wished to accomplish." *"Brother Woodrow,"* 127. Axson's colleague, Hardin Craig, agreed. *Woodrow Wilson at Princeton,* 49.

122. Princeton president Shirley Tilghman regards Wilson's goal of vertical integration as one of his major legacies to the modern university. Opening remarks at the conference on "The Educational Legacy of Woodrow Wilson: New Approaches," Woodrow Wilson School for Public and International Affairs, Princeton University, Oct. 16–17, 2009.

123. *PWW,* 17:185 (ca. June 6, 1907), 424 (Oct. 7, 1907), 19:289 (July 3, 1909).

124. For a discerning comparison, see Bruce Leslie's essay in this volume.

125. *PWW,* 20:165 (ca. Feb. 24, 1910), 334 (April 7, 1910).

126. *PWW,* 17:241 (July 1, 1907). See Bragdon, *Wilson: The Academic Years,* ch. 18; Mulder, *Wilson: Years of Preparation,* ch. 8; Axtell, *The Making of Princeton University,* ch. 7;

W. Barksdale Maynard, *Woodrow Wilson: Princeton to the Presidency* (New Haven: Yale University Press, 2008), chs. 12–14.

127. Craig, *Woodrow Wilson at Princeton,* 155–56.

128. Dodds's statement of beliefs about Princeton's future role at the final Bicentennial Convocation on June 17, 1947, could almost have been written by Wilson. For an excerpt, see Alexander Leitch, *A Princeton Companion* (Princeton: Princeton University Press, 1978), 140. Beginning in the mid-1930s, Dodds worked assiduously to commemorate Wilson's legacy at Princeton by building a home for the nascent School of Public and International Affairs and naming it for him; because of the Depression and World War II, the school was not renamed for Wilson until 1948 nor was the new building similarly dedicated until 1952.

129. "Wilson's Impact on Higher Education in the United States" address to the Woodrow Wilson Institute at Staunton, Virginia, April 26, 1956, in Raymond F. Pisney, ed., *Woodrow Wilson in Retrospect* (Verona, Va.: McClure Press, 1978), 68–73 at 68, 69, 72; reprinted in "Wilson as Educator," *Princeton Alumni Weekly,* Oct. 12, 1956, 9–10. See also Dodds, "The Educator," in Em Bowles Alsop, ed., *The Greatness of Woodrow Wilson, 1856–1956* (Port Washington, N.Y.: Kennikat Press, 1971 [1956]), 50–65.

130. See above, note 17; Samuel Eliot Morison, ed., *The Development of Harvard University since the Inauguration of President Eliot, 1869–1929* (Cambridge, Mass.: Harvard University Press, 1930), xlvii–xlix.

131. Alex Duke, *Importing Oxbridge: English Residential Colleges and American Universities* (New Haven: Yale University Press, 1996), ch. 4.

132. R. J. O'Hara, "Half of the Top 25 Universities Have Residential Colleges" (Aug. 20, 2006) and an international roster of collegiate-universities: http://collegiateway.org. The latest entrant abroad is the National University of Singapore, which will have four high-rise colleges for its freshmen and sophomores by 2012. Its planners, including five students, visited Harvard, Yale, and Princeton for their ideas about mixed faculty-student residences, small seminars, and multidisciplinary encouragement. Newley Purnell, "A Singapore University Plans Its First Residential Colleges," *Chronicle of Higher Education* (online), Dec. 14, 2010.

133. In 1946, professor of English George McLean Harper hoped that "some day perhaps a residential college such as [Wilson] envisioned will be incorporated in the University and named for him." "A Happy Family," in Myers, ed., *Woodrow Wilson: Princeton Memories,* 6.

134. "Welcome to Whitman College," *Princeton Alumni Weekly,* Nov. 21, 2007, 18–23; Catesby Leigh, "Traditional Style and Substance: Princeton's New Whitman Hall," *Wall Street Journal,* Sept. 25, 2007, D6; Richard Sammons, "Leaving the Dark Ages," [Clem Labine's] *Traditional Building* (Feb. 2008), 20–24; Ellis Woodman, "American Gothic," *Building Design,* 1080 (Feb. 29, 2008), 12–27; Shaina Li, "Butler Rising," *Daily Princetonian* (online), Feb. 20, 2009 (www.dailyprincetonian.com/2009/02/20); Lawrence Biemiller, "Princeton's Butler College Gets New Buildings—and May Lose an Old Nickname," *Chronicle of Higher Education,* Aug. 12, 2009 (http://chronicle.com/blogPost/Princetons-Butler-College/7655).

# Woodrow Wilson on Liberal Education for Statesmanship, 1890–1910

Adam R. Nelson

Throughout his years at Princeton, first as a professor and later as president, Woodrow Wilson asked one central question: how, in an era of rapid change, could the university prepare students for lives of national service, or, as he often called it, *statesmanship*? This question framed Wilson's sesquicentennial address, "Princeton in the Nation's Service" (1896), as well as his inaugural address, "Princeton for the Nation's Service" (1902). This essay traces Wilson's struggle to answer this question from the time he joined the Princeton faculty in 1890 to the year he left the presidency in 1910. A close look at his writings during this period suggests that his perspective on both liberal education and statesmanship changed over time. What began as a critique of abstract intellectualism and "de-nationalized" scholarship became, in the wake of the Spanish-American War, an impassioned call for a return to intellectualism and a reconceptualization of the purpose of liberal education in a global context. The modern American university, Wilson came to believe, had an urgent duty to prepare undergraduates for lives of both national *and* international statesmanship.

Although Wilson had been a proponent of "liberal education" from the start of his academic career, historians and biographers have overlooked the degree to which his perspective on the meaning and purpose of liberal education changed over time. In particular, they have ignored the ways in which his views shifted from a national to an international perspective after the United States' rise to a new role in world affairs. This change imposed new responsibilities on the American university. More than most of his contemporaries, who called on universities to bolster electives in technical, professional, or applied scientific education to secure the United States' military and economic supremacy, Wilson called for a prescribed literary and historical curriculum to give students the broad understanding they would need as leaders of national and international affairs. Dismissing applied science and professional training as the province of technical schools (and state universities), he called on Princeton to forge a different path. Only a revival of liberal humanistic education, he argued, could prepare a new generation of American statesmen for the difficult tasks of national and international leadership. Only a liberal education grounded in history, literature, politics, and "pure" (as opposed to applied) science could give the rising generation what he called a "statesmanship of mind."[1]

To be sure, Wilson's view of liberal education for statesmanship did not change suddenly after the Spanish-American War. It changed gradually as the implications of the United States' new position in the world became clear. "Ours is a day not of national so much as of *international* . . . forces," he had observed as early as 1891. "There is everywhere a free interchange of ideas, a wide community of intellectual and moral standards; there are common means of knowledge; there is quick intercourse and a general familiarity with the ends of the earth. No nation any longer lives apart; it is sharp give and take between the peoples of the world." This new, complex, and profoundly interconnected world placed new demands on the modern university. The question was, how could the university prepare students to *lead* this world?[2]

Surprisingly, the most prominent aspect of Wilson's public addresses in the 1890s was their relative neglect of international concerns in favor of a focus on nationalism. He gave countless speeches on nationalism, "Americanism," and the role universities could play in cultivating patriotic leaders. Among his many addresses were "Patriotism Begins at Home," "Spurious Versus Real Patriotism in Education," "Patriots and Politics," and "Patriotic Citizenship." Crisscrossing the country, giving dozens of speeches each year, he shared his thoughts on the subject of "true Americanism" with audiences young and old. While different speeches emphasized different aspects of his theme, all stressed the need for more patriotism in American life and the role universities could play in fostering a greater sense of national enthusiasm among students as well as future leaders. Despite—or perhaps because of—the United States' rapidly expanding role in the world,

Wilson returned again and again to nationalism as the key to a stronger and more unified country.[3]

In many speeches, Wilson noted the lamentable degree to which American universities had bowed in recent decades to European, especially German, models. In 1894 in *Forum* magazine he decried this foreign influence. "We have been so often bidden, by young and old alike, to make our university instruction like that of Germany, that we have more than half consented to try the experiment," he observed. But to what end? More often than not, the example of the German university had proven a poor fit in the American context. "There is a very heavy duty on imported ideals," he wrote. "It costs us more than they are worth to subject them to our customs and get them fairly on the market. There is no great demand for them." Rather than fawning after European models, Wilson urged, American universities should aim to serve uniquely *American* cultural and political needs. "Anybody can establish the modern sort of university, anywhere. It has no necessary nationality or character," he concluded. "But only in a free country with great traditions of enlightened sentiment and continuous purpose can a university have the national mark . . . of a deliberate espousal of the spirit of a noble literature and historic institutions. Such a university would be a National Academy—the only sort worth having."[4]

Echoing calls for a national university that went back at least a century, Wilson cast the modern university as an instrument of nation building. "In order to be national," he asserted, "a university should have at the centre of all its training courses of instruction in that literature which contains the ideals of its race and all the nice proofs and subtle inspirations of the character, spirit, and thought of the nation which it serves; and, besides that, instruction in the history and leading conceptions of those institutions which have served the nation's energies in the preservation of order and the maintenance of just standards of civil virtue and public purpose. These should constitute the common training of all its students, as the only means of schooling their spirits for their common life as citizens." In a tone Benjamin Rush and other Founding Fathers would have applauded, Wilson put the American university at the very heart of the national experiment. "A university should be an organ of memory for the State for the transmission of its best traditions," he told his readers. "We must look to the universities to see to it that we be not denationalized, but rather made more steadfast in our best judgments of progress."[5]

Wilson's fear of a "denationalized" university was arguably the defining feature of his educational thought in the 1890s. "Do we want universities of a distinctively American type?" he asked *Forum* readers. "It is the first impulse of most scholarly minds to reply with a plain and decided negative. Learning is cosmopolitan, and it would seem at first thought like stripping learning of its freedom and its wide prerogative to demand that the universities where [learning] makes its home should be national." While truth itself may be "without geographic boundary," Wilson conceded, universities had a distinctly national purpose. "All physical science is international, so are all formal parts of learning," he acknowledged. "But there is besides these a learning of purpose, to be found in literature and in the study of institutions; and this it is which should be made the means of nationalizing our universities, being given the central and coordinating place in their courses of instruction." Ultimately, he reasoned, "scholarship, though it must everywhere seek the truth, may select the truths it shall search for and emphasize. It is this selection that should be national." The challenge of the future was to make selections that prepared students for the responsibilities of national statesmanship.[6]

Much as Wilson lamented the "denationalization" of the modern university, the forces promoting this denationalization were themselves (ironically) nationalized in the form of the German university, which in Wilson's estimation represented a particular—and particularly damaging—strain of applied science and specialized research, both of which jeopardized the essentially "spiritual" quality he wished to preserve in American colleges. To understand Wilson's evolving perspective on the link between liberal education and national statesmanship, one must first understand his rather caricatured view of the German university. For most of the nineteenth century, he charged, American university leaders had "felt very strongly the influence of German universities, whose functions and objects are entirely different [from those of American universities]. It is almost the exclusive function of German universities to supply technical and professional education. They have no undergraduates, no colleges, no body of students who are going through the earlier stages of drill and initiation into the great subjects of study." Repeated attempts to graft the German university onto the American college had, in Wilson's view, "been very misleading to us in America in respect of genuine institutional growth and coordination." These efforts, he concluded, had done more harm than good.[7]

This unwelcome invasion of the German university model, based as it was on universalistic conceptions of scientific research, threatened to denationalize the American university, and indeed all modern universities, Wilson felt. Modern "scholarly culture," he told his students, "*tends always to denationalize*—at any rate to take away all intensities of habit or prepossession—*to universalize the habit of mind*—to produce *internationality* of thought and standard by substituting the broadly *human* for the narrowly local sympathy and comprehension." While such "internationality of thought" had its virtues, it also had serious drawbacks in that national character, for Wilson, hinged on "(a) *common ideals* of conduct . . . ; (b) a *common attitude towards institutions* and . . . ; (c) a *common attitude towards foreign systems* of government and foreign ideals of conduct." Distancing himself from enlightenment images of scholarly internationalism in favor of an updated romantic nationalism, Wilson claimed that higher education should be a "means of nationalizing the men whom the universities send forth to represent the power and worth of education." As he told a group of Princeton alumni in a particularly illuminating remark in 1897, "If you want a national university, you should build it out of nationality. Science has no nationality. If a university wants to breathe a national spirit, it must breathe the spirit of history and literature."[8]

Wilson, however, did not reject all forms of scholarly internationalism during these years. In an essay for *Century* magazine in 1895, he praised the cosmopolitan life of letters (and in the process gave a hint of his later call for an international "statesmanship of mind"). This essay, "On an Author's Choice of Company," described an idealized "community of letters," a peaceful realm where eternal principles and verities could be apprehended and appreciated in platonic abstraction. "Writers have liked to speak of the Republic of Letters, as if to mark their freedom and equality; but there is a better phrase, namely, the Community of Letters; for that means intercourse and comradeship and a life in common," he wrote; "for all, it is a bonny place to be," a place where the values of a liberal education reigned. Significantly for Wilson, this philadelphian community did not submerge national traits. "No doubt there are national groups. . . . Shakespeare is king among the English, as Homer is among the Greeks, and sober Dante among his gay countrymen. But their thoughts all have in common, though speech divide them; and sovereignty does not exclude comradeship or embarrass freedom." It was a commonality of thought—not a commonality of homeland—that united members of this community of letters.[9]

On the subject of liberal education, Wilson in the 1890s often seemed of two minds. On the one hand, he shared with many of his nineteenth-century predecessors a belief that universities must "nationalize" their students and that a liberal education grounded in national history, literature, and political institutions was the means to do so. On the other hand, he shared with other (or in some cases, the same) predecessors a belief that liberal education itself might *de*nationalize students and lead them *away* from a sense of national identity, sympathy, or loyalty. Thus, on the one hand, such education was a key to patriotism; on the other, it was an entrepôt to a culturally empty cosmopolitanism. Unfortunately, it was as unclear to Wilson as it was to his contemporaries how to encourage the former and evade the latter, even if success in this delicate task seemed essential to the education of citizen-leaders. To advance patriotism while avoiding cosmopolitanism (a realm, Wilson feared, "where sympathy is neither here nor there") seemed imperative to the education of future statesmen, but how could the American university provide a liberal education that would nationalize and not denationalize its students? In the 1890s, Wilson had no clear answer to this question.[10]

The basic tension between patriotism and cosmopolitanism—a tension arguably at the very heart of the modern university—figured into virtually everything Wilson published on the subject of liberal education in the 1890s. Typically, he framed this conflict in terms of a basic difference between the active patriotism of politicians and the passive cosmopolitanism of scholars. The opposition between "the politician" and "the writer" surfaced repeatedly in his speeches. "The men who act stand nearer the mass of men than do the men who write," he proclaimed in 1890 in a commencement speech at the University of Tennessee. "How can any man whose method is the method of artistic completeness of thought and expression, whose mood is the mood of contemplation, for a moment understand or tolerate 'the majority,' whose purpose and practice it is to strike out broad, rough-hewn policies, whose mood is the mood of action?" Statesmanship was impossible for the man of letters. "The literary mind conceives images, images rounded, perfect, ideal," Wilson argued. "It is not guided by principles, as statesmen conceive principles, but by conceptions. Principles, as statesmen conceive them, are threads to the labyrinth of circumstances; principles, as the literary mind holds them, are unities, instrumental to nothing, sufficient unto themselves." To prepare students for real, active statesmanship, Wilson insisted, American universities needed a new approach to liberal education: they needed to replace the passive cosmopolitanism of mere book-learning with a patriotic commitment to national service.[11]

In calling for a fresh view of liberal education, Wilson criticized the nation's universities for clinging to a tired, outmoded curriculum rooted in dull recitations and intellectual abstraction. This sort of "memoritor" curriculum, he maintained, was ill-suited to preparing active citizens and leaders. His ideal citizen-leader, Abraham Lincoln, was "the supreme American" precisely *because* he lacked a modern (read: denationalized and therefore soulless) university education. "He never ceased to be a common man: that was his source of strength," Wilson noted in the *Forum* in 1893. "[H]e was a common man with genius, a genius for things American, for insight into the common thought, for mastery of the fundamental things of politics that inhere in human nature and cast hardly more than their shadows on constitutions, for the practical niceties of affairs, for judging men and assessing arguments." Lincoln represented a "generalized American," a man who transcended sectional interests to unite the nation behind a shared identity and purpose. The challenge, Wilson felt, was to produce more Lincolns, but in the 1890s few American universities—distracted as they were by the siren calls of applied science, technical education, professional specialization, and the headlong pursuit of financial and physical "growth"—seemed ready to accept this challenge.[12]

To produce more Lincolns, the American university would have to revitalize its commitment to liberal education, but in a new form—a form that cultivated students' devotion to national service and, simultaneously, counteracted the dual threat posed by modern science: a denationalized cosmopolitanism on the one hand and a dangerous overspecialization on the other. Speaking in 1893 at the World's Columbian Exposition in Chicago, Wilson condemned "the disease of specialization by which we are now so sorely afflicted." "Our professional men are lamed and hampered by that partial knowledge, which is the most dangerous form of ignorance," he declared. "The empiric is the natural enemy of society . . . and it is imperative that everything should be done, everything risked, to get rid of him. Nothing sobers and reforms him like a (genuine) liberal education."[13]

But what constituted a genuine liberal education? Wilson began to craft his answer in 1896 in his landmark address, "Princeton in the Nation's Service," the keynote at Princeton's sesquicentennial anniversary. In this address, Wilson outlined his nascent vision of a new liberal education for statesmanship. "*The world,*" he began, "*has long thought that it detected in the academic life some lack of sympathy with itself, some disdain of the homely tasks which make the gross globe inhabitable—not a little proud aloofness and lofty superiority, as if education always softened the hands and alienated the heart.*" Acknowledging that "*books are a great relief from the haggling of the market, libraries a very welcome refuge from the strife of commerce,*" he argued that modern leaders nonetheless required far more than book-learning—more than intellectualism. In the future, he explained, Princeton would have to rediscover what Princeton men of revolutionary days had known: a "generous union . . . between the life of philosophy and the life of the state." The university's highest aim, he insisted, must be a *re*-nationalized education for statesmanship.[14]

Wilson's new liberal education for statesmanship put its emphasis squarely on humanistic, not scientific, learning. "Science," he felt, had to be humanized as well as nationalized. "No man more heartily admires, more gladly welcomes, more approvingly reckons the gain and enlightenment that have come to the world through extraordinary advances in physical science," Wilson held. "But I am a student of society, and I should deem myself unworthy of the comradeship of great men of science should I not speak the plain truth with regard to what I see happening under my own eyes. I have no laboratory but the world of books and men in which I live; but I am very much mistaken if the scientific spirit of the age is not doing us a great disservice, working in us a certain degeneracy." According to Wilson, science had denationalized the university, depleting its cultural sympathies and depriving its students of a sense of a common history and a common fate. "Science has bred in us a spirit of experiment and a contempt for the past," he stated. "*It has driven mystery out of the Universe; it has made malleable stuff of the hard world, and laid it out in its elements upon the table of every class room. . . . This is the disservice scientific study has done us: it has given us agnosticism in the realm of philosophy, scientific anarchism in the field of politics.*" How could a university with science at its center imbue students with a spiritual commitment to national service?[15]

"We have not given science too big a place in our education," Wilson noted, "but we have made a perilous mistake in giving it too great a preponderance in method in every other branch of study." Reiterating his fear that science abetted the denationalization of the university—partly because it represented forms of cosmopolitanism or internationalism that detached practitioners from local sympathies—Wilson called for a renewed commitment to national service in the American university. "Of course," he concluded, "when all is said, it is not learning but the spirit of service that will give a college a place in the public annals of the nation. It is indispensable, it seems to me, if it is to do its right service, that the air of affairs should be admitted to all its classrooms. I do not mean the air of party politics but the air of the world's transactions, the consciousness of the solidarity of the race, the sense of the duty of man toward man." Pointing to a post-frontier age in which American progress would become "intensive" rather than "extensive," Wilson called for a new patriotism in American colleges. "There is laid upon us the compulsion of the national life," he declared. "We dare not keep aloof and closet ourselves while the nation comes to its maturity. The days of glad expansion are gone. Our life grows tense and difficult; our resource for the future lies in careful thought, providence, and a wise economy; and the school must be of the nation."[16]

While most historians and biographers highlight the closing line of Wilson's sesquicentennial address—"Who shall show us the way to this place?"—as the first hint of his bid for the presidency at Princeton six years later, perhaps equally significant was the way in which this speech framed his understanding of the relationship between liberal education and statesmanship. Above all, it cast both liberal education and statesmanship in *national* terms, with the reinvigoration of national service as Wilson's foremost objective. Indeed, his overriding fear was the denationalization of the university under the powerful influence of modern science. "The science of the age was cosmopolitanism, has no home, no parallels of latitude," he wrote in 1897, the year after his sesquicentennial address; hence, the first priority of the American university must be to shore up a sense of nationality and reinforce students' commitment to national service . . . before it was too late. But in some ways, it was already too late. A very different world lay just around the corner—a new world that led Wilson to a dramatic reconceptualization of his views on both liberal education and statesmanship.[17]

In August 1898, six months after the sinking of the USS *Maine* brought the United States into war in Cuba and three months after Commodore George Dewey landed in the Philippines, Wilson drafted a short memo, asking: "What Ought We to Do?" His query applied not only to U.S. war aims but also to universities' role in the conflict. "A brief season of war has deeply changed our thought, and has altered, it may be permanently, the conditions of our national life," he wrote. "We shall be wise to assess the change calmly, if it be indeed inevitable, and to examine ourselves what it is we intend and by what means we hope to accomplish it. We have passed, it would seem, the parting of the ways: interest and prudence alike turn our thought to the new country we have entered." Reviewing the diplomatic complexities that had preceded the war, he urged leaders to weigh their actions carefully. "We had neither dreamed of nor desired victories at the ends of the earth, and the spoils of war had not entered our calculations," he insisted. "Whatever our judgments or scruples in these matters, the thing is done; cannot be undone; and our future must spring out of it. The processes of our modern life are swift: we cannot stay them by regrets. Only those nations shall approve themselves masterful and fit to act either for themselves or others in such a time which show themselves capable of thinking on the run and amidst the whirl of events."[18]

How, the professor wondered, could the American universities prepare their students for this new and "very modern world" in which nations had "become aggressive" in pursuit of global supremacy? "We have left the continent which has hitherto been our own field of action and have gone out upon the seas where the nations are rivals and we cannot live or act apart," he noted. "The question is not, shall the vital nations of Europe take possession of the territories of those [nations] which are less vital and divide the kingdoms of Africa and Asia? The question is, now, which nations shall possess the world?" Noting that Germany, France, Russia, and England were the chief "rivals in the new spoliation," he observed that, "of a sudden," the United States had joined this imperialist pack. "*What ought we to do?*" he asked. "It is not simply a question of expediency: the question of expediency is itself infinitely hard to settle. It is a question also of moral obligation. What *ought* we to do?" This question raised two corollaries for Wilson: first, *who* would decide what the United States ought to do? and second, *how* should these leaders be educated? How could American universities prepare a new generation of leaders for national and international statesmanship?[19]

In the winter of 1900, Wilson scrawled a few notes for a new speech on "Americanism"—notes he used many times over the next decade. "All the world just now is intensely conscious of the existence and the power of America," he wrote. "We do not have to prove that we are the chief nation of the world: we admit it! . . . We are conscious of a new turn in the plot—a dramatic situation, with all the world for audience." Defining *Americanism* the next day in Wilmington, Delaware, he added: "Now that the United States sets the pace for the nations it is necessary to examine it, and make it acceptable in the world's market by making it excellent and suitable for leadership in the world." Wilson repeated this message a year later in the *Atlantic Monthly* (which his friend Walter Hines Page edited after leaving the *Forum*). The great challenge, Wilson suggested, was no longer the *nationalization* but the *internationalization* of American statesmen, and it was up to American universities to see that future generations were prepared for global leadership. "We might not have seen our duty, had the Philippines not fallen to us by the willful fortune of war; but it would have been our duty, nevertheless, to play the part we now see ourselves obliged to play. The East is to be opened up and transformed, whether we will or no; the standards of the West are to be imposed upon it; nations and peoples which have stood still the centuries through are to be quickened and made part of the universal world of commerce and ideas which has so steadily been a-making by the advance of European power from age to age. It is our peculiar duty . . . to impart to the peoples thus driven out upon the road of change, so far as we have opportunity or can make it, our own principles of self-help; teach them order and self-control in the midst of change; impart to them, if it be possible by contact and sympathy and example, the drill and habit of law and obedience."[20]

Although his essay in the *Atlantic Monthly* said nothing explicitly about universities, it did reveal an important shift in Wilson's conception of statesmanship and, in turn, his conception of the form of *education* future statesmen required to prepare for the duties of global leadership. As his conception of statesmanship rose from a national to an international plane, so his conception of liberal education expanded from a national into an international endeavor. Liberal education for statesmanship became, for him, a project of preparing future leaders to spread the ideals and institutions of the United States to every corner of the earth. American ideals had to be exported; they had to be *internationalized.* "If we are to be statesmanlike, self-poised, and know the errand on which we have started," he wrote, "we must assess our qualities and get rid of the undesirable, perfect ourselves in those that make for power and know what sort of power we wish to possess, examine the brand of those we are carrying into the field of international politics and asking the world to admire." It was these qualities of international statesmanship that universities had to cultivate. "Some night the world will come to the threshold of a new century," Wilson concluded, "but, as far as our national life is concerned, we have passed the threshold. We stepped into the arena of the world since the Spanish war and entered a new century."[21]

It would not be too much to say that, for Wilson in the wake of the Spanish-American War, the greatest challenge facing the American university was no longer the de- or re-nationalization of the university but rather the *inter*nationalization of the university. No longer did he criticize the "internationality of thought"; now he embraced it. No longer did he condemn the "cosmopolitanism of science"; now he welcomed it. No longer he did he censure "abstract intellectualism"; now he praised it. The change was remarkable. After the war, he associated "practical" education with a "short-term" outlook and warned future leaders to be cautious amid the whirl of political affairs. No longer did he complain about the uselessness of book-learning or the passivity of scholarship; now he applauded the "statesmanship of letters." Gradually, the university became in his mind a place of quiet contemplation, a place set apart for disinterested thought and the articulation of "universal" values. While it would have been premature to interpret his appeal for the internationalization of the university as a philosophical shift toward international*ism* (he frequently called himself an "imperialist"), it was clear that his view of the American university—and specifically the purposes of liberal education for both national and international statesmanship—had changed.[22]

This changed view coincided with Wilson's inauguration in 1902 as Princeton's thirteenth president. His inaugural address, "Princeton for the Nation's Service," revisited many of the ideas that had preoccupied him in recent years but cast these ideas in a new light. "A new age is before us, in which, it would seem, we must lead the world," he asserted. "It is plain what the nation needs as its affairs grow more and more complex and its interests begin to touch the ends of the earth. It needs efficient and enlightened men. The universities of the country must take part in supplying them." The modern university, he explained, "is not for the majority who carry forward the common labour of the world, nor even for those who work at the skilled handicrafts which multiply the conveniences and the luxuries of the complex modern life. It is for the minority who plan, who conceive, who superintend, who mediate between group and group and must see the wide stage as a whole." For these future leaders, a liberal education in history, literature, and politics, as well as in pure science, was the key;

indeed, no other education would suffice. "Every considerable undertaking has come to be based on knowledge, on thoughtfulness, on the masterful handling of men and facts," Wilson noted. "The university must stand in the midst, where the roads of thought and knowledge interlace and cross, and building upon some coign of vantage, command them all."[23]

In the months after his inauguration, Wilson shared his new conception of liberal education with audiences across the country. Speaking to alumni in Washington, D.C., he drew an implicit connection between liberal education and world leadership. "What is the principal object of a liberal education?" he asked. "It is to liberate men from the dull round of one idea, to broaden their minds and their ability to conceive. The university is a little world of thought and action where we fit men for the larger world." He added in a particularly revealing metaphor: "People sometimes say that when a man goes through college he is ready to tackle the world. That is wrong. He has already tackled the world, on a small scale, when he has completed his course at college. The university is a world in miniature, and the larger the university the easier may this idea be realized." A few weeks later, after receiving an honorary degree at Brown, he summarized his view of liberal education for statesmanship: "To an educator in America is presented the task not only of scholarship, but of statesmanship, for with the leadership of educated men the country is ruled." Now it was time for American universities to blend the dual tasks of scholarship and statesmanship into one seamless intellectual and practical enterprise. Only a revival of liberal education could prepare a new generation of students for leadership both in the United States and overseas.[24]

Wilson's modern statesman was no denationalized cosmopolitan but, rather, a deeply *nationalized* leader who pursued distinctly national interests amid the complexities of global affairs. He was no less patriotic for having a global perspective. Speaking in Massachusetts in January 1902, Wilson stressed this point: "Men have dreamed of international patriotism, and they have spoken of the provincialism of the patriotism we have professed, and of the narrowness of keeping our patriotism to ourselves." Yet it seemed to Wilson that "international patriotism" was an oxymoron. At most, he speculated, two or more nations might share common sympathies based on ties of history or language, but the pursuit of a more general human solidarity would only strain these sympathies. Thus, when it came to American patriotism, he explained, "there's a boundary to it. It is easier for us to feel a quick impulse of sympathy with the nation across the ocean [i.e., England] because its people speak the same language we do, and because so many threads of history are run into our past, which is also their past, and there is the idea of kinship and solidarity of interests and purpose and ideals which lie at the bottom of it all." A similar bond with the people of the Philippines, he implied, was unlikely.[25]

Yet, just as Wilson could sometimes be of two minds on the link between liberal education and nationalism, he could also be of two minds on the subject of patriotism. On the one hand, he stressed the importance of local or regional ties as the foundation of "true patriotism." On the other hand, he frequently emphasized the importance of *transcending* local ties in the pursuit of more universal principles. Both points surfaced often in his speeches. In one speech, he might say that "Every man among us . . . is put upon his honor to understand and serve the community in which he lives, and the only true patriotism is that which is local in its rootage—vital patriotism begins at home; it is not a vague interest, spread out over the whole affairs of a whole nation [let alone the entire world], but a direct and definite identification of feeling and purpose with the interests of one's home and neighbors." Then, in another speech (given the same year), he could say, "We used to think there was a peculiar brand of human nature, known as the American. We now know that American human nature is exactly like any other human nature. We have had a special American past, but what that past has taught us, is that we are of the same blood as the rest of mankind." A liberal education, Wilson seemed to believe, was responsible for directing all these forms of human sympathy—local, regional, national, and international—toward one basic aim: *national* service.[26]

The chief obstacle to this aim, Wilson held, was sectionalism or "provincialism." "To rid our young men of provincialism," he told students at Cooper Union in New York, "I would have every young man of the North educated in the South and every young man of the South educated in the North. I would have every young man of the West educated in the East . . . and . . . every young man of the East educated in the West." Only in this way could each gain a truly national—and, ultimately, international—outlook. While "an exclusive home life bred provincialism," he explained in a related speech, "at college a man came into contact with men of all countries . . . and felt something of the life that circulated the world." This vision of a "life that circulated the world" recurred in many of Wilson's speeches in this period. Such cosmopolitanism was for him both a recollection of his beloved "community of letters" as well as an antidote to provincialism in the American university. "The danger of this country is provincialism," he told Wall Street bankers (whom he chided for their "eastern" parochialism) in 1902. "The mission of the university is to make its students citizens of the world of thoughtful men."[27]

To make students into "citizens of the world of thoughtful men," Wilson in the fall of 1903 launched a major overhaul of Princeton's curriculum, which was completed the following spring. With a mixture of required literary and scientific courses in the first year, followed by a choice of "concentration," the new curriculum institutionalized his idea of liberal education for statesmanship. "The world has changed by leaps and bounds . . . during the last generation," he wrote in one essay on his reforms. "The engineer nowadays, if he would rise to the top of his profession, must be something more than a mechanical expert; he must be ready to become a master of industry and of men, to assume charge of great undertakings in any quarter of the globe, under the most various and unlooked for conditions of law, of climate, of labor. His resources will be tried to the utmost, and he must have resources. . . . He needs the education of a general officer in the world's army of workers: and no sort of training or information will come amiss." In an era when the American engineer could well "be sent to build a bridge in India and use coolies as laborers," Wilson argued, every student needed an education for both national and international leadership.[28]

This new education for international statesmanship, Wilson came to believe, must be rooted in a thorough *literary* curriculum. In an important address, "The Statesmanship of Letters," delivered in 1903 at the Carnegie Institute in Pittsburgh, he made a case for literature and book-learning as the soul, or spirit, of the modern university. Uncharacteristically abstract, this address fundamentally reordered Wilson's conception of the relationship between practical and intellectual ends in undergraduate learning. In this speech, the man of letters became just as powerful in his view as the man of practical affairs. "We have established in our minds a sort of antithesis between what is literary and what is practical and have come to assume that there is no guidance in letters for the man of affairs," he maintained (perhaps downplaying his own role in the perpetuation of this antithesis). "But the fact is not so. If letters guide the thought and lead the imagination, they are an intimate part of the stuff the statesman deals with. Men have been subtly formed and singularly dominated by what they read, and those who form their reading for them are more truly their masters than their statesmen are. It behooves us to look into this matter, question some of the antitheses we have set up, and see life as it is."[29]

In "The Statesmanship of Letters," Wilson sought a new synthesis of literary and practical education. "The atmosphere of our time is not literary," he acknowledged. "The man of letters is made to feel by the challenges of the modern world that he must justify his existence, must prove himself not idle and bent upon a mere self-pleasing use of his faculties, but seriously and serviceably at work on what will advance the world's business." He continued: "We are apt to contrast science with letters and to suppose that the difference between them is that science handles concrete facts whereas letters handle only figments of the mind." Yet, he argued, letters and science—"in their higher range"—were simply different ways of expressing complex ideas. "Literature, if you conceive it broadly enough, is the conspectus of affairs outside the narrow path of what is merely technical or of the hand, and the literature of which this is true is the literature of science no less than the literature of imagination." No longer was book-learning for Wilson a selfish retreat from the world of practical affairs—what he once called a "cerebral involution." Now, a thorough literary education was the indispensable key to preparing undergraduates for national and international statesmanship.[30]

Dividing modern education into three branches—literary, scientific, and political—Wilson held that all three were essential to statesmanship and thus necessary components of the undergraduate curriculum. Literature, no less than science or politics, had the power to guide the affairs of state. "It is this power to guide which entitles the greater sort of writing to be called the literature of power," he asserted. "It takes hold upon the mind as the greater sort of oratory does, entering not merely the ear to please it but also the heart itself to quicken it as the source of action." Every undergraduate, he insisted, required a thorough education in this literature of power. "Great books have changed men's lives and altered the current of history," he told his listeners at the Carnegie Institute, adding that a "nation whose literature has sunk to inefficiency cannot expect to see its men masterful upon the field of action." Not only were books the most efficient instruments of education, Wilson concluded, but a liberal education based on books was a prerequisite for effective statesmanship.[31]

Yet, a literary education was only part of such preparation; a scientific education was also necessary. On this point, Wilson's thinking had changed no less than it had on the matter of literary education. For years, Wilson had condemned scientific education as merely technical; now, pure (non-applied) science gained a *spiritual* dimension that made it essential to international statesmanship. "Undoubtedly a profound knowledge of the processes of nature is necessary to the material greatness of an industrial people. . . . But we are not to stop there. . . . The nation must have spiritual success as well as material success; and some men somewhere must devote their energies to laying before . . . young minds . . . the library of the world's full range of thinking and experience." By such a library, he explained, "I mean not merely the classics of the world's literature . . . but also the books which contain record of the kind of thinking which underlies every process of the modern industrial world. Abstract science, by which I mean the science of the investigator whose object is not a commercial product but the discovery of the laws of nature and the exploration of every process which reveals nature in operation, must go before the practical application of the laws of nature in the factory and the shop."[32]

The shift in Wilson's perspective was striking. Written between his inauguration and his curricular reforms, "The Statesmanship of Letters" offered his most cogent summary of the link between literary education and statesmanship. "My conception . . . of the higher education is a conception broad enough to embrace the whole field of thought, the whole record of experience," he concluded, "but what I emphasize about it is that it is withdrawal from the main motives of the world's material endeavor. I maintain that it is part of the statesmanship of mind that there should ever [be] a certain seclusion of the mind that [must] precede the struggle of life, a certain period of withdrawal and abstraction, when no particular skill is sought, no definite occupation studied, no single aim or ambition dwelt upon, but only a general preliminary orientation of the mind. It is a process by which the young mind is, so to say, laid alongside the mind of the world." This emphasis on intellectualism, on a new "statesmanship of mind," expressed the core of Wilson's new conception of liberal education. In his words, "This captaincy upon the great high seas of intellectual enterprise is what I mean by the statesmanship of letters, that mastery of interpretation which shall penetrate the motives and the policies of the modern world."[33]

In the years after this speech, Wilson's vision of liberal education, and specifically the relationship between liberal education and international leadership, gained force and momentum. In a speech at Swarthmore in

1905, he framed statesmanship of mind in terms of the United States' new role in global affairs. "America is not the first to feel herself called to ruling the world," he noted, "but if she rules the world well, she will be the first to do that. . . . It is not because we will have and hold the fleetest ships and most irresistible armies that we shall deserve the annals we started out to write, but as we use these armies and navies to do the just thing and to serve mankind." He added in a speech in Montgomery, Alabama: "The coming citizens of manhood and philanthropy are to have international minds. Our cousins abroad must be searched, and it should be known what they are doing and what they are thinking. If we confine ourselves to the homes where we live and live and move only in their environment, we do not know where we are . . . and cannot tell where we are 'until we know what and where the rest of the world is.'" To give the rising generation the "international minds" they needed to "know what and where the rest of the world is," the American university had to offer a new form of liberal education—a form of literary education that prepared students for intellectual leadership on the national as well as the international stage.[34]

How, in an era of rapid change, could American universities prepare students for lives of national service? Wilson had been grappling with this question for a long time. As early as 1885, he had reflected on the pace of global change and the effects it would have on American education. Even as new institutions of higher education such as Johns Hopkins (where Wilson was then enrolled) had begun to emerge, he noted that "powerful forces for the diffusion and intercommunication of thought and information have been developing with equal rapidity. Through commerce and the press, steady trade-winds have sprung up which carry the seeds of education and enlightenment, wheresoever planted, to every quarter of the globe. No scrap of new thought can escape being borne away from its place of birth by these all-absorbing currents. No idea can be kept exclusively at home but is taken up by the trader, the reporter, the traveller, the missionary, the explorer, and is given to all the world in the newspaper, the novel, the memoir, the poem, the treatise, till every community may know not only itself and its neighbors, but all the world as well." It was a prescient statement—one that led Wilson to predict "a *new* democracy" shared among nations—but it hardly prepared him for the *educational* challenges that such a grand vision entailed.[35]

Two decades later, in December 1907 (as his famous "Quad" fight was just starting to heat up at Princeton), Wilson traveled west to speak on the future of the American university. While tempers flared over the placement of a new graduate school on campus as well as the role of eating clubs for undergraduates, he repeated his call for an international statesmanship of mind. "The trouble with America," he noted, "is that so many men are thinking in the terms of the things they are doing, that they cannot think in the terms of what other men are doing, and therefore cannot think in national terms of what the nation is doing." The solution, he claimed, was a reconceptualization of liberal education. "Liberal training is part of the training of the statesmanship of the mind for most people; it is a process of lifting men's minds above the level of their daily tasks and giving them a glimpse of the map of the world, so that . . . out of the ranks of the people there may constantly arise those who have knowledge of their day and generation and can speak to their people like prophets of things to come. It is for this reason we must give as many minds as possible a liberal education." And by *liberal education,* he added, "I mean an education which does not concentrate its attention upon particular individual interests but seeks to acquaint the mind with those great bodies of thought which are meant for the enlightenment of the world." Here, in short, was the link between intellectualism and both national and international statesmanship.[36]

"The life of the present day is incalculably complex," Wilson observed in 1909 in a New York speech on "The Meaning of a Liberal Education." Not only was modern life complex, but "its complexities are of such recent rise and origin that we have not yet had time to understand what they are or to assess the value of the new things that have come into our life." As life had become more complex, so had learning. "Modern learning has been so drawn into a score of consequences, has been so extended into a system of uses, that it is a sort of mirror held up to life itself, and the man of affairs now seeks . . . from the scholar, those . . . elements which shall guide him in accomplishing the particular material tasks which lie immediately under his hand." No longer was the scholar, for Wilson, a passive figure, aloof from active leadership; now the scholar was a central player in practical global affairs. In this new and "very modern world," he explained, "there is not the scholar on the one side with his door closed and his window open, and, on the other side, the manufacturer and man of commerce beating the seas with his ships and searching the distant markets of the world. . . . The man of learning has on his table a telephone that connects him with all the activities of the world . . . ; he feels that he is one of the many servants to carry on the great tasks of today, whether they be material or intellectual."[37]

The change was stunning. The very identity of the modern scholar had shifted for Wilson in the span of ten years. Where once he denounced the passivity of book-learning and the impracticality of "abstract intellectualism," he now appealed for the "intellectual liberalization" of the undergraduate curriculum. Where once he dreaded the denationalization of the American university and rejected the "internationality of thought," he now saw the fulfillment of the university's mission only in the internationalization of its work. The impetus for this dramatic change in perspective was the United States' rise to global power in the Spanish-American War—an event which, in Wilson's view, had exposed an urgent need for "a new breed of men" educated for national as well as international leadership. The nation's universities had to supply these men. Speaking in New York in 1909, Wilson asserted that, if the United States was to fulfill its destiny, "she must realize above all other things that she has ceased to be a closed and domestic nation. We have now to think in the terms of the world and not in terms of America. We have come out upon a stage of international responsibility from which we cannot retire." No other words so clearly summarized the shift in Wilson's perspective from a national to an international point of view. The war, he believed, had changed the United States' role in the world and, in turn, the role of the American university.[38]

Wilson knew the war had changed his views. Reflecting on his curricular reforms in 1910, he placed them explicitly in this context: "So long as we framed our policy for the college only, we were comparatively free," he wrote. "These were our domestic affairs. We could handle them independently, as the nation handled all its questions of domestic policy before the Spanish War drew it into the general field of international influence, the field in which nation reacts upon nation and it is necessary to have a policy whose connections are worldwide and accommodated to the great international forces of the day." The war changed everything. While at first the issues of curricular reform had appeared in a simple "domestic" light, the debate over graduate education placed the university in a global context. Wilson noted: "as with the nation after the Spanish War, when we came to university questions, questions that affected the training of professional scholars, questions of research, questions of professional study, we necessarily came out into the wide and general academic field, where the right policy was a matter of action and reaction between ourselves and the other universities of the country and of the world." In the wake of the war, he recognized, it "became necessary to relate ourselves very carefully to the rest of the great world of universities, to square our methods with the accepted methods of graduate study everywhere."[39]

Wilson's twenty years at Princeton had been guided by one key question—how could the university prepare its students for national service?—and his answer changed during these years. The watershed event was the Spanish-American War, which fundamentally reframed his conception of liberal education for statesmanship. Unlike contemporaries who called, after the war, for greater emphasis on applied sciences and specialized research, Wilson called for a new synthesis of literary and scientific education, a return to intellectualism, a statesmanship of mind. For him, the "very modern world" the United States entered in the twentieth century demanded a new, internationalized conception of liberal education. No longer could the American university define its work primarily in technical or professional terms; no longer could it define its mission in national terms. Now, the university's mission was global, and it had to prepare its students for both national and international leadership. Should it fail to do so—should it fail to cultivate an international statesmanship of mind—the nation would risk a dearth of leaders to serve its deepest interests both at home and abroad. Wilson (already hinting at the growing "material success" of industrial Germany) did not want to run that risk.[40]

NOTES

1. "The Statesmanship of Letters" (Nov. 5, 1903) in *The Papers of Woodrow Wilson,* ed. Arthur S. Link et al., 69 vols. (Princeton: Princeton University Press, 1966–94), 15:42 (hereafter *PWW*).

2. "Democracy" (Dec. 5, 1891), *PWW,* 7:348.

3. "Patriotism Begins at Home" (Dec. 10, 1897), *PWW,* 10:349–51; "Spurious Versus Real Patriotism in Education" (Oct. 13, 1899), *PWW,* 11:244–61; "Patriots and Politics" (Jan. 3, 1900), 11:356–57; "Patriotic Citizenship" (Sept. 29, 30, 1897), *PWW,* 10:320–21.

4. "University Training and Citizenship" (June 20, 1894), *PWW,* 8:587, 588, 595.

5. *PWW,* 8:588–89, 593.

6. *PWW,* 8:588.

7. "An Abstract of an Address in Brooklyn to the Princeton Alumni Association of Long Island" (March 21, 1910), *PWW,* 20:273. See also, for example, "A News Report of an Address in Harrisburg, Pennsylvania" (Feb. 20, 1903), *PWW,* 14:363: "Dr. Wilson declared with emphasis that we have been Germanizing too much in this country's institutions of learning. We have been specializing to too great an extent, which is not wise in a democratic country." See also "The Spirit of Learning," (July 1, 1909), *PWW,* 19:280. Of the new

"scientific research universities" in the United States in the late nineteenth century, Wilson wrote: "The teachers of this new regime, moreover, were most of them trained for their teaching work in German universities, or in American universities in which the methods, the point of view, the spirit, and the object of the German universities were, consciously or unconsciously, reproduced. They think of their pupils, therefore, as men already disciplined by some general training such as the German gymnasium gives, and seeking in the university special acquaintance with particular studies, as an introduction to special fields of information and inquiry. They have never thought of the university as a community of teachers and pupils: they think of it, rather, as a body of teachers and investigators to whom those may resort who seriously desire specialized kinds of knowledge. They are specialists imported into an American system which has lost its old point of view and found no new one suitable to the needs and circumstances of America."

8. "Notes for Lectures in a Course on the Elements of Politics" (March 5, 1898–April 29, 1900), *PWW,* 10:472; University Training and Citizenship," *PWW,* 8:595; "Prof. Woodrow Wilson the Guest of Honor at the St. Louis Club" (Dec. 31, 1897), *PWW,* 10:363.

9. "On an Author's Choice of Company" (Nov. 10, 1895), *PWW,* 9:344–45.

10. "Position and Importance of the Arts Course as Distinct from the Professional and Semi-Professional Courses" (Jan. 5, 1910), *PWW,* 20:716.

11. "Leaders of Men" (June 17, 1890), *PWW,* 6:646–47, 662. See also "A Newspaper Report of a Lecture on Walter Bagehot in Wilmington, Delaware" (Nov. 19, 1897), *PWW,* 10:341; and "Spurious versus Real Patriotism in Education" (Oct. 13, 1899), *PWW,* 11:260. The conflict between "the writer" and "the politician," the cosmopolitan "man of letters" and the patriotic "man of action," was a favorite trope in Wilson's speeches. See, for example, "An Address to the Princeton Alumni of New York" (c. March 23, 1886), *PWW,* 5:137; and "A Report of a Speech on Patriotism in Waterbury, Connecticut" (Dec. 18, 1899), *PWW,* 11:300.

12. "Should an Antecedent Liberal Education Be Required of Students in Law, Medicine, and Theology?" (July 26, 1893), *PWW,* 8:289 (see also "The Study of Politics"[Sept. 1891], *PWW,* 7:280); "A Calendar of Great Americans" (c. Sept. 15, 1893), *PWW,* 8:378; "Abraham Lincoln: A Man of the People" (Feb. 12, 1909), *PWW,* 19:41. See also "An Address to the Presbyterian Union of Baltimore" (Feb. 19, 1909), *PWW,* 19:55 and "An Address to the Presbyterian Union of Baltimore" (Feb. 19, 1909), *PWW,* 19:54.

13. "Should an Antecedent Liberal Education Be Required of Students in Law, Medicine, and Theology?" *PWW,* 8:290, 291, 287, 291–92. See also "Legal Education of Undergraduates" (c. Aug. 23, 1894), *PWW,* 8:648–49.

14. "Princeton in the Nation's Service" (Oct. 21, 1896), *PWW,* 10:21 (italics in original).

15. *PWW,* 10:28–29.

16. *PWW,* 10:30–31; "An Address in Indianapolis to the Indiana State Teachers' Association" (Dec. 27, 1907), 17:571.

17. "Princeton in the Nation's Service," *PWW,* 10:31; "Prof. Woodrow Wilson the Guest of Honor at the St. Louis Club," *PWW,* 10:363.

18. "What Ought We to Do?" (c. Aug. 1, 1898), *PWW,* 10:574, 575.

19. *PWW,* 10:575, 576.

20. "Notes for an Address on Americanism" (Dec. 6, 1900), *PWW,* 12:41; "Lecture at

New-Century Club" (Dec. 7, 1900), *PWW*, 12:42, 43; "Democracy and Efficiency" (Oct. 1, 1900), *PWW*, 12:11, 18. In a striking reversal of his earlier concern that many Americans were insufficiently "nationalized," Wilson now held that Americans were "unified" enough to bear the mantle of global leadership. In the years before the war, editor Walter Hines Page had asked Wilson for several articles on Americanism, nationalism, and patriotism and may have been a chief instigator of Wilson's preoccupation with these subjects. See, for example, *PWW*, 9:277–78 (May 23, 1895); *PWW*, 9:545–46 (June 22, 1896); *PWW*, 10:55–57 (Nov. 21, 1896): Wilson responded to Page's requests with "The Making of the Nation" (April 15, 1897), originally titled "Development of American Nationality," *PWW*, 10:71; the article was later retitled "Growth of American National Feeling," *PWW*, 10:194.

21. "Notes for an Address on Americanism" (Dec. 6, 1900), *PWW*, 12:41; "Lecture at New-Century Club" (Dec. 7, 1900), *PWW*, 12:42, 43.

22. See, for example, "Notes for Lectures in a Course on the Elements of Politics," notably the lecture on "Modern Political Ideas (4): Nationality and Humanity (Internationality)" (May 7, 1898), *PWW*, 10:472: "*Humanity* is *bred of intercourse and sympathy*—is killed by isolation and prejudice. Everything that fosters a common consciousness and enhances a sense of spiritual community amongst nations advances principles and sentiments of Humanity. Accordingly, these principles and sentiments have been enhanced. (1) *Slowly*, the centuries through, *by Christianity*—tho. the sweep and efficacy of its influence have been broken and interrupted by national, political, and sectarian separateness, rivalry, and antipathy. *Modern missions.* (2) The *liberal, humanitarian politics* which has transformed the political world since the American and French Revolutions. 'The Rights of Man.' (3) The *extension and liberalization of International Law* which has accompanied the international contests of the century of revolution. (4) *The intercourse of trade*, quickened and made universal by *steam* and *electricity*—railway, post, telegraph, telephone. (5) *Colonization:* the union and utilization of civilization of the ends of the earth by the great civilizing powers of Europe. (6) *Emigration:* interchange and transfer of populations." For Wilson's description of himself as an imperialist, see "An Address on Patriotism to the Washington Association of New Jersey" (Feb. 23, 1903), *PWW*, 14:366–67: "I am of the class of men who are described as *imperialists*." See also "A News Report of an Address in Syracuse, New York" (Feb. 17, 1904), *PWW*, 15:171: "I am an imperialist if you wish."

23. "Princeton for the Nation's Service" (Oct. 25, 1902), *PWW*, 14: 170, 174, 176, 185.

24. "A News Report of an Address to Princeton Alumni in Washington" (March 28, 1903), *PWW*, 14:402; "A News Report of the Conferral of an Honorary Degree by Brown University" (June 17, 1903), *PWW*, 14:495.

25. "A Newspaper Report of a Speech on Patriotism in Worcester, Massachusetts" (Jan. 30, 1902), *PWW*, 12:259–60. On the difficulty of sharing a common patriotism with the Philippines, see "The Ideals of America" (Dec. 26, 1901), *PWW*, 12:224; Wilson argued that, in some ways, the cultural heterogeneity of the United States also made "community feeling" difficult. See "Nature of Democracy in the United States" (May 10–16, 1889), *PWW*, 6:235. Two decades later, Wilson updated his views. See "After-Dinner Remarks in New York to the Friendly Sons of St. Patrick" (March 17, 1909), *PWW*, 19:105.

26. "A News Report of an Address on Civic Patriotism" (Dec. 3, 1903), *PWW*, 15:62–63; "A Newspaper Report of an Address at Lowell, Massachusetts" (Jan. 3, 1903), *PWW*, 14:315.

One way in which "American human nature" resembled human nature in general was in the spirit of conquest, Wilson noted. See "Democracy and Efficiency," *PWW,* 12:12–13: "We have shown ourselves kin to all the world, when it came to pushing an advantage. Our action against Spain in the Floridas, and against Mexico on the coasts of the Pacific; our attitude toward first the Spaniards, and then the French, with regard to control of the Mississippi; the unpitying force with which we thrust the Indians to the wall wherever they stood in our way, have suited our professions of peacefulness and justice and liberality no better than the aggressions of other nations that were strong and not to be gainsaid."

27. "A News Report of a Lecture in New York on Americanism" (Nov. 20, 1904), *PWW,* 15:536; "A News Report of an Address in Newark" (Dec. 6, 1902), *PWW,* 14:264; "A News Report of Remarks to the New York State Bankers' Association" (Dec. 19, 1902), *PWW,* 14:299; "A News Report of an Address in Newark, New Jersey" (April 11, 1905), *PWW,* 16:49. Wilson himself was not immune to sectional feeling. See "Leaderless Government" (Aug. 5, 1897), *PWW,* 10:288.

28. "Princeton's New Plan of Study" (Aug. 29, 1904), *PWW,* 15:453; "An Address in Memphis to the Princeton Alumni Association of Tennessee" (Nov. 9, 1907), *PWW,* 17:485. Historians and biographers have debated the impetus behind Wilson's curricular reforms. "If Wilson had much to say about the Princeton curriculum prior to his presidency, the documentary record does not disclose it," note the editors of *The Papers of Woodrow Wilson,* 15:287–88. "Two explanations have been advanced for Wilson's silence during the faculty debates [of 1901–1902]. Some persons have suggested that he knew that he was in line for the presidency of the university and did not wish to offend Dr. [Francis] Patton [the sitting president], who was still unenthusiastic about curricular reform. . . . Stockton Axson in later years offered the second explanation: Wilson kept quiet because he thought that the reforms proposed by the committee were mere patchwork. . . . Whatever reluctance Wilson may have had to becoming involved in the details of reform of the Princeton curriculum vanished after his election to the presidency." The analysis in this paper suggests a third explanation: the primary impetus for his interest in curricular reform was the United States' expanding role in global affairs, prompted by the Spanish-American War; only after the war did Wilson see a clear way forward in the arena of curricular reform.

29. "The Statesmanship of Letters," *PWW,* 15:33.

30. *PWW,* 15:34, 35; "The Eclipse of Individuality: A One-Sided Statement by Axcon Mayte [pseudonym]" (April 7, 1887), *PWW,* 5:478.

31. *PWW,* 15:38–39. For a different view expressed several months earlier, see "An Address on Patriotism to the Washington Association of New Jersey" (Feb. 23, 1903), *PWW,* 14:376.

32. *PWW,* 15:39–40.

33. *PWW,* 15:36, 40–41.

34. "The University and the Nation" (Dec. 15, 1905), *PWW,* 16:268; "A News Report of an Address in Montgomery, Alabama" (April 22, 1905), *PWW,* 16:74, 76.

35. "Memoranda for 'The Modern Democratic State'" (c. Dec. 1–20, 1885), *PWW,* 5:72, 80; see also "Nature of Democracy in the United States" (May 10, 1889), *PWW,* 5:225–26.

36. "An Address in Indianapolis to the Indiana State Teachers' Association" (Dec. 27, 1907), *PWW,* 17:576. See also "My Ideal of the True University" (July 6, 1909), *PWW,* 19:295–

96: "But practice is always the best definer; and practice is slowly working out for us in America a sufficiently definite idea of what a university is. It is not the same idea that has been worked out in England or Germany or France. American universities will probably, when worked out to the logical fulfillment of their natural development, show a type distinct from all others. They will be distinctive of what America has thought out and done in the field of higher education."

37. "The Meaning of a Liberal Education" (Jan. 9, 1909), *PWW,* 18:594–95.

38. "After-Dinner Remarks in New York to the Friendly Sons of St. Patrick," *PWW,* 19:107. See also "Abraham Lincoln: A Man of the People," *PWW,* 19:41: "Can we have other Lincolns? . . . We must have the leadership of the sane, genial men of universal use like Lincoln, to save us from mistakes and give us the necessary leadership in such days of struggle and of difficulty. And yet, such men will hereafter have to be produced among us by processes which are not characteristically American, but which belong to the whole world. There was something essentially native, American, about Lincoln; and there will, no doubt, be something American about every man produced by the processes of America; but no such distinguished process as the process, unique and separate, of that early age can be repeated for us."

39. "An Abstract of an Address in St. Louis to the Western Association of Princeton Clubs" (March 26, 1910), *PWW,* 20:293.

40. "After-Dinner Remarks in New York to the Friendly Sons of St. Patrick," *PWW,* 19:107: "Germany knows some of the ways of material success, for example, a great deal better than we do. Germany does not need to be drawn into the tutelage of America to learn how to make money, but every nation of the world needs to be drawn into the tutelage of America to learn how to spend money for the liberty of mankind; and in proportion as we discover the means for translating our material force into moral force shall we recover the traditions and the glories of American history." See also "An Address in Indianapolis to the Indiana State Teachers' Association," *PWW,* 17:573: "The fact that the label, 'Made in Germany,' commends wares on our markets, whether it be truly put upon the wares or not, is in itself a condemnation of our methods of education. There ought to be nothing made in Germany better than it is made in America; and if there is anything better made in Germany than it is made in America it is because Germany recognizes the distinction between the technical education which must be given to a large majority of the young people and the liberal education which only a small minority of the children can get. Let us be done, then, once and for all, with the futile effort of trying to combine the two theories."

# Princeton in the National Spotlight

## *Woodrow Wilson in the Era of the University Builders, 1880–1910*

John R. Thelin

University presidents in the late nineteenth and early twentieth centuries were praised by journalists (and themselves) as heroic builders and pioneers. A century later this presidential cohort still elicits envy and awe from contemporary presidents of the prestigious research universities that belong to the Association of American Universities (AAU). The circle of university presidents from a century ago persists in projecting an iconography of "giants," with the inference that they set the standard by which today's university presidents measure their own stature as academic leaders.[1] This conclusion prompts us to ask: What were the public images of the various institutions within that prestigious circle in the early 1900s as their presidents jockeyed for attention? And how did Woodrow Wilson and Princeton fare in the glare of their reflected glory?

Laurence Veysey observed in *The Emergence of the American University* that there was little cooperation among the heroic presidents. More often than not, except perhaps for selected instances among the "Big Three" of Harvard, Yale, and Princeton after 1900, a university president advanced his own project by denigrating others—and by hoarding resources and ideas that otherwise might be siphoned off by rivals. According to Walton Bean, rivalries for reputation included Stanford alumni calling their alma mater the "Harvard of the West," with the added chauvinism that Harvard was the "Stanford of the East."[2] Veysey argued that most of the leading presidents of the emerging universities did *not* talk or write much about the underlying ideas or curricular plans which purportedly would shape or animate their respective campus construction projects and master plans. In other words, their polemics were not always built on coherent educational philosophies. Each pioneering president seemed to be certain that *his* respective vision for the Great American University was *the* right one. Lack of reflection stands out in this era of institutional expansion. As Veysey wrote, "The most striking thing about the American university in its formative period is the diversity of mind shown by the men who spurred its development. Herein lies the excitement of their story. Those who participated in the academic life of the late nineteenth century displayed sharply dissonant attitudes. Their outlook offered no smooth consensus, despite the eventual efforts of an official leadership to create one. Instead, theirs was an arena of continual dispute, of spirited conflicts over deeply held ideas, of partisan alignments and sharp individual thrusts, which gentlemanly loyalties might soften but could never wholly subdue."[3]

The dynamic leadership of university presidents was underwritten by the happy coincidence of large-scale philanthropy in the late nineteenth and early twentieth centuries. This relationship seems obvious in retrospect, but at the time it was not inevitable that new or expanded universities would necessarily be the primary focus of giant gifts and benefactions. In the first three quarters of the nineteenth century, American voluntary support of projects spread far and wide across an array of hospitals, schools for the deaf and blind, churches, museums, private libraries, and colleges. The period of great industrial wealth, starting roughly around 1870, brought unprecedented donations in which all charities and eleemosynary institutions gained.[4] Most striking, however, were the disproportionate gains shown by universities. Many of the large donors had little prior experience or association with a campus. Some, such as Andrew Carnegie, had doubts as to whether a college or university was the optimal site for investment in new scientific research.[5]

Exactly why the creation of a university suddenly took precedence over, say, a commitment to the funding of a park, hospital, or library was neither clear nor preordained. In 1922 Jesse Brundage Sears documented the remarkable surge by higher education within the rising tide of generosity between 1893 and 1906. Annual bequests for all charitable and service activities nationwide went from $14 million to $90 million. Gifts to education accounted for more than 40 percent of all private giving.[6] The presidents and academics who advocated the creation of great American universities enjoyed a perfect rainbow in their timing and ability to attract the interest of a new generation of donors. Johns Hopkins, Ezra Cornell, Matthew Vassar, Cornelius Vanderbilt, Paul Tulane, Jonas Clark, William Marsh Rice, Andrew Carnegie, Jane and Leland Stanford, and John D. Rockefeller were the new figures of industrial and commercial wealth whose major donations created a modern institutional category that Sears called "the endowed university." Some donors gained enduring fame as the namesakes of the new institutions often characterized by magnificent campus architecture. Perhaps the ideal donor from the perspective of an ambitious university president was one who did not meddle in academic planning. By this standard, Vanderbilt was the best of the lot because he was too ill during the last two years of his life to visit the new university campus in Nashville named in his honor.[7] Yet the new universities had no monopoly on the philanthropy and energy of the era. Established universities such as Harvard, Yale, and Brown shared in this abundance, even though they kept intact their historic names, which often honored founders or donors drawn from mercantile wealth in the seventeenth and eighteenth centuries. Philanthropy extended as well to public or state institutions, such as the Hearst family's generous support of capital projects on the campus of the University of California.[8]

The large-scale philanthropy bestowed on higher education between 1880 and 1910 made it a fortuitous time to be a university president. It was a situation that fostered confidence and academic imagination. To understand the self-assurance and egoism of the university advocates, the autobiography of the first president of Cornell University, Andrew D. White, who worked closely and harmoniously with donor Ezra Cornell, stands out. In 1905 White recalled how the "Cornell Idea" had formed in his mind decades earlier:

> Every feature of the little American college seemed all the more sordid. But gradually I began consoling myself by building air-castles. These took the form of structures suited to a great university: with distinguished professors in every field, with libraries as rich as the Bodleian halls, as lordly as that of Christ Church or of Trinity, chapels as inspiring as that of King's, towers as dignified as those of Magdalene and Merton, quadrangles as beautiful as those of Jesus and St. John's. In the midst of all other occupations, I was constantly rearing these structures on that queenly site above the finest of the New York lakes, and dreaming of a university worthy of the commonwealth and of the nation. This dream became a sort of obsession. It came upon me during my working hours, in the class-rooms, in rambles along the lakeshore, in the evenings when I paced up and down the walks in front of the college buildings, and saw rising in their place and extending to the pretty behind them, the worthy home of a great university.[9]

White was not alone in his self-assured quest to build a great American university. A good sequel to his academic vision surfaced in 1884 in a book written by John W. Burgess on the burning question: "The American University: When Shall It Be? Where Shall It Be? What Shall It Be?"[10] Burgess, one of the more scholarly and thoughtful of the university builders, concluded that the truly great American university ought to be urban in location, private in its governance and control, and defined primarily by its devotion to advanced graduate studies and doctoral programs. It was no coincidence that the institution where Burgess was a professor and dean of the graduate school—Columbia University—was all of those things. At the new University of Chicago, opened in 1892, founding president William Rainey Harper relied on the generosity of John D. Rockefeller along with support from local mercantile wealth to introduce so many new features to academic life that his university was nicknamed "Harper's Bazaar."[11]

Where did Princeton fit into this era of academic expansion and polemics? Before Wilson's presidency, Princeton had changed regularly yet cautiously. In the 1880s, President James McCosh sided with Yale's president, Noah Porter, at meetings of New England college presidents that, according to minutes, often degenerated into heated shouting matches, with McCosh and Porter allied against the chaos, godlessness, and elective system associated with new-modeled Harvard and its brash young president, Charles W. Eliot. But Princeton's position would change both in its values and visibility over time, becoming less identified with the "collegiate ideal" and more associated with becoming a "university" during the presidency of Frances L. Patton from 1888 to 1902. This was, of course, signaled by its name change from the College of New Jersey to Princeton University in 1896 and by creating a graduate school in 1900. McCosh's successor, Patton, did prompt Princeton to edge toward university standing by hiring new scholarly faculty (including Woodrow Wilson) and completing several campus building projects.[12] Woodrow Wilson was a participant-observer in this institutional transformation, first as an influential professor and then, in 1902, when he was inaugurated as Princeton's president.

One occasion when the emerging universities did cooperate was in 1900 when fourteen presidents gathered to form the Association of American Universities, with the shared intent to enhance Ph.D. programs in quality and within the university.[13] Because Princeton was a charter member of the AAU, Woodrow Wilson was immediately part of the elite presidential group. Princeton's inclusion in the AAU two years before Wilson's inauguration was no mean accomplishment and was certainly not inevitable. Princeton not only lagged in offering graduate programs and conferring Ph.D.s; it lacked a large endowment because it had not enjoyed the transformational gift of a major donor comparable to Rockefeller's multimillion-dollar investment in the University of Chicago.[14] Evidently Princeton, under Wilson's predecessor, had demonstrated enough promise to be invited to join with thirteen other founding members.

Many institutions were not invited to join the AAU in 1900, despite their claims to university status.[15] The universities of Wisconsin and Michigan, for instance, were the only state universities in the Midwest initially included. University building was a high-risk venture, and some promising institutions actually fell in reputation. A telling example of this uncertainty was Clark University, whose founding president, G. Stanley Hall, had pioneered behavioral sciences as part of graduate studies in the late nineteenth century. Although eleven-year-old Clark was a charter member of the AAU in 1900, its meteoric rise in 1889 had been followed by an equally dramatic eclipse, in part because of over-investments in bricks and mortar while under-budgeting for annual operating expenses. The episode illustrated the competitive character of ambitious university builders, as Clark's misfortunes were an opportunity for the University of Chicago to recruit most of Clark's top professors with generous salaries.[16] Presidents such as William Rainey Harper of Chicago, Andrew White of Cornell, Charles Eliot of Harvard, Seth Low of Columbia (later replaced by the long-serving Nicholas Murray Butler), David Starr Jordan of Stanford, and Benjamin Ide Wheeler of the University of California were the presidents identified as major leaders of the university movement at the turn of the century.

To promote healthy town-gown relations and to generate good press, the powerful university presidents were involved in local organizations and affairs. Harper in Chicago, Eliot in Boston, and Butler in New York all worked closely with public-school boards and gave frequent talks to local clubs and civic groups. These "Captains of Erudition," as Thorstein Veblen called them, were comfortable with and often in the company of "Captains of Industry."[17] A typical newspaper photograph in 1901 showed Harper, the University of Chicago's president, in academic regalia striding beside his major donor, John D. Rockefeller Sr., who, in a rare public appearance, was dressed in top hat and formal wear at commencement exercises. The photograph confirmed Harper's nickname among Chicago's mercantile and industrial leaders as a "Young Man in a Hurry."[18]

University presidents were also colleagues of national political figures. Benjamin Ide Wheeler, president of the University of California, "had the endorsement and admiration of both the academic and political world of New York and Washington" and "could count among his good friends both Grover Cleveland and Theodore Roosevelt."[19] Roosevelt took time to accept a personal invitation from Wheeler to travel cross-country to Berkeley to speak at the University of California's 1911 Charter Day. His address was a good example of a public pronouncement on the vision of the modern university playing an integral role in American progress. Roosevelt praised the founding of the University of California as a "major step in the evolutionary march to a new and dominant culture in the world." Now, according to Roosevelt, the United States "had on the Pacific Coast of America great universities looking across the last of the great oceans, looking across to the ancient civilizations of Asia" in its quest to build "deep and high a finer civilization than anything the world had yet seen."[20] Roosevelt's public appearance at the University of California extended beyond academic ceremony. He also used the trip to meet with Wheeler and California's governor, Hiram Johnson, to discuss presidential campaign strategies, further indication of the presence of university presidents in the political life of the nation.[21]

For Wilson as the new president of Princeton, membership in the AAU conferred gilt by association, more prestige than publicity. The AAU was a small circle of influential university presidents and deans who met to discuss standards in graduate education. Princeton's inclusion as a charter member meant that Wilson inherited the strategic advantage of automatic membership in the major-university club. Had Princeton not been an AAU member when Wilson became president in 1902, his distinctive campaign for a "liberal university" would have been conducted in relative isolation from the foremost universities. Princeton might have been regarded by the public as another Dartmouth, an institution that was successful, popular, and distinctive but categorized as a college rather than a university.[22]

The AAU did not work through the press to influence public opinion, nor was it designed to be a political lobbying group. Rather, its collective aim was to gain academic legitimacy in the evaluations made by scholars in European universities. By contrast, George Atherton, a political economist who had moved from a professorship at Rutgers to become president of Pennsylvania State College, used the vehicle of group identity in a markedly different way. Atherton surveyed the weak federal funding and underachievement of land-grant colleges designated by the Morrill Act and proceeded to organize his fellow presidents of land-grant institutions to concentrate on establishing a formal, collective lobbying presence in Washington, D.C. The resulting Association of American Agricultural Colleges and Experiment Stations conceded doctoral prestige to the AAU and opted instead for power and patronage in its collective pursuit of research and development sponsored by the federal government in an era when such programs were rare. The land-grant college association was effective in gaining for its member institutions substantial and enduring funding for applied research in agricultural sciences and experiment stations via major legislation such as the Hatch Act (1887), the second Morrill Act (1890), and the Smith-Lever Act (1914).[23]

One university that enjoyed the best of both worlds was the University of Wisconsin. It was the strongest of the state universities and gave notice that it did not have to defer to the historic institutions of the East Coast. Under long-time president Charles Van Hise, Wisconsin could boast outstanding faculty in such fields as economics and history while gaining recognition as the foremost institution in providing statewide extension services in agriculture and engineering. The "Wisconsin Idea" had great public appeal, as Lincoln Steffens proved in "Sending a State to College," a long, illustrated article in the *American Magazine.*[24]

Publicity was also important and increasingly available for ambitious university presidents, thanks to what historian Daniel Boorstin has called a "graphics revolution."[25] Graphics and national publications flourished together between 1880 and 1910. Instead of the etchings and line drawings typical of *Frank Leslie's Illustrated Weekly,* by 1900 American magazines blossomed with sophisticated layouts, graphics, and photos. Newspapers also enjoyed a renaissance. It was not unusual to have five or more competing newspapers published daily in the same metropolitan area. The prominence of sports journalism in the daily newspapers provided a big gain in free publicity for some universities. Intercollegiate football gained coverage not only in the sports section, but often on the front page as headline stories as well. According to Michael Oriard, the popularity of college games induced a new generation of Americans to "learn to read football," an initiation that included acquiring skills ranging from understanding a new prose style with a vocabulary characterized by hyperbole and clichés to paying sustained attention to dramatic stories over several days, culminating in the playing of the "big game" and, of course, the postgame headline stories on Sunday morning.[26]

Even though some professors and presidents decried the popular attention and press coverage given to college football, most university presidents accepted the publicity as a phenomenon that could not be ignored and might even be used to promote one's university.[27] Harper at the University of Chicago was a master at this. He hired and paid well a football coach, Amos Alonzo Stagg, whose many years of championship teams became a major source of public relations in the city, a campaign that included sellout crowds at a new stadium and using football to cultivate a following among Chicago's business leaders. Harper gave free rein and a large budget to Stagg, who served simultaneously as head football coach and athletic director. Stagg did not have to submit a proposed annual operating budget through normal university channels, for example. His administrative autonomy was so great that he even expressed outrage when the university comptroller questioned some of the athletic expenditures.[28] Meanwhile, on the East Coast, Yale, Harvard, and Princeton led the nation in football victories, attendance, and press coverage with or without the blessings of the university presidents.[29]

Thus, when Wilson became president of Princeton in 1902, he gained mightily from the disparate academic and athletic domains: membership in the prestigious AAU and press coverage given to Princeton's powerful football teams. By 1905 the abuses of college football gave Wilson and Princeton an unexpected boost in national attention. Brutality, injuries, and even fatalities on the football field led President Theodore Roosevelt to summon the presidents of Harvard, Yale, and Princeton to the White House to discuss ways to curb college football's excesses. Although far removed from curricular innovations and academic excellence, this kind of association simultaneously placed Wilson in the headlines and consolidated Princeton's historic membership in the "Big Three."[30]

Furthermore, the journalistic habit of heightening the dramatic tension between opposing teams soon provided a model for some press coverage of academic affairs: university rivalries and disputes were often covered as if they were intercollegiate sporting events. Journalist Edwin Slosson playfully asked: "If we are to have intercollegiate contests in intellectualism, what form will they take? Will there be public disputations, in the style of the schoolmen? Will the two sides alternately propound to each other mathematical puzzles and logical subtleties? Will the Association of American Universities prescribe the rules and the Carnegie Foundation and General Education Board offer the prizes? And will the public take the same interest in the contest that they now take in baseball"? His futuristic account envisioned a contest in New York City in which Columbia and Cornell matched their dissertations. Park Row was "packed with upturned faces watching the bulletin boards . . . So, the contest goes on hour by hour, while the popular excitement grows more intense, and extras of the yellow journals, with portraits of the winning men and explanatory diagrams of their theses, spread the news to the suburbs." "Big Three" debating contests did take on such agonistic coloration.[31]

While daily newspapers served a mass local audience, high-quality monthly magazines were distributed nationwide and intended for a specific, educated constituency. *The Century* magazine and *The Independent* joined the ranks of the more familiar but equally transformed *Atlantic Monthly* and *Harper's*. Here was topflight, widely circulated journalism intended for an educated, enthusiastic, and optimistic middle-class readership. Many articles were devoted to the latest developments in higher education—architecture, curricula, student life, controversies, and reform.[32]

As press coverage of American universities expanded in the early 1900s, institutions developed their own sophisticated efforts at public relations. Ambitious Columbia and Chicago were among the first to put themselves forward. At Chicago, President Harper appointed sociologist Albion Small to head up a new publicity office charged with distributing brochures and stories. As Small told his boss in 1901, "We must obey the first and last law of advertising—Keep everlastingly at it."[33] By 1910, the University of Pennsylvania had created a Bureau of Publicity, "consisting of an accommodating young man, some typewriter girls, and a suite of rooms in Houston Hall containing all sorts of statistical and historical data relating to the university, the diagrams and exhibits that had been prepared for various expositions, sets of university publications and files of photographs, all carefully indexed." Of the fourteen major universities journalist Edwin Slosson had visited, "no other university," he exclaimed, "has such a complete and convenient collection of material for the present and future study of the institution."[34]

While Slosson was focusing on the University of Pennsylvania and the University of Chicago for their innovations in public relations, he failed to note that Princeton also was right in the mix. In 1906 it established a serious press bureau, hoping to outdo a once-active "Literary Bureau" begun in the 1880s. It also sought to scoop its own student Press Club, which had fed university stories to metropolitan papers and national wire services since 1900. In 1905 the university had also published at a posh press in New York a richly illustrated, 150-page *Handbook of Princeton*, to which President Wilson contributed a seven-page introduction.[35] Princeton was at the forefront of communications aimed at alumni. Indeed, from 1900, the *Princeton Alumni Weekly* was an influential medium for keeping young and old grads informed about alma mater. The *PAW* and alumni magazines at other universities also became convenient sources for reporters in search of ideas and information for their own stories.[36]

As might be expected, the *Princeton Alumni Weekly* was influential in launching favorable publicity for Wilson when he was inaugurated as Princeton's president in late October 1902. But its influence went well beyond the campus when editor Jesse Lynch Williams published a celebratory profile, "Woodrow Wilson—The New President of Princeton University," in the national *McClure's Magazine* as soon as Wilson was inaugurated. Williams predicted Wilson's success on the basis of the new president's conviction that Princeton's classrooms must be open to "the air of [public] affairs" and that its students should be "citizens and the world's servants."[37]

For a number of reasons, the American campus captured the fancy of the reading public. The drama and melodrama of the new American university provided abundant material for correspondents and photographers. When the Columbian Exposition opened in Chicago in 1893, it was hailed as "The Great White City." At the same time, the grand opening of the new University of Chicago was proclaimed "The Great Gray City."[38] This was a fitting tribute to the instant neo-Gothic campus whose spires and quadrangles led one journalist to marvel that "The American university appears to grow older as it is newer."[39] The alchemy of the heroic university builders was that they enveloped their bold new ventures in higher learning in an array of historic motifs. Now one could have the modern convenience of office buildings, laboratories, observatories, and dormitories fitted with plumbing and electricity, then wrapped in medieval stone, Georgian brick, or classical marble.

The boosterism of the new American university was often arrogant and biased. What easier target to hit than the "old-time college," followed quickly by praise of the new-model "university." Wilson's plans for Princeton could easily have been rejected and he ejected from the "university builder" group. Thanks to his speeches and articles, Princeton escaped that fate. Not only was Wilson quotable, his insights into problems calling for reform at Princeton resonated nation-wide, with implications for American colleges and universities in general. Both his 1896 speech, "Princeton in the Nation's Service," and his 1902 inaugural address, "Princeton for the Nation's Service," were quoted and invoked for years beyond the Princeton campus. His memorable, influential comments included his observation on the undue primacy of student life and extracurricular activities: "So far as the colleges go, the sideshows have swallowed up the circus, and we in the main tent do not know what is going on. And I do not know that I want to continue under those conditions as a ringmaster."[40] He gained fame for taking on the formidable task of reforming a Princeton that had been described as "the most pleasant country club in America."[41] The cumulative result of his public statements was a steady flow of articles in which the Princeton experience was showcased as having national importance. As late as 1913, John Corbin's extended article on "The Struggle for College Democracy," published in *The Century* magazine, put forward now-U. S. President Wilson's former plan for reforming Princeton's social system as a solution to the growing exclusion and snobbery on America's campuses.[42]

In sum, it was Wilson's powerful combination of oratory and prose, followed by press coverage of his vision for a distinctive American university, that made his plan for Princeton too important to be ignored by the other university builders. Newspaper editors, primarily in New York but throughout the North and West, assigned reporters to attend and write articles on Wilson's local speeches. When Wilson traveled to cities such as St. Louis or Pittsburgh to address Princeton alumni, major newspapers in those cities covered his appearances with feature articles. Time and again his talk to a civic group or alumni gathering gained larger influence simply because many newspaper editors deemed his commentary to be important. The benefit to Princeton was that even an impromptu talk by Wilson drew coverage far and wide. With a president of lesser presence than Wilson, Princeton might have been left out of the media portrait of great American universities.

By 1910 journalist Slosson had noted that one now could identify the "SAU"—the Standard American University. But its hallmarks of graduate programs, vocational schools, teaching hospitals, medical centers, and law schools were nowhere to be found in the university model advanced by

Woodrow Wilson for *his* Princeton. Why Wilson's ideal was not ignored persists as a pivotal development in the academic publicity of the era. Wilson had been lucky in dealing with the scrutiny of advocates of a genuine American university. In his role as president of the Carnegie Foundation for the Advancement of Teaching (CFAT), Henry Pritchett had chided Wilson in 1906 that Princeton had been deficient in offering serious and sufficient graduate courses. Wilson's response was equivocal at best, as he plea-bargained that Princeton had worked to offer advanced studies in some, albeit not all, fields that Princeton offered. He then noted that new hiring of outstanding faculty in such fields as mathematics and physics showed signs of Princeton's earnest commitment to advanced scholarship—and graduate programs. What he was reluctant to admit was that Princeton had some difficulty retaining its new faculty stars, some of whom were lured to Harvard and other universities with an established record in doctoral programs.[43]

Press coverage of Wilson's later years as president of Princeton revealed the simultaneous strengths and weaknesses of his tenure. His internal squabbles with graduate dean Andrew Fleming West and alumni donors about the future of Princeton's eating clubs and undergraduate social system and then about the governance and philosophy of the Graduate School resulted in a large measure of controversy in the *Princeton Alumni Weekly.* These local accounts soon became lively copy for numerous New York and Philadelphia dailies. The coverage of academics tended to mirror that of athletics in that each paper adopted a partisan stance, either supporting Wilson or his wily adversary, Dean West. Again, Princeton gained conspicuous news coverage, regardless of the reporter's or editor's point of view.[44]

Wilson's contests with alumni and major donors over the eating clubs, and then battles with Dean West about the location of the new Graduate College, were dramas that tended to obscure shared ground.[45] Arguments between Wilson and West took place in an arena of shared belief in a university that emphasized liberal education for undergraduates. It was not, as it might have been two or three decades earlier, a debate that pitted the sciences against the classics. However important the particulars were to Wilson or West, Princeton had committed to becoming a liberal university that, unlike many other prestigious AAU members, would not neglect its historical pledge to the liberal arts and undergraduates.

The best source of insight into the character and condition of American universities, including Princeton, during this period of growth comes from Edwin Slosson's anthology, *Great American Universities.* Published in 1910, this anthology of detailed, illustrated profiles of fourteen universities originally appeared as a series of monthly articles in the national magazine *The Independent.* Editor Hamilton Holt assigned writer Slosson to spend a year visiting the emerging, distinctive universities and to write about them individually and collectively. Slosson, a Midwesterner who had graduated from the University of Kansas and was one of the first recipients of a Ph.D. in chemistry from the University of Chicago, paid little deference to the historic institutions of the Atlantic seaboard. On the contrary, his background in scientific research, combined with an egalitarian streak, tended to make him critical and cautious in assessing whether historic universities such as Harvard, Yale, Princeton, the University of Pennsylvania, and Columbia could, indeed, transform themselves into genuine universities that would compare favorably with universities in Germany and elsewhere on the European continent. Furthermore, in contrast to the original roster of AAU institutions of 1900, by 1910 there were signs that Midwestern state universities such as Illinois and Minnesota were worthy of joining Wisconsin and Michigan in the small circle of premier universities.[46]

In some of his campus profiles, Slosson devoted attention to the new campus architecture that housed an unprecedented array of facilities, including laboratories, observatories, libraries, lecture halls, gymnasiums, and football stadiums. In the case of Columbia University, President Seth Low's orchestration of the move to and building of a new campus in Morningside Heights in Manhattan epitomized the excitement of architecture in reshaping an historic institution. For most of the university presidents, external relations and institutional promotion were central to their role, whether persuading governors and state legislatures to provide adequate and stable annual appropriations or courting prospective donors. At the University of Chicago, President Harper was persistent and effective in forging a bond between the immediate metropolitan community, its business leaders, and the energetic, new university campus.

Slosson's coverage of Princeton adhered roughly to this campus-profile formula. He also commented at length on the peculiarities and excesses of student life and extracurricular activities that dominated Princeton early in the twentieth century. Then he suddenly shifted to give extended attention to the curricular visions and plans of Wilson, nearing the end of his relatively short presidency at Princeton. The visions and the plans were not identical but, to Slosson as to Wilson, they were inseparable. Slosson noted in his opening remarks about Princeton, "What I like about Princeton is that it has an ideal of education and is working it out. It is not exactly my ideal, but that does not matter to anybody but me. The remarkable thing is that here is a university that knows what it wants and is trying to get it. Many universities seem to me to be drifting. Some of them are trying in vain not to drift. Some of them are bragging about the speed they are making, when they are really being borne along by the current of affairs, and not keeping up with it at that. But Princeton is steering a pretty straight course toward a port of its own choice, regardless of wind and current, perhaps even heading a trifle upstream."[47]

Whether one agreed with or embraced the educational ideals being realized at Princeton, one had to acknowledge that Wilson was a president who had subjected his university to critical academic scrutiny and was making a bold attempt to have his institution define itself as a *uniquely* great university. Slosson and others had written about the trend toward consolidation and homogenization by 1910—the so-called Standard American University—in which the disparate experiments and innovations of ten or twenty years earlier had now started to harden into conformity. Princeton during Wilson's presidency did not conform to this model.

The era in which one compares and contrasts the various emerging American universities is important. Forty years ago historian James Axtell documented convincingly that in the 1880s and 1890s many of the aspiring "universities" that claimed bold departure from the moribund "old-time colleges" often overstated their achievements.[48] Nowhere was this exaggeration more pronounced than in the state universities of the Midwest, where the record rather than the rhetoric shows that the universities of Michigan, Illinois, Indiana, Iowa, and Ohio State stumbled and scrambled to survive, with catalogues listing Ph.D. programs that had scant existence in reality. Attempts to build a new, great state university did not always enjoy full support or understanding. For example, the original Illinois Industrial University was often mistaken for a state prison. According to Slosson, "Graduates of the institution applying for employment were liable to be asked, 'What were you sent up for?' " So in 1885 the name was changed to the University of Illinois.[49]

The paragon of university building since the 1870s had been Johns Hopkins University. Almost every feature cited to distinguish a university from a college had been initiated there, so much so that historian Hugh Hawkins called Johns Hopkins the "Pioneer."[50] Its contributions were formidable: emphasis on graduate, especially doctoral, programs; establishing the first university press in the nation; sponsoring numerous academic journals; de-emphasizing undergraduate life; and integrating professional schools, especially medicine, into the academic structure and culture of the genuine university. But this profile became more complicated by 1910.

When Edwin Slosson sorted data for his roster of fourteen Great American Universities, Johns Hopkins appeared as a sentimental favorite, like the uncle fallen on hard times who comes to Sunday dinner in threadbare clothes. The university builders by 1910 had overestimated or, more likely, simply overstated their forays into advanced scholarship and doctoral programs. Johns Hopkins was distinctive in that it was the only institution—after the decline of Clark University in 1892—to follow this bold agenda. The statistics showed that by 1910 it, like Clark, had paid dearly for its pioneering commitments to German ideals at the expense of American realities.

The institutional statistics of the era provide one explanation for Hopkins's slide in prestige. Slosson wished to balance description with systematic data. It was a priority advocated by the directors of the CFAT, who were passionate about dispassionate numbers. Their belief was that raising standards required standardization, and this meant collecting and analyzing institutional and collective data on enrollments, endowments, per capita expenditures, library holdings, and so on.[51] In retrospect, it was risky to place confidence in these uneven, dubious data. Nonetheless, they were revealing in 1909 and remain so a century later. The surprise is that two institutions at opposite ends of the spectrum of Great American Universities—Johns Hopkins and Princeton—actually tend to converge and overlap in Slosson's statistical tables. In the roster of fourteen universities, both Princeton and Johns Hopkins bring up the rear in several categories:

| *Total Annual Income* | |
|---|---|
| Harvard University | $1,827,789 |
| Columbia University | $1,675,000 |
| University of Chicago | $1,304,000 |
| University of Illinois | $1,200,000 |
| Yale University | $1,088,921 |
| Cornell University | $1,082,513 |
| University of Michigan | $1,078,000 |
| University of Wisconsin | $998,634 |

| | |
|---|---|
| University of Pennsylvania | $889,226 |
| University of California | $844,000 |
| Stanford University | $850,000 |
| University of Minnesota | $515,000 |
| Princeton University | $442,232 |
| Johns Hopkins University | $311,870 |

| *Total Number of Students* | |
|---|---|
| University of Chicago | 5,070 |
| University of Michigan | 4,282 |
| Columbia University | 4,087 |
| Harvard University | 4,012 |
| University of Minnesota | 3,889 |
| University of Pennsylvania | 3,700 |
| Cornell University | 3,635 |
| University of Illinois | 3,605 |
| Yale University | 3,306 |
| University of Wisconsin | 3,116 |
| University of California | 2,987 |
| Stanford University | 1,583 |
| Princeton University | 1,311 |
| Johns Hopkins University | 651 |

| *Total Instructional Staff* | |
|---|---|
| Harvard University | 573 |
| Columbia University | 559 |
| Cornell University | 507 |
| University of Illinois | 414 |
| University of Pennsylvania | 375 |
| Yale University | 365 |
| University of California | 350 |
| University of Minnesota | 303 |
| University of Wisconsin | 297 |
| University of Chicago | 291 |
| University of Michigan | 285 |
| Johns Hopkins University | 172 |
| Princeton University | 163 |
| Stanford University | 136 |

The problem with this one-year snapshot is that it does not reveal patterns, trajectories, or qualitative explanations for the quantitative data. Princeton and Johns Hopkins show a comparable statistical profile on many counts but for different reasons. Princeton was small in size and focused in mission by design; Johns Hopkins was small by default. At the end of the era of university building, Johns Hopkins, once the outstanding exhibit of advanced scholarship, was an institution in distress. If Princeton's precarious feature was that Wilson underemphasized the place of doctoral programs and advanced research in his vision of a great American university, then for Johns Hopkins hubris went to the other extreme. Hopkins overestimated its ability to create and maintain a university without a strong, vital undergraduate core. It had, in effect, inverted the pyramid. Wilson's Princeton was by design the opposite. Elsewhere, the Midwestern state universities stumbled as they talked the talk of advanced programs but walked the walk of undergraduate programs, especially entry-level professional schools. Slosson pegged it right—Princeton, more than any other American university of the era, had transformed a vision into a plan.

Many university presidents put their emphasis on graduate programs and advanced scholarship as defining features to set them apart. In 1909 the largest total student enrollments were about five thousand, led by Columbia, Harvard, Chicago, Michigan, the University of Pennsylvania, Cornell, and Wisconsin. Only one university, Columbia, could claim that graduate students represented more than 10 per cent of total enrollment. Medical school enrollments at several universities were high both in numbers and as a percentage of total enrollments. But medical study was not considered advanced work because it often did not require a bachelor's degree as a prerequisite. Indeed, the University of Michigan was the home of *two* medical schools—namely, one for "medicine" and the other for "homeopathy," which illustrates the capacity of American universities to accommodate diverse, even conflicting, educational philosophies with little concern for clarity of institutional mission or high academic standards.[52]

University production of Ph.D.s remained uneven and often minuscule from 1898 to 1909. What we know today as the Big Ten institutions were not so big as far as doctoral programs were concerned. The universities of Michigan, Illinois, and Minnesota had a combined eleven-year total of just 132 doctorates. In California, productivity might have been robust for agricultural crops, but Clark Kerr's "Knowledge Factory" was still a pipedream years away from realization. Berkeley and Stanford conferred, respectively, a total of 47 and 19 Ph.D.s in the same period.[53]

Most press coverage of the university-building era focused on the excitement and energy of campus expansion and innovation. By 1910, however, it was timely to give some attention to the departures of the heroic presidents. The end point of the university-building era was also 1910, coincidentally the last year of Woodrow Wilson's presidency of Princeton. Woodrow Wilson's leaving Princeton was personally troubling to him. Atypical of his customarily thoughtful speeches, he lost some support from Princeton alumni and from newspaper reporters with his vitriolic talk to an alumni gathering in Pittsburgh when he lashed out at his adversary, Dean West.[54] On balance, newspaper articles gave sufficient attention to his long-term accomplishments at Princeton and to his new ventures into New Jersey state politics so that his disappointments did not tarnish his public image unduly. In marked contrast to Wilson's transition, William Rainey Harper departed the University of Chicago with the same enthusiasm, energy, and optimism that had characterized the start of his presidency. With his usual commitment to place the university and himself in the public spotlight, Harper even on his deathbed in 1906 made elaborate plans for his funeral, including instructions for Chicago faculty to march wearing full academic dress.[55]

For the university builders and presidents, from Harper to Wilson, their plans and visions coexisted with the inescapable fact that both colleges and universities as late as 1910 were heavily committed to providing bachelor's degree programs for undergraduates, many of whom were not academically inclined. University presidents devoted many of their speeches and articles to the zenith of university programs. At the same time, they knew that the academic operation depended on tuition payments for financial fuel and on undergraduates as a source of future graduate and professional students. Woodrow Wilson stood out among the presidents of the Great American Universities in that he did not take undergraduate education and students for granted. The undergraduate liberal arts college was not merely the financial base of a modern university. To Wilson, it was the heart and soul of the university, not an afterthought. A legacy of Wilson's Princeton presidency, then, was that in the decades after 1910 those university presidents who failed to take the undergraduate course of studies seriously or to scrutinize the dominance of a sprawling extracurriculum would pay a heavy price.

Abraham Flexner, famous as the author of the CFAT's scathing report on medical schools in 1910, turned his attention to the American university twenty years later. He found that the prototypical American university had lost its center.[56] The result was that high attrition and low bachelor's degree completion rates, combined with a lack of academic purpose, would persist as a continual source of internal consternation and curricular neglect. Particularly disappointing for the presidents of AAU member institutions was that Flexner's book was based on his travels and observations in Europe and England, culminating in a series of lectures at Oxford University, where the shortcomings of American universities were cast in bold relief against the English and German universities, the precise group whose respect the American presidents had long sought. Despite the triumphant publicity associated with the creation of the new Great American University that had flourished from 1880 to 1910, an enduring and sobering message was that the educational problems Wilson confronted at Princeton persisted nationwide long after the heady era of heroic growth had subsided.

## NOTES

1. See, for example, the essays based on conference presentations by the presidents of Princeton and the University of Chicago in the late 1990s: Harold T. Shapiro, "University Presidents—Then and Now," and Hanna H. Gray, "On the History of Giants," in William G. Bowen and Harold T. Shapiro, eds., *Universities and Their Leadership* (Princeton: Princeton University Press, 1998), 65–100, 101–15.

2. Walton Bean, *California: An Interpretive History* (New York: McGraw-Hill, 1968), 268.

3. Laurence R. Veysey, *The Emergence of the American University* (Chicago: University of Chicago Press, 1965), vii.

4. Robert H. Bremner, *American Philanthropy*, 2d ed. (Chicago: University of Chicago Press, 1988), 100–115.

5. Merle Curti and Roderick Nash, *Philanthropy in the Shaping of American Higher Education* (New Brunswick, N.J.: Rutgers University Press, 1965), 107–35.

6. Jesse Brundage Sears, *Philanthropy in the History of American Higher Education* (Washington, D.C.: U.S. Government Printing Office, 1922), 53–80. See also Bremner, *American Philanthropy*, 100–115.

7. James Howell Smith, "Honorable Beggars: The Middlemen of American Philanthropy" (Ph.D. diss., Dept. of History, University of Wisconsin, 1968), 175–82. See also Paul K. Conkin, *Gone with the Ivy: A Biography of Vanderbilt University* (Knoxville: University of Tennessee Press, 1985), 17–18, 21.

8. Verne A. Stadtman, *The University of California, 1868–1968* (New York: McGraw-Hill, 1970), 119–20; John Aubrey Douglass, *The California Idea and American Higher Education: 1850 to the 1960 Master Plan* (Stanford: Stanford University Press, 2000), 100–103.

9. Andrew D. White, *Autobiography*, 2 vols. (New York: Century Company, 1905), 1:288–90.

10. John W. Burgess, *The American University: When Shall It Be? Where Shall It Be?*

*What Shall It Be?* (Boston: Ginn, Heath, 1884), excerpted in Richard Hofstadter and Wilson Smith, eds., *American Higher Education: A Documentary History,* 2 vols. (Chicago: University of Chicago Press, 1961), 2:652–66.

11. Veysey, *Emergence of the American University,* 311. See also Edwin E. Slosson, *Great American Universities* (New York: Macmillan, 1910), ch. 13.

12. Thomas Jefferson Wertenbaker, *Princeton, 1746–1896* (Princeton: Princeton University Press, 1946), ch. 10; Henry Wilkinson Bragdon, *Woodrow Wilson: The Academic Years* (Cambridge, Mass.: Belknap Press of Harvard University Press, 1967), ch. 11; Alexander Leitch, *A Princeton Companion* (Princeton: Princeton University Press, 1978), 354–57.

13. Hugh Hawkins, *Banding Together: The Rise of National Associations in American Higher Education, 1887–1950* (Baltimore: Johns Hopkins University Press, 1992), 10–15; William K. Selden, "The Association of American Universities: An Enigma in Higher Education," *Graduate Journal* [University of Texas], 8:1 (1968): 199–209.

14. Roger L. Geiger, *To Advance Knowledge: The Growth of American Research Universities, 1900–1940* (New York: Oxford University Press, 1986), 200–202; Curti and Nash, *Philanthropy in the Shaping of American Higher Education,* 143.

15. Making accurate sense out of the invitations to be a charter member of the Association of American Universities is problematic. For example, the 2010 website for the AAU includes a reprint of the original January 1900 letter with the editorial note that the letter was sent from five university presidents (of Harvard, Columbia, Johns Hopkins, Chicago, and California) to "nine of their colleagues" (http://www.aau.edu/about/history_centennial.aspx). However, the text of the letter listing all invitees (California, Chicago, Clark, Columbia, Cornell, Harvard, Johns Hopkins, Michigan, Pennsylvania, Princeton, Stanford, Wisconsin, and Yale) totals only thirteen. Who was the fourteenth and why was it omitted? The answer to the first question is Catholic University. The second question remains unanswered. AAU records from its early years are limited, since files usually were housed with the president, who was selected as acting secretary and, often were never delivered to the AAU's central office or archives.

16. Veysey, *Emergence of the American University,* 165–70; William A. Koelsch, *Clark University, 1887–1987: A Narrative History* (Worcester, Mass.: Clark University Press, 1987), ch. 1.

17. Thorstein Veblen, *The Higher Learning in America: A Memorandum on the Conduct of Universities by Business Men* (New York: B. W. Huebsch, 1918).

18. Milton Mayer, *Young Man in a Hurry: The Story of William Rainey Harper, First President of the University of Chicago* (Chicago: University of Chicago Alumni Association, 1957); Richard J. Storr, *Harper's University: The Beginnings—A History of the University of Chicago* (Chicago: University of Chicago Press, 1966), photo opp. 238; Thomas Wakefield Goodspeed, *William Rainey Harper, First President of the University of Chicago* (Chicago: University of Chicago Press, 1928).

19. Douglass, *The California Idea and American Higher Education,* 104.

20. Ibid., 113. See also Bean, *California,* 329–39.

21. See Mark R. Nemec, *Ivory Towers and Nationalist Minds: Universities, Leadership, and the Development of the American State* (Ann Arbor: University of Michigan Press, 2006) and Nemec's essay in this volume for the emerging trend in university-state engagement.

22. See, for example, Marilyn Tobias, *Old Dartmouth on Trial: The Transformation of the Academic Community in Nineteenth-Century America* (New York: New York University Press, 1982). By 1900, thanks to the leadership of innovative president William Jewett Tucker, Dartmouth had achieved relatively large enrollments, generous financial support from increasingly affluent alumni, scholarly contributions by its faculty, national success in its football victories against major universities, and popularity in newspaper and magazine press coverage—all without relinquishing its deliberate identity as a college. Its popularity as an American favorite was enhanced, for example, by its highly publicized upset football victory over Harvard in the inaugural game of Harvard's state-of-the art football stadium, Soldiers Field, in 1904. Maintaining identity as a college as distinguished from a university did not necessarily shunt an ambitious president and institution to the background in popular images and opinion. However, even though a "collegiate" categorization might have provided a reasonable fit for Princeton University, including popularity and prestige in 1900, it was a categorization the institution had consciously rejected in 1896, a decision that both allowed and required Wilson to play in the "university" arena.

23. Roger L. Williams, *The Origins of Federal Support for Higher Education: George W. Atherton and the Land-Grant College Movement* (University Park: Pennsylvania State University Press, 1991). See also Earl F. Cheit, *The Useful Arts and the Liberal Tradition* (New York: McGraw Hill, 1975), ch. 3.

24. Lincoln Steffens, "Sending a State to College: What the University of Wisconsin Is Doing for Its People," *American Magazine*, 62:4 (Feb. 1909), 349–64.

25. Daniel J. Boorstin, *The Image: A Guide to Pseudo-Events in America* (New York: Harper Colophon, 1964), 181–239.

26. Michael Oriard, *Reading Football: How the Popular Press Created an American Spectacle* (Chapel Hill: University of North Carolina Press, 1993).

27. Frederick Rudolph, *The American College and University: A History* (New York: Alfred A. Knopf, 1962), ch. 18; John Sayle Watterson, *College Football: History, Spectacle, Controversy* (Baltimore: Johns Hopkins University Press, 2000), chs. 1–6.

28. Robin Lester, *Stagg's University: The Rise, Decline, and Fall of Big-Time Football at Chicago* (Urbana and Chicago: University of Illinois Press, 1995), 40–41.

29. John R. Thelin, *Games Colleges Play: Scandal and Reform in Intercollegiate Athletics* (Baltimore: Johns Hopkins University Press, 1994), 15–22; Oriard, *Reading Football*, 117–25.

30. Ronald A. Smith, *Sports and Freedom: The Rise of Big-Time Athletics* (New York: Oxford University Press, 1988), ch. 14 and pp. 92–95; John Sayle Watterson, "The Football Crisis of 1909–1910: The Response of the Eastern 'Big Three,'" *Journal of Sport History*, 8:1 (Summer 1981), 33–49; Oriard, *Reading Football*, 191–228.

31. Slosson, *Great American Universities*, 508, 509; Roberta J. Park, "Morale, Mind, and *Agon*: Intercollegiate Debating and Athletics at Harvard and Yale, 1892–1909," *Journal of Sport History*, 14:3 (Winter 1987), 263–85, esp. 279–82; Charles G. Osgood et al., *The Modern Princeton* (Princeton: Princeton University Press, 1947), 23.

32. See, for example, James C. Stone and Donald P. DeNevi, eds., *Portraits of the American University, 1890–1910* (San Francisco: Jossey-Bass, 1971), table of contents.

33. Albion W. Small to William Rainey Harper, Jan. 20, 1901, quoted in Veysey, *Emergence of the American University,* 326.

34. Slosson, *Great American Universities,* 345.

35. Moses Taylor Pyne to Woodrow Wilson, June 13, 1903, in *The Papers of Woodrow Wilson,* ed. Arthur S. Link et al., 69 vols. (Princeton: Princeton University Press, 1966–94), 14:490 and nn3–4 (hereafter *PWW*); Alexander Leitch, *A Princeton Companion* (Princeton: Princeton University Press, 1978), 377–78; John Rogers Williams, *The Handbook of Princeton* (New York: Grafton Press, 1905). (Thanks to James Axtell for these references.)

36. James D. Startt, *Woodrow Wilson and the Press: Prelude to the Presidency* (New York: Palgrave Macmillan, 2004), 19–40. J. I. Merritt, ed., *The Best of PAW: 100 Years of the Princeton Alumni Weekly* (Princeton: Princeton Alumni Weekly, 2000), vi-vii.

37. Jesse Lynch Williams, "Woodrow Wilson: The New President of Princeton University," *McClure's Magazine,* 19:6 (Oct. 1902), 534, reprinted in Stone and DeNevi, *Portraits of the American University,* 134.

38. Jean F. Block, "Prologue: The Gray City and the White City," *The Uses of Gothic: Planning and Building the Campus of the University of Chicago, 1892–1932* (Chicago: University of Chicago Library, 1983), 2–8. See also A.D.F. Hamlin, "Recent American College Architecture," *The Outlook,* 74 (Aug. 1, 1903), 790–99.

39. Slosson, *Great American Universities,* 429.

40. Quoted in Slosson, *Great American Universities,* 506.

41. W. Barksdale Maynard, *Woodrow Wilson: Princeton to the Presidency* (New Haven: Yale University Press, 2008), 113–28. For an excellent portrait of undergraduate life at Princeton from the perspective of students in the decade before World War I, see John Davies, *The Legend of Hobey Baker* (Boston: Little, Brown, 1966).

42. John Corbin, "The Struggle for College Democracy," *The Century,* 87 (Nov. 1913):80–87.

43. *PWW,* 17:511–12 (Nov. 21, 1907), 527 (Nov. 27, 1907), 545–46 (Nov. 29, 1907).

44. James D. Startt, *Woodrow Wilson and the Press: Prelude to the Presidency* (New York: Palgrave Macmillan, 2004).

45. Veysey, *Emergence of the American University,* 246–47.

46. Slosson, *Great American Universities,* 474–525.

47. Ibid., ch. 3, esp. 75–77.

48. James Axtell, "The Death of the Liberal Arts College?" *History of Education Quarterly,* 11:4 (Winter 1971), 339–52.

49. Slosson, *Great American Universities,* 282.

50. Hugh Hawkins, *Pioneer: A History of the Johns Hopkins University, 1874 to 1889* (Ithaca: Cornell University Press, 1960).

51. Ellen Condliffe Lagemann, *Private Power for the Public Good: A History of the Carnegie Foundation for the Advancement of Teaching* (Middletown, Conn.: Wesleyan University Press, 1983).

52. Slosson, *Great American Universities,* 185. See also Howard H. Peckham, *The Making of the University of Michigan, 1817–1967* (Ann Arbor: University of Michigan Press, 1967), 59–60, 71–72. To place the University of Michigan's configuration of schools for health-

related professions such as medicine, homeopathy, pharmacy, and dentistry into national perspective as a model of accommodation without academic coherence, see Abraham Flexner, *Medical Education in the United States and Canada* (New York: Carnegie Foundation for the Advancement of Teaching, 1910), bulletin no. 4.

53. Slosson, *Great American Universities*, 485.

54. Startt, *Woodrow Wilson and the Press*, 35–39.

55. Veysey, *Emergence of the American University*, 379–80.

56. Abraham Flexner, *Universities: American, English, German* (New York: Oxford University Press, 1930).

# Dreaming Spires in New Jersey

## *Anglophilia in Wilson's Princeton*

W. Bruce Leslie

After his first day in Oxford, Woodrow Wilson breathlessly reported to Ellen that "a mere glance at Oxford is enough to take one's heart by storm. . . . I am afraid that if there were a place for me here Am[erica] would see me again only to sell the house and fetch you and the children."[1] Six years later, reporting from his Princeton University–funded European fact-finding trip, Dean Andrew West confided to Wilson, "If I could forget Princeton anywhere, it would be here in Oxford."[2]

These are clearly serious cases of Anglophilia. This diagnosis is unsurprising, but the meaning of these appeals to foreign models is not necessarily straightforward. Well known as Wilson's and his rival West's proclivities are, the role such reverence played merits examination and evokes speculation.

They were not carrying a rare disease. Anglophilia infected wide swaths of upper- and upper-middle-class fin de siècle America. Woodrow Wilson's career at Princeton overlapped a period when British models carried immense cultural authority in America. In an era of exceptionally rapid social and cultural change driven by industrialization, urbanization, and immigration, attaching to the venerability of a more mature culture conveyed prestige on the new industrial elite and provided confidence to an emerging upper-middle-class spawned by the rapid increase in professional, corporate, and governmental white-collar occupations.

At the height of its imperial power and cultural influence, Britain offered a particularly useful and compelling model. The astute English observer James Bryce cited many cases of "Anglomania" and was amazed that Americans were often more familiar with English literature than were his fellow countrymen.[3] In secondary education, the new "prep" schools drew inspiration from the revived English "public schools," and *Tom Brown's School Days,* an idealized rendition of life at Rugby School under Thomas Arnold, sold well in America. Although some aspects of the prep schools had indigenous roots, they had a strong English accent.[4] Britain, and especially England, also influenced American upper- and upper-middle-class lifestyles. The Episcopal and Presbyterian churches drew many of the American elite to their pews. The new phenomenon of country clubs and the sport at its core, golf, were imported from Britain. Brooks Brothers introduced the button-down collar, emulating English polo players' garb, and the Oxford suit and Oxford-cloth shirts became fashionable labels.

From the early years of Harvard, American academe drew inspiration and practices from Britain. Strongly influenced by alumni of the University of Cambridge, Harvard's founders adopted its curriculum and renamed the surrounding area "Cambridge." The other eight colonial colleges also drew heavily on British practice. If the American Revolution briefly frayed the mystic chords of memory, early-nineteenth-century romanticism repaired them. Harvard Yard especially evoked the language of English pastoralism. James Russell Lowell in 1854 recalled his Harvard as "essentially an English village, quiet, unspeculative, without enterprise, sufficing to itself." Later, after several decades in England, Henry James took refuge at Harvard as a safe harbor from which to look out at an America no longer familiar. At Harvard, English pastoralism was already merging with college nostalgia.[5]

The mystique of Oxford and Cambridge (conventionally conflated into "Oxbridge") intrigued generations of Americans. Mid-century English academic novels sold well in America, especially the *Mr. Verdant Green* series and *Tom Brown at Oxford.* First-person accounts by American visitors were also popular. In 1852, Charles Astro Bristed described his Cambridge experience in *Five Years in an English University.* Just after the Civil War, William Everett's lectures and his book *On the Cam* (1866) attracted large audiences and readership.[6] Oxbridge continued to inspire popular novels and magazine stories and to influence styles through the rest of the century.

Early white-collar railway commuters leaving for work in American cities could tuck Harper Brothers' handy little 2½″ × 4″ "Half-Hour Series" into their pockets. Most volumes were British and American literary and historical classics by the usual suspects, Eliot, Thackeray, Hardy, Tennyson, Trollope, James, and Macaulay. But in 1880, Harper published one in a quite different genre, *British and American Education: The Universities of the Two Countries Compared.*[7] In this slim volume, Mayo Hazeltine offered an upbeat tour of British academe with particular attention to Oxbridge. Harper's inclusion of Hazeltine's volume in the series reflected the American upper-middle-class's curiosity about, and romance with, the "dreaming spires." Hazeltine's praise of Oxford's and Cambridge's honors degrees no doubt resonated with his readers.

Soon American academe began changing rapidly, evoking nostalgia for seemingly stable pasts. Thus the intersection of tradition and modernity, American and British, would not lack for irony. Although Cornell University epitomized American philistinism to Matthew Arnold, the poet who dubbed Oxford "the city of dreaming spires," Cornell's founding president, Andrew D. White, lyrically recounted his repeated visits to Oxford. "Then and at later visits, both to Oxford and Cambridge, I not only reveled in the architectural glories of those great seats of learning, but learned the advantages of college life in common—of the 'halls,' and the general social life which they promote; of the 'commons' and 'combination rooms,' . . . of the quadrangles, which give a sense of scholarly seclusion, even in the midst of crowded cities."[8]

Although connections to Oxbridge stretched back to the origins of American academe, a rival model appeared in the mid-nineteenth century, one that many felt offered a superior guide to the future. As Daniel Rodgers argues, Americans may have been unusually open to foreign influences in the period between antebellum democratic assertiveness and emergence as a superpower.[9] At least in academe, Americans customarily framed fin de siècle debates in terms of two dueling foreign models, English and German.

Like American society generally, late-nineteenth-century higher education was undergoing rapid, even traumatic change. With traditional colleges having difficulty adjusting to the knowledge explosion and to demands for technical training, the search for new models and a new order was on. The German university offered a plausible solution—a university based on research and an academically specialized professoriate who taught only advanced students. Over nine thousand young Americans crossed the Atlantic to see the academic future, although Woodrow Wilson was not among them. Many returnees championed a curricular model that marginalized, if not eliminated, the American traditions of a common core curriculum and of developing students' characters as well as their minds.

The impact was considerable. Faculty reorganized knowledge, curricula, and professional organizations by disciplines while seeking to shift their duties from student oversight to research. Impressive new universities and some older ones such as Harvard adopted the spirit and practices brought back by the returning scholars. Although the converts selectively chose from their German experiences, which were often brief, superficial, and acquired in diverse locales with different faculty over various periods, the perception of a "German" model gained credence.

These innovations threatened American colleges' existence. Many agreed with Columbia's John Burgess that "I am unable to divine what is to be ultimately the position of Colleges which cannot become Universities and which will not be Gymnasia. I cannot see what reason they have to exist."[10] While institutional inertia suggested that colleges would survive in some form, the way forward was not clear.

Several issues demanded resolution: the professorial balance of research and teaching; the amount of specialization in the curriculum; the college's responsibility for students outside the classroom and laboratory; and the relationship of the bachelor's degree to professional training. Those determined to retain the traditional American commitment to college faculty as teachers first, to curricular breadth and the primacy of the bachelor of arts degree, and to education of the "whole man" needed an alternative model. Oxbridge provided it.

Through the 1890s and the years leading up to World War I, debates over the shape of America's mushrooming higher education were frequently framed by competing perceptions of English and German universities.[11] After the founding of Johns Hopkins University in 1876 as primarily a graduate institution, the German model initially swept all before it. Harvard, newly endowed private universities (especially Chicago, Clark, and Stanford), and a number of state universities embraced versions of the German model. Meanwhile, traditional colleges grasped for a curricular solution that would accommodate the rapid expansion of knowledge while preserving their role and values.

Those like Wilson, who sought to revive the collegiate ideal with appeals to Oxbridge, were aided by Britain's cultural prominence in the Anglophonic world. Queen Victoria presided over a massive empire that displayed its grandeur in ceremonies for her diamond jubilee, funeral, and son's coronation. In the year after her death, the Rhodes scholarships were announced to considerable attention on both sides of the Atlantic.[12] Also in the last year of Victoria's reign, John Corbin published his popular *An American at Oxford,* an intelligently loving account.[13] The Tom Brown books continued to make money for Macmillan publishers, and the YMCA, an English invention, was the dominant student campus organization. Symbolically "Pomp and Circumstance" was first performed at a Yale commencement in 1905. Adopted by Princeton two years later, its performance at graduations soon became an American tradition, though not one adopted in composer Edward Elgar's homeland.

Wilson articulated the common rhetorical dichotomy in his famous Phi Beta Kappa speech at Harvard in 1909. For him, American academe had lost its way due to German-trained faculty who "have never thought of the university as a community of teachers and pupils. . . . They are specialists imported into an American system which has lost its old point of view and found no new one suitable to the needs and circumstances of America."[14]

Anglophilic rhetoric was already the lingua franca as Wilson emerged as a leader at Princeton. A lavish book recounting the university's 1896 sesquicentennial celebration rejoiced that "the colleges of America, like many in the mother-country, owe their existence to the wise forethought and devoted liberality of private individuals."[15] Wilson would soon deftly employ the relationship with the "mother-country" to encourage further financial liberality to transform the campus educationally and physically.

Expanding campuses provided an opportunity to physically manifest links to eight centuries of European university culture. For the first time, American colleges had the resources to plan their development and choose a coordinated style for new buildings. Some opted for neoclassical or neo-Georgian formality, but Collegiate (or Tudor) Gothic, with its allusions to Oxford and Cambridge, became the style of choice for institutions in the East.[16]

Wilson had encountered pioneering Collegiate Gothic structures while teaching at Bryn Mawr in the mid-1880s and was charmed by real and neo-Gothic on his two visits to Oxford and Cambridge before assuming Princeton's presidency. It was fortunate that the style resonated with him, because as college president he inherited a stylistic fait accompli. In addition to changing its name at its 1896 sesquicentennial, the newly christened "Princeton University" planned a physical makeover and selected Gothic as a style for its imminent expansion. The trustees apparently saw no irony in selecting a style derived from medieval Catholicism, presumably because it was associated with Protestant Oxbridge. Princeton hired Cope and Stewardson, the same firm that had designed Bryn Mawr's buildings and was the leading practitioner of Collegiate Gothic, to design a campus of dreaming parapets and spires.

Although not party to the original architectural decision, Wilson was a true believer. Appealing to Chicago alumni to help fund his preceptorial system, he informed them that "from the Tudor style of building one gets the spirit of the tradition of the old English learning."[17] Indeed, his interest in campus aesthetics probably exceeded the architects' desires. He even forced one to top Patton Hall with a replica of Oxford's Magdalen Tower.[18]

Choosing Collegiate Gothic fostered more than mere aesthetic consistency. It invoked the prestige of the world's superpower and the cultural stature of venerable traditions, as Wilson boasted to alumni in New York City: "By the very simple device of constructing our new buildings in the Tudor Gothic style we seem to have added to Princeton the age of Oxford and Cambridge; we have added a thousand years to the history of Princeton by merely putting those lines in our architecture which point every man's imagination to the historic traditions of learning in the English-speaking race."[19]

The gift of the Mather Sundial exemplified the romantic connection between Princeton and Oxbridge. When an English industrialist donated a replica of the sundial in the courtyard of Corpus Christi College, Oxford, its dedication in 1907 attracted the distinguished British Ambassador, James Bryce, who extolled the yet-to-be-named "special relationship" between England and America.[20]

Wilson's architectural and educational visions overlapped. When McCosh Hall was on the drawing board, he intervened to elongate faculty offices to facilitate his vision of student preceptorials, adapted from Oxbridge tutorials. When pitching his preceptorial system, Wilson employed appeals to Oxbridge pedagogy as well as architecture. In Chicago, the *Daily Tribune* reported that he informed alumni that "American colleges should follow more closely the English system of education by tutors and make the university examination more of a judgment day for the students." He urged them to help underwrite his plan to hire "a body of tutors like the English tutors."[21] In his first annual report, Wilson prescribed the cure for Princeton students' intellectual torpor to be making "use, in a modified form, of the English tutorial system. Under that system men are examined . . . upon subjects which they are expected to get up for themselves, and upon which they are tested by outside examiners. Tutors superintend and assist their reading, show them the best books in which to get at the subjects assigned, act as their coaches and advisors in their preparation for the general tests which await them."[22]

The new curriculum he championed and Princeton inaugurated in 1905, with a major in a discipline, was inspired by the reputation of Oxbridge students who pursued Honors degrees. The specialized expertise they achieved by the time of their climactic examinations went beyond what American students could hope to emulate but provided a model for upper-class specialization following two years of general studies.

Wilson combined backing for the preceptors and the new curriculum in a 1903 lecture to New York–area schoolmasters. He lauded Balliol's Honors course and talked of the men who "have found their souls at Oxford University. Now I venture to say that no man ever found his soul in a recitation or at a lecture."[23] He also employed Oxbridge references to recruit faculty. While trying to convince Robert Root to accept a preceptorship, he bragged that he was "instituting in Princeton a Tutorial system based upon that at Oxford."[24] Seeking Frederick Jackson Turner's assistance in locating candidates, he explained that he hoped to put into practice, "in modified and Americanized form, the Oxford Tutorial system."[25] Similarly, he informed *Harper's Weekly* readers that he was introducing "the tutorial system of Oxford adapted to American conditions and to the traditions of America colleges."[26] A Princeton alumnus working at the Cambridge Observatory promoted his application for a preceptorship by reporting that "what I have seen of the tutorial system at Cambridge has put me in very hearty sympathy with what I read of the proposed preceptorial system at Princeton."[27]

But his borrowing from Oxbridge may have been too selective. Even his Harvard ally, Abbott Lawrence Lowell, later commented that importing the tutorial system without instituting general examinations resembled playing football without the goalposts.[28] The precepts certainly brought undergraduates into sociable personal contact with young faculty, but they functioned as a pleasant way to prepare for regular classes rather than encouraging broader integrative study. In the library, use of reserve readings rose, but general circulation declined in the first years of the preceptorial system, suggesting that students' increased attention to required texts was not accompanied by an increase in independent reading.[29]

Wilson never visited Oxford or Cambridge while classes were in session, yet he held up their colleges as the epitome of a system that enabled students to feel at home and facilitated close contact with faculty. In an article in *Youth's Companion,* he urged his young readers to read *Tom Brown at Rugby* to understand the spirit of great teachers. To provide that experience in higher education, he explained that English universities solve the problem by dividing students into small colleges, each of which is "a little community apart, a little academic family . . . and nowhere, probably in all the academic world, is the contact between the two more natural, more constant, more influential than there."[30]

His December 1906 "Supplementary Report" to the trustees proposing his ill-fated quadrangle plan surprisingly fails to mention Oxbridge, but the derivation was unmistakable. He labeled the new units "colleges," which he envisaged as largely self-governing entities overseen by a resident master and preceptors who would dine with undergraduates. Wilson had been enraptured by the enclosed quadrangles when he toured Cambridge and Oxford, spending most of his time gauging their atmosphere rather than pedagogical specifics. His correspondence with architect Ralph Adams Cram regularly referred to the Oxbridge colleges as models for the abortive plan.[31] Wilson had also conceived Dean West's initial Graduate College proposal in terms of "a great quadrangle in which our graduate students should be housed like a household . . . under a master whose residence should stand at a corner of the quadrangle in the midst of them."[32]

Wilson also admired British faculty. In 1904 he wrote to his colleague and close friend, John Grier Hibben, that "the scholars on the other side [of the Atlantic] are a little broader and more human men, a little more like all-round gentlemen, a little more marked by refinement and a broad and catholic taste for the most excellent things of scholarship and conduct, than the typical man of our faculties."[33]

Wilson envisioned Preceptors (a name Wilson adopted from the Inns of Court in London) as gentlemen and social equals of the students, presumably replicating his image of Oxbridge dons. A letter to historian Frederick Jackson Turner about a preceptor candidate inquired about his scholarship and "even more particularly about his personality and antecedents."[34] In interviews, Wilson checked candidates' table manners and asserted that "if their characters as gentlemen and as scholars conflict, the former will give them the place."[35] His preference for Anglo-gentility may explain why three of fifteen new instructors appointed in 1907 had recently returned from three years at Oxford as Rhodes scholars and why, after listing all the candidates' degrees, he highlights those three and adds their Oxford college affiliations.[36] His emphasis on character finally drove his dean of the faculty, Henry Fine, to protest before hiring criteria were rebalanced in favor of a more "German" emphasis upon specialized expertise.[37]

However much Wilson romanticized Oxbridge tutors' social graces, he reported one flaw: they are hired for life and burn out or "go to seed," in his words.[38] Thus his preceptors would be hired for only five years before proceeding to more traditional academic status or other career paths. Since 37 of the first 49 preceptors had doctorates, presumably partly owing to Fine's influence, Wilson's image of gentlemen on the first step of a career ladder collided with the reality that most faculty were already trained in the "German" system.[39]

The battle over the location and control of the Graduate College that finally drove Wilson from Princeton was also saturated with Anglophilic overtones and ironies. Wilson glowingly endorsed West's elaborate 1903 report that was replete with romantic sketches of Oxford, especially dreamy interior and exterior views of Magdalen College. In words he must have deeply regretted and that foreshadowed their later struggle, he gushed that "this is not merely a pleasing fancy of an English college placed in the midst of our campus to ornament it. In conceiving this little community of scholars set up at the heart of Princeton, Professor West has got at the real gist of the matter, the real means by which groups of graduate students are most apt to stimulate and set the pace for the whole University."[40] It is plausible that Wilson gave the contents of West's book only passing attention, but his Anglophilic feelings make it likely that he would have been comfortable with the contents. Wilson's visits to Oxford and Cambridge are full of similarly romantic statements and a tendency to value ambience over educational content.[41]

Although British ambassador James Bryce lamented that England's failure to develop graduates studies had cost it "a golden opportunity" to influence future American academic leaders, neither West nor Wilson was apparently bothered by the irony that they were modeling their Graduate College on two English universities that had steadfastly resisted awarding the Ph.D.[42] This paradox may be explained by the claim in West's proposal that the Graduate College would reduce the need to recruit new faculty from other graduate schools. By training their own, the "true Princeton tradition will be perpetuated with as much purity and strength as has been attained even in the old universities of Oxford and Cambridge."[43] Oxbridge's ability to produce gentlemen-scholars apparently trumped its rejection of the degree that had become the union card for American research universities. Later in his presidency, Wilson, again influenced by Dean Fine, began enthusiastically recruiting faculty from Cambridge, Glasgow, and American research universities.[44] But his endorsement of West's proposal plausibly fits his earlier commitment to hiring "clubbable" gentlemen as faculty, Wilson's later denial notwithstanding.

In the bitter debate over the Graduate College's location, both sides invoked Oxbridge. Wilson used the seclusion offered by Oxford's colleges bordering busy streets to challenge West's call for separating graduate students from both the central campus and its undergraduates. In turn, Henry Van Dyke defended West's site beyond the golf course on the basis that a similar distance separated St. John's College from the Fitzwilliam Museum in Cambridge.[45]

Wilson's architectural interest continued to the end of the battle. In March 1909 he defended building an elaborate tower in honor of recently deceased former president Grover Cleveland, even though "such a memorial tower would be of no monetary value to the university," on the grounds that "many of the most beautiful at Oxford and Cambridge had such an origin." Echoing West's proposal six years earlier, he recommended Founders Tower of Magdalen College to Ralph Adams Cram as a desirable model.[46]

That Wilson promoted and defended his dramatic remake of Princeton with Anglophilic rhetoric is beyond doubt. The source of his judgments and the accuracy of his pronouncements, however, are less clear. To reach those determinations we must briefly look at his earlier intellectual development and then examine his experiences in the Britain Isles.

Wilson's affinity for British, especially English, literature and politics began early. His father introduced him to English and Scottish writers and subscribed to the *Edinburgh Review.* As a teenager Wilson composed an elaborate constitution for an imaginary Royal United Kingdom Yacht Club and in adulthood created several real organizations with distinctly British derivations. As a freshman at Princeton he conscientiously collected quotations, largely from British literary and political figures. At graduation he orated on "Our Debt to England." Wilson's first significant publication was an article titled "Cabinet Government in the United States." It and his first book, *Congressional Government,* both drew admiringly on Walter Bagehot's *The English Constitution* and argued passionately that American government should morph into a system closer to the British parliamentary style. Although his political and literary tastes were Anglophilic from childhood, *The Papers of Woodrow Wilson* have virtually no references to English higher education before his 1896 trip.[47]

Wilson's academic Anglophilia developed as he became an academic leader and was based almost entirely on Oxford and Cambridge. Other British universities held little interest for him. Neither did the Scottish academic tradition seem to have attracted him, even though Glasgow was his port of call several times, his Scotch-Irish ancestry was a source of great pride, and representing Princeton at a University of Glasgow celebration was his first European experience. Even the greater breadth of the Scottish curriculum, closer to his values than English specialization, did not grab his attention. And although his hero and early intellectual model, Walter Bagehot, had been rejected at Oxbridge on religious grounds and graduated from the University of London, Wilson showed little interest either in it or in the emerging "Red Brick" universities of the Midlands. Oxford and Cambridge were his sole models.

On his first trip in 1896, he dutifully visited several universities, partially to recruit speakers for Andrew West, who was organizing Princeton's sesquicentennial celebration to be held later in the year. He visited Glasgow and Edinburgh universities and twice passed through Cambridge. After his first brief sojourn in Cambridge, he told Ellen that "the town seemed to me rather mean, but the colleges most of them beyond measure attractive,—some of them exceedingly beautiful."[48] His return trip was disappointing. Initially he planned to arrive for the beginning of Cambridge's University Extension Society's Summer School and to have several days "to look the ground over,—see what sort of men are to be engaged, what the plans are, of how much consequence the thing is to be." But when he realized that none of the faculty was distinguished and he was not interested in the courses offered, he left the next morning, preferring to continue bicycling across the countryside.[49]

But he fell in love with Oxford at first sight. "A mere glance at Oxford is enough to take one's heart by storm," he declared to Ellen before laying out his fantasy of moving to England if there were a position for him.[50] He spent three days and was smitten.

Returning to England three years later with Ellen's brother, Stockton Axson, he lyrically mused to her from Cambridge about what their life could be like in England. Wilson reported to Ellen that "Today we 'did' Cambridge. . . . There is much more architectural consistency here than at Oxford,—with the result that there are no monstrosities here such as there are at Oxford, but a sameness of satisfying style." His approach was "not so much to study the colleges individually, as to get the topography of the place clearly in mind and be able to take away a clear conception of it as a whole."[51]

He visited fifteen colleges seeking to understand "the place in its entirety,—a place *full* of quiet chambers, secluded ancient courts, and gardens shut away from intrusion,—a town full of coverts for those who would learn and be with their own thoughts. I bring away from it a very keen sense of what we lack in our democratic colleges, where no one has privacy or claims to have his own thoughts."[52]

Then on to Oxford. He was no less charmed the second time around. He informed his middle daughter, Jessie, that Oxford "is England's great university town. We hope Princeton will be like it some of these days,—say about two hundred years from now."[53] He reported to his wife, Ellen, "I have, of course, gone about Oxford this time looking about me with the keenest and most constant interest, turning into quads.; penetrating beyond quads. to delightful secluded gardens; peeping now into one and again into another quaint corner, and seeing a great deal."[54] He attended Prof. Albert Dicey's University Extension lecture comparing English and American constitutions, possibly the only instruction he ever observed in Britain. The only other faculty contact he reported to Ellen was a distasteful encounter with someone he mistook for a Balliol don.[55]

After crossing the Irish Sea to visit Dublin and being suitably impressed by the immensity of Trinity College's quadrangles, he headed home via Glasgow. On the return trip, his ship, *The City of Rome,* hit an iceberg—giving us cause to wonder how different world history, and not merely Princeton's, might have been.

Four years later, in 1903, he crossed the Atlantic again, this time as Princeton's president. Ellen accompanied him for the first time; consequently we know far less about this trip.[56] He presumably enjoyed showing her the jewels of England's academic crown, spending about five days in each. In Cambridge he visited the colleges he had missed on the previous trip and walked enough to require shoe repair. In Oxford he recorded visiting the standard sites.[57] Unfortunately, without his long, loving missives to Ellen, we know little about these wanderings. As far as we know, he never returned to either Oxford or Cambridge.

In 1906 Princeton's trustees granted him a sabbatical to recover from a serious stroke. He and Ellen rented a house in Rydal, north of Lake Windermere in the Lake District near Wordsworth's cottage. There they spent some of the happiest days of their lives. A decade earlier he had pedaled through Rydal and given his lifelong love of the romantic poets full vent, describing to Ellen "a region so complete, so various, so romantic, so irresistible in its beauty." His pleasure was only limited by feeling he would "be haunted, and perpetually *hurt* by it all till I get you here,—and shall we ever get away again when I do?"[58] He confided to his friend, classmate, and ally on the Board of Trustees, Cleveland Dodge, that he has "learned to love Rydal like another home. I have not stirred from this enchanting region once since the tenth of July, except to go to Edinburgh to see the doctors and get [to know] our new Professor of Psychology, Norman Kent Smith." This was the only academic contact he recorded in three months. In addition to regaling his friend Cleve with details of his isolated idyll, he informed him that "the summer has brought to maturity the [quadrangle] plans for the University which have for years been in the back of my head but which never before got room enough to take their full growth."[59] Curiously, although he was formulating his controversial plan which he would promote using Oxford and Cambridge as models, he did not bother to revisit them.[60]

On his fifth trip, in 1908, fortunately (for historians) Ellen did not accompany him, bequeathing us better records. He bicycled south from Glasgow to their beloved Lake District and, except for visiting Andrew Carnegie in Skibo Castle, remained there for the entire time. Ralph Adams Cram had suggested that they meet at Oxford and Cambridge, an offer Wilson did not take up even though he was returning to the climactic battles over the Graduate College and quadrangles.[61] In more than two months he apparently never set foot on university grounds and confessed to his daughter Jessie his pleasure at having "only casual thoughts of Princeton and its too complicated affairs."[62] He continued to glory in the atmosphere of the Romantic poets and delighted in meeting descendants of Coleridge and

Wordsworth. A sense of inability to cross cultural barriers, and perhaps frustration with English culture, crept into his letters. To Jessie he confided annoyance that the lack of real interest in America displayed by most English prevented meaningful relationships. In contrast, "with an American I can really grapple."[63] To Ellen he complained that "it requires a life time to know an Englishman thoroughly. I shall never have time enough on this side the water to attain the slow intimacy."[64]

On his five European trips, Wilson travelled beyond the British Isles only once. His triumphal postwar entrance into Paris was only his second venture beyond the Anglophonic world. From August 24 to September 13, 1903, he and Ellen toured France, Switzerland, and Italy; perhaps tellingly, his "grand tour" itinerary omitted Germany. His few days in Luzern and Basel constituted his only experience in a German-speaking region. There is no indication he visited any university on the Continent. Ironically, in 1902, Andrew West had visited Princeton alumni at German universities and thoroughly enjoyed his time there.[65]

Several points are striking. First, Wilson's primary interest apparently was architecture and ambience; few meetings with faculty are reported. Indeed, it seems to have been West who carefully inspected the tutorial system at Oxford.[66] Second, his visits always took place during the universities' summer vacation and were relatively brief. Third, his interest in visiting declined dramatically; he saw neither Oxford nor Cambridge again after 1903, just as his rhetorical use of them soared. Neither was he eager to meet with academics, especially on his later trips.

Wilson's trips overseas always had an element of escapism and in two cases (1896 and 1906) he was recovering from serious ailments. His sojourns were neither long enough nor of a character to grasp daily realities. Wilson no doubt observed England through rose-colored glasses, and his last two trips, centering on the Lake District, echoed his childhood interest in Coleridge and Wordsworth. When it looked as if he had lost the 1912 Democratic nomination, he and Ellen consoled themselves with the thought of vacationing in Rydal again.[67]

The nature of Wilson's contact with British culture invites the question of how closely his ideas and rhetoric jibed with reality at Oxbridge. Oxbridge's claim to pedagogical fame rested on the students reading for Honors. They read widely in the period leading up to the all-important exams and gained impressive command of their subject, aided by close supervision from tutors. Virtually all observers praised the tutorial system as the gold standard in education, and Wilson explicitly drew on the Honours courses to push the creation of majors at Princeton.

But the first half of Princeton's new curriculum bore no relation to Oxbridge's. The honors curriculum, except in Oxford's famous classical "Greats" degree, tended to be very specialized, often in a single subject after 1880. The Cambridge tripos was similarly limited. In the early 1800s, Oxford created the "responsion" exam and Cambridge the "previous" exam to guarantee some breadth of knowledge in the students' preparation. But in the period when Wilson and similar-minded educators were fighting to retain the collegiate tradition of a broad and at least partially shared curriculum, Oxford and Cambridge were moving in the opposite direction, slowly phasing out the exams.[68]

American universities and Oxbridge were also going in opposite directions in their approaches to professional training. After the 1893 opening of the Johns Hopkins Medical School, where admission required a bachelor's degree, its competitors began requiring prior undergraduate work if not a degree. Schools training in the other two medieval professions, theology and law, soon followed suit, adding baccalaureate study to their admissions requirements.

In his 1880 comparison of *British and American Education,* Mayo Hazeltine praised Oxford's requirement that its final medical exams not be taken until students had gained four years' experience after receiving a B.A. He urged Harvard to adopt a similar requirement, holding up Oxbridge as a model at a time when his alma mater accepted medical students with no prior college study. He got his wish, but Harvard and other American universities, including Princeton, were passing Oxbridge going in the opposite direction.

Wilson and West salivated at the opportunity to draw architectural inspiration from Oxbridge for the Graduate College. But their longing was deeply ironic. Oxbridge had steadfastly resisted the Ph.D., seeing it as a Trojan horse for pedantic German scholarship. They awarded doctoral degrees (D.Sc. and D.Litt.) toward the end of professorial careers, but had no equivalent of the Ph.D. as the union card and did not begin awarding them until World War I.

Although imperial Britain was at the zenith of its power, it viewed the flourishing republic across the Atlantic with trepidation. American economic power was all too evident as Yankees appeared to be buying up Britain, including the London Underground. Only government action blocked Americans from purchasing Britain's flagship Cunard Line. Frederick McKenzie's widely read 1902 exposé, *The American Invaders*, forecast a cultural takeover, with American products and tastes overwhelming English culture.[69] In a famous spoof on the first Rhodes Scholars, an avaricious father is convinced to support his son's Rhodes application and send him to learn more about England because "when a big nation perposes to eat up a little nation, she begins by sendin' missionaries and traders to study the language and habits of the natives. And when the eatin' begins, it's the man that knows most about them that gets the biggest chunk."[70]

In higher education, just as partisans of the American liberal arts college and defenders of collegiate community went into battle under an English flag, many English critics were looking elsewhere for champions, especially to the United States. Cultural insecurity is not a zero-sum game. From the turn of the last century, delegations crossed the Atlantic to observe Yankee academe in action. The universities of Birmingham and Reading both drew heavily on American practice, and Ruskin College at Oxford was created by Americans. In 1904, Oxford even raided Johns Hopkins to recruit Dr. William Osler for the Regius Chair of Medicine.[71]

Meanwhile, in England criticism of Oxbridge was growing, including of its college system. Although Wilson portrayed his proposed adaptation of the college system as a democratic reform, in England it was being attacked as a bulwark of elite privilege. In 1907, the year Princeton's quad fight erupted, the House of Lords debated a proposal for a royal commission to investigate Oxbridge and especially the role of colleges.[72] As American journalist Edward Slosson observed, "The particular thing that we are most anxious to get from Oxford and Cambridge, their separate residential colleges, is what the reformers of these universities are most eager to break up."[73]

James Bryce's famous *American Commonwealth* arguably provides the most informed and balanced Anglo-American comparison in the period. Bryce shared Wilson's admiration of Oxbridge honors degrees and thought no American studies equaled them. But he believed that American students worked more consistently and harder than non-honors students in Oxbridge and most students in Europe. He also lamented that the extracurricular "sideshows" were running away with the academic circus in

Europe as in America. Bryce was so impressed by the new American universities that in 1894 he predicted they would soon surpass their European equivalents and at least equal Oxbridge.[74] Few Americans in the mid-1890s shared his confidence in their system.

We are left with the question of the extent to which Anglophilia became a useful past that Wilson, and indeed others, used as a rhetorical weapon, especially with trustees and alumni. Curiously, his papers contain few references to European universities before he became president of Princeton, though his admiration of the parliamentary system was long-standing and deep-rooted. Volume 12 of the *Papers of Woodrow Wilson,* which covers his last two years as a professor, lists no references to Oxford or Cambridge. With his ascendancy to the presidency of Princeton in 1902, he began peppering his speeches and letters with references to Oxbridge.

Indeed, he and West sang from the same hymnal for a long time, sharing a misty romanticism about Oxbridge. In the Graduate College fight, both sides used Oxbridge references to support their case. They had become a lingua franca, perhaps one whose reality receded over time. Wilson and his rival no doubt believed much of their own rhetoric, but their flourishes may have been encouraged by the knowledge that they were addressing those Americans most likely to share their admiration of Britain. Most donors lived in the world of golf, country clubs, prep schools, English styles, Episcopalian and Presbyterian churches, and trans-Atlantic marriages.

Wilson's initial reforms drew on Oxbridge fairly accurately, aided by Dean West's extensive investigation.[75] His preceptorial proposal drew on the tutorial system but adapted it to an American curriculum. Likewise, the upper-class major in Princeton's new curriculum was inspired by the honors degree work at Oxbridge. But Wilson's view of English academe appears to have become increasingly distant and romanticized. His failure to visit either Oxford or Cambridge after 1903 is striking, especially in 1908, when Cram offered to meet him at both and such a visit might have added clarity and credibility to his quadrangle advocacy.

Wilson focused primarily, even obsessively, on the ambience and appearance of Oxbridge's residential colleges and ignored critical disjunctures with American institutions, such as the power of academic departments.[76] Wilson's quadrangle plan had only a vague connection to the curriculum. He seems to have put his faith in creating the right social and physical atmosphere. In his conception of the Graduate College, he was almost as fixated on replicating Oxbridge architecture as West was.

It is difficult to measure the mixture of informed observation, selective vision, romanticism, and opportunistic rhetoric in Wilson's academic Anglophilia. Whatever the mix, it is not surprising that the role of foreign models evolved as American academe changed rapidly during Wilson's time at Princeton.

From Wilson's leap into prominence at the sesquicentennial celebration until he resigned the presidency, Anglophilia pervaded Princeton. Oxbridge was invoked for almost every cause and sometimes on both sides of debates. But the meaning of such invocations changed over that decade and a half.

Jackson Lears has suggested that antimodernism, with Gothic architecture and Anglophilic trappings as principal manifestations, shifted from a meaningful search for answers into more formulaic enunciations of established positions. Symbols appropriated for an American present eventually lost their original meaning.[77] His insight offers a clue to understanding the role played by Anglophilia at Princeton.

In the 1890s, America faced exceptional uncertainty, worsened by a deep depression. By 1910, a new social order was emerging and the world looked safer. The upper class had established institutions—urban clubs, country clubs, elite vacation areas, prep schools, social registers—that confirmed and protected their privilege. The rapidly growing upper-middle-class was developing an identity illustrated in magazines and lived in suburbs. Both classes evolved symbiotically with colleges. They supplied most of the students and philanthropy that enabled private colleges to live in the style to which they wished to become accustomed. In turn, colleges offered halfway houses to adulthood that played on romantic images and increasingly offered facilities that fulfilled them. The "English" model gave colleges a common language with those classes, especially in the East, and helped save the college from its predicted decline, and even demise.

By 1910, American colleges and universities were dramatically better off than fifteen or twenty years earlier. Enrollments grew as magazines touted the "college man" and "college woman," and college life became a rite of passage for affluent youth. While images of Oxbridge still appeared, magazines increasingly depicted American colleges, implying that they blended the best of Europe into an American model in tweeds. Frank Merriwell and Dink Stover provided suitably American and democratic successors to Tom Brown.[78]

Collegiate Gothic developed a distinctively American variant. Adjusting to open space and lack of a college system, American architects shifted from seeking to imitate Oxbridge to paying more attention to materials and craftsmanship. The Mather Dial provides a symbolic example. Situated inside a small quadrangle in Oxford, at Princeton it sits in ample open space with buildings on only three sides. Near the dial, preceptors met their students in McCosh Hall, accessed across an open space rather than an enclosed quadrangle. Ironically, the Graduate College, whose planning poisoned the last years of Wilson's presidency, gave Princeton the one quadrangle that would have looked at home as a college in Oxford or Cambridge.

Curricularly, American colleges were changing in ways that Wilson influenced with reforms he promoted by drawing on Oxbridge's prestige. The baccalaureate degree was regaining its position as the precursor to professional training, and undergraduate curricula increasingly echoed Wilson's formula. The ascendancy of his friend and ally, Abbott Lawrence Lowell, to Harvard's presidency in 1909 suggested they were starting to carry the debate. The upper-class major bore the genes of Oxbridge's honors curriculum, but the breadth of freshman and sophomore years lacked foreign parentage. The amalgam was uniquely American.[79]

Alongside the victories for those championing the "English" model, faculty life was being reshaped by those who appealed to a "German" approach. The national academic professions were structured by national disciplinary organizations and campus departments. Research became the coin of the realm for professional prestige, and graduate programs proliferated. But unlike the German practice, graduate schools were added to colleges, as a follow-up to the baccalaureate degree and the "real" college life. While most colleges initially experimented with doctoral and professional programs, by 1910 a growing number were deciding that their core business was undergraduate education. Thus decades of lauding presumed German practice yielded a distinctly American model in which only a small minority of institutions awarded doctoral degrees.

The German influence dramatically affected academic life, but largely in a professional culture invisible to the public. German culture was respected in America but lacked the ability to evoke the same feelings of cultural inferiority as did the English. While Americans read English authors voraciously, German literature was not well known. Moreover, the German Empire looked increasingly uninviting as the Kaiser's militarism became more apparent after the turn of the century.

As with the English model, champions of the German model drew selectively from their time abroad. American visitors found a system that appeared to provide alternatives at a time when the knowledge explosion was rendering the prescribed curriculum untenable, students were chafing under the strictures of Victorian Protestantism, and the utility of Latin and Greek was being questioned. Over nine thousand American students had sampled German universities, and many found an attractive environment, intellectually and socially. The German label carried considerable prestige. In the 1840s, Horace Mann had praised Prussian education in his widely circulated reports and cited it as a model for many of his "common school" reforms that swept across the country. The crushing German victory over France in the 1870–71 war seemingly demonstrated the superiority of the universities in the newly unified country, as scientific achievement began to be associated with national prestige. It is indicative that the trustees of Johns Hopkins sent their new president, Daniel Coit Gilman, to Germany before opening the doors of Wilson's future graduate school in 1876. For the academic pilgrims, "German" came to mean specialization, a scientific approach to knowledge, research as the first priority, and one's academic discipline as the primary professional identity. Having studied in Germany was a valuable credential in many fields, and the expertise brought back shaped several emerging fields.[80]

As with English universities, the reality was usually more complicated. Most American visitors spent less than a year in Germany, attended lectures rather than seminars or labs, and floated among several universities. Few spoke German fluently, spent much time with faculty, or gained a real understanding of the structure and organization of German universities. Although most praised them in public, private judgments were often more critical. The resulting American graduate school bore little resemblance to German practice, but owed much to the research spirit it conveyed to scholars like Wilson's dean, Henry Fine.[81]

Inside Germany, Wilhelmine universities were viewed by many as in crisis at the same time their praises were being sung in the United States and elsewhere in Europe (though not in Britain). A wide gulf opened between an increasingly specialized, socially elite faculty and more career-oriented, more bourgeois students. The university was increasingly isolated from German society.[82]

Ironically, Wilhelm von Humboldt's ideal of a well-rounded education was more truly fulfilled in the Oxbridge and American colleges than in German universities.[83] But his notion of *Bildung* or personal cultivation was not the version of German tradition brought back by academic pilgrims returning to the United States.

In Laurence Veysey's term, American higher education was showing "symptoms of crystallization" by 1910. It was more secure and confident and had reached solutions that drew on European models, real and imagined. Appeals to foreign models had become part of academic dialogue but were increasingly formulaic and less part of fundamental debate. Thus Wilson could go into battle for an Anglophilic image whose reality he had not seen in years, if ever.

Anglophilia and the associated images of Oxbridge were effective weapons in the fin de siècle battle for the soul of American academe. Virtually all bets had been off in a country searching for order in the aftershocks of industrialization, urbanization, and immigration and the resulting class re-formation. In academe, older institutional forms looked increasingly anachronistic as new ones materialized. But from that turmoil emerged a unique approach to higher education that borrowed semblances of foreign models to create something very American.

In the 1890s, the spirit and institutional forms represented as German were carrying the day, wiping out collegiate traditions and threatening institutions. Counterattacking, Woodrow Wilson and others deployed an English model that resonated with an Anglophilia familiar to the eastern upper and upper-middle classes. A revived liberal arts college and its special mutation at Princeton, "the university college," preserved older colleges and the core of their ethos. As seems typical of most cultural borrowing, Wilson cherry-picked attractive aspects of Oxbridge, especially the tutors, the honors degrees, the college system, and the quadrangles.

Wilson's continued rhetorical use of Oxbridge obscures his evolution. At the beginning of his Princeton presidency, his views of academe and his romantic views of Oxbridge differed little from Andrew West's. They shared limited views of graduate education, and Wilson's concern with "clubbable" preceptors reflected a continuing distance from the emerging research university world. But in the second half of his presidency, he threw himself into recruiting faculty with distinguished research credentials and began to imagine a modern graduate school, albeit in a university with a college at its core.

Paradoxically, clashing appeals to supposed foreign models helped shape distinctively American practice. Closer attention to the reality of German and English practice might have obstructed the shaping of indigenous traditions. Selectively choosing from a romanticized Oxbridge and linking it to a broader Anglophilia initially informed debate and continued to be an effective rhetorical tool after its heuristic value faded.

In cultural borrowing, Wilson's romantic invocations may have been more useful than nuanced Anglo-American comparisons in transforming Princeton and influencing American academe. His close friend and correspondent, Edith Reid, later observed, "Cambridge and Oxford had put dreams into his head which were to become a nightmare and were to be his undoing."[84] Dreams of spires informed and facilitated the successes that became Wilson's educational legacy, even if they also led to nightmares.

NOTES

The author wishes to thank Harold Silver, James Axtell, John Thompson, and the University of Virginia Press's anonymous readers for their generous and insightful editorial guidance.

1. Woodrow Wilson (hereafter WW) to Ellen Axson Wilson, July 9, 1896, in *The Papers of Woodrow Wilson,* ed. Arthur S. Link et al., 69 vols. (Princeton: Princeton University Press, 1966–1994), 9:537–38 (hereafter *PWW*).

2. *PWW,* 14:139 (Oct. 4, 1902).

3. James Bryce, *The American Commonwealth,* 2 vols. (New York: Macmillan, 1910), 2:chs. 109, 112.

4. James McLachlan, *American Boarding Schools: A Historical Study* (New York: Charles Scribner's Sons, 1970), 149–57, 203–5.

5. Elisa Tamarkin, *Anglophilia: Deference, Devotion, and Antebellum America* (Chicago: University of Chicago Press, 2008), 316–22, quote at 322.

6. Tamarkin, *Anglophilia,* 257.

7. Mayo W. Hazeltine, *British and American Education: The Universities of the Two Countries Compared,* Harper's Half-Hour Series (New York: Harper and Brothers, 1880).

8. Richard Hofstadter and Wilson Smith, eds. *American Higher Education: A Documentary History,* 2 vols. (Chicago: University of Chicago Press, 1961), 2:550–51. See also W.H.G. Armytage, *The American Influence on English Education* (London: Routledge and Kegan Paul, 1967), 38–39.

9. Daniel T. Rodgers, *Atlantic Crossings: Social Politics in a Progressive Age* (Cambridge, Mass.: Belknap Press of Harvard University Press, 1998), 1–7.

10. Rodgers, *Atlantic Crossings,* 655.

11. For example, John Corbin, *An American at Oxford* (Boston: Houghton Mifflin, 1902), 1–3, 301–9.

12. Thomas and Kathleen Schaeper, *Rhodes Scholars, Oxford, and the Creation of an American Elite* (New York: Berghahn Books, 1998), ch. 2.

13. Corbin, *American at Oxford.*

14. *PWW,* 19:280 (July 1, 1909).

15. *Memorial Book of the Sesquicentennial Celebration of the Founding of the College of New Jersey and of the Ceremonies Inaugurating Princeton University* (New York: Charles Scribner's Sons, 1898), 1.

16. Charles Z. Klauder and Herbert C. Wise, *College Architecture in America* (New York: Charles Scribner's Sons, 1929), 2–16, 43–45.

17. *PWW,* 14:227 (Nov. 29, 1902).

18. Benjamin W. Morris to WW, Aug. 16, 1904, *PWW,* 15:445.

19. *PWW,* 14:269 (Dec. 9, 1902).

20. *Daily Princetonian,* Nov. 1, 1907, in *PWW,* 17:462–65.

21. *Chicago Daily Tribune,* Nov. 29, 1902, in *PWW,* 14:226–27.

22. *PWW,* 14:153–54 (Oct. 21, 1902).

23. *PWW,* 15:96–97 (Dec. 12, 1903). Although the idea of a major originated at Johns Hopkins and had been adopted by Bryn Mawr and other colleges, Wilson clearly preferred to attribute curricular innovations to Oxbridge rather than his doctoral alma mater or domestic rivals.

24. *PWW,* 16:37 (March 23, 1905).

25. *PWW,* 16:58 (April 15, 1905).

26. WW, "New Plans for Princeton," *Harper's Weekly,* June 24, 1905, in *PWW,* 16:146–49 at 148.

27. Henry Russell to WW, April 27, 1905, *PWW,* 16:83.

28. Henry Wilkinson Bragdon, *Woodrow Wilson: The Academic Years* (Cambridge, Mass.: Belknap Press of Harvard University Press, 1967), 360.

29. Bragdon, *Woodrow Wilson,* 360.

30. *PWW,* 17:325–33 at 332 (ca. Aug. 1, 1907).

31. *PWW,* 16:523 (Dec. 13, 1906), 17:119 (April 25, 1907).

32. *PWW,* 14:157–58 (Oct. 21, 1902).

33. *PWW,* 15:421 (July 23, 1904).

34. *PWW,* 16:58 (April 15, 1905).

35. Bragdon, *Woodrow Wilson,* 305.

36. *PWW,* 17:557 (Dec. 13, 1907).

37. Anthony Grafton, "The Precept System: The Myth and Reality of a Princeton Institution," *Princeton University Library Chronicle,* 64:3 (Spring 2003), 467–503.

38. *Chicago Daily Tribune,* Nov. 29, 1902, in *PWW,* 14:227.

39. Bragdon, *Woodrow Wilson,* 305.

40. *PWW,* 14:158 (Oct. 21, 1902).

41. Bragdon, *Woodrow Wilson,* 367; on 483–84n41, Bragdon discusses Wilson's later denial that he read West's proposal. Bragdon's charitable interpretation of Wilson's denial fails to consider how much West's book reflected Wilson's own observations.

42. Bryce, *American Commonwealth,* 2:787.

43. *The Proposed Graduate College of Princeton University* (Princeton: Princeton University, 1903), 9.

44. *PWW,* 16:156–57 (July 18, 1905).

45. *PWW,* 17:590 (Jan. 9, 1908), 19:739 (Jan. 6, 1910).

46. *PWW,* 19:126–28 (March 29, 1909), 537–38 (Nov. 29, 1909).

47. John M. Mulder, *Woodrow Wilson: The Years of Preparation* (Princeton: Princeton University Press, 1978), chs. 2–4, offers excellent insights into, and examples of, Wilson's early attitudes toward Britain. Also useful is Bragdon, *Woodrow Wilson,* chs. 2–7. See also Woodrow Wilson, *Congressional Government* (Boston: Houghton, Mifflin, 1885) and Walter Bagehot, *The English Constitution* (London: Chapman and Hall, 1867).

48. *PWW,* 9:521 (June 19, 1896).

49. *PWW,* 9:547–48 (July 26, 1896).

50. *PWW,* 9:537–38 (July 9, 1896).

51. *PWW,* 11:185–86 (July 23, 1899).

52. *PWW,* 11:189 (July 26, 1899).

53. *PWW,* 38:681 (July 30, 1899).

54. *PWW,* 11:207 (Aug. 6, 1899).

55. *PWW,* 11:197 (July 30, 1899), 207 (Aug. 6, 1899).

56. No journals from Wilson's trips survive. Thus we are dependent upon his correspondence, especially to Ellen, to trace and understand his overseas experiences.

57. *PWW,* 14:530–32 (Aug. 1903).

58. *PWW,* 9:528–29 (June 29, 1896); W. Barksdale Maynard, *Woodrow Wilson: Princeton to the Presidency* (New Haven: Yale University Press, 2008), 135.

59. *PWW,* 16:453–54 (Sept. 16, 1906).

60. In similar fashion, he had not visited Congress while writing *Congressional Government,* even though he was living only a short train ride away in Baltimore. His friend and pedagogical ally, Abbott Lawrence Lowell, believed that Wilson neglected careful research and was prone to making judgments "through the haze of his own preconceptions." Bragdon, *Woodrow Wilson,* 137; John Milton Cooper Jr., *Woodrow Wilson: A Biography* (New York: Alfred A. Knopf, 2009), 51.

61. Ralph Adams Cram to WW, June 1, 1908, *PWW,* 18:314.

62. *PWW,* 38:687 (July 28, 1908)

63. *PWW,* 18:391–92 (Aug. 4, 1908).

64. *PWW,* 18:406 (Aug. 20, 1908).

65. *PWW,* 14:245 (Nov. 29, 1902).

66. *PWW,* 14:139–40 (Oct., 4, 1902); Andrew Fleming West, "The Tutorial System in College," *Short Papers on American Liberal Education* (New York: Charles Scribner's Sons, 1907), ch. 1, esp. pp. 3–7.

67. Maynard, *Woodrow Wilson,* 273.

68. M. C. Curthoys, "The Examination System," in M. G. Brock and M. C. Curthoys, eds., *Nineteenth-Century Oxford, Part 1,* vol. 6 of *The History of the University of Oxford,* gen. ed. T. H. Aston (Oxford: Clarendon Press, 1997), 356–59.

69. Frederick Arthur MacKenzie, *The American Invaders* (London: Grant Richards, 1902).

70. George Calderon, *The Adventures of Downy V. Green: Scholar at Oxford* (London: Smith, Elder, 1902), 16.

71. Armytage, *American Influence,* 45.

72. Bayard Henry to WW, Aug. 16, 1907, *PWW,* 17:347–48 n1.

73. Edwin E. Slosson, *Great American Universities* (New York: Macmillan, 1910), 421.

74. Bryce, *American Commonwealth,* 2:663–94.

75. West to WW, Oct. 4, 1902, *PWW,* 14:139–40.

76. In this respect, Wilson shared a tendency of other North American academic importers of Oxbridge practices. Alex Duke, *Importing Oxbridge: English Residential Colleges and American Universities* (New Haven: Yale University Press, 1996), 88–89.

77. T. J. Jackson Lears, *No Place of Grace: Antimodernism and the Transformation of American Culture, 1880–1920* (New York: Pantheon Books, 1981), 300–302.

78. Daniel A. Clark, *Creating the College Man: American Mass Magazines and Middle-Class Manhood, 1890–1915* (Madison: University of Wisconsin Press, 2010), chs. 2, 3, 5. John R. Thelin, *A History of American Higher Education* (Baltimore: Johns Hopkins University Press, 2004), 150–62.

79. Julie A. Reuben, *The Making of the Modern University: Intellectual Transformation and the Marginalization of Morality* (Chicago: University of Chicago Press, 1996), 230–43.

80. For instance, in economics, Rodgers, *Atlantic Crossings,* 76–111.

81. Anja Becker, "For the Sake of Old Leipzig Days: Academic Networks of American Students at a German University, 1781–1914" (Ph.D. diss., Dept. of History, University of Leipzig, 2006); Becker, "Southern Academic Ambitions Meet German Scholarship: The Leipzig Networks of Vanderbilt University's James H. Kirkland in the Late Nineteenth Century," *Journal of Southern History,* 74:4 (Nov. 2008), 855–86; Edward Shils and John Roberts, "The Diffusion of European Models Outside Europe," in *Universities in the Nineteenth and Early Twentieth Centuries (1800–1945),* ed. Walter Rüegg, vol. 3 of *A History of the University in Europe* (Cambridge: Cambridge University Press, 1992), 163–75; James Turner and Paul Bernard, "The 'German Model' and the Graduate School: The University of Michigan and the Origin Myth of the American University," *History of Higher Education Annual,* 13 (1993), 69–98; Konrad Jarausch, "American Students in Germany, 1815–1914," in Henry Geitz et. al., eds., *German Influences on Education in the United States to 1917* (Washington, D.C.: German Historical Institute and Cambridge: Cambridge University Press, 1995), 195–211.

82. Christophe Charle, "The Crisis of the German Model," in Rüegg, *Universities,* 57–61.

83. Rüegg, *Universities,* 11–12.

84. Edith Reid, *Woodrow Wilson: The Caricature, the Myth, and the Man* (New York: Oxford University Press, 1934), 100–101.

# Conservative among Progressives

## *Woodrow Wilson in the Golden Age of American Women's Higher Education*

Victoria Bissell Brown

In the spring of 1894, near the end of his ninth year as a college professor, Woodrow Wilson responded to an old friend's query about the merits of coeducation. Reformers at the University of Virginia, the all-male institution at which Wilson had begun his study of the law, were considering the admission of women as undergraduates. Charles William Kent, a law school fraternity brother and now professor at Virginia, sought Wilson's view of the matter. Speaking from his safe perch as a teacher of Princeton's all-male student body, Wilson claimed "just enough experience of co-education to know that, even under the most favourable circumstances, it is most demoralizing."[1]

Wilson's concern did not center on intellectual or physical deficits among women. Nor was his warning centered on the fear that coeducation "leads to vice, though occasionally it does." The core problem, said Wilson, was that coeducation "*vulgarizes* the whole relationship of men and women." This "generalization is a *fact*" in every setting, asserted Wilson, but he predicted that especially "in the South it would be fatal to the standards of delicacy as between men and women which we"—meaning Wilson and other southerners—"most value." Besides, Wilson reasoned, "where is the necessity? Women now have excellent colleges of their own, where their life can be such as is fit for women."[2]

Brief though it is, this letter captures the key features of Woodrow Wilson's notably unchanging views on female education in the years between 1883 and 1910. He was, let us be absolutely clear on this point, in favor of education for women, including higher education for those who wanted it.[3] Wilson enjoyed intellectually lively, literate women who were conversant on politics and the arts; he flirted with, courted, married, and fathered such women. But at the heart of his letter to Charles Kent is Wilson's opposition to any educational arrangements that threatened either the romance or the power of patriarchy. Wilson's comments about gender in the decade before and the decade after his 1894 letter to Kent make clear his belief that the tender balance of devotion and domination which Wilson so cherished in heterosexual relations would be "vulgarized"—exposed and diminished—by the workaday familiarity and academic competition inherent in coeducation. Like many other opponents of coeducation, Wilson feared that mixed classes at the college level caused men to cease protecting women and caused women to cease deferring to men. According to this argument, patriarchy's "standards of delicacy" were destroyed in promiscuous chemistry labs beyond high school.[4]

By endorsing the era's "excellent" female colleges, Wilson signaled that he did not reject rigorous collegiate coursework for women; he simply believed that intellectual endeavor shielded from heterosexual competition was requisite to produce men who were "intelligently manly" and women who were "intelligently womanly," both "specially fitted" by segregation "for the parts they are to play in the country's life."[5] The part that the educated woman was to play was a private, domestic one, lovingly subordinate to and supportive of an educated man's career and interests. It was out of these convictions that Wilson dismissed coeducation in his letter to Kent as the "gratuitous folly" of "an age . . . going out of its way to seek change!"[6]

Read in the larger context of 1894, Wilson's embrace of all-female colleges as consistent with patriarchy and his treatment of coeducation as a passing fad appear to be dead wrong on both counts. In the quarter century between 1870 and 1894, women's colleges had become America's nursery for female independence, training women for professional lives and creating a sororal culture that encouraged or, at least, enabled half of the graduates not to marry. Contrary to Wilson's claim, women's colleges in the late nineteenth century did not steep women in the life that Wilson thought "fit for women"; they encouraged women to live without dependence upon or deference to men.[7]

But this was only half of Wilson's apparent misunderstanding of the situation in 1894. Anyone paying attention to actual data that year would have known that sex-segregated colleges were not the growth industry in U.S. higher education. In the years between 1870 and 1890, coeducational institutions grew from 29 percent of all colleges to 43 percent and 70 percent of all female college students were enrolled in coeducational schools.[8] Far from being a fad, coeducation was, by 1894, firmly established as the method by which American higher education was going to be organized, vulgar though it might be. Single-sex education was dominant in only one region of the country: New England.[9]

From the viewpoint of a feminist educator in 1894, American women were living in a golden age. Since 1870, the number of women enrolled in institutions of higher education had increased from 11,000 to almost 60,000, and women constituted over 36 percent of all students enrolled in colleges and universities and were increasing their participation in higher education at a much faster rate than were men.[10] Moreover, women were proving to be successful competitors in academia; in the University of Chicago's first decade, for example, its female students earned 56 percent of the Phi Beta Kappa awards while comprising just 40 percent of the student body.[11]

To be sure, the national collegiate population was less than 5 percent of women, as it was less than 5 percent of men, but that did not take away from the fact that in post-Civil War America, women experienced an expansion of educational opportunity unprecedented in human history and a concomitant expansion in the potential to use their education for independent pursuit of professional, artistic, scholarly, technical, and civic endeavors.

The popular literature of the era tells us that this dramatic growth in female opportunity was hotly debated. Dozens upon dozens of books and magazine articles, speeches and pamphlets were published in these years extolling—or decrying—the social and individual effects of female education. Woodrow Wilson was not a vocal participant in this contest. Women's education was not like a football game at Wesleyan or Princeton where Professor Wilson could be seen "running up and down the side-lines . . . moving his closed umbrella in the air and cheering encouragement at the top of his lungs."[12] In the debate over women's education, he was quietly resigned to the fact that "the higher education of women is certain to be settled in the affirmative, in this country at least, whether my sympathy be enlisted or not."[13] He confessed to Charles Kent that he wished he "could write all my heart contains on the matter," but he chose not to devote rhetorical energy to the public debate over the educational fortunes of half the U.S. population.[14]

We can define Wilson's position in this debate, however, and discern the factors shaping his position by analyzing three sets of sources: the love letters he exchanged with Ellen Axson before their marriage in 1885 and in subsequent years; the published record of his experiences at Bryn Mawr College and Wesleyan University; and his Princeton-era essays and speeches on the humanities and on the purpose of liberal arts education. The argument growing out of these documents defines Wilson as a romantic, androcentric, conservative in the female education debate. He did not align with reactionaries in opposing female education; nor did he align with liberal feminists in supporting a woman's right to use her education in any way she wished.

Wilson supported female education as long as it served men's interests, as long as it protected male dominance. He applauded education for enhancing a woman's ability to sympathize with her husband's endeavors, and he took romantic and sexual pleasure in the notion that an educated woman, though equipped for independence, chose selfless devotion to one man's career and household. Wilson was more conservative than most other Americans of his era insofar as he persistently opposed coeducation as a route to this androcentric goal. But he was not unique in wanting to train women to serve men, nor were his allies only men; many women, including his wife, embraced the romance and the respect attendant upon female selflessness. Wilson's stance did not alter in the years between 1883 and 1910, but there is an ironic arc to the education story that unfolded around him. He and his fellow opponents lost the battle of coeducation, but they won the war over patriarchal power in academe. As it turned out, Wilson's 1894 comments to Charles Kent on women's colleges and coeducation proved true. Within twenty years of his description of women's colleges as prep schools for domesticity, they had become precisely that; in the same span of time, coeducational institutions had designed enough curricular and extracurricular sex-segregation to contain heterosexual competition, reduce the vulgar possibility of sexual equality, and instate the female student as a sexualized "coed" seeking a "Mrs." degree. By the time Wilson was president of the United States and called for war with Germany, over 60 percent of female professors at coeducational institutions were teaching home economics, regardless of their Ph.D. training. The androcentric position had become the mainstream position.[15]

Between 1883 and 1910, American women's great gains in access to education served to intensify the debate over what women would actually do with their education. That fight was over more than access to classrooms and books. It was over privilege and rights, masters and subordinates, love and sacrifice, sex and children, jobs and money. The goal of female independence was defeated in that era's contest, and patriarchal control of the means and ends of women's education was the victor. Wilson was not an active agent in patriarchy's conservative collegiate victory in the 1910s, but his story illuminates the emotional and intellectual complexities in that contest. For those who study gender history, Wilson's unbending assumption of male privilege, despite his devotion to human freedom and opportunity, testifies to patriarchy's power to encourage the androcentric presumption of male-as-human and female-as-the-servant-of-humanity. For those who study Wilson, attention to his entitled stance toward female education can enrich any analysis of his intellectual philosophy and style of leadership.

Woodrow Wilson and Ellen Axson met when he was twenty-seven and she was twenty-three years of age. Their fathers' acquaintance as southern Presbyterian ministers occasioned a chance encounter in early April 1883, but the seventy miles that separated Wilson's home in Atlanta from Ellen's in Rome meant that the young couple reunited for just one carriage drive in late May and one picnic in mid-June. But they corresponded that summer and were engaged by mid-September.[16]

The speed and success of their courtship served, for both of them, as a tribute to love's mysterious power to defy reason and justify the impetuous leap of faith that feminist critics of Victorian marriage cautioned against. The young, passionate couple spent the two years between their engagement in September 1883 and their marriage in June 1885 glorying in the serendipity of their union.[17] They lived quite distant from each other in those two years: Wilson was in graduate school at Johns Hopkins, in Baltimore, while Ellen coped, in Georgia, with her father's mental illness and probable suicide. She then used her inheritance money not to attend college but to study for a year at the Art Students' League in New York City. During their two-year separation, Wilson and Ellen wrote hundreds of letters in which they sounded out the depth of their compatibility. Three months before their wedding, Ellen wrote:

> My darling, I want to tell you too that when you speak of ours being kindred spirits you touch one of the deepest sources of the ever-growing joy which fills my heart to over-flowing. I too have had an ever-deepening sense of the

> inborn sympathy there is between us in all matters of importance; we look at life in the same way, our ideals and aspirations are in harmony . . . it is this sympathy which, together with the greatness of my love, makes me hope now that in spite of all my unworthiness I was indeed "meant" for you . . . I do indeed seem to understand you, dear, without interpretation . . . because it is my native tongue you speak.[18]

Wilson replied the next day, using his pet name for her, "Eileen," to express his "unspeakable delight" over her deservedness and his prescience:

> What with admiration of its wonderful womanly sense and delight at its still more wonderful womanly *love*, my heart is even yet almost too full to trust itself to speak. Oh, Eileen, what a happy, God-sent inspiration it was that made me love you at first acquaintance! My heart knew at once the treasure it had found, and ever since my slower head has been daily discovering, with increasing amazement and delight, fresh proofs of my heart's instinctive wisdom.[19]

At the center of the Wilsons' impassioned compatibility was a shared excitement over the incandescent beauty of female devotion to male ambition. The young lovers built an intimate home in each other's hearts through mutual rapture over Ellen's intellectual, psychological, and ideological commitment to "untiring service" to a "really worthy" cause: Woodrow Wilson's life and career.[20]

The point here is not to doubt or denigrate the thirty-year love affair between Ellen and Woodrow Wilson. On the contrary, the point is that the Wilsons' marriage was so satisfyingly central to Woodrow Wilson's lived experience that it reaffirmed all of his sanguine assumptions about the natural mutuality of male dominance and female service. Some attention to his marriage is vital to understanding Wilson's resistance to female independence and nondomestic uses of female education. Shared delight in traditional gender roles (and shared disdain for nonconforming women) fueled the Wilsons' marital romance; harmony on the "woman question" sealed their conjugal pact and cemented their domestic bond long before they actually lived together. To ignore his marriage when discussing Wilson's views on female education is to underestimate the depth of his emotional investment in patriarchy as a fundamental structure in human life.[21]

A reading of the letters Ellen and Woodrow Wilson exchanged in the

1880s, informed by some familiarity with love letters of the day, makes clear that the Wilsons were typical in seeking constant assurances of the other's love and in articulating particular areas of interest and vulnerability.[22] Ellen constantly sought assurance that she was intelligent enough and educated enough to serve as the wife of a man who believed that without her "aid and companionship I shall never do any of the great things of which my ambition has dreamed."[23] Wilson, in turn, constantly sought assurance that he was magnificent enough to inspire Ellen to dedicate her entire life to his advancement; "The beginning of my real career," he wrote, "hangs upon the sacrifice you may be willing to make in my behalf, provided it be a sacrifice to marry."[24]

Though she frequently fretted over her lack of education, Ellen was the graduate of a female seminary, so she was among the better-educated southern women of her day. From age eleven until eighteen she studied math, science, French, German, English literature, and art at Rome Female College.[25] Her easy epistolary references to Shakespeare, Wordsworth, Carlyle, and Ruskin make clear that she was as comfortable in the Victorian world of literature as she was in the world of visual art. Wilson told a male friend that Ellen "grew up in that best of all schools—for manners, purity, and cultivation—a country parsonage." In addition to her abilities as an artist, from which she had earned some money in local portrait painting, Wilson said, "She is also devoted to reading of the best sort: so that, without any pretense to learning and without the slightest tinge of pedantry, she has acquired a very remarkable acquaintance with the best literature. If you add to this, the fact that she is in her tastes the most *domestic* of maidens, you will see how well fitted she is to become a *student's* wife." But Wilson hastened to add that his was not a "dispassionate" story of calculating Ellen's fitness as a "proper help-meet for a professor." Rather, his was a story of falling head-over-heels in love "because of her beauty, and gentleness and intelligence; because she was irresistibly lovable."[26] In Wilson's mind, the wonderful twist in this romantic tale was that he had followed his heart in choosing Ellen and was rewarded with a partner who had the intelligence to sympathize with his scholarly pursuits.

In assuring Ellen that her intellect was perfectly pitched for his marital tastes, Wilson emphasized the beauty of sexual difference, complementarity, and female sympathy. He did not want a scholarly colleague in marriage, not "a woman such as John Stuart Mill married," who ministered "not to his love but to his logical faculty."[27] Wilson wanted Ellen because she had "acquired a genuine love for intellectual pursuits without becoming bookish, without losing her feminine charm"; her mind "had been cultivated without becoming stiffened or made masculine"; she could "enter into men's highest pleasures without becoming at all like men."[28] Ellen's intelligence was womanly, Wilson explained, because she could "reflect the sentiments and opinions" he expressed "like a mirror without a flaw!" She helped him to think, not by having her own ideas but "by showing me in the clear depths of her woman's mind what I had thought!"[29]

Wilson's intellectual guide in the matter of marriage and female partnership was Philip Gilbert Hamerton, a prolific and respected British intellectual of the mid-nineteenth century whose 1873 book, *The Intellectual Life,* devoted several chapters to the role of "Women and Marriage" in advancing a male scholar's pursuits. Both Wilson and Ellen read—and quoted—from Hamerton, who presented the intellectual with just two choices: he could marry a "simple" woman who would manage his domestic life, "make no demands on his time or society," and regard his work as "unknown, or to her uncongenial." Or he could choose a wife possessed of the intelligence to "reverently [follow the man] she loves, however arduous be the path." According to Hamerton, "the whole universe is changed" for the solitary intellectual possessed of a sympathetic wife "who will always be accessible by day and night" to listen and understand.[30]

Wilson confessed that, before meeting Ellen, he had read Hamerton's chapters on marriage "with great disquietude," fearing that his passionate nature would cause him to fall for a pretty, but simple, woman and that fatal choice would lead to his intellectual "ruin." Indeed, he had despaired of ever finding the ideal woman Hamerton described. But discourse with Ellen about Eliot's *Middlemarch* had "thrilled" him with the "discovery" that she "knew what sort of wife I needed" and was prepared "to give me all the intellectual sympathy I desire." Wilson assured Ellen that he did not expect "my darling to go back with me into those prehistoric times in which government originated," but he delighted in the confidence that "she will not frown at my abstraction in such studies."[31]

Wilson made clear that he did not want Ellen competing with him in their shared pursuit of his scholarly goals; he jokingly sought assurance, for example, that she did not "know much about the Constitution of the United States for I know marvelously little about art." According to his lighthearted patriarchal calculation, if Ellen knew about "both subjects how am I to be the head of the house?"[32] Ellen assured Wilson that she did not know about the Constitution and made clear that she seriously embraced the auxiliary role Wilson defined for her. She exulted in the "power of love" to bring together, "in such full sympathy," "two natures so different as yours and mine (or say those of men and women)," but she insisted that this "perfect union" was only possible because men and women were different; women could not give such sympathy if "we were not 'the complement of man.' "[33]

Coquetry was surely at play in Ellen's demure denials of her ability to satisfy Wilson's intellectual needs (and her doubts and his assurances about intellectual harmony may have doubled as a conversation about sexual harmony).[34] But there is little doubt that Ellen shared Wilson's enthusiasm for the female role of sympathetic subordinate and equally little doubt that she enjoyed showing Wilson her readiness for that role. In one deft page of a letter written just three months before their wedding, Ellen quoted Hamerton to assure herself that "a woman helps a man not so much by adding to his ideas as by understanding him" and quoted Portia in *Merchant of Venice* to say she was "an unlessoned girl, unschooled, unpractis'd" but "happy" that she was "not bred so dull but she can learn" and, "happiest of all" that she was ready to be "directed as from her lord, her governor, her king." Embellishing the point with a bit of Robert Browning, Ellen closed this testament to her happy intellectual subordination by promising, "I *will* be the cricket on the lyre."[35]

In return for his assurances of Ellen's intellectual ability, Wilson regularly sought assurance that she was happy to sacrifice her artistic career for the sake of his domestic comfort and professional advancement. It was not as though Wilson actually believed that a feminine woman like Ellen had any choice but to marry; "the family relation" was a dictate of God and nature and "*only* women whom God has intended for old maids" chose against it. Nor did he really believe that the sacrifice women made was so great; he had only "contempt for the view which would have it that marriage *belittles* a woman."[36] But Wilson heightened the pleasure and intensity of his romantic life by, first, imagining Ellen as a gifted artist, one whose "powers" could "leave some immortal portraits" to the world and, next, confessing how "guiltily selfish" he felt because of the "fact . . . that marriage will take away almost all of your chances for work of that kind."[37] Constructing Ellen's situation in this way set her outside the circle of crass women who schemed to marry or needed to marry; Wilson insisted that marriage was not "in any true sense an economic question."[38] This construction of Ellen as a great (and, implicitly, self-supporting) artist meant that she was choosing Wilson out of love, not necessity, but it also meant she was sacrificing her own potential career for his. There was no thought of domestic compromise on that point, leaving plenty of room for the drama of sacrifice as a testament of love.

The discussion of Ellen's sacrifice reached a crescendo in the spring before their June 1885 wedding. "Ah, sweetheart, this thing has torn my heart more than once!" Wilson cried out. "I *hate* selfishness, it hurts me more than I can tell you to think that I am asking you to give up what has formed so much of your life and constituted so much of your delight. And yet," he quickly added, universalizing their arrangements, "that is what is involved in becoming a wife." Wilson begged to know "what my darling thinks" on this subject; "I would give my life for you," he closed, "and yet I am asking you to give your life to me—for me, to be merged in mine."[39]

Ellen's response testifies to their emotional and ideological compatibility, serving as a reminder that Wilson's home life never challenged his assumptions about normal female nature and abnormal female ambition. Ellen not only denied ever having any "ambition" to paint "immortal portraits"; she also argued that her "woman's heart with all its natural impulses and cravings" would have "cried bitterly" if she had "chosen to sacrifice" marriage and family to the "vanity and vexation" of an artistic life.[40] In generalizing from her desires to all women's desires, Ellen echoed an earlier commentary on the northern, feminist claim to " 'a woman's right to live her own life.' " The claim, thought Ellen, was foolish because "we haven't enough faith in ourselves, we women," to be "sure" that women's own pursuits were of "real use to anyone." Ellen did not question why this was the case. She simply concluded that "the best way to still all doubts about the worthiness of our ambitions, . . . our power to achieve them . . . [and] the uses and meaning of our life, is to merge that life with *another* about which there *can* be no such doubt" and then devote "untiring service" to that other's life.[41] She argued that it was only because he was a man that Wilson saw Ellen's choices as a sacrifice; if he were a woman (or what Ellen and Wilson jokingly referred to as a "sure enough woman") he would understand that giving up an outside pursuit like painting was "*nothing*, because however much of her life" that pursuit "constituted, it was not her *true* life, the life for which she was made."[42]

From her rhetorical position as the representative of all women, Ellen thanked Wilson for giving her life meaning and purpose and for being so unselfish as to feel selfish.[43] Having deflated his dramatic balloon of sacrifice, Ellen assured Wilson that she wished marriage were a sacrifice, "or that I could make *any* sacrifice which would prove how much I love you." Mirroring her beloved's closing language, she exclaimed, "My darling, it would not be a sacrifice to *die* for you, how then can it be one to live for you?"[44]

Romantically speaking, this was pretty heady stuff. Anyone caught up in it, and Ellen and Wilson were sincerely caught up in it, would naturally defend the integrity of their marital ideology against any criticism, direct or implied. In America in 1885, the odds were good that the Wilsons could enjoy, unchallenged, their faith in patriarchal bliss. Indeed, had Wilson's early career led in any number of directions, had the newlyweds settled in any number of academic communities, he and Ellen would not have been forced to deal with critics of female sacrifice, womanly dependence, and wifely sympathy. As luck would have it, however, Woodrow Wilson's first academic position was at Bryn Mawr College, and that made all the difference.

Bryn Mawr College had not even opened its doors when, in November 1884, the new school's president and dean, James Evans Rhoads, approached Woodrow Wilson about a position as the first professor of history. He had been recommended by his Johns Hopkins mentor, Herbert Baxter Adams. Wilson, writing excitedly to Ellen about the job prospect, emphasized the "several things that would make a position at Bryn Mawr very advantageous." The trustees of the Quaker college, located ten miles west of Philadelphia, were closely associated with Johns Hopkins, so "reputation made under their auspices would be reputation *well-placed,* so to speak." As the sole professor of history at the new school, Wilson would be empowered to create the department, to "*organize* it, and give it direction and plan." The offer of an academic job, not contingent upon receipt of the Ph.D. (whose value Wilson had come to doubt), and not located "far away from these eastern centres of educational work and from the great libraries" looked like a great launching pad for "a youngster who wants to gain a reputation and make his work tell as soon as possible." Bryn Mawr's administration was intent on attracting a faculty of scholars and giving them sufficiently light teaching loads to afford "leisure" for research and writing. Finally, of course, a salaried position, assuming it was "enough for us to live on," meant that Wilson and Ellen could get married and start their real lives.[45]

There was just one "very serious" objection, and Ellen zeroed in on it immediately: the mission of Bryn Mawr was to provide women "of the higher and more refined classes of society" with "all the advantages of a college education which are so freely offered to our young men."[46] Moreover, the college's first dean was to be a female, M. Carey Thomas, a Ph.D. from Zurich and the daughter of one of the trustees. Right from the start, Thomas persuaded the trustees that Bryn Mawr should be different from other women's colleges by not even pretending to offer a feminized education; Bryn Mawr should demonstrate that women "*can compete* with man in the grand fields of literature and science," and should be "proud if it gives to such of its women as are scholars not only a training but a career."[47]

Ellen did not know all of this when she read Wilson's first letter about Bryn Mawr, but she had the nose to sniff trouble. Deploying her most sympathetic voice and assuring Wilson that if he were "satisfied and pleased" with the position then she would be "equally pleased and satisfied," Ellen warned against allowing his "impatience for some sort of a position [to] lead you to decide hastily in favour of a disagreeable one." Her reactions were only "feelings," she assured "her lord, her governor, her king," and not "matured, deliberate settled *convictions,*" but Ellen wondered:

> Do you think there *is* much reputation to be made in a *girls school*—or as it please you, a "woman's college"? Can you be content to serve in that sort of an institution? . . . Can you bring yourself to feel thoroughly in sympathy with that kind of thing—with the *tendencies* and *influences* of such an institution? Can you, with all your heart, cooperate with the strong-minded person who controls it? The "Dean"! How ridiculous! If they are going to have "prudes for proctors, dowagers for deans" it would be more consistent to . . . exclude men altogether—on penalty of death! Seriously, dear, I fear you would find it very unpleasant to serve, as it were, under a *woman!* It seems so unnatural, so jarring to one's sense of the fitness of things—so absurd, too. I may be very silly to say so, but it seems to me that it is rather beneath *you* to teach in a "female college."[48]

Over the course of the previous year, Ellen and Wilson had solidified their bond by sharing their doubts about women in public positions. Just a month before his first meeting with M. Carey Thomas, Wilson had described the "chilled, scandalized feeling that always comes over me when I see and hear women speak in public" as well as his sense of "whimsical delight" at the spectacle.[49] In response, Ellen had confessed that the sight of "representative women in medicine, the pulpit, and the law" opining from a platform sometimes made her "too indignant to see the funny side." How, Ellen wondered, could such clever women "make themselves so absurd?"[50] Still, they were both willing to listen to women who preserved a feminine style, who were "motherly" or "jolly" or "graceful" in their carriage.[51] Indeed, Ellen had been pleasantly surprised at an "address by a woman," Mrs. Hannah Whitall Smith, who demonstrated "good taste" and "tact" in her public performance. Ellen might have revised her opinion had she known that Smith was M. Carey Thomas's aunt and, at the very time she delivered her tactful speech on Christianity in Savannah, Georgia, was also lobbying Bryn Mawr's board of trustees to appoint her niece the president—not merely the dean—of the new college.[52]

Having signed on as Wilson's sympathetic subordinate, Ellen was in no position to stop her confident fiancé from persuading himself that M. Carey Thomas was "altogether attractive," that he would "not be under a woman" but, rather, under the college's president, James Rhoads, and that Thomas was merely a "disciplinary officer—necessarily a woman in a girl's school." He contradicted this definition of Thomas's role in the same letter by reporting that he would be meeting the next day with "Miss Thomas" to lay out his "special" approach to the pedagogical work at Bryn Mawr and to inform her that if she found his plan "incompatible" with the college's mission "she can prevent my appointment."[53] The record does not reveal what transpired at that meeting, but a week later Wilson reported to Ellen on a working dinner with the "Dean" (Wilson's quotation marks), where he found her "critical and a whit superior." Undaunted, he bragged to Ellen that he had established his "intellectual equality" with the Zurich Ph.D. and rendered her "ready to defer to me in everything." Six weeks later, he agreed to "surrender" to Bryn Mawr's terms at a meeting at "Dean Martha's."[54] While Wilson admitted that he would "rather" teach "*men* anywhere" than "girls . . . anywhere," the fact was that he had no job offers from all-male schools and he had "none of the same objections" to Bryn Mawr that he had "to *co-educational* institutions." Wilson's mentor, Herbert Baxter Adams, had begun his own teaching career at Smith College and thought Wilson's appointment to Bryn Mawr would be "an exceptional honor." That assessment from someone who had moved from a woman's college to Johns Hopkins assuaged Wilson's (and Ellen's) fear that starting out at a woman's college would jeopardize his later prospects "in some man's college" and convinced him that a first job among women would allow him to "learn *how* to teach before seeking a more conspicuous place." Besides, he reminded Ellen, he did not expect to spend his life teaching but in "literary work"; it is "my writing, not my teaching, that must win me reputation."[55]

During the eight-week negotiation over the position, Wilson won his father's endorsement and agreed to a salary of $1,500—up from the initial $1,200 offer, less than the $2,000 he asked for, but $500 more than Dean Thomas was earning, despite the fact that Thomas had a Ph.D. and Wilson did not.[56] He told Ellen that she had "the first right to be consulted, and your judgment in the matter is more vital to me than any one else's can be," but he prefaced that remark by saying "there can be no question about the advisability of my accepting the offer."[57] Wilson signed the Bryn Mawr contract in January 1885, sealing his own fate and Ellen's. In keeping with their gender pact, she had been allowed to comment but not to vote. It was two months later that Ellen wrote of her willingness to live, or die, for Wilson. The wedding came off in June of that year, and the newlyweds moved to Bryn Mawr in September.

There was awkward, joking banter about the new job in Wilson's correspondence with male friends during the months before the move to Bryn Mawr. While M. Carey Thomas labored to create a haven for women's scholarly ambitions, Wilson thought his friends would be "*amused* to hear" of his agreement to "furthering the higher education of women!" Simultaneously elevating and demoting the new school's stature, he explained that Bryn Mawr was modeled so closely on Johns Hopkins that the "wits" were "dubbing" it " 'the Miss Johns Hopkins' or the 'Johanna Hopkins.' " The record does not reveal whether Wilson cringed (or even replied) when a friend sought confirmation that "the Johanna Hopkins with the unpronounceable name" was actually a "female annex where the future mothers can be instructed." The description certainly fit Wilson's view of female education but not his lofty notions of the intellectual work he had imagined undertaking at Bryn Mawr.[58]

In the spring after signing his job contract, Wilson was tempted by a "vague" and "secret" hint of a faculty position at the famously coeducational University of Michigan. Charles Kendall Adams, a historian at Michigan, was impressed by Wilson's just-published first book, *Congressional Government,* and lobbied Wilson to consider annulling the Bryn Mawr contract on the grounds that work at a women's college would not offer "adequate scope" for one with Wilson's "kind of talent." Adams, who taught women at Michigan, meant "no disparagement whatever of women's ability," but "after all . . . [it] is not of the kind that is quite at home in the acute analysis of political institutions." Despite Ellen's and his parents' admonishment that he pursue the possibility of work at a prestigious (albeit coeducational) university, Wilson maintained that it would not be "honourable to *seek* another place." If Michigan wanted to make a serious offer, he would void the Bryn Mawr contract, but he would not actively pursue a job possibility having signed the Bryn Mawr contract.[59]

Writing from Johns Hopkins, Herbert Baxter Adams regarded the position at Bryn Mawr to be "about as near Paradise as a young man can expect to come." As things turned out, the post was not "Paradise" for Wilson or his bride.[60] Their three-year stint at Bryn Mawr, between 1885 and 1888, did not turn the Wilsons against female education, but it did deepen their antipathy to female independence and female entrance on to any field of direct, equal competition with men. So it is useful to consider the particular disappointments the Wilsons endured at Bryn Mawr and to understand how the experience both reflected and deepened their prejudice against the egalitarian ideals that the college and M. Carey Thomas represented. Three years after assuring Ellen that "there could not be a better berth for me" than Bryn Mawr (leaving "out of sight the fact that the college is to be for women"), Wilson confessed, "I hate the place very cordially for you are the *only* woman hereabouts of your genuine, perfect sort!"[61]

Looking at the situation from the Wilsons' point of view, it is undeniable that Bryn Mawr presented a chilly climate for both family life and intellectual life. Ellen, just three months married, was already quite sick from pregnancy when they arrived on campus. Having failed to find suitable living quarters in the area, the young couple spent their first year, before and after the baby was born, residing in the sort of communal faculty rooming house that M. Carey Thomas thought wonderfully liberating from all domestic cares. Thomas dictated that even Bryn Mawr students would not so much as make their own beds, thereby announcing that female scholars were just as superior to such menial tasks as male scholars. Ellen had spent two years dreaming of housekeeping for Wilson, but she was now under the administrative control of a woman who disdained domestic work. Adding insult to injury, Thomas enjoyed the privacy of home life with her partner, Mamie Gwinn, in "the Deanery," a separate, fully staffed abode next door to the rooming house.[62] It was years later that

Thomas said "only" Bryn Mawr's "failures" married, but Ellen could not have missed that sentiment in the 1880s.[63] Thomas's particular war for sexual equality left her with no sympathy for women like Ellen who crossed over the battle lines into marriage and motherhood. In 1900, Thomas denied a part-time teaching position to the academically qualified wife of Wilson's successor, Charles McLean Andrews, because Mrs. Andrews, though a Bryn Mawr alumna, was a mother and therefore professionally unreliable.[64]

Ellen exchanged the "masculine standard" of Bryn Mawr for the comforting southern culture of her aunt's home in Gainesville, Georgia, to give birth to her first daughter, Margaret, in April 1886 and her second daughter, Jessie, in August 1887.[65] When Ellen returned to Bryn Mawr with Jessie, the family moved into the large Baptist parsonage across Gulph Road from the college. There, Ellen could care for her daughters, for her brother, Stockton, who had come to live with them, and for her cousin, Mary Hoyt, whom the Wilsons were supporting as a student at Bryn Mawr. Imagining that busy life while reading a former student's recollection of Ellen Wilson as "aloof and retiring" offers some measure of the chasm between campus and the Wilsons' home.[66] The culture at Bryn Mawr College was as jokingly disdainful of the Wilsons' cherished domesticity as the Wilsons were of strong-minded women. M. Carey Thomas's cousin, Alys Smith (the first woman Bertrand Russell divorced), looked back on Ellen Wilson as "very dull and not good enough for him," despite the curious fact that "he seemed devoted to her." The Wilsons' dear friend Edith Reid looked back on Ellen as a "Southern wife [who] could hold to old traditions with a will quite as inflexible as the Dean's."[67] Even if the Wilsons did not grasp the romantic nature of the relationship between M. Carey Thomas and Mamie Gwinn, they certainly did not like Gwinn. Years later, Wilson found Gwinn to be "as affected a nincumpoop as ever (bah!)."[68]

Exacerbating the Wilsons' domestic discomfort at Bryn Mawr was the professional discomfort. In assuring himself and everyone else that the college suited him because it was modeled after Johns Hopkins, Wilson conveniently forgot that he was not intellectually happy at Johns Hopkins. The university's determined assertion of male privilege fit Wilson's proclivities, but its embrace of the Germanic approach to scholarship did not. Daniel Coit Gilman, the legendary president of Hopkins, barred female competition from his own classroom doors but still encouraged Carey Thomas's desire to incorporate the Germanic approach to scholarship into the design of her female school.[69] As a professor and president at Princeton, Wilson would articulate his strong criticism of this approach to scholarship, but that criticism is discernible in his Bryn Mawr record and tightly wound up with his emotional recoil from M. Carey Thomas and her particular brand of feminism.

At its core, Wilson's critique was that the scholarly style of the day, borrowed from German universities, deconstructed human experience into such small research bits that the overall humanity was lost. As a graduate student, he had rebelled against the data-thick, detail-rich approach at Hopkins, explaining to Ellen that he had "no patience for the tedious toil of what is known as research"; he found "digging . . . into the dusty records" of the past "very tiresome." Disdaining the "sober methods of the scholar," Wilson valorized his "passion for interpreting great thoughts to the world." Wilson aspired to joining "a great movement of opinion" in which he would choose the facts he wanted for illustrating big themes but would not be a slave to minutiae.[70] By sharp contrast, M. Carey Thomas had earned her Ph.D. in philology, the detail-driven, minutiae-laden study of the origins and evolution of language. Her highly technical dissertation subjected the fourteenth-century romantic poem *Sir Gawain and the Green Knight* to a painstaking process in which she "counted common words . . . [and] demonstrated similarities of rhymes" in order to reveal the poem's French roots.[71]

In her youth, Carey Thomas had entertained notions of "literary" scholarship that were quite similar to Wilson's. But as a woman in the early 1880s, the only place she could earn a Ph.D. was in Europe, and to get a European degree she had to play by the Germanic rules of scientific research—rules that the American-based Wilson had the courage, but also the male privilege, to ignore. He could even decide, in the months before he married, not to pursue the Ph.D. degree yet still publish his nonempirical study, *Congressional Government,* and secure a job at Bryn Mawr. Thomas, by contrast, could never have won her position at Bryn Mawr without the Ph.D. To get that degree, she travelled first to Leipzig, Germany, where she learned that the university there no longer granted Ph.D.s to women. She transferred to the university at Göttingen and fulfilled all of the university's course requirements while drily deconstructing Sir Gawain, only to be told that her special petition to the faculty for the Ph.D. had been rejected solely because she was a woman. Thomas then transferred to the University of Zurich, submitted her dissertation to new scrutiny, wrote a supplementary paper on a different topic, and passed grueling oral exams on both the theory and grammar of Indo-Germanic linguistic evolution. At the end of it all, the examining committee awarded Thomas the Ph.D. and declared her summa cum laude, a rare honor and one never before given to a woman at Zurich. Still, Thomas's sober mentors declared that she faced yet more digging in the dusty records before she could publish her argument about Sir Gawain's French ancestors.[72]

The record does not reveal how much Thomas knew of the distinct differences between her battle to gain the Ph.D. and the accommodations Johns Hopkins made to Wilson in granting him the degree. He had dismissed the value of the Ph.D. when in graduate school because he recoiled from the type of work required for the exams and a scholarly thesis. In his first year at Bryn Mawr, however, Wilson recalculated the degree's value, realizing that it could give him equal status with his immediate colleagues and improve his academic opportunities in the future.[73] What did Thomas think when she learned that Johns Hopkins agreed to accept the well-reviewed *Congressional Government* as his dissertation, even though it did not conform to the Hopkins' empirical approach, even though Wilson had written this American riff on Walter Bagehot's parliamentary study without ever visiting an archive, much less the U.S. House of Representatives?[74] Did she know of Wilson's worry that his cognitive style did not lend itself well to cramming great hunks of information into his head for a comprehensive exam? Did she (who had been grilled for hours in her Ph.D. exam, in German, on arcane philological details) have any hint that Wilson's professors at Johns Hopkins relieved Wilson of his worry by assuring him ahead of time, "There is no chance of your being plucked"? Did she know that Herbert Baxter Adams promised Wilson that he and Professor Richard Ely would "conduct your examination, both written and oral, in a manner at once considerate and just" and that "just" in this instance meant Wilson could "rest assured" of success?[75] Even if Thomas did not know these details, did she still sense the dimensions of the difference between male mentors' encouragement of her talent and his? In the great calculus of tensions between Wilson and Thomas, one wonders how this particular gender gap figured.

Initially, Carey Thomas had not even planned for a history position on the Bryn Mawr faculty since she did not regard history as a sufficiently rigorous discipline to require collegiate training. She had envisioned Bryn Mawr as a veritable school of philology, supplemented by the sciences.

President Rhoads and the trustees insisted on including historical study at Bryn Mawr, but Rhoads interviewed Wilson solely to ascertain that the young man from Johns Hopkins "believed that the hand of Providence was in all history."[76] When talking themselves into taking the Bryn Mawr offer, Wilson and Ellen had imagined that sole control of the history program would give him freedom to create his own sort of program. But the reality at Bryn Mawr was that Wilson was an intellectual orphan. Among the nine professors initially hired to teach the college's first thirty-six students, four faculty members were hired to teach science or math; four were to teach English, Greek, philology or the Romance languages. Wilson was the sole professor of history, political science, and political economy—and the only one who had not studied in Europe.[77]

Before starting his work at Bryn Mawr, Wilson told Ellen that he intended to "lecture" the students on Hegel's "beautiful conception" that women "can find their true selves only in the love and devotion of family life," that "women *have* a right to live their own lives" but that "life must *supplement* man's life." This destiny, he intended to explain to his students, implied no subordination to men, only a reflection of the fact that if women did not take care of children and housekeeping then men would have to do so, a notion Wilson capped with an exclamation point. Wilson's surviving notes for his "history of society" lectures do not include any section on the purpose and importance of gender roles in civilized society, so we do not know if he ever used class time to openly challenge his female dean by declaring the importance of patriarchy for preserving men's unalienable right to have both love and work.[78]

Looked at from both personal and professional standpoints, it is not difficult to appreciate Wilson's discomfort at Bryn Mawr College. He worked enormously hard during his three years there, his first years of marriage and fatherhood, and he did so in unaccustomed and unpleasant isolation from colleagues. Despite—or perhaps because of—his intention to move beyond Bryn Mawr, Wilson labored over his multiple course preparations, disappointed to realize that his assigned responsibility for Greek, Roman, medieval, modern European, and American history left little of the time that Dean Thomas had promised for scholarship. Though his male colleagues beyond Bryn Mawr publicly praised *Congressional Government* as a visionary work of political theory, it is unlikely that any of his colleagues at the college even read the book.[79]

Wilson's alienation from Bryn Mawr was so great that he managed to convince himself that he was not behaving unethically when he ignored the terms of his contract and, in June 1888, accepted a position at Wesleyan University in Middletown, Connecticut. Back in 1885, he had nipped a budding springtime interest from the University of Michigan, having already signed with Bryn Mawr. The month of June, he told Michigan colleagues, "was too late" to ask Bryn Mawr to find a fall replacement for him. Now, in the spring of 1887, he justified secret pursuit of the Wesleyan job and a June resignation with the bogus claim of a contractual breach by Bryn Mawr. That excuse was accompanied by an honest admission that Wesleyan offered more time, more money, and "classes . . . composed almost exclusively of men, who from the nature of the case are necessarily much more directly interested in the topics of Political Science than women are." No historian who has ever looked at the contractual details of this case has ever defended the suddenness of Wilson's resignation.[80] The fact that he always depicted himself as the victim in this story suggests that he so resented M. Carey Thomas's college that he viewed the last-minute job as a providential deliverance to which he was entitled.

A year after leaving Bryn Mawr, Wilson criticized the school's "administration" for pursuing "new educational 'fads' " rather than "tested educational wisdom." At the same time, he snickered with Ellen about news of another male faculty member's departure, wondering if it was "*very* naughty to be just a little pleased" to hear of "trouble of just the sort" that the Bryn Mawr leadership "most deserve to have!" Six years after leaving, he reported to Ellen on a social encounter with the "astonishingly cordial" Miss Thomas, noting that the now-president of Bryn Mawr sent Ellen "her love—or something like it (I don't suppose she has any love!)." Just a year after that, in 1895, he prayed to Ellen that Thomas "may soon be thoroughly exposed" or brought to a "doom" of "ruin."[81] His prayers were not answered, but fully twenty years after his departure from Bryn Mawr, when he was president of Princeton, Wilson wrote to Ellen from England about meeting a woman whose memory of teaching for just one year under M. Carey Thomas caused "her lips and nostrils alike" to grow "taut and tense and utterable things came into her eyes." In short, reported Wilson, he "enjoyed" his conversation with the woman "very much."[82] One need hold no brief for Thomas, nor deny her legendary conflicts with far less sexist individuals than Woodrow Wilson, in order to suspect that Wilson's enduring contempt for her arose, in part, from that old "chilled, scandalized feeling" he felt toward women who presumed to occupy his field of play.[83] A woman like M. Carey Thomas, who was every bit as arrogant as Wilson, was not simply a scholarly competitor with whom he disagreed; she was also, for Wilson, an *illegitimate* competitor in the world of academia. We have little documentary evidence of Thomas's view of Wilson, but in her notes for her autobiography, the only words she wrote under his name were a quote from Tennyson: "Put thy sweet hand in mine and trust in me."[84]

Looked at from the viewpoint of the women who Wilson was hired to teach at Bryn Mawr, his conduct while on faculty does not suggest any growth in his empathy for the serious ambitions of individual women. He spoke often to Ellen about his own dreams for his future as a scholar and a public intellectual, and certainly worried over whether he would achieve his literary goal of capturing people's real lives and real desires in his political writings, but Wilson never seems to have imagined what it would feel like to be a person with his dreams and have those dreams denied because of sex. Wilson never rose above his personal antipathy toward M. Carey Thomas to absorb the broader dimension of her realistic fears of a world in which "women lived a twilight life, a half-life apart," consigned to subordination in "a man's world," with "men's laws . . . a man's government . . . [in] a man's country."[85]

As ambitious as he was, as aware as he was of the grave unhappiness he would suffer if he could not test his talents in competition with other intellectuals, Wilson never expressed empathy for ambitious females who were excluded from that same competition. His male friends' snickers over the "Johanna Hopkins" may have caused Wilson to worry about starting his career at a women's college but never inspired him to write about the injustice of mocking women for wanting the intellectual life he so treasured. Even his great friend Edith Reid, in her very sympathetic memoir about Wilson, spoke of his lack of appreciation for the struggles faced by women like M. Carey Thomas. "We must," insisted Reid, "give this dauntless, able woman the admiration Wilson never could give her."[86]

Bryn Mawr was unique among women's colleges in providing funds for five graduate "fellows." Lucy Salmon, a University of Michigan graduate, was one of Wilson's three graduate students during his three years at Bryn Mawr. Salmon went on to a career of pedagogical innovation as a history professor at Vassar, where she was known for creatively engaging students in what Wilson regarded as the "tedious" process of historical investigation.[87] Charles Kendall Adams, the Michigan historian who told Wilson that women were not "quite at home in the acute analysis of political institutions," also told Salmon not to anticipate too much help from young Professor Wilson. "Indeed," Adams predicted, based on his reading of Wilson's book, "I shall be very much surprised if you find that he knows nearly so much history as you do." Adams's parting advice on how to handle Wilson proved prescient: "Remember," he counseled, "it is more blessed to give than to receive."[88]

Four decades after working with Woodrow Wilson at Bryn Mawr, Lucy Salmon drily and devastatingly described him as a man who lacked "the capacity for vicariousness."[89] During private, regular meetings intended to discuss Salmon's research, Wilson indulged in self-centered monologues, "apparently unconscious of the presence of others, except as they served as an audience to whom he could express his views." Such views included, Salmon recalled, the idea that "a woman who had married an intellectual, educated man was often better educated than a woman who had had college training." Wilson expressed this opinion to a woman with a B.A. and an M.A. degree from a prestigious university who, assuredly, presented herself as someone not intending to marry. He was, Salmon decided, a man incapable of adapting his thoughts "to the presumable opinions of others." As the female graduate of a coeducational institution who had enjoyed an egalitarian relationship with her brother, Salmon concluded from Wilson's conduct and comments that he "never had any of the normal relationships of life with women, he assumed that women were quite different from men, and he made, I felt, no effort to understand them. He always assumed that they were intellectually different from men and that, therefore, they would not interest him."[90]

Even if the tone of Salmon's "acid" recollection was tainted by her activism in the suffrage movement, Salmon's particular focus on Wilson's incapacity for "vicariousness" still offers a striking confirmation of the impression Wilson leaves in all of his other comments on educated women.[91] Salmon, of course, never read Wilson's letters to Ellen on the beauty of sexual difference and women's unique ability to "reflect the sentiments and opinions one pours into their ears."[92] Nor did she know that Ellen referred to Wilson's first graduate student, Jane Bancroft, as an "exasperating . . . old lady."[93] Lucy Salmon did know that Bancroft, who was nine years older than Wilson and a professor of French literature at Northwestern, had found Wilson patronizing toward her work, which included an already-accepted Ph.D. dissertation on France's parliaments.[94]

Salmon may also have known that Bancroft, whose family shared the Salmon family's abolitionist background, felt distant from this southern professor "who had no special sympathy for Negroes as human beings." Assuming Salmon's recollection of her meetings with Wilson is accurate, she just let him talk and talk, figuring, she said, that "the best way of getting on comfortably was to express no pronounced opinions, to be entirely passive and colorless, and to be a good listener."[95] Her Michigan professor had, after all, counseled his smart female student that it was "better to give than to receive." Wilson's conduct made clear to Salmon that vicariousness was a trait he expected of women, not a pedagogical virtue he intended to acquire for himself.[96]

The terrible irony of Wilson's teaching experience at Bryn Mawr is that, as Henry Bragdon observed over forty years ago, "he expected docility" from these female students "and then he complained when he got it"; he dominated the rooms he shared with female students and then complained to Ellen about "what a strain and a bore" it was to be "dominating" all the time.[97] Two issues lay at the heart of his problem with the Bryn Mawr undergraduates: first was the conflict between Wilson's sincere desire to be preparing youth for political action by teaching "governmental topics" and his absolute inability to see females as participating citizens in the democracy. Second was the contradiction between Wilson's theoretical position that democracy requires the "greatest possible freedom of discussion" and his personal talent for classroom lecture, not for leading discussion—certainly not discussion among women.[98] In his first year, Wilson reported that the students were "docile, intelligent and willing." In the fall of 1886, Wilson began holding weekly "news-meetings" at which he would comment upon "current events" and their relationship to "historical antecedents." The disenfranchised American women at Bryn Mawr were not required to attend these extracurricular meetings, but Wilson reported in June 1887 that "interest proved so great that the attendance much outgrew the limits" of the classroom space.[99]

Despite students' reported fascination with his lectures and news commentary, Wilson confided to his journal, in the fall of his third year at Bryn Mawr: "Lecturing to young women of the present generation on the history and principles of politics is about as appropriate and profitable as would be lecturing to stone-masons on the evolution of fashion in dress. There is a painful *absenteeism* of mind on the part of the audience. Passing through a vacuum, your speech generates no heat."[100] That same semester, as he began to nose around for another job, Wilson complained to a Princeton chum that "teaching young women (who never challenge my authority in any position I may take) is slowly relaxing my mental muscle." His late-spring justification for trading Bryn Mawr for Wesleyan echoed this sentiment, claiming that male students were "from the nature of the case . . . much more directly interested in the topics of Political Science than women."[101]

Before departing Bryn Mawr, Wilson did consider the possibility that the "absenteeism of mind" he encountered in lectures was "due to undergraduateism, not all to femininity." But he did not revisit this possibility when he ran into similar mental vacuity among males in his classes at Wesleyan or when the vitality of the school's fraternities sapped enthusiasm for the House of Commons–style debating society he tried to revive among the men there. Wilson did not rethink his gender analysis when he found the Wesleyan classroom, which he dominated with lectures, to be "insufficiently stimulating." Now, instead of the "the plentiful lack of inspiration in teaching young women politics," Wilson ascribed the problem to Wesleyan men's moderate social class and poor preparation for college.[102]

Wilson had been "hungry for a class of *men*" when he went to Wesleyan, and though his male students there did not respond as enthusiastically as he had hoped to the stimulus of political history and theory, he and Ellen were enormously happy in the male-dominated Wesleyan community. There was football to cheer for at Wesleyan, and proper academic families to befriend, and zesty faculty politics to organize.[103] Ellen did not leave Connecticut for Georgia during her third pregnancy, which her doctor had warned would have to be her last. So when she gave birth to the Wilsons' third daughter, Eleanor, she had the company of her husband as she faced the fact that she would never bear him a son.[104] Still, life in Middletown, Connecticut, was good. Thomas Dixon, the Johns Hopkins friend who would gain fame celebrating the racial purity of Southern white womanhood, wrote to Wilson in the happy certitude that "you must enjoy your classes of boys now, after your siege with girls only."[105]

Technically, Wesleyan University in 1888 was a coeducational institution, but there were only fifteen females among the school's two hundred male students. Wilson made no mention of female students in his published letters from Wesleyan, though he later claimed his experience in Middletown, between 1888 and 1890, as the source of his expertise on the problems with coeducation. It is true that, in the 1890s, a fast-growing population of Wesleyan women suffered hostile jibes from fraternity boys. It is also true that, by 1911, the male alums' fear that Wesleyan was being "feminized" resulted in the expulsion of all women.[106] But these gender hostilities, part of the national backlash against women's growing numbers and successful performance on coed campuses, emerged in the 1890s, after Wilson had left Wesleyan. The 1880s appear to have been an accommodating moment for the handful of women on campus, half of whom married Wesleyan men. Despite Wilson's personal comfort at Wesleyan and the record of apparent coeducational quiescence during his tenure there, he drew on these years to warn others away from sex-integrated education.[107]

We are left, then, with the curious fact that Wilson spent a miserable three years at an all-female college and a very happy two years at a coeducational college, but these experiences did nothing to alter his support for all-female education or his opposition to coeducation. As a faculty member at Princeton, as a father, and as president of Princeton, Wilson continued to advocate the separation of male and female students. In returning to where this essay began and moving toward a conclusion, it is useful to ask why Wilson stood fast against coeducation during his years at Princeton. What do his direct—and indirect—comments tell us about who or what he was protecting in all-male collegiate enclaves?

In his 1894 letter to Charles Kent opposing coeducation at the University of Virginia, Wilson denied that he feared actual "vice" as an outcome, but Wilson does seem to have drawn on his own "anatomical" experience with "the riotous elements in my own blood" when "keenly" fearing "what even the most honorable young fellows might be tempted by mere beauty to do where there is no restraint."[108] The only "riotous" event Wilson knew of at Wesleyan involved a fraternity boy impregnating a domestic servant. That event did not lead him to call for all-male cleaning staffs in fraternity houses, but it may have underscored—in his mind—the dangers men faced when exposed to women.[109] Perhaps Wilson attributed the lack of vulgarity among the coeducated at Wesleyan to the school's rule barring its female students from various social activities. When his friend J. Franklin Jameson wrote in 1892 for advice about the imminent faculty vote on coeducation at Brown University, Wilson responded that his "chief objections" did not apply if women "would live away from the college," if they were not integrated into the men's campus lives but, rather, kept visibly on the margins. Wilson's letter to Jameson makes clear that he knew the college population of women in the United States was growing, and he correctly perceived that, as college became more common for women, it was attracting not only the brainy pioneer types of earlier decades but also the more "easy going and sociable" girls who sought college for "enjoyment." Wilson regarded this transformation in the profile of the female college student as a "danger" best contained by preserving sex segregation at the college level.[110]

Wilson's loyal colleague and friend, Raymond Fosdick, told a story about Wilson in his memoir that was intended to demonstrate Wilson's "lively wit," not his views on gender. However precise the recollection, the general attitude rings true. Fosdick reported that "the mother of one of his students urged [Wilson] to make Princeton a coeducational institution." According to Fosdick, Wilson asked why, and the mother argued that coeducation would "remove the false glamor with which the two sexes see each other." Instantly, Wilson "shot back, 'that is the very thing we want to preserve at all costs!' "[111]

So Wilson based his opposition to coeducation, in part, on fear of the temptation that "sociable" girls posed for "honorable young fellows" and fear that everyday familiarity on campus and in the classroom would spoil the "glamor" of off-campus encounters with exotic members of a different breed. If the cost of preserving male honor and heterosocial romance was that elite females were confined to private women's colleges and the mass of the nation's daughters were denied access to more affordable state institutions, so be it. Wilson told an interviewer in 1908 that "a woman should have all the protection that is legitimately possible," but implicit in that claim was the desire to protect men's apparently fragile honor and romantic fantasies.[112]

The Wilsons' three daughters were products of their parents' beliefs about the structure and purpose of female education. When Margaret, Jessie, and Nell were between the ages of five and nine, Ellen jokingly observed that her husband would be "grieved to hear . . . that they all propose to go to college!"[113] By the time they were of college age, the zeal for that endeavor had been properly shaped by years of home schooling, followed by tutelage at Miss Fine's all-female secondary school in Princeton. As they matured, the Wilson girls gave up playing war games and trying to be the "hero," activities that Wilson, in line with G. Stanley Hall, associated with little boys' "recapitulation" of the race's evolution, not little girls' development.[114] Margaret, the spitting image of a father who openly doted on pretty girls, spent two years at Women's College of Baltimore (later renamed Goucher) but—in contrast to her father's youthful experience—was not expected to return to school after a bout with her "nervous condition." Nell (Eleanor), the pretty baby of the family and her father's pet, had no particular yearning for college but went to an Episcopal junior college in North Carolina, where an old friend of Ellen's was the hovering "school mother."[115]

Only Jessie, the middle child with what Wilson called a "real literary flair," finished a four-year program at Women's College of Baltimore, graduating Phi Beta Kappa. Ellen was happy that Jessie won the honor "without your making any special effort."[116] When Jessie briefly considered transferring to Bryn Mawr out of anger at the sorority snobbery in Baltimore, she and her mother apparently agreed that the extra year of study to meet Bryn Mawr requirements was not worth the time or trouble.[117] Wilson spoke at Jessie's college graduation in 1908, telling the female audience that the "danger in a democratic country" lay in being penalized for having "the courage to be different," and praising "the man who will not sell his independence." These remarks were a not-so-subtle defense of Jessie's battle with campus elitism, but there is no additional evidence that Wilson ever encouraged any of his daughters to take the road less travelled or even to engage seriously in the sort of scholarship that he was actively promoting at Princeton.[118] He did not live to see Margaret, his least educated and only unmarried daughter, follow a very independent path to the ashram of Sri Aurobindo in Pondicherry, India; nor was he alive when Nell divorced. His daughters did, in the years after Ellen's death, lobby their father on the subject of woman suffrage, but not in defiance of women's domestic role. As far as Wilson knew when he died in 1924, Margaret was a respectable spinster pursuing her love of vocal music, and Jessie and Nell were properly wed and settled in traditional marriages.[119]

Wilson's commitment to traditional heterosexual unions and female dependence need not have translated into opposition to coeducation. Indeed, his position on this issue during his Princeton career ran counter to the dominant American resolution of the conflict between female education and female subordination. While Wilson was calling "sociable" girls a "danger" and insisting that segregation was the answer, most American educators, parents, and students were adopting the view that heterosociality on campus could be used to contain female achievement and ensure the adoption of precisely the "manly" and "womanly" roles that Wilson endorsed in the notes he made when preparing for his address at Jessie's graduation. Wilson's experience with Bryn Mawr College and M. Carey Thomas could, quite logically, have sent him into the arms of the coeducators. By 1900, they were consciously deploying Wilson's beloved football—along with fraternities and sororities, domestic science and social work programs for women, engineering and business programs for men, and male privilege in student government—to institutionalize virility and femininity in the curricular and extracurricular life of higher education.[120] The fact that Wilson did not embrace coeducation, despite the fiercely patriarchal direction in which it was heading by 1900, suggests that he was protecting more than just heterosocial romance.

One of Wilson's great achievements at Princeton was his courageous defense of the humanities in an era that seemed to be in the thrall of science and professional specialization. In a series of memorable essays and addresses, from "Mere Literature" in 1893 and the Princeton Sesquicentennial speech in 1896 to his inaugural speech as president of Princeton in 1902 and his *Scribner's Magazine* essay, "What Is College For?" in 1909, Wilson made a powerful case for the importance of the humanities in training men for all forms of leadership.[121] Most male students, he explained, would not be scholars; most were to be "citizens and the world's servants in every field of practical endeavor." For that reason, argued Wilson, "their instruction [at] the College must use learning as a vehicle of spirit, interpreting literature as the voice of humanity—must enlighten, guide, and hearten its sons, that it may make men of them. If it give them no vision of the true God, it has given them no certain motive to practice the wise lessons they have learned."[122]

In the 1890s, when Wilson was settling into Princeton and shaping this argument, women were pouring into American colleges, especially coeducational colleges. By 1900, there were more than twice as many women in coeducational colleges as in women's colleges. Though females comprised only one quarter of all students in U.S. coeducational colleges and universities, they typically dominated the humanities classes and majored in English, history, philosophy, classics, Romance languages.[123] This was due in part to the fact that modern science defined women as insufficiently logical or rigorous for scientific pursuits and traditional culture defined women in precisely the spiritual terms that Wilson associated with the humanities. Such social prejudices influenced women's choices and shaped the bias toward hiring women for humanities teaching jobs in secondary schools. Ignoring these social realities, Charles Van Hise, president of the

University of Wisconsin, invoked the "sex repulsion" theory to explain that women were "pushing the men out" of the College of Liberal Arts due to "natural segregative laws."[124]

Natural or not, the crowding of female students into the humanities intensified the association of the humanities with femininity, a source of tremendous anxiety for male humanities professors, who had legitimate reasons to fear that association with women would diminish the value of their fields of study. The reactionary effort to either expel women from coeducational schools, as Wesleyan did in 1911, or internally segregate schools by creating different tracks and programs for men and women, as the University of Chicago attempted to do in 1902, was all part of a response to women's numbers and success in coeducational schools and the fear of their dominance in the humanities. Indeed, said M. Carey Thomas in a 1904 speech to the General Federation of Women's Clubs: "When you hear it sometimes said that coeducation is not a success, what is really meant is that its success has been too great; and when, as in Chicago University [*sic*] women are beginning to be taught in separate classes, it is in reality an effort to segregate men from the academic competition of women."[125]

Analyzed in this broader context, Wilson's determined assertion of the virility of the humanities and the significance of liberal arts training as preparation for manly leadership appears to be, in part, a heartfelt response to the feminizing effects of coeducation. Heard through the din of the contentious gender debate swirling around him, Wilson seems to be calling for all-male schools as protected terrain where young men could study the literature and languages required for visionary leadership without the diminishing effects of feminization—or feminism.

When he was president of Princeton, Wilson did not use his academic bully pulpit to lecture explicitly on womanhood. Even when he spoke at schools such as Vassar, Wellesley, and Mt. Holyoke, as he occasionally did in these years, Wilson never addressed the "woman question," or woman suffrage or feminism. He spoke about "Americanism" and "Democracy," always using male pronouns to describe the actors in those panoramic national dramas. In defining the challenges of liberty at Vassar in 1902, for example, Wilson explained that "we have the same sort of human nature that Adam had," and are still trying to figure out "how to hold certain persons in check without choking them to death." Wilson did not enlighten the Vassar students on women's place in this political wrestling match. By publicly ignoring the woman question, Wilson telegraphed that education for leadership in a democracy was about men, and men's education had to include sensitive, humane literary studies pursued in a manly atmosphere.[126]

Ostensibly, the inspiration for Wilson's stinging essay, "Mere Literature," was a single disdainful remark about literary works by a Johns Hopkins philologist. The editors of the *Papers of Woodrow Wilson* did not doubt the story or that Wilson's reply was "I'll get even with him." But they did question whether this one angry moment could account for the production, two years later, of such a sweeping indictment of the philological approach to literature. In seeking to understand the strong emotions that fueled "Mere Literature," it seems useful to recall that M. Carey Thomas was a philologist, that Wilson had suffered three long years in the atmosphere that her intellectual enthusiasms created at Bryn Mawr, and that he was bitter about that experience for decades afterward.[127] When Wilson wrote that students of literature "must have a heart" in order to "handle with real mastery the firm fibre" of Burke or Browning, Dryden or Swift, he was asserting that it takes masculine power to appreciate the "authentic products of literature," for those products were like "a beautiful woman." When he sneered at Germanic scholars for lacking a heart, or a "pulse," or "any blood" and having to "make shift" in literary study by counting words, putting "rhythm into a scale of feet," and running "their allusions—particularly their female allusions—to cover," Wilson was drawing on his anger at the kind of philological analysis that M. Carey Thomas extolled.[128]

"Mere Literature" is a passionate indictment of what Wilson saw as the modern, scientific deconstruction of ineffable human genius, of spiritual essences. In it, he paints philology as a sterile angel of death, systematically destroying our capacity to embrace the "immortal essence of truth" in literature. An appreciation for Wilson's deep well of anger at the intersection of philology and feminism in the person of M. Carey Thomas helps to inform an analysis of this essay. Wilson railed against the scientific, philological claim that "man's nature submits to man's circumstances," that literary products are "a product of man's circumstances rather than a sign of a man's mastery over circumstance." Such philological claims characterized Thomas's particular brand of feminism. She was of the school that saw patriarchal gender arrangements as purely a product of historical circumstance, not an expression of any "immortal essence of truth" or Eden-born sexual dynamism.[129] Wilson was far too dedicated to the romantic notion, shared with Ellen, that their sexual complementarity was a natural expression of divine will to allow for the pedestrian idea that circumstances and self-interests had constructed the path to their marriage bed.

Wilson was willing to consider—and alter—circumstance when it came to training men. In "What Is College For?" he told his readers in 1909 that "college is meant to stimulate" ambitions for leadership in "a considerable number of men" when only a few would be stimulated if we relied purely on "nature and circumstances." But when it came to women, Wilson advocated no such social agency; "whether by nature or circumstance," he shrugged in a private letter the previous year, women simply could not be sufficiently "safe-guarded"—or relieved of domestic duties—to gain the worldly experience necessary to exercise wise leadership.[130]

There are multiple ironies in all of this. M. Carey Thomas abandoned the humanistic approach to literature when she was a young woman in order to earn the academic badge of sexual equality afforded by a Germanic Ph.D. Wilson, a humanist, denied Thomas that equality because he refused to see a woman's spiritual essence as anything but feminine and subordinate. When it came to women, Wilson lacked the heart, the blood, the eyes, and the imagination which he named as vital to grasping the full humanity of great literature. In her attempt to gain equality and authority in academe, M. Carey Thomas adopted a male-identified form of feminism that embraced science (even as science denigrated women) and perversely sought to prove Bryn Mawr's intellectual worth by hiring more male professors than female.[131] In his attempt to regain masculine control of the humanities, Wilson extolled the emotionalism and spirituality typically tied to the feminine. As an advocate of sex difference, Wilson loathed Thomas's encroachments upon literature and leadership, where her cold-blooded claims to equality seemed to defy a universe of warmth, love, and sensuality. Their antipathies illustrate the ways in which gender was coded in academic battles that grossly conflated research methodology with feminist theory and literary humanism with manliness. Such complex conflict prohibited rational consideration of an obvious alternative to America's history of higher education: the sorting of students not by sex but by scholarly commitment.

At the start of the twentieth century, Woodrow Wilson grasped that colleges like Princeton, aspiring to the highest intellectual standards, were swimming against a populist tide of students flooding onto campuses with more interest in sports and parties than books and research. M. Carey Thomas was facing the same problem at Bryn Mawr, so was Charles W.

Eliot at Harvard and Caroline Hazard at Wellesley. They all looked down their noses at coeducational state universities for the diluted intellectualism they smugly blamed on mixed-sex classes, but the truth was that their same-sex student bodies were just as caught up in what Wilson famously referred to as "side shows."[132] Wilson was courageous in raising academic standards at Princeton, resisting a wholly elective curricular system, proposing the quadrangle system, insisting that graduate and undergraduate education be integrated, and centering professional training in the liberal arts. But his academic imagination could not admit of an obvious response to the sideshow problem: create highly selective universities that admitted only the most dedicated, able scholars—regardless of sex. Given Wilson's (and Thomas's) academic aspirations, the answer to their struggles with side shows and sociability could logically have been the creation, at their institutions, of coeducational havens for the nation's premier students.

The final irony, then, is that Wilson and M. Carey Thomas totally agreed on matters of strict entrance exams, a balance of requirements and electives, the stupidity of "applied" courses in a liberal arts environment, and the value of undergraduate access to graduate students.[133] If they had not despised each other's sexual politics and if they had not been similarly autocratic in their leadership style, they could have been great allies in educational innovation, offering America's young scholars democratic access to rigorous study undiluted by sophomoric high jinks. But only historical fantasy can alter the "ifs" of reality.

In reality, Wilson tied his faith in the humanities to his belief in universal certainties. "Colleges ought surely to be," he explained at Princeton's Sesquicentennial, "the best schools of the progress which conserves." Six years later, at his inauguration as Princeton's thirteenth president, he linked young men's education for leadership to their knowledge of "what has been settled and made sure of."[134] For Wilson, women's subordinate, sympathetic place in the universe was an unquestionable verity. He did not allow his belief in individual freedom and opportunity or his experience with educated, ambitious women to disrupt that view, and the most intimate women in his life encouraged his emotional attachment in it.[135] Examination of Wilson's unbending stand on female education is certainly a useful vehicle for exploring the androcentric, egocentric nature of his gender assumptions. To realize the potential of such analysis, however, the evidence of his sexism cannot be isolated as a separate compartment of Wilson's life. Analysis of Wilson's particularly intense, entitled masculinity can profitably be integrated into the larger stories of his intellectual philosophy and political leadership.

NOTES

1. Woodrow Wilson (hereafter WW) to Charles William Kent, May 29, 1894, in *The Papers of Woodrow Wilson,* ed. Arthur S. Link et al., 69 vols. (Princeton: Princeton University Press, 1966–94), 8:583–84 (hereafter *PWW*).

2. WW to Charles William Kent, May 29, 1894, *PWW,* 8:584.

3. WW to Charles Andrew Talcott, March 25, 1885, *PWW,* 4:413. In telling this good friend from Princeton about taking a teaching position at Bryn Mawr College, Wilson wrote, "I do not mean to identify myself with the higher education of women, much as I sympathize with it."

4. WW to Charles William Kent, May 29, 1894, *PWW,* 8:584. For discussions of opposition to coeducation in these years, see: Thomas Woody, *A History of Women's Education in the United States,* 2 vols. (New York: Science Press, 1929), 2:294–30; Mabel Newcomer, *A Century of Higher Education for American Women* (New York: Harper & Brothers, 1959), 5–51; Lynn D. Gordon, *Gender and Higher Education in the Progressive Era* (New Haven: Yale University Press, 1990); Ruth Bordin, *Women at Michigan: The "Dangerous Experiment," 1870s to the Present* (Ann Arbor: University of Michigan Press, 1999), 7–39; Rosalind Rosenberg, "The Limits of Access: The History of Coeducation in America," in John Mack Faragher and Florence Howe, eds., *Women and Higher Education in American History* (New York: W. W. Norton, 1988), 107–29. For examples of popular magazine articles dealing with the dangers of coeducation, see Ely Van de Warker, "Is the Education of Women with Men a Failure?" *Harper's Weekly,* 48 (Aug. 20, 1904), 1288–89; H. T. Finck, "Why Coeducation Is Losing Ground," *The Independent,* 55 (Feb. 5, 12, 1903), 301–305, 361–66; Wardon Curtis, "The Movement Against Coeducation at the University of Wisconsin," *The Independent,* 65 (Aug. 1908), 323–26; G. Stanley Hall, "The Question of Co-Education," *Munsey's Magazine,* 34 (Feb. 1906), 588–92; "R.O.," "The Pros and Cons of Co-Education," *The Nation,* 76 (April 2, 1902), 267–68.

5. "Notes for a Commencement Address," June 3, 1908, *PWW,* 18:318. Prepared for Jessie Wilson's graduation from Woman's College of Baltimore.

6. WW to Charles William Kent, May 29, 1894, *PWW,* 7:584.

7. Patricia Palmieri, *In Adamless Eden: The Community of Women Faculty at Wellesley* (New Haven: Yale University Press, 1995); Gordon, *Gender and Higher Education in the Progressive Era;* Helen Lefkowitz Horowitz, *Alma Mater: Design and Experience in the Women's Colleges from Their Nineteenth-Century Beginnings to the 1930s* (New York: Alfred A. Knopf, 1984).

8. Barbara Miller Solomon, *In the Company of Educated Women: A History of Women and Higher Education in America* (New Haven: Yale University Press, 1985), 44; Newcomer, *A Century of Higher Education for Women,* 49.

9. M. Carey Thomas, "Education of Women," in Nicholas Murray Butler, ed., *Monographs on Education in the United States* (Albany, N.Y.: J. B. Lyon, 1900). See Thomas's chapter in online edition at http://books.google.com/books?id=ZisLAAAAIAAJ&printsec=frontcover&source=gb#v=onepage&q&f=false, 1:3–40 (321–58).

10. Solomon, *In the Company of Educated Women*, 63.

11. Ibid., 58.

12. Carl F. Price, *Wesleyan's First Century, with an Account of the Centennial Celebration* (Middletown, Conn.: Wesleyan University, 1932), 161–62.

13. WW to Ellen Louise Axson, Nov. 30, 1884, *PWW*, 3:499. Ellen Axson hereafter referred to as "EAW" (for Ellen Axson Wilson).

14. WW to C.W. Kent, May 29, 1894, *PWW*, 8:584.

15. For the story on the backlash against women in both higher education and secondary schools, see Solomon *In the Company of Educated Women*, chs. 6–7; Palmieri, *In Adamless Eden*, chs. 12–13; Gordon, *Gender and Higher Education in the Progressive Era*, chs. 2–3; Victoria Bissell Brown, "The Fear of Feminization: Los Angeles Schools in the Progressive Era," *Feminist Studies*, 16 (Fall 1990), 493–518.

16. Frances Wright Saunders, *Ellen Axson Wilson: First Lady Between Two Worlds* (Chapel Hill: University of North Carolina Press, 1985), 3–8.

17. WW to EAW, Nov. 26, 1887, offers one of many possible examples. Wilson wrote: "I didn't seek your promise in order to satisfy myself afterwards that you were the woman I wanted. The thing sounds monstrous even in the denial! What I did I did simply because I couldn't help it. It was an imperative heart-instinct that brought me to your feet. But, my love, our intercourse since then has furnished the *proof* that we did not mistake our hearts—that we *had* found our true destiny." *PWW*, 3:488. My analysis of the Wilsons' courtship letters is based on a careful reading of the hundreds of letters they exchanged between their engagement in September 1883 and their marriage in June 1885.

18. EAW to WW, March 29, 1885, *PWW*, 4:434.

19. WW to EAW, March 30, 1885, *PWW*, 4:434–35.

20. EAW to WW, Feb. 27, 1885, *PWW*, 4:307. There has been a well-intentioned effort since the early 1980s to modernize the image of Ellen Axson Wilson by equating the clear evidence of her intelligence with a leaning toward feminist-style independence before she married Wilson and to suggest that her artistic efforts might have made her self-supporting. It is beyond the scope of this study of Wilson and female education to review all of the premarital data on Ellen Axson, but the use of her romantic attachments to female friends in her youth, her interest in painting, and her postponement of a wedding date do not constitute strong evidence of deviance from the female norms of her generation. Setting Ellen Axson up as an independent female who would not have married had she not met Woodrow Wilson risks adopting, rather than analyzing, the Wilsons' own narrative. The evidence testifying to Ellen Axson's strong intelligence does not preclude her well-bred proclivity to marry or her ideological commitment to a subordinate role for wives. See Saunders, *Ellen Axson Wilson*, 15–31; August Heckscher, *Woodrow Wilson* (New York: Charles Scribner's Sons, 1991), 72–75.

21. The argument offered here questions John Mulder's view that Woodrow Wilson's abiding love for Ellen made him less likely to "aggrandize his own authority" or less "rigid" in his "adherence to just principles." John M. Mulder, *Woodrow Wilson: The Years of Preparation* (Princeton: Princeton University Press, 1978), 108.

22. Karen Lystra, *Searching the Heart: Women, Men, and Romantic Love in Nineteenth-Century America* (New York: Oxford University Press, 1989). Lystra's study of love letters exchanged by members of the white, middle-class offers a basic context for understanding

the Wilsons' letters. While they were typical in seeking assurances from one another, they were more harmonious on the subject of female subordination than many white couples of their class.

23. WW to EAW, April 24, 1884, *PWW,* 3:145.

24. WW to EAW, May 1, 1884, *PWW,* 3:157.

25. Saunders, *Ellen Axson Wilson,* 15–17.

26. WW to Richard Heath Dabney, Feb. 17, 1884, *PWW,* 3:27.

27. WW to EAW, Oct. 18, 1883, *PWW,* 2:482.

28. WW to EAW, July 16, 1883, *PWW,* 2:388–89.

29. WW to EAW, March 31, 1885, *PWW,* 4:437.

30. Review of Philip Gilbert Hamerton, *The Intellectual Life* (Boston: Roberts Brothers, 1873), *New York Times,* July 14, 1873, available at http://query.nytimes.com/mem/archive. The editors of the *Papers of Woodrow Wilson* described Hamerton in footnotes as one of Wilson's "favorite authors," pointing to *Round My House: Notes of Rural Life in France in Peace and War* (Boston: Roberts Brothers, 1876) and *Graphic Arts* (1882) as Hamerton works that Wilson read and shared with Ellen. But the editors offered no bibliographical information on his or Ellen's references to Hamerton's views on marriage in *The Intellectual Life,* which was a much more important aspect of Wilson's personal history. A letter from Wilson to Ellen, in which he referenced both Hamerton and Walter Bagehot on the subject of marriage, received an editorial note only on Bagehot. WW to EAW, Nov. 22, 1884, *PWW,* 3:471–74; WW to Philip Gilbert Hamerton, Jan. 4, 1887, 5:428–29.

31. WW to EAW, Nov. 22, 1884, *PWW,* 3:473; WW to EAW, Oct. 18, 1883, 2:481–82. Wilson also referred, in this letter to Ellen, to an essay about Percy Bysshe Shelley by Walter Bagehot, "my master." According to Wilson, Bagehot argued that Shelley's ill-chosen first wife, Harriet Westbrook, could have made an ordinary man happy but could not make a genius like Shelley happy because she lacked the capacity to sympathize with his eccentricities or understand that writing was actual work. WW to EAW, Nov. 22, 1884, 3:471–73. Wilson again referred to Bagehot's theories on compatible marriage in the first letter he wrote to persuade Ellen of the virtues of the position at Bryn Mawr College. WW to EAW, Nov. 27, 1884, 3:491.

32. WW to EAW, April 15, 1884, *PWW,* 3:132–33. In this letter, Wilson mocked a married Wellesley graduate in his rooming house who, he said, was "versed in several languages and on speaking terms with one or two sciences" but was a "*very* amateur artist" who kept "neither her person nor her room tidy and will certainly convince her husband of the necessity of a divorce when she undertakes to keep house for him."

33. EAW to WW, April 21, 1884, *PWW,* 3:140; EAW to WW, March 4, 1885, 4:332. In her April 21 letter, Ellen playfully claimed to be "shocked, grieved, and mortified" that Wilson, "a disciple of learning," would "hope" she did not know about the Constitution. "Who would have anticipated such conduct in a professor!" Ellen exclaimed. She quickly added, "But you don't profess to teach women," and assured him she did not know about the Constitution and had "no personal interest" in the subject.

34. Wilson told Ellen that she was the "only pupil I ever have had or shall have in this delightful study of love-making; and if, after marriage (which we may call your graduation, the close of your preparatory training in the art), you should show no ardor in putting my

instruction into delighting practice, how overwhelmingly I should be convicted of failure!" WW to EAW, May 26, 1885, *PWW,* 4:664. See, too, WW to EAW, May 22, 1885, 4:616.

35. EAW to WW, March 7, 1885, *PWW,* 4:340. Wilson quoted back the same line to Ellen two months later. WW to EAW, May 15, 1885, 4:594.

36. WW to EAW, March 1, 1885, *PWW,* 4:316.

37. WW to EAW, March 27, 1885, *PWW,* 4:420–21.

38. WW to EAW, April 27, 1884, *PWW,* 3:146; WW to EAW, Dec. 9, 1884, 3:528.

39. WW to EAW, March 27, 1885, *PWW,* 4:420–21.

40. EAW to WW, March 28, 1885, *PWW,* 4:429.

41. EAW to WW, Feb. 27, 1885, *PWW,* 4:307.

42. EAW to WW, March 28, 1885, *PWW,* 4:431.

43. EAW to WW, Feb. 27, 1885, *PWW,* 4:307; March 28, 1885, 4:429.

44. EAW to WW, March 28, 1885, *PWW,* 4:431.

45. WW to EAW, Nov. 27, 1884, *PWW,* 3:490; WW to EAW, Nov. 30, 1884, 3:499; WW to Richard Heath Dabney, Feb. 14, 1885, 4:249.

46. EAW to WW, Nov. 28, 1884, *PWW,* 3:494. It is in this letter that Ellen refers to the "very serious" objection to "a 'woman's college.' " For the Bryn Mawr mission, see Helen Lefkowitz Horowitz, *Alma Mater,* 111; Helen Lefkowitz Horowitz, *The Power and Passion of M. Carey Thomas* (New York: Alfred A. Knopf, 1994), 193; Henry Wilkinson Bragdon, *Woodrow Wilson: The Academic Years* (Cambridge, Mass.: Belknap Press of Harvard University Press, 1967), 143.

47. Bragdon, *Woodrow Wilson,* 144; Horowitz, *Power and Passion of M. Carey Thomas,* 164.

48. EAW to WW, Nov. 28, 1884, *PWW,* 3:494–95. Ellen had borrowed Portia's speech in The *Merchant of Venice* to explain her commitment to Wilson; that speech concluded with a reference to "her lord, her governor, her king." EAW to WW, March 7, 1885, 4:340.

49. WW to EAW, Oct. 31, 1884, *PWW,* 3:389.

50. EAW to WW, Nov. 1, 1884, *PWW,* 3:395.

51. WW to EAW, Oct.31, 1884, *PWW,* 3:389.

52. EAW to WW, Feb. 25, 1884, *PWW,* 3:46; Horowitz, *Power and Passion of M. Carey Thomas,* 183–84.

53. WW to EAW, Nov. 27, 1884, *PWW,* 3:491; WW to EAW, Nov. 30, 1884, 3:499.

54. WW to EAW, Dec. 6, 1884, *PWW,* 3:517; WW to EAW, Jan. 19, 1885, 3:621.

55. WW to EAW, Dec. 6, 1884, *PWW,* 3:517–18; WW to EAW, Nov. 30, 1884, 3:499; WW to EAW, Dec. 1, 1884, 3:504.

56. Joseph Ruggles Wilson to WW, Dec. 2, 1884, *PWW,* 3:505; WW to EAW, Dec. 4, 1884, 3:513; Joseph Ruggles Wilson to WW, Jan. 15, 1885, 3:612–13; Bragdon, *Woodrow Wilson,* 145; Horowitz, *Power and Passion of M. Carey Thomas,* 189.

57. WW to EAW, Jan. 13, 1885, *PWW,* 3:604–605. Ellen had been mollifed by Wilson's arguments. While she felt "its being a school for women *must* remain an objection," she conceded that the advantages to Wilson's career "*do* counterbalance that one drawback," and she felt that having "a man for a President," made the job "less *disagreeable.*" EAW to WW, Dec. 1, 1884, 3:504.

58. WW to Albert Shaw, Jan. 28, 1885, *PWW,* 4:195; WW to Richard Heath Dabney,

Feb. 14, 1885, 4:248; WW to Charles Andrew Talcott, March 25, 1885, 4:413; William Battle Phillips to WW, May 12, 1885, 4:583; Albert Shaw to WW, May 24, 1885, 4:624; WW to EAW, Nov. 30, 1884, 3:500.

59. WW to EAW, March 4, 1885, *PWW,* 4:331; Charles Kendall Adams to WW, March 12, 1885, 4:357; Janet Woodrow Wilson to WW, March 17, 1885, 4:376; EAW to WW, March 19, 1885, 4:388; EAW to WW, March 24, 1885, 4:410–11; WW to EAW, March 18, 1885, 4:382. Woodrow Wilson, *Congressional Government* (Boston: Houghton Mifflin, 1886). See, too, draft letter, WW to Charles Kendall Adams, March 19, 1885, 4:384–85 and WW to EAW, March 21, 1885, 4:393–94. Wilson confessed to Ellen in the March 18 letter that "my ambition kicks against the pricks." He assumed the Bryn Mawr trustees would have to "release" him for this great Michigan opportunity if it were offered, but he refused to "coquet with these chances."

60. Herbert Baxter Adams to WW, April 9, 1887, *PWW,* 5:484.

61. WW to EAW, Nov. 30, 1884, *PWW,* 3:499–500; WW to EAW, Oct.4, 1887, 5:605.

62. EAW to WW, March 29, 1885, *PWW,* 4:428; Bragdon, *Woodrow Wilson,* 146–47; Horowitz, *Alma Mater,* 119; Horowitz, *Power and Passion of M. Carey Thomas,* 197, 202–3.

63. Horowitz, *Power and Passion of M. Carey Thomas,* 129, 385.

64. Reel Guide and Index to the Microfilm Collection, the Papers of M. Carey Thomas in the Bryn Mawr College Archives, compiled by Lucy Fisher West, 71. For a general view of Thomas's attitudes on women who married, see Horowitz, *Power and Passion of M. Carey Thomas,* 301–5. For evidence that Thomas had to trim her views to fit post-1900 fashions, see "Marriage and the Woman Scholar," in *The Educated Woman in America: Selected Writings of Catharine [*sic*] Beecher, Margaret Fuller, and M. Carey Thomas,* ed. Barbara M. Cross (New York: Teachers College Press, 1965), 170–75.

65. EAW to WW, April 26, 1885, *PWW,* 4:530, regarding Bryn Mawr's "masculine standard." Saunders, *Ellen Axson Wilson,* 68.

66. Mary Hoyt to EAW, May 4, 1885, *PWW,* 5:502; Bragdon, *Woodrow Wilson,* 147–48; Stockton Axson, *"Brother Woodrow:" A Memoir of Woodrow Wilson,* ed. Arthur S. Link, (Princeton: Princeton University Press, 1993), 58–59. Heckscher, *Woodrow Wilson,* 89, draws on unpublished letters from Mary Hoyt to note that she had "ruefully calculated" that her rate of pay as a schoolteacher in Athens, Georgia, would accrue the savings to attend college by the time she was seventy-five years old. Hoyt was enormously grateful to the Wilsons for making her college education possible. Clearly, Wilson had direct experience with the economic difficulties unmarried women faced in a world that undervalued their labors.

67. Bragdon, *Woodrow Wilson,* 146. While providing this useful quote from Alys Smith, Bragdon attributes it to "a student" without identifying that student as Thomas's cousin, the daughter of Christian feminist Hannah Whitall Smith and ex-wife of Bertrand Russell. These two identifiers provide context for Smith's attitude toward women in general and Mrs. Wilson in particular. Edith Gittings Reid, *Wilson: The Caricature, the Myth, and the Man* (New York: Oxford University Press, 1934), 46–47.

68. WW to EAW, Feb. 4, 1894, *PWW,* 8:454. For a full discussion of Thomas's complicated, thirty-year relationship with Mary Gwinn, see Horowitz, *Passion and Power of M. Carey Thomas.*

69. Horowitz, *Passion and Power of M. Carey Thomas,* 186–88, 193. Bryn Mawr College, M. Carey Thomas, and Johns Hopkins University were interconnected in multiple ways. Thomas had attempted graduate work at Johns Hopkins in 1877, but she found humiliating and isolating the rule that excluded her from participation in any seminars and restricted her to private study with those professors who would meet with her. Moreover, Hopkins would not grant a graduate degree to a female. Members of the Johns Hopkins Board of Trustees, including Thomas's own father, were active in the design of Bryn Mawr College, as was Johns Hopkins president Daniel Coit Gilman. Christine ("Carrie") Ladd, Thomas's great friend in adolescence, subsequently married Fabian Franklin, a professor of mathematics at Johns Hopkins in 1882. That same year, she completed all of the work necessary for a Ph.D. in mathematics at Hopkins but was denied the degree. Ladd-Franklin went on to do significant work in symbolic logic. Mary Garrett, M. Carey Thomas's second life partner, after Mamie Gwinn, was the daughter of a very wealthy member of the Johns Hopkins Board of Trustees. In 1887, as the heir to the Garrett fortune, Mary Garrett partnered with M. Carey Thomas in making her financial support for the university's new medical school contingent upon acceptance of women. This "bribe" made the Johns Hopkins University Medical School the only part of the university to accept women for several years. Florence Bascomb, a geologist, was the first woman to be granted a Ph.D. there, in 1893; she became one of the few full-time, long-term female faculty members at Bryn Mawr College. Women were not accepted at Johns Hopkins as undergraduates until 1969. See discussions of Ladd-Franklin, Garrett, and the medical school in Horowitz, *Passion and Power of M. Carey Thomas.* See also Elizabeth Scarborough and Laurel Furumoto, *Untold Lives: The First Generation of American Women Psychologists* (New York: Columbia University Press, 1987), 109–29; Hugh Hawkins, *Pioneer: A History of the Johns Hopkins University, 1874–1889* (Ithaca: Cornell University Press, 1960); Abraham Flexner, *Daniel Coit Gilman, Creator of the American Type of University* (New York: Harcourt, Brace, 1946).

70. WW to EAW, Oct.16, 1883, *PWW,* 2:479–80; WW to EAW, Feb. 24, 1885, 4:287 and April 27, 1885, 4:532.

71. Horowitz, *Passion and Power of M. Carey Thomas,* 145–46.

72. Ibid., 144–53. Thomas never did publish the dissertation.

73. Joseph Ruggles Wilson to WW, Oct. 29, 1884, *PWW,* 3:385; WW to EAW, Nov. 8, 1884, 3:415; WW to EAW, Feb. 17, 1885 and Feb. 20, 1885, 4:263, 271–72; WW to Herbert Baxter Adams, April 2, 1886, 5:150–51; Reid, *Wilson,* 47.

74. John Milton Cooper Jr., *The Warrior and the Priest: Woodrow Wilson and Theodore Roosevelt* (Cambridge, Mass.: Belknap Press of Harvard University Press, 1983) 50; Bragdon, *Woodrow Wilson,* 107, 124–40; Mulder, *Woodrow Wilson,* 78–81.

75. WW to EAW, April 22, 1884, Oct. 14, 1884, Oct. 25, 1884, Oct.27, 1884, Nov. 8, 1884, *PWW,* 3:144, 353–54, 371, 378–79, 415; WW to Herbert Baxter Adams, April 2, 1886, 5:150–51; Herbert Baxter Adams to WW, April 7, 1886, 5:154.

76. Horowitz, *Power and Passion of M. Carey Thomas,* 158, 160, 186; Edith Finch, *Carey Thomas of Bryn Mawr* (New York: Harper & Brothers, 1947) 150; WW to EAW, Nov. 27, 1884, *PWW,* 3:490.

77. EAW to WW, Nov. 28, 1884, *PWW,* 3:494; WW to EAW, Jan. 13, 1885, 3:604; *Bryn Mawr College Catalog,* 1885–1886

78. WW to EAW, March 1, 1885, *PWW,* 4:316–318. Wilson's notes for his public law class at Princeton a decade later trace the origins of the state to the patriarchal family, where the father's power was based "primarily *upon power*; by derivative conception, *upon Religion.*" Wilson did not delve into his view that this arrangement was a product of divine will and natural law. Lecture Notes on Public Law, Sept. 22, 1894, 9:7.

79. WW to Richard Heath Dabney, Feb. 14, 1885, *PWW,* 4:248. For discussions of the tremendous amount of attention Wilson received from public intellectuals and scholars for *Congressional Government,* see Bragdon, *Woodrow Wilson,* 121, 134–40.

80. Draft of a letter to Charles Kendall Adams, March 19, 1885, *PWW,* 4:385; Agreement Between the Trustees of Bryn Mawr College and Woodrow Wilson, Ph.D., March 14, 1887, 5:468–69; WW to Robert Bridges, Nov. 30, 1887, 5:632–33; WW to John M. Van Vleck and WW to James E. Rhoads, June 7, 1888, 5:735–36; From the Minutes of the Executive Committee of the Bryn Mawr Board of Trustees, June 27, 1888, 5:739–40; WW to the President of the Board of Trustees of Bryn Mawr College, June 29, 1888, 5:743–47; James E. Rhodes to WW, July 7, 1888, 5:749. Wilson argued that Bryn Mawr had violated its contract by not hiring an "assistant" professor in the History Department, but the contract said the college would do so "as soon as practicable," and, indeed, hired Williston Walker in May 1888. See Williston Walker to WW, May 28, 1888, 5:730–31. See Bragdon, *Woodrow Wilson,* 161; Heckscher, *Woodrow Wilson,* 93. M. Carey Thomas was not involved in deliberations over Wilson's resignation because her mother had just died in Baltimore. Horowitz, *Power and Passion of M. Carey Thomas,* 242–43.

81. WW to Horace Scudder, March 31, 1889, *PWW,* Addendum, 8:658; WW to EAW, March 18, 1889, 6:159; WW to EAW, Feb. 4, 1894, 8:454; WW to EAW, Feb. 17, 1895, 9:203. In the 1895 letter, Wilson was complaining about M. Carey Thomas and Mary Garrett's administration of the Bryn Mawr School, a private girls' school in Baltimore, which Garrett had founded and supported with her considerable wealth. "Doom" at the Baltimore school would have meant unemployment for Wilson's two cousins by marriage, Mary and Florence Hoyt, both of whom taught at the Bryn Mawr School.

82. WW to EAW, Aug. 9, 1908, *PWW,* 18:395.

83. WW to EAW, Oct. 31, 1884, *PWW,* 3:389. For more detail on others' conflicts with Thomas, see Horowitz, *Power and Passion of M. Carey Thomas,* and Margaret Farrand Thorp, *Neilson of Smith* (New York: Oxford University Press, 1956), ch. 5. William Allan Neilson served, unhappily, as an English professor at Bryn Mawr for one year, 1898–99, before moving on to Smith College, where he eventually became president. Since Neilson spent his career serving female students, it is unlikely that contempt for women in general caused him to view Thomas, according to Thorp, as "autocratic, high-handed, [and] devious in her methods." But Neilson's jocular, poetic put-down of Thomas's administrative style did mock her insufficient femininity. Thorp, *Neilson,* 77, 82. Wilson was not unique in measuring all women by the yardstick of femininity.

84. Finch, *Carey Thomas of Bryn Mawr College,* 175. Bragdon draws on letters to him from two alumnae to claim that Thomas and Wilson were alike in their "ambition, strength of will, and sense of superiority," but Thomas found Wilson's "southern attitude toward women sentimental and degrading." *Woodrow Wilson,* 160. As the focus of this article is on Wilson, not Thomas, it does not go into the public record of Thomas's retorts to educators

like Charles W. Eliot, president of Harvard University, who argued for a separate and different education for women. See, for example, M. Carey Thomas, "The College," *Educational Review,* 10 (Jan. 1905), 1–16; Cross, ed., *The Educated Woman in America,* 139–70; Horowitz, *Power and Passion of M. Carey Thomas,* 317–18.

85. Horowitz, *Power and Passion of M. Carey Thomas,* 404.

86. Reid, *Wilson,* 45–46.

87. WW to EAW, Feb. 24, 1885, *PWW,* 4:287; Salmon recalled, in a letter to Ray S. Baker, that Wilson had told her of writing *Congressional Government* without ever going to Washington, D.C., from Baltimore to view Congress in action. In reporting on this letter, Henry Bragdon indicates that Salmon remembered this as a boast of Wilson's. Lucy Salmon to Ray S. Baker, Jan. 6, 1926, cited in Bragdon, *Woodrow Wilson,* 127

88. Charles Kendall Adams to WW, March 12, 1885, *PWW,* 4:357; Charles Kendall Adams to Lucy Salmon, June 3, 1886, cited in Louise Fargo Brown, *Apostle of Democracy: The Life of Lucy Maynard Salmon* (New York: Harper & Brothers, 1943), 101. Wilson was acquainted with, and unimpressed by, Salmon's work before she arrived at Bryn Mawr. He had reviewed her M.A. thesis from the University of Michigan, "History of the Appointing Power of the President," at a meeting of the Johns Hopkins Seminary of Historical and Political Science, March 6, 1885. Wilson, who favored theory over empiricism, found that Salmon's work showed "great industry and carefulness" in the data collection and presentation but lacked analysis and failed to address Wilson's interests in Congress and in comparisons between the United States and Britain. *PWW,* 4:336. A perusal of the thesis today indicates that it offered considerable analysis in its data-driven historical narrative, but her mentor on the M.A. thesis, Charles Kendall Adams, may have shared Wilson's assessment since his March 12, 1885, remark to Wilson that women were not "quite at home in the acute analysis of political institutions" was penned while Salmon was working with Adams, 4:384–85. See Salmon, "History of the Appointing Power of the President," in *Papers of the American Historical Association,* 1:5 (New York: G. P. Putnam's Son, 1886), available at: Hathi Trust Digital Library, http://babel.hathitrust.org.

89. Bragdon, *Woodrow Wilson,* 152.

90. Brown, *Apostle of Democracy,* 101–2. Salmon's remarks call to mind a letter that Wilson wrote to his middle daughter, Jessie, in 1908, when she was visiting England with her mother and, apparently, finding the British attitude toward Americans unsettling. Wilson's remarks in this letter about the British stance toward Americans capture the essence, if not all the particulars, of his stance toward women:

> It is not exactly an attitude of condescension, but it is an attitude of tolerant curiosity: as if they would *like* to know what Americans are like and what they think and how they talk and act and feel about the ordinary things of existence, but are not very *keen* about it—do not regard it as *very* interesting, and would, on the whole, rather talk to their own kind about their own things. Quoted in Bragdon, *Woodrow Wilson,* 334.

91. Bragdon, *Woodrow Wilson,* 152. See also Chara Haeussler Bohan, *Go to the Sources: Lucy Maynard Salmon and the Teaching of History* (New York: Peter Lang, 2004), 18–23.

92. WW to EAW, March 31, 1885, *PWW,* 4:437.

93. EAW to WW, June 7, 1886, *PWW,* 5:294.

94. Bragdon, *Woodrow Wilson,* 152. According to a letter quoted in Bragdon, Wilson told

M. Carey Thomas that Bancroft had committed an "indiscretion" by taking on too hefty a topic. See "Jane Bancroft Robinson," *Notable American Women, 1607–1950: A Biographical Dictionary*, vol. 3, P-Z, ed. Edward T. James, Janet Wilson James, and Paul S. Boyer (Cambridge, Mass.: Harvard University Press, 1971), 183; Jane Bancroft, "A Study of the Parliaments of Paris and Other Parliaments of France," Ph.D. diss., Syracuse University (Evanston, Ill.: Northwestern University, 1884), available on Google Books, http://google.books.com.

95. Bragdon, *Woodrow Wilson*, 151–52; Brown, *Apostle of Democracy*, 101–2.

96. Wilson promised Salmon that he would read her thesis "with much pleasure and care" but then ignored it for three months before graciously apologizing and praising the "painstaking" work (if not the "style"). In the interim, Wilson told Ellen that he gave Salmon "constant encouragement" and wailed, "I'm *tired* of carrying female Fellows on my shoulders!" WW to Lucy Salmon, Aug. 10, 1887, *PWW*, 5:548; WW to Lucy Salmon, Nov. 23, 1887, 5:630–31; WW to EAW, Oct. 4, 1887, 5:605.

97. Bragdon, *Woodrow Wilson*, 152. WW to EAW, Oct. 4, 1887, *PWW*, 5:605.

98. Notes for Four Lectures on the Study of History, IV: The Value of Discussion, Sept. 29, 1885, *PWW*, 5:22; Woodrow Wilson, "The Modern Democratic State," unpublished treatise, Dec. 1–20, 1885, 5:71, 90; Woodrow Wilson, "Spurious Versus Real Patriotism in Education," *School Review*, 7 (Dec. 1899), 599–620. In this article, Wilson argues for training students in a democracy to question and debate authority.

It is beyond the scope of this essay to analyze the ways in which Wilson's teaching style contributed to his pedagogical disappointments at Bryn Mawr and Wesleyan. See Bragdon, *Woodrow Wilson*, 148–49, 167–71 for Wilson's successes as a lecturer at both schools. Bragdon offers evidence of Wilson's difficulty with students at Wesleyan who challenged his views. He had once told Ellen, "I have a sense of power in dealing with men collectively which I do not feel always in dealing with them singly." WW to EAW, Dec. 18, 1884, *PWW*, 3:553. Frederic C. Howe, *The Confessions of a Reformer* (New York: Charles Scribner's Sons, 1925), 6, 36, described Wilson as "our greatest lecturer" when Howe was a student at Johns Hopkins University and Wilson delivered lectures on government for five weeks each year in the 1880s. But, said Howe, "He dealt in abstractions" and "fraternized abstractly" with the graduate students. In her study of Lucy Salmon's pedagogy, Chara Bohan reports that Salmon believed that Wilson lacked the "essential characteristics" of a true teacher. Bohan acknowledges that Wilson's lecture classes at Bryn Mawr and Wesleyan were enormously popular, if passive, exercises. She argues, in line with Henry Bragdon, that Wilson sought to correct for his own pedagogical weaknesses as president of Princeton when he introduced the "preceptorial system" of small discussions between undergraduates and newly minted Ph.D.s. Bohan, *Going to the Sources*, 22; Bragdon, *Woodrow Wilson*, 205–10, 304–10.

99. WW to Richard Heath Dabney, Jan. 25, 1887, *PWW*, 5:437; Editorial notes, "Wilson's Teaching at Bryn Mawr, 1886–1887," "Wilson's Description of His Courses at Bryn Mawr College," Nov. 27, 1886, "Wilson Reviews His Course Work at Bryn Mawr," June 1, 1887, 5:349, 409, 512–13.

100. From Wilson's Confidential Journal, 1887, *PWW*, 5:619.

101. WW to Robert Bridges, Nov. 30, 1887 and Woodrow Wilson to the President and Trustees of Bryn Mawr College, June 29, 1888, *PWW*, 5:633, 743.

102. From Wilson's Confidential Journal, 1887, *PWW*, 5:619. An editorial from the

*Wesleyan Argus* called for a revival of the spring's "flagging interest in the House of Commons," but Wilson's effort at arousing interest in political debate never took hold among the Wesleyan men, Oct. 9, 1889, 6:401; David B. Potts, *Wesleyan University, 1831–1910: Collegiate Enterprise in New England* (New Haven: Yale University Press, 1992), 108, 140–41; WW to Robert Bridges, Jan. 27, 1890, 6:481.

103. WW to Robert Bridges, Aug. 26, 1888, *PWW,* 5:764; Potts, *Wesleyan University,* 140–41; Price, *Wesleyan's First Century,* 164–65; Reid, *Woodrow Wilson,* 51–54; Saunders, *Ellen Axson Wilson,* 77; Bragdon, *Woodrow Wilson,* 163–73; From the Minutes of the Conversational Club, Middletown, Conn., Oct. 14, 1889, *PWW,* 6:403.

104. Eleanor Wilson McAdoo, ed., *The Priceless Gift: The Love Letters of Woodrow Wilson and Ellen Axson Wilson* (New York: McGraw-Hill, 1962), 171. McAdoo wrote about herself in the third person in editorial notes about her birth, stating that "everybody was disappointed" she was not a boy. She claimed that her father had declared, "No child of ours shall be unwelcome," but also claimed that, as a child, she overheard her mother telling Mary Hoyt, "She had cried when the doctor told her that her third baby was a girl." Eleanor claimed that, as a result of hearing this, she "brooded secretly for years over her misfortune." There is no way to test the accuracy of these recollections, but it is certain that McAdoo chose to include them in her collection of her parents' letters in order to make some point about gender preferences in her family.

When the Wilsons' second daughter, Jessie, was born in Georgia in 1886, Wilson wrote to assure Ellen that he was not "very much disappointed that she wasn't a boy . . . At first—at the very first—I was a little disappointed. I found that I *had,* after all, been hoping a little that it would be a boy. But, my dear, that regret did not last 24 hours." WW to EAW, April 29, 1886, *PWW,* 5:184. At the time of Eleanor's birth, her paternal grandfather wrote to Wilson, "Somehow I had—unreasoningly of course—hoped for a boy—but the divine Father, who has events in His own hand, moulds all things for the best." Joseph Ruggles Wilson to WW, Oct. 30, 1889, 6:408

105. Thomas Dixon Jr. to WW, Nov. 8, 1888, *PWW,* 6:19.

106. J. Franklin Jameson to WW, Feb. 16, 1892, *PWW,* 7: 442; WW to J. Franklin Jameson, Feb. 21, 1892, 7:444. Potts, *Wesleyan University,* 166–67, 197–220; "The Shame of Wesleyan," *The Independent,* 66 (March 4, 1909), 494–95.

107. Louise W. Knight, "The Feminine Ideal," *Wesleyan University Alumnus,* 59 (Winter 1975), 24; "The Prestige Factor," *Wesleyan University Alumnus,* 60 (Winter 1976), 21–23. See also "Pressing the Damsels," *Wesleyan University Alumnus,* 59 (Spring 1975), 17–19. These articles were based on Knight's B.A. honors thesis at Wesleyan, " 'The Quails': The History of Wesleyan University's First Period of Co-Education, 1872–1912" (1972).

108. WW to EAW, March 15, 1892, *PWW,* 7:487; WW to EAW, March 10, 1892, 7:467.

109. Elmer Truesdell to WW, Feb. 19, 1889, *PWW,* 6:108.

110. WW to J. Franklin Jameson, Feb. 21, 1892, *PWW,* 7:444. J. Franklin Jameson to WW, Feb. 16, 1892, 7:442–43. For evidence of these male scholars' inability to see women in anything but a sexual light, see their joking exchange about Brown University's choice of Jameson to represent Brown at Vassar College's 25th anniversary ceremony—simply because he was unmarried. J. Franklin Jameson to WW, May 28, 1890, 6:634; WW to J. Franklin Jameson, June 6, 1890, 6:639.

111. Raymond B. Fosdick, *Chronicle of a Generation: An Autobiography* (New York: Harper & Brothers, 1958), 49.

112. Woodrow Wilson interview with the *Royal Gazette* of Hamilton, Bermuda, March 3, 1908, *PWW*, 18:4. In the interview, Wilson made a curiously contradictory comment in arguing, seven years before his conversion on suffrage, that women did not really want the franchise: "It may be that women in various parts of the world have to fight against severe odds, but in America, at least, they are almost too protected. Not that I would have this otherwise, because I think a woman should have all the protection that is legitimately possible." At the time he gave this interview in Bermuda, Wilson was failing to protect his wife, choosing, instead, to satisfy his own romantic impulses by launching his dalliance with Mary Allen Hulbert Peck. The Peck flirtation was, according to Ellen's biographer, "the only unhappiness which her husband had caused her during their entire married life." Saunders, *Ellen Axson Wilson*, 200–202.

113. EAW to WW, Jan. 26, 1895, *PWW*, 9:135.

114. EAW to WW, Feb. 13, 1895, *PWW*, 9:194–95; EAW to WW, July 2, 1896, 9:531; Saunders, *Ellen Axson Wilson*, 119, 126–27. Miss Fine's School was open to girls and boys in the lower grades but was open only to girls at the secondary level.

In the summer after leaving Bryn Mawr, Wilson corresponded with Moses Slaughter, who had been an "instructor" in Latin at the college during Wilson's last two years there. In 1888, Slaughter took a job teaching young men at the Collegiate Institute in New Jersey and wrote to Wilson for advice on "teaching boys Caesar." Wilson replied with a full, enthusiastic description of ways to get "boys" engaged with the realities of Caesar's lived experience. The entire exchange was premised on the assumption that a teacher of male students should approach this subject entirely differently than a teacher of females. Now that Slaughter was going to teach boys, he could think about evoking the sights, smells, and noises of military camps, explaining the "reality" of Caesar's evolution from a young "fop and a lady-killer" to a "sure-enough man" and allow the students to enact the campaigns. Wilson's pedagogical point was a sound one, but it reveals that he did not attempt to reach Bryn Mawr students with such evocative material, assuming that "boys like generals, like fighting, like accounts of battles," and thought it was pointless to attempt to engage girls in such vivid human experiences. Moses Slaughter to WW, July 25, 1888, 5:755–56.

Evidence of Wilson's subscription to G. Stanley Hall's developmental theories can be found in his recommendation, at a teaching conference, of John Johnson's *Rudimentary Society Among Boys* (Baltimore: Johns Hopkins University, 1884) as a guide to teaching precollegiate history. Minutes of Madison Conference, Dec. 28–30, 1892, *PWW*, 7:65. Hall's theories fit well with Wilson's focus on separating male and female students at adolescence. According to Hall's "ontogeny recapitulates phylogeny" theory, it is at adolescence that young people reach the civilized state in human history and, at that point, males and females evolve in utterly different directions. See Janice Law Trecker, "Sex, Science, and Education," *American Quarterly*, 26 (Oct. 1974), 352–66; Elizabeth Fee, "The Sexual Politics of Victorian Social Anthropology," *Feminist Studies*, 1 (Winter-Spring 1973), 23–39; Flavia Alaya, "Victorian Science and the Genius of Woman," *Journal of the History of Ideas*, 38 (April-June 1977), 260–80; G. Stanley Hall, *Adolescence* (New York: D. Appleton, 1904); Patrick Geddes and J. Arthur Thompson, *The Evolution of Sex* (London: W. Scott, 1889).

115. Saunders, *Ellen Axson Wilson,* 147, 165, 169–70.

116. From Wilson's Diary, Jan. 5, 1904, *PWW,* 15:118; Saunders, *Ellen Axson Wilson,* 189.

117. EAW to Mary Hoyt, June 12, 1906, 16:423.

118. "Dr. Woodrow Wilson Speaks to Woman's College Graduates," *Baltimore Sun,* June 4, 1908, in *PWW,* 18:318–20. In 1915, former U.S. president William Howard Taft expressed the hope that his daughter, Helen, after graduation from Bryn Mawr, would "do graduate work at Yale," believing that "a professorship, now that women are coming more to the front, is not beyond her reasonable ambition." Helen Taft, later Manning, bucked the odds of her era: she taught in her field of specialty, American history, rather than being forced to teach domestic science, and she actually got a teaching position at Bryn Mawr College, which was rare for women. Manning was also a wife and mother, making her even more unusual for academic women of her day. M. Carey Thomas was active in advancing Manning's career, and her approval of Manning's marriage and motherhood in the 1920s indicates how social pressure and academic realities forced Thomas to revise her opposition to the combining of career and family. Manning served as dean of Bryn Mawr College in the last years of Thomas's presidency. Her published works on British government in the colonial era represented just the sort of dogged, archival research that Woodrow Wilson had disdained as a young academic. Ishbel Ross, *An American Family: The Tafts* (Cleveland: World Publishing, 1964), 279–83, 293–94, 301, 307, 319–21, 346, 351, 413–14. See discussion of Manning's career at Bryn Mawr in Horowitz, *Power and Passion of M. Carey Thomas;* Finch, *Carey Thomas of Bryn Mawr.*

119. Saunders, *Ellen Axson Wilson,* 224, 262–63, 271–72; "Mrs. Eleanor Wilson McAdoo, President's Daughter, 77, Dies," *New York Times,* April 7, 1967; a play by playwright-actress Aurovilian Seyril Schochen, "Nishtha," traces Margaret Woodrow Wilson's path into eastern mysticism. See http://www.auroville.org/art&culture/theatre/nishtha.htm. Wilson's friend and colleague from Princeton, Bliss Perry, described Wilson as "strict with his children" and "a trifle old-fashioned" in regard to women. *And Gladly Teach: Reminiscences by Bliss Perry* (Boston: Houghton Mifflin, 1935), 153–54.

120. "Notes for a Commencement Address," June 3, 1908, *PWW,* 18:318. Lynn D. Gordon, "The Gibson Girl Goes to College: Popular Culture and Women's Higher Education in the Progressive Era, 1880–1920," *American Quarterly,* 39 (Summer 1987), 211–30; Patricia A. Graham, "Expansion and Exclusion: A History of Women in American Higher Education," *Signs,* 3 (Summer 1978), 759–73; Joan Zimmerman, "Daughters of Main Street: Culture and the Female Community at Grinnell, 1884–1917," in Mary Kelley, ed., *Woman's Being, Woman's Place: Female Identity and Vocation in American History* (Boston: G. K. Hall, 1979), 154–70; Patricia Searles and Janet Mickish, "A Thoroughbred Girl: Images of Female Gender Roles in Turn-of-the-Century Media," *Women's Studies,* 10 (1984), 261–81; Christina Simmons, "Companionate Marriage and the Lesbian Threat," *Frontiers,* 4 (1979), 54–59; Frank Stricker, "Cookbooks and Law Books: The Hidden History of Career Women in 20th-Century America," *Journal of Social History,* 10 (Fall 1976), 1–19. For parallel developments in secondary schools, see Brown, "Fear of Feminization." For examples of popular magazine articles that touted the heterosocial benefits of coeducation, see Anne Allinson, "The Present and Future of Collegiate Co-Education," *The Nation,* 88 (April 22, 1909), 404–6; James R. Angell, "Coeducation in Relation to Other Types of College Education for

Women," NEA *Proceedings* (1904), 548–49; "Comrades and Sweethearts," *The Independent,* 67 (Oct. 28, 1909), 989–91; "Be Clever, Sweet Maid," *The Independent,* 70 (May 4, 1911), 952–55; Richard Rice Jr., "The Educational Value of Co-Education," *The Independent,* 73 (Dec. 5, 1912), 1304–6; W. A. Curtis and M. E. Cook, "Coeducation in Colleges," *The Outlook,* 72 (Dec. 13, 1902), 887–91.

In a courtship letter to Ellen, Wilson had commented on "the frequent mistakes" in marital choices (by folks "less extraordinary" than they) owing to "the fact that intellectual young men" were "kept apart" from "general society . . . until they reach the most susceptible age, and then thrown into associations which ensure their falling in love with the first pretty woman they meet." WW to EAW, Nov. 22, 1884, 3:473.

121. Woodrow Wilson, "Mere Literature," *Atlantic Monthly,* 72 (Dec. 1893), 820–28, reprinted in *PWW,* 8:240–52; Woodrow Wilson, "Princeton in the Nation's Service," commemorative address delivered at Princeton University's sesquicentennial celebration, Oct. 21, 1896, reprinted in *Forum,* 22 (Dec. 1896), 447–66 and *PWW,* 10:11–31; Woodrow Wilson, "Princeton for the Nation's Service," address delivered on occasion of Wilson's inauguration to presidency of Princeton University, Oct. 25, 1902, 14:170–85; Woodrow Wilson, "What Is College For?" *Scribner's Magazine,* 46 (Nov. 1909), 570–77, reprinted in *PWW,* 19:334–47.

122. Wilson, "Princeton in the Nation's Service," Oct. 21, 1896, *PWW,* 10:21. According to the editors of the *PWW,* Wilson cut this section from his long text for the purposes of the spoken address, but the section was published in *The Forum,* 22 (Dec. 1896). See editorial introduction to sesquicentennial address, *PWW,* 10:11–12n1 and *Selected Literary and Political Papers and Addresses of Woodrow Wilson,* vol. 3 (New York: Grosset & Dunlap, 1926), 56.

123. U.S. Office of Education, *Report of the Commissioner of Education for the Year 1900–1901,* vol. 2 (Washington, D.C.: Government Printing Office, 1902), 1234.

124. Solomon, *In the Company of Educated Women,* 59–60.

125. "Chicago University Methods," *The Independent,* 54 (Sept. 4, 1902), 2153; "Coeducation at the University of Chicago," *The Nation,* 75 (Aug. 21, 1902), 147–48; "The Shame of Wesleyan," 494–95; Knight, "The Prestige Factor," 21–23; Potts, *Wesleyan University, 1831–1910,* 213–20; M. Carey Thomas, "Educated Women in the 20th Century," speech delivered to the General Federation of Women's Clubs at the Louisiana Purchase Exposition, St. Louis, Sept. , 1904, Bryn Mawr College Archives, M. Carey Thomas Papers. In addition to works cited in note 15, see Roberta Frankfort, *Collegiate Women: Domesticity and Career in Turn-of-the-Century America* (New York: New York University Press, 1977); Charlotte W. Conable, *Women at Cornell: The Myth of Equal Education* (Ithaca: Cornell University Press, 1977); John R. Thelin, *A History of American Higher Education* (Baltimore: Johns Hopkins University Press, 2004), 182–86; and Horowitz, *Power and Passion of M. Carey Thomas,* chs. 16–19, for the negative reaction to female scholarly achievement and the fear of feminization in academia.

126. Woodrow Wilson, "Democracy," a lecture completed on Dec. 5, 1891 and delivered at Vassar College in Jan. 1893, *PWW,* 7:344–69, 8:76–77; WW to EAW, Feb. 19, 1895, and "Political Liberty," commencement address at Wellesley College, June 26, 1895, 9:98, 491; Founder's Day Address, May 3, 1902, 12:359–62; Woodrow Wilson, "What Is College For?"

*Scribner's Magazine,* 46 (Nov. 1909), 570–77. In this article for *Scribner's Magazine,* Wilson asked, "Why would a man send his son to college?" *PWW,* 19:335.

127. Editorial note, "Mere Literature," *PWW,* 8:239.

128. Wilson, "Mere Literature," *PWW,* 8:241, 243–44, 246. G. Stanley Hall, a longtime opponent of education that would promote female equality or independence, echoed Wilson's critique of philology and explicitly linked philology to both antifeminism and male humanists' fear of feminism in "The Kind of Women Colleges Produce," *Appleton's Magazine,* 12 (Sept. 1908), 3313–19.

129. Wilson, "Mere Literature," *PWW,* 8:245–46.

130. Wilson, "What Is College For?" *PWW,* 19:336; WW to Frederic Yates, Sept., 1908, 18:417. Wilson supported woman suffrage in 1915, after his gubernatorial experience taught him that women could be womanly, domestic, and civic actors. See Victoria Bissell Brown, "Did Woodrow Wilson's Gender Politics Matter?" in John Milton Cooper Jr., ed., *Reconsidering Woodrow Wilson: Progressivism, Internationalism, and Peace* (Washington, D.C., and Baltimore: Woodrow Wilson Center Press/Johns Hopkins University Press, 2008), 125–62.

131. Horowitz, *Power and Passion of M. Carey Thomas,* 195–97. Thomas's goal as a young academic had been to create opportunities for other female scholars to pursue a scholarly life. But a survey of faculty names in Bryn Mawr College catalogues, 1885–1910, reveals that of the 85 classroom professors who were listed in regular faculty positions, only 13—that is, 15 percent—were female. Those hired for lesser positions, such as "readers," laboratory "demonstrators," and "assistants," were almost entirely female. Bryn Mawr College Archives.

132. Woodrow Wilson, "Address to the Presbyterian Union of Baltimore," Feb. 19, 1909, *PWW,* 19:57–58; "The Spirit of Learning," July 1, 1909, *PWW,* 19:286–87; "What Is College For?" 19:340–45; James Axtell, *The Making of Princeton University: From Woodrow Wilson to the Present* (Princeton: Princeton University Press, 2006), ch. 5; Cornelia Meigs, *What Makes a College: A History of Bryn Mawr* (New York: Macmillan, 1956), ch. 7; Hugh Hawkins, *Between Harvard and America: The Educational Leadership of Charles W. Eliot* (New York: Oxford University Press, 1972); Palmieri, *In Adamless Eden.*

133. Though Wilson disliked the Germanic tilt of the Bryn Mawr curriculum, his own policies at Princeton aligned with Bryn Mawr's in regard to electives, dedication to liberal arts, and integration of graduates with undergraduates. Without any apparent sense of irony, W. Bruce Leslie postulates that "Wilson may have derived some of his ideas from his former employer, Bryn Mawr." *Gentlemen and Scholars: College and Community in the "Age of the University," 1865–1917* (University Park: Pennsylvania State University Press, 1992), 178. M. Carey Thomas, "Should Higher Education of Women Differ from That of Men?" *Educational Review,* 21 (1901), 1–10; M. Carey Thomas, "College Entrance Requirements," Address, Association of Collegiate Alumnae, Nov. 10, 1900, *Publications of Collegiate Alumnae,* ser. 3, no. 4 (Feb. 1901), 23–35; Horowitz discusses Thomas's choice to create a curriculum that was a "compromise between the elective system pursued at Harvard and the traditional classical curriculum," *Power and Passion of M. Carey Thomas,* 193. See also Cooper, *The Warrior and the Priest,* 90–97; Axtell, *The Making of Princeton University,* 59–71; Bragdon, *Woodrow Wilson,* ch. 15.

134. Wilson, "Princeton in the Nation's Service," 23; Wilson, "Princeton for the Nation's Service," 178.

135. As indicated in note 21, the argument offered here questions John M. Mulder's view that Woodrow Wilson's abiding love for Ellen made him less likely to "aggrandize his own authority" or less "rigid" in his "adherence to just principles." Mulder, *Woodrow Wilson,* 108. His own close friends, Edith Gitting Reid and Bliss Perry, suggest in their memoirs of Wilson that Ellen Wilson's cosseting adoration of her husband increased his sense of entitlement to authority in discussions and decisions. Reid, *Woodrow Wilson,* 46–51; Perry, *And Gladly Teach,* 153–54.

# Politics and Wilson's Academic Career

John Milton Cooper Jr.

Woodrow Wilson remains the only president of the United States who has risen to the very top in a profession removed from public life. In fact, he rose to the top in two private callings. He became one of the leading scholars of his time in any field, and he still ranks among a small coterie—slightly more than a handful—of truly great political scientists whom America has produced. He also became the outstanding educational leader of his era, and he still ranks among another small coterie—again only slightly more than a handful—of truly great university presidents whom America has produced.[1]

This private, academic prelude to Wilson's political career has spawned a great deal of inquiry and argument, as scholars and other writers have ransacked his life as a professor and college president for clues to his performance as president. This enterprise got started early, shortly after Wilson's death, with testimony from his brother-in-law and faculty colleague, Stockton Axson, and another faculty colleague, George McLean Harper. Separately, they told his first biographer, Ray Stannard Baker, that the fight over the Graduate College at Princeton prefigured the great political fight over the League of Nations. Soon afterward, reviewing the first two volumes of Baker's biography, the literary critic Edmund Wilson (no relation, but a student at Princeton shortly after Woodrow Wilson's time) drew the same comparison publicly. After that, many historians and biographers drew the same parallels. Others, however, have disagreed, pointing out that the Graduate College and League fights were vastly different affairs, played out in totally different arenas, with Wilson losing the earlier one through bad luck at a critical moment.[2]

Some interpreters have also sought to link his fight against the exclusivist eating clubs at Princeton and his clashes with wealthy trustees to his espousal of progressive reform in politics. But others, most notably James Axtell, have pointed out that Wilson's initial opposition to the clubs sprang from intellectual concerns—he saw them as distractions from the university's principal aim, which was to make the students into what he often called "reading men." One of Wilson's chief supporters among the trustees, Melanchthon Jacobus, repeatedly urged him to link his fight against the clubs with Theodore Roosevelt's and other progressives' battles against wealth and privilege, but the university president resisted these entreaties until after he had reoriented himself politically.[3]

Necessary as the search for academic prefiguration of Wilson's political career has been, it is just as necessary to turn the matter around and explore how his interest in politics informed his work as a scholar and educator. As is well known, academic life was not Wilson's first choice of a career. Right after he entered graduate school at Johns Hopkins, he told his fiancée, Ellen Axson, "The profession I chose was politics; the profession I entered was law. I entered the one because I thought it would lead to the other." But his experience with practicing law had shown him that long years of grinding toil at the bar would render him unfit for the kind of high-minded politics he wished to pursue. He concluded, therefore: "A professorship was the only feasible place for me," because it would allow him to study and write about politics. "Indeed I knew very well that a man without independent fortune must in any event content himself with becoming an *outside* force in politics, and I was well enough satisfied with the prospect of having whatever influence I might be able to exercise felt through literary and non-partisan agencies."[4]

That may have been how Wilson saw things as he embarked on his academic career, but he was letting his memory play tricks on him. Law had been a bad fit for him from the outset, and he gave it a try mainly to satisfy his father, who had worldly ambitions for his older son and once chided him for wanting "a mere literary career."[5] From the time he experienced his intellectual awakening as an undergraduate at Princeton and discovered the writings of the recently deceased English journalist, Walter Bagehot, he wanted to write about politics and perhaps also to try his hand at imaginative literature. In his senior year, he began to satisfy that urge by getting an article accepted for publication in a Boston-based journal edited by a young Harvard instructor named Henry Cabot Lodge. With his literary appetite thus whetted, young Wilson held his nose as he approached the study and practice of law, and he spent much of his time during that period reading and writing about politics.[6]

Likewise, when he abandoned his legal practice after the briefest of tries, it was by no means clear that "a professorship was the only feasible place" for him. It seems puzzling that he did not choose high-toned journalism. Not only had his inspiration, Bagehot, been that kind of journalist, but also his most satisfying activity as an undergraduate at Princeton, even more than public speaking, had been editing the newly founded student newspaper, *The Princetonian.* Moreover, his best friend from Princeton, Robert Bridges, was already pursuing a journalistic career, and he would gladly have helped his friend break into the field.

Wilson appears to have rejected journalism in part because he doubted whether he had the quickness of mind for it and because he did not think journalism would strike his father, a Presbyterian minister and former seminary professor, as a sufficiently respectable alternative to the law. A professorship would offer such an alternative in the eyes of his family, and he knew that colleges afforded him a congenial environment. Still, just as he was completing his two years of graduate work at Johns Hopkins, he had second thoughts about academia and put out feelers about a newspaper job and an appointment in the State Department. He also fretted about losing touch with the world of affairs and becoming impractical and doctrinaire in his teaching and writing. Clearly, Wilson never aspired to ascend into what later would be called the ivory tower.[7]

Yet Wilson did become more of a detached academic than he planned to be. Instead of the para-political career that he suggested to Ellen, teaching and writing on scholarly topics and nonpolitical subjects absorbed him, and he rarely commented on current policies and debates. His first and best book, *Congressional Government,* published in 1885, was highly critical of the legislative branch and saw it in need of reform, but it was far more a work of analysis than of prescription. Likewise, although he wrote the book while he was a graduate student at Johns Hopkins, it apparently never occurred to him to take a short train ride from Baltimore to Washington to see Congress in action. His second book, *The State,* a textbook published in 1889, continued in a vein Wilson had been mining since his undergraduate days—comparative government, in which he was a pioneer—by unfavorably judging the American system of separated legislative and executive powers against the merger of those powers in parliamentary systems. Wilson also pioneered in the study of public administration, publishing a seminal article in this field in 1887, but he did not pursue this breakthrough with subsequent work either.[8]

Much of Wilson's writing in the last decade of the nineteenth century and first two years of the twentieth was not in political science. He wrote three books in American history. The first was *Division and Reunion,* published in 1893, a volume in Albert Bushnell Hart's American Nation series, covering the period from 1829 to 1877. It was a sound work of scholarship, predictably long on politics but also incorporating insights Wilson had garnered from the young historian Frederick Jackson Turner, whom he had gotten to know while teaching part-time at Johns Hopkins in the early 1890s. His other two books in history were slapdash efforts that he produced for money. A short biography of George Washington, published in 1896, rested on slender research and employed a saccharine, flowery style that was out of character for his writing. *A History of the American People,* though in five volumes in 1902, was of the same low caliber and earned from a Princeton faculty colleague the sobriquet of "gilt-edged potboiler."[9] Nor did those books comprise everything Wilson wrote for money. He also turned out a stream of articles for higher-class magazines; usually based on previously delivered paid public lectures, some of those articles did not address politics at all.

By the middle of the 1890s, Wilson spread himself so thin with outside speaking and writing that he suffered a small breakdown and had to spend a summer abroad resting and recuperating. Perhaps in part because of that breakdown, he turned back to his study of politics. He had already been reflecting again on his other great political inspiration, Edmund Burke, and he was steeping himself anew in Burke's anti-ideological, antitheoretical conception of politics. As the twentieth century dawned, Wilson was planning to make that conception the basis for what he wanted to make his magnum opus, what he called "Philosophy of Politics." He wanted to turn from the "how"—how power really worked—to the "why"—why different systems grew in different times and places and why some succeeded and others failed in providing stability and liberty. Before that could happen, however, fate and the choice of the trustees intervened, and he became president of Princeton.[10]

During his years as a professor, Wilson never did become a completely detached academic. He spoke occasionally at political rallies, including one for a reform mayoral candidate in Baltimore, where he shared the platform with a rising Republican politician, Theodore Roosevelt. The two men struck up a mutually admiring acquaintanceship, which lasted for over a decade, but ended in 1906 when Wilson started sticking his toes in the political waters and criticizing Roosevelt and his policies as president. One area where he agreed with his new acquaintance was foreign policy. From 1898 onward, Wilson became an ardent imperialist, too, and some of his speeches and writings sound uncannily like what Roosevelt was proclaiming. During the few months in 1901 that Roosevelt was vice president, he invited professors from Harvard, Yale, and Princeton to meet with him and discuss ways to interest their students in public service. The Princeton professor whom he invited was Wilson.[11]

Yet those involvements were exceptions during Wilson's scholarly career. He almost never commented on current politics, not even to share publicly his repugnance toward the turn that his party, the Democrats, had taken in 1896 toward William Jennings Bryan and free silver. In his teaching, he did admonish students to involve themselves in public life, and he rejected the currently fashionable disdain for politics and politicians as unworthy pursuits and unfit company for high-principled gentlemen. But Wilson set no example of involvement himself, and he rarely gave specific advice about how, where, and why the young men he was teaching should get involved. His sesquicentennial speech "Princeton in the Nation's Service" was not, as is commonly thought, a call to public service; rather, it was a recounting of how the newly renamed university had always been in such service. His inaugural speech as president, "Princeton for the Nation's Service," did issue a call for public service, but, again, only in general terms.

In sum, for Wilson's career as a scholar and teacher, his original vocation for politics served mainly as a backdrop. He cared about public affairs deeply, and he sought to communicate that concern to students and readers, but he did not use his professorship as a platform for current commentary or perch for policy advising. The truly significant influence of his original vocation for politics on his scholarship lay in providing him with his subject. Wilson's early pursuit of the question of how power really worked and, as a corollary, how it could be made to work more efficiently and accountably would later serve him well when he entered politics. No career in American history would better vindicate the study of politics as preparation for the practice of politics than Wilson's.

Between the scholar of politics and the scholar in politics fell Wilson's other successful private career—as a university president. The link was important both because it provided valuable experience for public life and because it shaped his behavior as an educational leader. At first, Wilson's attraction to politics played the same role for him as an administrator as it had done for him as a scholar—as a backdrop. During his first three years as president of Princeton, he fell silent on public issues. He gave many more off-campus speeches than his predecessors, but he nearly always talked about either Princeton or educational matters. When he began to speak out about political matters in 1906, the initiative came from others, namely the magazine editor George Harvey and other conservative Democrats who spotted him as a potential champion for their battered political ranks. The Princeton presidency gave Wilson a lot of public visibility, which made him attractive to these would-be patrons.

Flattered by their attention and intrigued with the possibility of pursuing his first vocational love, Wilson put on a brave show of trying to be a spokesperson for the state-rights, limited-government views of the Grover Cleveland wing of the Democrats. He abandoned this fling after about three years, and he made the switch admittedly for opportunistic reasons. Progressivism was the rapidly rising tide in American politics then, and Wilson wanted to be on the winning side. At one point he declared, "I never heard of a man in his senses who was fishing for a minority." His years in academia had not stifled the would-be politician in him.[12]

Yet Wilson was also a genuine intellectual, and ideas were equally important to him in choosing which side of the political fence he believed suited him. In his early thirties, Wilson had told the Harvard historian Albert Bushnell Hart, for whom he was about to write *Division and Reunion:* "Ever since I have had independent judgments of my own I have been a Federalist(!)" By that, he meant that he liked strong, centralized government and admired Alexander Hamilton, who was always his favorite among the Founders. During his three-year fling with the conservative Democrats, Wilson put himself through intellectual contortions in an effort to reconcile those beliefs with the limited-government creed of those conservative Democrats. It was no use, and he let out an almost audible sigh of relief when he came out as a progressive.[13]

Along the way, he did sometimes mix politics with his leadership at Princeton. In 1907, he wrote to a wealthy conservative alumnus, Adrian Joline, "Would that we could do something, at once dignified and effective, to knock Mr. Bryan once and for all into a cocked hat."[14] Wilson made that remark as part of an unsuccessful effort to curry favor with Joline, who soon became one of the most outspoken opponents of his reforms at Princeton and who later let this letter be published in an unsuccessful effort to embarrass Wilson in the eyes of Bryan and progressives. By the opposite token, even after he started mixing his newfound progressivism with Princeton issues—such as attacking the clubs' social exclusiveness and the influence of wealthy donors—Wilson still tried to raise money from such tycoon-philanthropists as John D. Rockefeller and Andrew Carnegie. Revealingly, it was in the midst of his pursuit of Carnegie that Wilson joined the American Peace Society, one of Carnegie's favorite causes. This move did not jibe with his earlier imperialist outburst and his near-total lack of interest in foreign affairs between that time and after he entered the White House.

One other major public concern also occasionally—and, in the long run, detrimentally—intruded on Wilson's Princeton presidency. This was race. Despite his southern birth and upbringing, he held racial views that much more closely resembled those of the majority of white northerners at that time. He paid little attention to race relations, aside from applauding Booker T. Washington's nonthreatening gradualism. In fact, Wilson so admired Washington that he invited the Tuskegee principal to his inauguration as president of Princeton. This offended one of his southern-born wife's aunts, who "said if she had known he was to be there she wouldn't have gone." Wilson, by contrast, said to his family about the inaugural ceremonies that he thought Washington's "speech was the very best at the dinner afterwards bar none."[15]

If anyone thought that gesture portended a new day in race relations at the university, that person would soon be disappointed. Unlike most of the country's older, socially prestigious colleges and universities, Princeton had admitted no African Americans. Two years into his presidency, Wilson discouraged an inquiry from a black applicant, saying that no rules barred such an application, but "the whole temper and tradition of the place are such that that no negro has ever applied for admission, and . . . [it] seems extremely unlikely that the question will ever assume a practical form." Time did not soften that view. After another three years, he discouraged another application from an African American who was aiming for a career in the ministry by instructing his secretary to write: "Regret to say that it is altogether inadvisable for a colored man to enter Princeton. Appreciate his desire to do so, but strongly recommend his securing education in a Southern [Negro] institution perhaps completing it with a course at the Princeton Theol. Sem., which is under an entirely separate control from the Univ."[16] His attitudes toward white ethnic and religious minorities were different. He did not discourage Jews and Catholics from applying, and in faculty hiring he banished the last vestiges of Presbyterian orthodoxy and appointed the first Jew and Catholic to teach at Princeton.

Privately, Wilson deplored President Roosevelt's appointment of an African American to a government post in South Carolina and raised the specter of "intermarriage." Yet he spoke sometimes to black audiences, and he became an acquaintance of the head of Hampton Institute, Robert Moton, who succeeded in getting him belatedly to denounce lynching as president. Wilson also continued to praise Washington's work at Tuskegee and that of "many smaller institutions conducted along similar lines."[17] He would carry these attitudes into the White House, where he would sanction attempts to introduce racial segregation into the federal workplace but would count Catholics and Jews among his closest political associates and appoint one of them, Louis Brandeis, to be the first Jewish justice of the Supreme Court.

The biggest impact of his previous attraction to politics on Wilson's university presidency did not lie in the influence of big public issues. Rather, that attraction shaped his fundamental approach to the job. Preparing for his inauguration, which was to include "Princeton for the Nation's Service," he told his wife, "I feel like a new prime minister getting ready to address his constituents." That remark revealed Wilson's instinctive equation of educational leadership with political leadership. It never occurred to him not to regard his university presidency as the equivalent to a political office. Furthermore, his comparative studies of politics had led him to esteem the prime minister in a parliamentary government as the best kind of political leader.[18]

This approach bore fruit from Wilson's first days at the helm of Princeton. As an admirer of how parliamentary regimes melded legislative and executive functions, he liked the way those governments often prepared programs in advance for enactment. This approach also resonated with one of his strongest character traits, which had previously found few outlets—a penchant for bold action. Even before his inauguration, he presented the Princeton trustees with plans for improvements, reforms, and expansion, and he put a breathtaking price tag on his program. He proceeded slowly for a while, concentrating on curricular reforms, and he enlisted his friend from undergraduate days on the *Princetonian,* the mathematician Henry B. Fine, as his chief lieutenant. Wilson also devoted time to the aspect of his new job that he liked least—fundraising, which he regarded as a form of begging. Most important from his point of view, he started working what he regarded as his main constituency—the alumni. He began travelling around the Northeast and Midwest to address alumni groups, with whom he shared his vision of a new and better Princeton. With the same goal in mind, he likewise talked to educational and civic groups as a way of advertising his plans for his university.

It might seem surprising that Wilson did not also regard the students as a constituency, but few, if any, people in higher education in those days gave much thought to catering to or seeking support from students. Already Princeton's most popular lecturer, Wilson enjoyed enthusiastic, near-unanimous approval from the student body, at least until he attacked the clubs in 1907. It did hurt that the student paper, now called the *Daily Princetonian,* which "Tommy" Wilson and "Harry" Fine had once edited, now turned against them over the clubs. The editors feared that ceding control over the clubs under the quad plan would cause "a change so radical that Princeton as it is today would cease to exist and another, a strange and an unknown Princeton would rise in its place."[19] Yet for every club member or aspirant whose support he lost, he gained fervent adherents from among those who had bad experiences or faced poor prospects with those organizations.[20]

As both professor and president, he often befriended individual students. Two of his special favorites were members of the class of 1905, Raymond Fosdick and Norman Thomas. Interestingly, both were ministers' sons from the hinterlands who had earlier attended other colleges; both were excellent, intellectually serious students who were also socially personable. In them, Wilson could see a later generation's incarnation of himself. Both of these students reciprocated the president's regard for them. Fosdick became a lifelong friend, political supporter, and sometime diplomatic aide, and after Wilson's death he devoted himself to the Woodrow Wilson Foundation and played the major role in launching *The Papers of Woodrow Wilson* under the editorship of Arthur S. Link. Thomas later parted company with Wilson over World War I and became the Socialist Party's perennial presidential candidate. Three years after his graduation, however, he wrote Wilson, "Every day I live I am more thankful that I am a Princeton man. My only regret is that I graduated in the Dark Ages before the preceptorial system and other good things of the present!"[21]

If, in Wilson's parliamentary view, the alumni were his constituency, then the trustees were his cabinet and the faculty were his backbenchers. He practiced different brands of politics with them. He tried to be collegial with both groups, at least up to a point. Given the indolence of Wilson's predecessor, Francis Landey Patton, the trustees had grown accustomed to running Princeton to a large degree. The best example of this came when they set up the graduate school as an autonomous unit, with its dean, Andrew Fleming West, reporting directly to them, not the president. Similarly, the trustees' curriculum committee had been drawing up lists of possible faculty members and presenting them to the president. That was the way Wilson himself had been hired in 1890: the initiative and the money for his appointment had come from wealthy trustees, notably Moses Taylor Pyne and Wilson's classmate, Cyrus McCormick. The new president put a stop to those hiring practices; he picked recruits himself, and he made the trustee committee his rubber stamp. This usurpation caused some grumbling among the trustees, but the new president got off to such an impressive start and attracted such stellar new professors that he encountered far less resistance than might have been expected. Clipping West's wings was another aspect of asserting his prerogative, and this was an important aspect of the feud over the location of the Graduate College.[22]

In treating the trustees like his cabinet, Wilson met frequently with the full board, various committees, and individually with influential members. He usually did well in each forum. At board meetings, he sometimes displayed his gifts as a speaker. None of his speeches to those meetings has survived in the minutes, but a hint of their power came from a trustee who had second thoughts about the president's biggest reform effort, the quad plan: "Wilson's eloquence over-persuaded us."[23] With individual trustees, he showed his equally great but less well-known gift for one-on-one persuasion. Oddly, he never gave sufficient attention to the critical task of choosing loyal supporters as members of the board. Early in his presidency, one sympathetic trustee warned Wilson against "elect[ing] two or three more very rich men simply because they are rich men,"[24] The president heeded that advice up to a point with a few appointments, but he never made a systematic effort to pack the board with loyalists. Lack of support among the trustees ultimately hobbled him in his two biggest fights to transform Princeton.

With the faculty, Wilson acted in different ways with different members. He readily acknowledged his own lack of knowledge of the sciences, and he gladly gave Dean Fine a virtual free hand in running that part of the university. This offered a foretaste of the way he treated most of the members of his cabinet in Washington. He made his closest friend, John Grier Hibben, his main advisor and deputized Hibben to serve as acting president when he took a medical leave in 1906. This was not, however, a relationship between equals, as with Fine. Hibben and his wife grew to resent what they saw as Wilson's domineering ways, and in 1907 Hibben broke painfully and publicly with the president over the quad plan. Wilson treated some faculty luminaries, particularly the ones he and Fine recruited, with respect and deference, and he stood firm against West on the Graduate College in part out of a desire to satisfy them.[25]

The president was polite and usually cordial toward most of his faculty colleagues. He presided over meetings with a light hand and no appearance of domination—another foretaste of the way he would act in Washington. He also exercised his eloquence when he thought the occasion demanded it. In two faculty meetings in 1907, he spoke about the quad plan so movingly that even his opponents applauded him. According to those present, he gave low-key presentations, standing and holding the head of a mallet poised on the desktop. Fragmentary notes record that he ended his second speech with the peroration, "I BEG OF YOU TO FOLLOW ME IN THIS HAZARDOUS, BUT SPLENDID ADVENTURE."[26]

Hiring and firing showed another side of his dealings with the faculty. Toward those whom he considered duds as scholars or teachers, he often used the soft approach of easing the older ones into retirement. In some cases, he forced resignations, and once he fired a man who enjoyed popularity among students for his easygoing ways and was a second-generation faculty member.[27] Recruitment of new faculty afforded Wilson further opportunities to shine at individual persuasion. One younger recruit recalled, "Had Woodrow Wilson asked me to go with him to a new university in Kamchatka or Senegambia I would have said 'yes' without further question."[28] Senior stars reacted the same way. When the biologist Edwin Grant Conklin, who came from the University of Pennsylvania, met the classicist Edward Capps, who came from Chicago, Capps asked him, "What brought you to Princeton?" Conklin answered, "Woodrow Wilson, and what brought you here?" Capps responded, "The same."[29]

On balance, Wilson's political conception of his university presidency served him well. It gave him scope for the bold actions and publicizing that made him the brightest star of American higher education. He never envisioned his job as a matter of placidly presiding over a venerable institution. He enjoyed the bricks-and-mortar side of his presidency, and he appreciated the need for efficient administration, which included hiring a business manager and appointing a dean of students. Yet Wilson readily admitted to wanting to do more. At the end of his presidency, he told his brother-in-law and faculty supporter, Stockton Axson, "I am not interested in simply administering a club. Unless I can develop something I cannot get thoroughly interested."[30] In sum, it was Wilson's political conception of his office that impelled him to strive to transform Princeton into a front-rank modern university

Conversely, his approach to the office also served him and his institution ill at times. Impatience was the corollary to Wilson's boldness, and he sprang his two biggest reforms on Princeton with almost no advance notice. Those were the preceptorial system and the quad plan. The precipitous approach worked well with the precepts, mainly because he was adding resources all around and not taking anything away from anybody. The approach fell flat with the quads. After he achieved apparent initial success in persuading the trustees to adopt the plan, a storm of student and alumni protest turned a majority of the board and its most influential member, Pyne, against it. There followed a gradual but soon bitter estrangement between this kingpin of the trustees and the president. It is easy to fault Wilson for misjudging the situation, for moving too fast, and for not securing financial backing before coming out for the quads. One of Wilson's biographers has attributed these misjudgments to the health crisis that he had suffered in 1906 because of a retinal hemorrhage that sprang from arteriosclerosis. For a while after this incident, he did seem to think he might be in a race with time and his own mortality. That was not a good frame of mind in which to commence such a far-reaching reform program.[31]

In the Graduate College fight, Wilson's political gifts usually served him well, despite his ultimate defeat. In that fight, he engaged in an academic duel to the death with Pyne and West, but this was not a quarrel of his choosing. Moreover, he lost on the verge of victory because fortune unexpectedly smiled on West in the form of a big bequest from an aged alumnus. In the quad fight, besides being impatient and not preparing the ground in advance, Wilson erred mainly in not appreciating the need to raise money beforehand. In that instance, his political model for a university presidency did not serve him well. Campaign finance was one subject he had never studied as an academic political scientist, and later, in his campaigns for governor and president, he gladly left money matters to others. Moreover, fund-raising was a new dimension of academic leadership, and Wilson's failing to grasp its full importance was perhaps understandable.

Unquestionably, his university presidency gave him his first taste of practicing politics. It was a special kind of politics—academic politics—but he believed that it prepared him well for the "real thing." On numerous occasions, he remarked on the differences between the two kinds of politics. When he was running for president in 1912, he commented that "politicians in the field of politics . . . play their hand rather openly," whereas "the college politician does it carefully. He plays it very shrewdly, and he has such a gift of speech that he could make black sound as if it were white any time that he chooses."[32] Another time, Wilson observed, "After dealing with the college politician I find the men I am dealing with now seem like amateurs."[33] He had West in mind when he said that.

Happy and fulfilled as Wilson became after his entry into politics, he did not entirely forget academic life. In 1914, at the height of his legislative success as president and before the outbreak of World War I, he confessed to his confidant, Colonel Edward M. House, that he still had nightmares about "some of his old Princeton enemies." House also observed, "Whenever we have no governmental business to discuss, somehow or other, we drift into his life at Princeton and his troubles there, showing . . . how deeply the iron entered his soul." Nearly a decade after House made those comments, in the last three months of his life, Wilson approached Raymond Fosdick, who was then working for the Rockefeller Foundation, about what he called "an educational matter." He told Fosdick he believed that his greatest contributions lay not in politics but as a teacher and college president, and he wanted to try his hand again at reforming a university. Nothing came of this scheme, which Fosdick later called "the nostalgic dream of an old and crippled warrior as he thinks over the battles of his younger days."[34]

In fact, Wilson did not die disenchanted with politics and longing for academic life. Soon after he broached his idea to Fosdick, he started planning to run again for president in 1924, and he laid out a policy program for another term in the White House. Mercifully, death intervened to quell those fantasies and spare him from witnessing the Democrats' internecine warfare and debacle of that year. Going to his grave dreaming about both academia and politics brought a fitting end to Wilson's life. This most successful of presidents in private pursuits owed those successes in large measure to his political vocation, and his achievements as an academic had propelled and guided him to his triumph and tragedy in public life.

## NOTES

1. The other great political scientists would include Charles E. Merriam, Harold Lasswell, Robert Dahl, V. O. Key, and Quincy Wright. The other great university presidents would include Charles William Eliot (Harvard), Daniel Coit Gilman (Johns Hopkins), William Rainey Harper (Chicago), David Starr Jordan (Stanford), Andrew D. White (Cornell), Robert M. Hutchins (Chicago), Kingman Brewster (Yale), and perhaps also Clark Kerr (California–Berkeley) and Robert F. Goheen (Princeton).

2. See Stockton Axson, "The Princeton Controversy," Feb. 1925, Ray Stannard Baker Papers, Library of Congress, box 99 [hereafter Baker Papers, LC]; George McLean Harper interview, Nov. 12, 1925, ibid., box 107; Edmund Wilson, "Woodrow Wilson at Princeton," *New Republic,* Nov. 30, 1927, in Wilson, *The Shores of Light: A Literary Chronicle of the Twenties and Thirties* (New York: Farrar, Straus and Giroux, 1952), 298–324. For two interpretations that draw this parallel at length, see Alexander L. George and Juliette L. George, *Woodrow Wilson and Colonel House: A Personality Study* (New York: John Day, 1956), and Sigmund Freud and William C. Bullitt, *Thomas Woodrow Wilson: Twenty-eighth President of the United States: A Psychological Study* (Boston: Houghton Mifflin, 1967). For an example of the disagreement, see John Milton Cooper Jr., *Woodrow Wilson: A Biography* (New York: Alfred A. Knopf, 2009).

3. See James Axtell, *The Making of Princeton University: From Woodrow Wilson to the Present* (Princeton: Princeton University Press, 2006), 14; for Jacobus's advice to Wilson (hereafter WW), see, for example, *The Papers of Woodrow Wilson,* Arthur S. Link et al., eds., 69 vols. (Princeton: Princeton University Press, 1966–1994), 17:458–59 (Oct. 29, 1907) (hereafter *PWW*).

4. WW to Ellen Axson, Oct. 30, 1883, *PWW,* 2:500–501.

5. Joseph R. Wilson to WW, Dec. 22, 1879, *PWW,* 1:589.

6. On Wilson's intellectual and literary awakening and his stab at the law, see Cooper, *Wilson,* 26–41.

7. For Wilson's last-minute inquiries about journalism and a government job and his concerns about losing touch with real world affairs, see Cooper, *Wilson,* 54, 57.

8. Although much has been written about Wilson's work as a political scientist, nearly all of it has been within the confines of trying to predict his later career in elective office and does not evaluate much on its own merits. The best account of his contributions to the field can be found in Henry Wilkinson Bragdon, *Woodrow Wilson: The Academic Years* (Cambridge, Mass.: Belknap Press of Harvard University Press, 1967). See also Wilson, *The State: Elements of Historical and Practical Politics. A Sketch of Institutional History and Administration* (Boston: D. C. Heath, 1889);"Editorial Note: Wilson's 'The State,' " *PWW,* 6:244–52; "Editorial Note: Wilson's 'The Study of Administration,' " *PWW,* 5:357–59.

9. Edward S. Corwin interview by Henry W. Bragdon, June 6, 1939, Henry W. Bragdon Collection, Seeley G. Mudd Library, Princeton University Library, Box 1.

10. Wilson's breakdown in 1896 has spawned speculation and argument about whether this was an early symptom of the cardiovascular condition that led to his major stroke in 1919. For assertions that this stroke did stem from such a condition, see *PWW*. 9:507n2; Edwin M. Weinstein, "Woodrow Wilson's Neurological Illness," *Journal of American History*, 57:2 (Sept. 1970), 333, and *Woodrow Wilson: A Medical and Psychological Biography* (Princeton: Princeton University Press, 1981), 140–49. These assertions and the larger ascription of neurological illness have been attacked in several articles by Alexander and Juliette George. For a summary and analysis of the controversy, see Dorothy Ross, "Woodrow Wilson and the Case for Psychohistory," *Journal of American History*, 69:3 (Dec. 1982), 659–90. On Wilson's reimmersion in Burke and the promise of "P.O.P." see Cooper, *Wilson*, 73, 76–77.

11. On the early connection and similarity with Roosevelt, see John Milton Cooper Jr., *The Warrior and the Priest: Woodrow Wilson and Theodore Roosevelt* (Cambridge, Mass.: Harvard University Press, 1983), esp. 59–62.

12. WW speech, Nov. 16, 1907, *PWW*, 17:500.

13. WW to Hart, June 3, 1889, *PWW*. 6:243. On Wilson's conservative fling and its abandonment, see Cooper, *Warrior and Priest*, 118–29, and *Wilson*, 91–92, 105–109.

14. WW to Joline, April 29, 1907, *PWW*, 17:124.

15. Jessie Wilson Sayre interview, Dec. 1, 1925, Baker Papers, LC, box 121; Jessie W. Sayre to Baker, [April 25, 1927], ibid.

16. WW to John Rogers Williams, Sept. 2, 1904, *PWW*, 15:462; WW memorandum, ca. Dec. 3, 1909, *PWW*, 19:550. Princeton would not grant an undergraduate degree to an African-American until 1947, but the applicant Wilson discouraged in 1909 did go on to receive a degree from the Princeton Theological Seminary.

17. Mary Yates diary entry, July 31, [1908], *PWW*, 18:386; *Daily Princetonian*, April 3, 1909, *PWW*, 18:149. For a more extended treatment of Wilson's racial attitudes and actions, see Gary Gerstle, "Race and Nation in the Thought of Woodrow Wilson," in John Milton Cooper Jr., ed., *Reconsidering Wilson: Progressivism, Internationalism, War, and Peace* (Baltimore: Johns Hopkins University Press, 2008), 93–124, and Cooper, "American Sphinx: Woodrow Wilson and Race," in Cooper and Thomas J. Knock, eds., *Jefferson, Lincoln, and Wilson: The American Dilemma of Race and Democracy* (Charlottesville: University of Virginia Press, 2010), 145–62.

18. WW to Ellen Axson Wilson, July 19, 1902, *PWW*, 14:27.

19. *Daily Princetonian* editorial, "The Quad System," [Oct. 2, 1907], quoted in *PWW*, 17:140.

20. For a poignant expression of parental dislike of the clubs, see a letter from the father of three sons who had varied experiences with them: James A. Green to WW, June 17, 1910, *PWW*, 20:536–38.

21. Norman Thomas to WW, June 11, 1908, *PWW*, 18:335–36.

22. On Wilson's being hired at Princeton, see Cooper, *Wilson*, 61–62. On Wilson's hiring practices and treatment of the faculty, see Axtell, *The Making of Princeton University*, 49–61.

23. Henry B. Thompson to Moses Taylor Pyne, July 30, 1907, *PWW*, 17:308.

24. David B. Jones to WW, March 15, 1904, *PWW*, 15:191–92.

25. On Wilson's relationship with Hibben, see Cooper, *Wilson*, 70, 93–94.

26. Andew F. West, "Abstract of President Wilson's Speech to the Faculty," Oct. 7, 1907, *PWW*, 17:424. See also entries in William Starr Myers's diary, Sept. 30, Oct. 7, [1907], *PWW*, 17:408–409, 424.

27. On the firing, see Axtell, *The Making of Princeton University*, 55–58.

28. Robert K. Root, quoted in William Starr Myers, ed., *Woodrow Wilson: Some Princeton Memories* (Princeton: Princeton University Press, 1946), 13–14.

29. Myers, ed., *WW: Princeton Memories*, 58–59.

30. Axson, "The Princeton Controversy," [Feb. 1925], Baker Papers, LC, box 99.

31. The connection between Wilson's health and his behavior after 1906 is made most strongly in Weinstein, *WW: Medical and Psychological Biography*, 165–80.

32. WW speech, Sept. 2, 1912, *PWW*, 25:68.

33. WW speech, May 25, 1911, *PWW*, 23:93.

34. Edward M. House diary, entries for Dec. 12, 1913, and Jan. 22, 1914, *PWW*, 29:33–34, 163; WW to Fosdick, Oct. 22, 1923, *PWW*, 68:451; Fosdick, *Chronicle of a Generation: An Autobiography* (New York: Harper & Brothers, 1958), 23–31. On Wilson's academic and political schemes at the end of his life, see James Axtell, "The Bad Dream: Wilson on Princeton—After Princeton," *Princeton University Library Chronicle*, 69:3 (Spring 2008), 401–36, and Cooper, *Wilson*, 590–94.

# The Unappreciated Legacy

## *Wilson, Princeton, and the Ideal of the American State*

Mark R. Nemec

Despite its interdisciplinary ambitions, this essay remains a product of its disciplinary home, political science, and its subfield, American political development. American political development posits that three major forces drive public policy and political action: interests (individual and collective), institutions (governmental and societal), and ideas (public and private). At the confluence of the later two, institutions and ideas, my larger work on universities and the leaders who guided them has resided.[1]

In assessing Woodrow Wilson's impact upon the development of American higher education and its relationship to the American state, one is reminded of Emerson's declaration that "an institution is the lengthened shadow of one man."[2] While social scientists and historians might quibble about the specific implications of this assertion, it provides a useful touchstone for our broader consideration of Wilson's legacy.

Upon first glance, Wilson's time as academic executive and political leader can suggest a pall as much as a shadow. While guiding Princeton, Wilson experienced several early successes.[3] But the latter half of his tenure was also marked by some significant disappointments, most notably in attempting to reform campus intellectual life and to develop a first-class graduate school at the heart of the campus.[4] After a number of pitched battles (primarily with Dean Andrew Fleming West and his allies), Wilson's tenure came to an "abrupt and acrimonious end."[5] In the White House, Wilson undertook even grander initiatives to reform civil service and the party system. Similar to his tenure in academia, however, his efforts often fell short. Seeking to reform both the contemporary practice and perception of public administration, he struggled to achieve his full vision. Specifically, in regard to governmental structure, Wilson "could do little to secure the integrity of the Civil Service Commission or the professional ideal," and he "failed to place relations between party and bureaucracy on a new plane. His programmatic achievements remained personal and circumstantial and left this basic structural tension between party power and administrative modernization unresolved."[6]

More broadly in the realm of public opinion, Wilson found that "the complexity and subtly of the ideas . . . [he] had developed did not lend themselves to effective translation into political speech intended for a general public audience, or to the political practice necessary for governing the diverse, contentious, 'multiform' American polity."[7] These assessments are typical of institutional and policy scholars in the field of American political development. A common theme in their appraisal of Wilson's academic and political leadership is that his middling execution inhibited his ability to achieve his lofty ambitions.

At the same time, Wilson's steady progression from university president to governor to chief executive of the United States is rightly recounted as representing a high point for the "collegiate ideal."[8] Whatever his shortcomings in execution, through his biography (professor, university administrator, political leader) and his progressive philosophy, Wilson has come to embody the era's movement to apply knowledge to public affairs. Yet, to view Wilson's presidency at Princeton as primarily a preamble to his time as governor of New Jersey and later president of the United States is to miss the fact that his tenures connect not only personally but institutionally as well. In other words, although Wilson's legacy at individual postings may have been marked by narrow successes, Wilson's shadow is longer, his impact greater, if we view it in the context of advancing higher education's place within, as well as support of, one larger institution, the modern American state.

Fundamental to our evaluation of Wilson's legacy is that he significantly advanced the idea of a burgeoning national state and an emerging university closely connected to it. In the long evolution of political development and state building, defining rhetorical and ideological gains is as influential as short-term organizational and policy victories. This is especially true in the American context, where political ideas are essential to our national conceit. As political theorist Eldon Eisenach noted, "Our only source of a common American identity is political; our fundamental political ideas are largely constitutive of our personal ideas as Americans. If the moral and intellectual integrity of our most basic political ideas is in doubt, so, too are its ideological products and the authority of political groupings organized around those ideologies."[9] Wilson exemplified this idea while speaking in Chicago on "The Relation of University Education to Commerce" in 1902. "Every man who fights under the flag of the United States fights under an abstraction," Wilson commented. "He fights for a thing he never saw and he never can see. He fights for a poetic idea, and when we speak of the nation, we speak as men who are ignorant, unless we have some imaginative and sympathetic conception of the parts of the country in which we do not live."[10] Recognizing the intellectual underpinnings of the state means that as we assess Wilson's legacy of connecting institutions of higher learning and institutions of government, we must look to his public pronouncements as much as his policy initiatives. We must also look to his rhetorical power and efficacy. Early in his career when discussing the British Liberal statesman John Bright, Wilson acknowledged the importance of being substantively articulate: "Eloquence is not of the lips alone. Eloquence is never begotten by empty pates. Groveling minds are never winged with high and noble thoughts. Eloquence consists not in sonorous sound or brilliant phrases. Thought is the fibre, thought is the pith of eloquence. Eloquence lies in the thought, not in the throat. . . . It is persuasion inspired by Conviction."[11]

At the end of his Princeton tenure, Wilson's fluent persuasiveness was recognized by the Princeton faculty in their departing commendation: "Throughout his administration it has been his practice to devote his extraordinary powers of speech and debate to the public discussion of leading questions of educational and national interest. It is not too much to say that in this function he has won a national reputation and has brought fame to Princeton and secured for her a position of leadership in the educational movements in the country."[12] But for all his elocution, Wilson's greatest rhetorical impact was in legitimating the conception of American universities in service to, and as an extension of, the national state.

To properly assess Wilson's legacy, we must define what is meant by the modern American state. Scholars of American political development have long recognized that while universities were structurally independent from formal government, they were inextricably linked to governmental apparatus and authority. The emergence of the American university and the building of the new American state were not simply correlated, they were causally and institutionally linked. Considerations of the state from Max Weber onward have underscored that "the state must be considered as more than the 'government.' It is the continuous administrative, legal, bureaucratic, and coercive systems that attempt not only to structure relationships *between* civil society and public authority in a polity but also to structure many crucial relationships within civil society as well."[13] Educational institutions that structure ideas and define expertise come to be extensions of the state itself. In broadest terms, "the knowledge basis of state action, as well as the process by which the state itself influences the development and application of social knowledge, are . . . of central importance."[14] Taking this idea one step further, Mary Douglas emphasized that when considering political institutions, "half of [the] task is to demonstrate this cognitive process at the foundation of the social order. The other half is to demonstrate that the individual's most elementary cognitive process depends on social institutions."[15] Both streams of scholarship conclude that the state is an intellectual construct as much as an institutional one. Thus, the university can be seen as an extension of the state itself.

Wilson's own writings anticipated and popularized this conception—he was a scholar of politics, after all. While president of Princeton, Wilson had occasion to address the New Jersey State Teachers' Association in 1909 on "The State and the Citizen's Relation to It." He told the educators assembled, "You work in the stuff of the human mind when you conduct a state," and, "The process of the life of the State is a great organic process of the mind."[16] For Wilson, the state drew upon both intellectual underpinnings and institutional structure to achieve its legitimacy. In that same address Wilson extended the sentiment he had expressed more than a decade earlier in his notes on the "Philosophy of Politics": "The only brief and adequate definition of the State that I have been able to find, is that which describes it as 'a people organized for law within a definite territory.' It seems to me that that is an enlightening definition; because it states so clearly and succinctly what the object of the State is. The object of the State is institutions, is law, is those arrangements upon which we can all agree, in which we can all be ranked and harnessed in order to accomplish some common object."[17]

Significantly, in this definition, the power of the state lies as much in the shared conceptions of its people and its intellectual underpinnings as in its formal authority and institutional structures.

In the American context, especially the era of the new American state (ca. 1877–1920), this confluence was heightened as the movement to build new national institutions and to reorient existing ones in a nationalist fashion "was taken up . . . by an emergent intelligentsia rooted in a revitalized professional sector and a burgeoning university sector. These intellectuals championed a fundamental reconstruction of the mode of governmental operations to be centered in an administrative realm possessing 'finish, efficacy, and permanence.' "[18] This intelligentsia solidified the link of the university to the state by inventing a "conception of citizenship that stipulated that the possession of social knowledge entailed the duty of reflecting on and articulating ideas of national public good," and by demanding that universities and other quasi-state institutions had a "special responsibility" to promote the public good. These universities "served as something like a national 'church'—the main repository and protector of common American values, common American meanings, and common American identities."[19] Although the separation of church and state has long defined American political development, so too does the link of our national church—the university—to the state.

In the broadest context, Wilson's legacy reflects what might be called the transitive theory of American political development. Universities are essential to political participation and activity. The single largest influence upon likelihood and nature of participation in the electoral process is level of education.[20] As Tocqueville first observed, political participation and activity are crucial to our national institutions and identity. Therefore, if both of these statements are true, then universities are integral to our national institutions and identity.

Wilson's words and actions contributed to this construct in a major way. In his speeches Wilson advanced a notion of administration that depended on universities to educate and refine. Additionally, not long removed from Reconstruction, he emphasized the role of universities in crafting a truly national identity and concept of citizenship. As a leader, he sought to dedicate Princeton to "the nation's service" and, finally, as President of the United States, he enlisted the nation's universities in the war effort.

The son of a minister who first matriculated at Presbyterian Davidson College in North Carolina, Wilson could naturally take the pulpit of one parish (Princeton) and call upon it to serve a greater public good. Likewise, the Progressive movement for reform which he promoted as governor and president pursued efficiency as "a moral concept. . . . Efficient administration was 'good'; inefficient administration was 'bad.'"[21] These were not discrete movements. The moral dimension of the effort to build a new American state resided as much in academic as in religious institutions.

From his earliest days in academia, Wilson thought that higher education needed not just to serve the state but to help define it as well. "Higher education should be made an ally of the state," he said. Praising the University of Berlin as one of the best examples of a beneficial interaction between government and higher learning, he recognized the "body of able and disinterested critics" produced by the university who found themselves "at the very doors of the gov[ernmen]t." These critics could "see the small technical things which the nation could never see" and could function as "the eyes of the nation in finding out the personal and particular features of administration."[22] At the start of his career, Wilson himself sought to be those eyes of the nation, though not, as one might expect, through the civil service. In 1887, while at Bryn Mawr, Wilson wrote somewhat overeagerly to University of Michigan president James Burrill Angell asking for his assistance in securing an appointment under Secretary of State Thomas Bayard, with whom Angell was currently working on the International Commission on Canadian Fisheries. Angell politely wrote back suggesting that Wilson pursue a more appropriate posting, given his limited experience. Humbled, but still seeking to explain himself, Wilson stressed that his ambition was to "vivify my chosen studies. . . . I love the stir of the world; that stir is what I chiefly desire to study and explain and I know I cannot scarcely explain it from Teufelsdrockh's tower."[23]

In this private correspondence Wilson extended the argument he had made publicly concerning the need for applied rather than simply scholarly expertise in an article on "The Study of Administration" earlier that same year.[24] Rather than merely emphasizing that the developing American state needed academic insight, Wilson's letter to Angell acknowledged that his scholarship itself (and implicitly that of all who study politics and public affairs) needed administrative experience to be fully effective. In this individual effort, Wilson embodied the larger institutional efforts of university presidents throughout the state-building era. Universities did not simply wait to be tapped to offer their service. Rather, the institutional entrepreneurs who guided the nation's leading universities actively sought opportunities to help the new American state navigate rising challenges of the modern era. Similar to these soon-to-be peers, Wilson advanced a conception of the relationship between universities and the national government which was bi- rather than uni-directional. This vision meant that universities were not simply to be subjects of the state, but rather extensions of it, affirming administrative knowledge and its uses that would buttress governmental authority.

Wilson pursued this theme throughout his early academic career in speeches and writings. This singular focus was sometimes bemoaned by those attending speeches that were ostensibly on other topics. In 1903, for example, a Boston reporter covering Wilson's speech on state education noted that those in the "audience learned little on (the topic)," but they did learn a great deal about "the relation of education to political life and development."[25] Consistent with this conceit, while addressing the New Jersey State Teachers' Association in 1909 on "The State and the Citizen's Relation to It," Wilson emphasized the intellectual basis of state authority and action before arguing that the education that helped foster this intellectual basis was not just about the transfer of knowledge, but was rather a "process of association." Considering education and the state in concert, Wilson continued:

> Education consists in getting out of people this narrowness [regionalism], this localization, this pettiness, this provincialism of mind. Obviously, this is a function of society.
>
> What I am trying to argue is that the State is not merely an artificial arrangement which we have thought convenient. It contains in it almost all the vital processes of the human mind, all the simulations, all those things which quicken the mind to be something big instead of something little, all those things which enable men to think in terms of masses, in terms of movements, in terms of great moral advances, in terms of great intellectual conceptions.[26]

In concluding his remarks, he stressed to those assembled, "as teachers we ought to remind ourselves. . . . What education does is to knit the fabric together."[27] For Wilson, educational institutions were central threads that held the tapestry of state together.

Given his stature as a political scientist and a university president, Wilson was uniquely positioned to apply his theorizing about education's relationship to the state. He sought to apply this concept more broadly in concert with his peers at the Association of American Universities (AAU).

Founded in 1900 by fifteen of the nation's leading research universities, the AAU sought to coordinate policies and standards much like a national university.[28] During his time at Princeton, Wilson's attendance at AAU's annual meetings was somewhat limited by his personal rivalry with Andrew Fleming West, who by virtue of his status as dean of the graduate school was also invited to participate and did so actively.[29] However, in January 1910, Wilson accepted an invitation from A. Lawrence Lowell to present a paper on the "Position and Importance of the Arts Course as Distinct from the Professional and Semi-Professional Course," and undertook the multi-day journey to Madison, Wisconsin, for the AAU's annual meeting.

Given its subject, one would not expect Wilson's presentation to give any consideration to the intellectual underpinnings of the American state. But because Wilson saw educational institutions naturally linked to the state, he began his talk on the specifics of curriculum with a general discussion of the state and its citizens:

> You do not need to be told how practically all difficulties of our national life, all the difficulties in the field of statesmanship, I mean, arise out of the jealousies and the competitions of special interests and the lack of understanding between them or of a common object. . . .
>
> [I]t [is] the business of a college to regeneralize each generation as it [comes] on, to give it a view of the stage as a whole before it [is] drawn off to occupy only a little corner of the stage and forget the rest.[30]

Effective statesmanship began with common understandings. It was the mission, "the business," of institutions of higher learning to convey these understandings to their students.

Wilson argued that these understandings were not simply patriotic sentiments. Rather they were practices that allowed for dispassionate assessment and administration. "I believe that the most desirable discipline for the rising youth is that he should by education be able to acquire the habit and the discrimination which must underlie the habit of stating a fact without stating a opinion."[31] Furthermore, the complexity of the times demanded that this habit be shared broadly and by all university students. As Wilson stressed, "The discipline, therefore, that the modern man needs is the discipline of general preparation for the difficult tasks of our own day."[32] In this sentiment, Wilson extended the consideration he had made two years earlier, when delivering the presidential address to the Association of Colleges and Preparatory Schools of the Middle States and Maryland. "There is another sort of education which this age needs, and needs more than any preceding age: that kind which for many ages has borne amongst us the name of liberal education. If ever an age stood in need of the statesmanship of the mind, this is that age; if ever an age stood in need of men lifted above their fellows in their point of view, who can see the significance of knowledge and of affairs, this is the age."[33]

Strikingly, in both talks, Wilson did not presume that such education must come from a prescribed course of study dedicated to public affairs. In fact, "for my own part," he claimed, "I must say that in my own studies, in the field of politics, I have found more true political interpretation in the poets, than I have ever found in the systematic writers on political science."[34] Coming from someone whose seminal article, "The Study of Administration," still reverberates through the scholarly study of politics and public administration, this claim can perhaps best be described as poetic license.[35] At his core, Wilson believed that through general studies and detailed courses, the university could lay the groundwork for thoughtful and effective statesmanship and state action: "When we speak, therefore, of the relation of the arts course to the professional courses, we are speaking of the relation of the foundations to the edifice, we are speaking of the relation of the understanding to the career. It is the relation between comprehension and action, and you cannot establish this relationship successfully in any other way."[36] Wilson understood that the intellectual foundations of the new American state needed to be laid by the nation's universities in a way that ensured common understandings and structured collective actions.

The mutual understanding necessary to build the American state did not simply require an educated citizenry sharing a common framework for assessment and action. Equally important was the intellectual base and supporting institutional structures that fostered a shared national identity. By virtue of his words, his actions, and his biography, Wilson promoted the consecration of the university as a "national church" closely linked to the American state.

Though somewhat difficult to follow because it does not exhibit his usual rhetorical panache, Wilson's notion of national identity is expressed in his notes for an address in December 1902 at Brooklyn's Lafayette Avenue Church entitled "The University and the Country." He begins by framing his discussion around the core elements of national identity. For Wilson, "our pride in the past of our race and country, [has been defined] not so much because of individual achievement as of the *motive* of individual achievement,—*idealistic, common effort,* unselfish and for the whole." Thus, for Americans, " '*Public spirit*' has become our word." Interestingly, Wilson then notes that "the University has served these ideals and methods . . . by being a *community* of ideals." He further emphasizes that the university has achieved this through the fostering of ideas and support of institutions as much as by its instruction, suggesting that "not learning so much as the *Spirit of learning* has made our universities seed ground."[37] In summary, Wilson believed that universities stood "beside the Church as *vehicles of spirit.*" They did so by propagating: "1) the influence of individual idealists, 2) national rather than provincial sympathies, 3) the spirit of affairs, and 4) the central religious idea of *service.*"[38] When Wilson spoke of spirit and service, he was speaking of concepts consistent with his second point, extended beyond regional boundaries in an effort to define national identity. This concept of national identity was a cornerstone of the new American state and universities' connection to it.

The scourge of provincialism and the American university's role in reducing it was a recurring theme for Wilson. Speaking just weeks before he drafted his notes, Wilson found occasion to share such sentiments when addressing a collection of Chicago businessman on the relationship of the university to commerce. "You know gentlemen, as well as I do, that the great incubus upon this country is its provincialism. . . . It is downright provincial not to have an imaginative conception of what the rest of the country is like, and that is the imaginative conception the university is meant to give to men."[39] He gave this theme its fullest expression in April 1903 with an address to the Princeton Club in Philadelphia entitled "National and University Life." According to a news report, Wilson highlighted universities' relation to national identity. "Professor Wilson began his address by referring to the greatness of national life in this country, and how its character can be set forward in many ways by the universities." He recognized the extent to which this effort exemplified American exceptionalism. " 'In the midst of this life the university stands and asks what can it do. In no other country is the university called upon to do this.' " To Wilson, the university was a cornerstone of American exceptionalism and national identity, " 'I love to think of a university in this country as a community of ideals. The same ambitions, the same attitudes towards the national life. You cannot do this without a community life.' " The university was both the intellectual foundation and institutional magnet for the national community. The university must attract students from "all parts of the country" and "create . . . a national type of man" to fulfill its vision, mission, and purpose.[40] Wilson saw the university as part of a tapestry creating a national citizenry through the formulation of national ideas and the extension of national institutions.

Wilson identified the manifestation of this national identity not only in the university but in the apparatus of government as well. In a speech before the New York Southern Society in December 1906, Wilson emphasized that both civic duty and modern social challenges "required an ever-present catholicity of sympathy and of judgment to think of this country, as every citizen should, as a single whole, a thing to be served not merely in its parts and separate interests, as the states are intended to serve it, but also in its entirety as the Federal Government is intended to serve it, keeping all interests harmonious, all powers cooperative."[41] This subtle expression of nationalism is important for two reasons. First, the magnitude of the institutional setting cannot be overemphasized. Asking the audience of a social club dedicated to "cherish[ing] and perpetuat[ing] the memories and traditions of the Southern people" to look beyond their local ties and praising the federal government at a formal gathering less than a generation removed from Reconstruction was, to say the least, bold.[42] Second, Wilson articulated a vision of government that did not dictate terms to the citizenry, but rather harmonized the various interests of society. Implicitly, this vision necessitated that the state play a coordinating function by weaving the support of various institutions into an authoritative whole.

Though the leading universities could and did in many ways coordinate through the Association of American Universities, the United States did not effectively coordinate its whole educational system. The federal Bureau of Education was buried in the Department of Interior, and its longtime leader, William T. Harris, was so ineffective that in 1904 University of Chicago president William Rainey Harper sought to remove Harris by convincing his fellow presidents to create a lectureship to entice him from office.[43] Wilson did not actively participate in this failed effort, but he did express frustration with the inability of the country to produce a national system to link all of its educational institutions. In his presidential address to the Association of Colleges and Preparatory Schools of the Middle States and Maryland, he emphasized that "in the purpose and method there is no difference between school and college. We have neglected the union and organization of forces. We have divided our learning as if we had done away with our Union of States and had dissolved the federal government into a body of local principalities; *and so we have neglected the very genius of our race, which is the genius of organization*"[44] In this formulation, we see both the promise and the limitations of the new American state. Universities could shape a national identity and extend our national institutions because they stood beyond local governmental structures. But local school districts were often tied to what Stephen Skowronek refers to as the state of courts and parties, and as such did not necessarily coordinate or extend national state authority.[45]

Leading universities were central institutions for the creation of national authority, and Wilson sought to place Princeton squarely among its peers in the narrative of state-building even before he ascended to its presidency. In his address, "Princeton in the Nation's Service," given in conjunction with the university's 150th-anniversary celebration in 1896, Wilson called upon the newly renamed institution to "do its right service" and to embrace "the presence of men in every problem, of the significance of truth for guidance as well as for knowledge, of the potency of ideas, of the promise and the hope that shine in the face of all knowledge." The tenor of the times required no less. Wilson closed his remarks by reminding not just the audience but all of those in higher education of "the compulsion of the national life. We dare not keep aloof and closet ourselves while a nation comes to its maturity."[46] As the faculty speaker, Wilson did not directly acknowledge the curricular shift implicit in Princeton's titular emergence as a university.[47] Nonetheless, in this speech he did begin to articulate a new vision not just for Princeton, but for American higher education in general.

Six years later, at his inauguration as Princeton's president, he provided a fuller vision. The subtle evolution in title from the slightly subservient "Princeton *in* the Nation's Service" to the more active "Princeton *for* the Nation's Service" gave a fair hint of this. Harkening back to his sesquicentennial speech, he began by taking some artistic license and recalling his primary task for that talk as being "to speak of the memories with which

Princeton men heartened themselves."[48] Wilson's 1896 address was more than a simple exercise in nostalgia. Nonetheless, in comparing his previous speech, Wilson found his present task "more delicate" and "more difficult." Whatever the merits of Wilson's assessment, there is no denying that the nationalist ambition for higher education had been advanced in the previous six years. The founding of the AAU in 1900 and a last final push for a congressionally supported national university by perpetual proponent and former Wyoming governor John W. Hoyt in 1899–1900 had both elevated the question of how the emerging university would serve as a national institution in coordination with the American state.

Wilson was uniquely qualified to define the intellectual framework, if not the actions necessary, for the university to embrace this role. His stated goal was to "assess our present purposes and power and sketch the creed by which we shall be willing to live in the ideas to come." He used his platform to propose a slew of initiatives focusing on instruction, curriculum, and advanced education. Yet he emphasized that "when planning for Princeton, we are planning for the country. The service of institutions of learning is not private, but public." The complexity of the era demanded that universities produce a steady supply of "efficient and enlightened men" to serve the nation."[49]

More importantly, by defining the universities' "creed" of service, Wilson had moved beyond the simple notion of university as factory, filling orders for national needs. Rather, he trumpeted an agenda-setting role whereby Princeton would tackle public problems that called for thoughtfulness and devotion as well as efficiency and would seek to "not merely release the faculties of men for their own use, but also to quicken their social understanding, instruct their consciences, and give them the catholic vision of those who know their just relations to their fellowman." Thus, Wilson concluded dramatically, Princeton could support the intellectual apparatus so necessary for the national state: "Every concrete thing that [America] has done has seemed to rise out of some abstract principle, some vision of the mind. And in days quiet and troubled alike Princeton has stood for the nation's service, to produce men and patriots. . . . A new age is before us, in which, it would seem, we must lead the world. No doubt we shall set an example unprecedented not only in the magnitude and telling perfection of our industries and arts, but also in the splendid scale and studied detail of our university establishments: the spirit of the age will lift us to every great enterprise."[50] The ambitions of this effort were significant both for Princeton institutionally and Wilson personally. As W. Barksdale Maynard notes in his biographical treatment of Wilson's Princeton years, "to reenvision the American college completely, to restructure it, gave Woodrow Wilson what he had long been seeking, a poetical and oratorical outlet from the cramping confines of academic life. More than ever before, he would act the role of an *educational statesman*. He would dream up great ideas and make them practical."[51]

Wilson was not the only academic leader of this era to pursue or be placed in the role of educational statesman. Arthur Twining Hadley of Yale, Nicholas Murray Butler of Columbia, James Burrill Angell of Michigan, and Charles Van Hise of Wisconsin were among those who linked their universities to the new American state as institutional entrepreneurs. However, one could argue that as the only bona fide scholar of politics in the group, Wilson was the one "educational statesmen" who used the university pulpit to spread an emerging narrative. Upon taking office, Wilson worked diligently to ensure that Princeton could meet the promise of what he described in his inaugural as a new age. Beyond his administrative duties, Wilson also continued to refine and evangelize his vision for higher education by advancing the notion that university building was state building and that academic reforms were political reforms.

Wilson did not see his newness to the role as requiring contrition. As the *New York Times* noted while reporting a speech given at the Brooklyn Institute of the Arts in the first months of his tenure, Wilson had begun "with the statement that being one of the newest of college Presidents, he was probably better able to theorize regarding the functions of the university than an older president, who was handicapped by fact and experience." He concluded his talk by noting that "the function of the University of the United States is the service of the nation, the preparation of specialized minds, not in the sense of being narrowed but in the sense of being tempered for hard and delicate use."[52] Wilson was not shy about his conviction that Princeton was uniquely situated to arguably be the "University of the United States." During April 1903, in an effort to solicit funds for a school of law and public institutions, he told Andrew Carnegie, "you have been kind enough to express your interest in Princeton as what I believe she really is, the college most saturated with the traditions and political beliefs which have made America great and democracy triumphant."[53]

Despite the attitude expressed in his Brooklyn speech about fact and experience, Wilson continued to speak on the functions and uses of the university, both Princeton specifically and its peer institutions more generally, far beyond his "novice" years. Reiterating his Brooklyn Institute ideas seven years later while giving the Phi Beta Kappa address at Harvard, Wilson referred to colleges as the "root of our intellectual life as a nation" which lay at the "heart of American social training and intellectual and moral enlightenment."[54] Wilson was often outspoken while advancing his views regarding the university and its role in furthering the new American state. When University of Michigan regent Walter Sawyer was inquiring about Wilson's viability as a replacement for retiring president Angell, Franklin Giddings of Columbia's school of political science replied that to some Wilson had "hurt himself by talking too much about various things." At the same time, Giddings stressed to Sawyer that he would give Wilson a most heartfelt endorsement because he stood for the very highest ideals in "education, in public duty and in national policy."[55]

Though there was general agreement among AAU peers that Wilson stood for the highest ideals in education, there was some dispute among other academics about where the institution Wilson had guided stood. Most notably, Henry Smith Pritchett, former M.I.T. president and head of the Carnegie Foundation for the Advancement of Teaching (CFAT), discussed Princeton's history in the foundation's second annual report published in 1907. He wrote somewhat churlishly, "On October 22, 1896, the college celebrated its 150th anniversary of the signing of the first charter, and on that occasion adopted the title Princeton University. The reasons for this step are not entirely clear."[56] Pritchett proceeded to critique Princeton and to disparage the AAU when he compared Princeton and Johns Hopkins: "Both [are] noble institutions, both are centers of intellectual and moral influence, but one is in its spirit, its methods, its atmosphere essentially a university, the other a great college. To bring together as an 'Association of American Universities' institutions differing so widely in their essential characteristics means agreement only on generalities, a process which is not likely to raise the standards of the weaker."[57]

Needless to say, Wilson took issue with this characterization and was blunt in his response. Acknowledging that Princeton's renaming in 1896 might have been overly ambitious, Wilson responded that Pritchett's "intimations that Princeton is less entitled to name than some others who have long borne it without question is not justified." Wilson acknowledged that there was a "great confusion of standards," and "some of our universities are universities in the German sense and some are not." Nonetheless, he argued "it does not seem to me a single standard, introduced virtually by the Johns Hopkins, should settle the question in the face of innumerable historical circumstances."[58] Wilson concluded by noting that Princeton had made great strides in the last decade, was deserving of the university title and that he would one day "insist on having you [Pritchett] down here to find out what we are really doing."[59]

Regardless of such contemporary critiques, Wilson's imprint in elevating Princeton as a modern university is undeniable. As John Milton Cooper concludes when discussing Wilson's Princeton tenure, "Wilson had not labored in vain. [Henry] Fine judged his legacy correctly when he told Wilson's first biographer in 1925, '[W]hen all is said and in spite of the controversies, Wilson *made* Princeton. . . . He gave it its intellectual stimulus.' "[60] In "making" Princeton, Wilson not only established its preeminence as an institution of higher learning; he also created an institution that would fulfill his vision of the university as connected with and supportive of the American people, American ideals, and the American state.

Wilson's educational legacy did not abruptly end when he left Nassau Hall. For though both the governorship and the presidency offered little formal authority to shape education, Wilson's conception of and interest in the university's relation to the state meant he could still exert great influence. Just as significantly, with the advance of the First World War, Wilson's drafting of universities for military training and preparation embodied his vision of universities as extensions of the national state.

Now possessing the power of the presidency, Wilson maintained his view of education and its role in driving the intellectual and community basis of state authority. Delivering the commencement address at the Naval Academy in 1914, for example, Wilson told the new graduates, "you are not serving a government, gentlemen; you are serving a people."[61] Echoing the generalist themes articulated in a number of his previous speeches, Wilson recognized that though these graduates were unlike the university graduates to whom he usually spoke in that they were "trained for a special thing," he did not want them to adopt the narrowness of the professional point of view and instead hoped they would connect their specialized training and education to the broader American state and its ideals.[62] Wilson emphasized the need for a generalist sensibility even for those graduating from the nation's most proscribed and particularized course of study. However, when the United States participation in the Great War dragged into its second year, Wilson saw the need to have all of the nation's universities and their scholars dedicated to the military professions.

The First World War brought massive disruption to America's campuses because of mobilization. Educational historian Roger Geiger offers a useful summary: "American colleges and universities were involved in World War I for longer than the nineteen months of officially declared hostilities. Campuses were particularly sensitive to the call for American preparedness as the conflict in Europe dragged on."[63] University preparedness first materialized in 1914 and 1915 with initiatives such as the War Department's summer camps. In the fall of 1915, Yale president Arthur Twining Hadley praised them: "I have no hesitation in saying that, wholly aside from their military value in preparing a reserve of trained officers for possible service in event of war, the [camps] have an educational value that much more than justifies their organization and its maintenance."[64] As hostilities increased, universities escalated their commitment to the war effort. They coordinated through ad hoc organizations such as the Advisory Committee of University Presidents and through formal organizations such as the AAU, whose 1916 annual meeting agenda included a lengthy discussion of "Military Training in Universities and Colleges." This resulted in the formation of the Reserve Officers' Training Corps (ROTC) in the summer of 1916 and the formation of the Students' Army Training Corps (SATC) in 1918.

Although enabled by university presidents who enthusiastically volunteered their institutions, the SATC was a radical intrusion. "Campuses were nationalized almost as completely as the railroads had been in order to provide training grounds."[65] In its original conception, the SATC would have been little more disruptive than the ROTC. However, a German surge in the summer of 1918 led in August to the lowering of the draft age to eighteen. To avoid the complete evisceration of the student population from universities, enrollment in the SATC was made compulsory.[66] "On October 1, 1918, some 140,000 college men on four hundred American campuses were simultaneously inducted into active duty in the U.S. Army. The colleges and universities at which they were stationed had become units of the SATC."[67] In words addressed to the nation's university students upon their induction, Wilson left little doubt as to the totality of their commitment. "The step you have taken is a most significant one. By it you have ceased to be individuals. . . . You have joined yourselves with the entire manhood of the country and pledged, as did your forefathers, 'your lives, your fortunes, and your sacred honor' to the freedom of humanity."[68] Wilson was also signaling the formalization of the university's position as an extension of the mobilizing national state. For Wilson this effort would be "a difficult one. This is not a war of words; this is not a scholastic struggle. It is a war of ideals, yet fought with all the devices of science and with the power of machines."[69] With the advent of the SATC, it was now the mission of the university to train men in such devices and their power.

The signing of the armistice less than six weeks later led to the disbandment of the SATC almost as soon as it began. But its short-term impact had been pronounced, if not notorious. As Geiger highlights, "Normal university instruction was thoroughly undermined as courses were ludicrously foreshortened for soon-to-depart soldiers and as military duties often took priority over class attendance. Faculty members had to show passes to student guards to gain admittance to university buildings."[70] The final plan for the SATC did not originate with Wilson; he had initially envisioned a slightly less elaborate scheme. But even with his less intrusive concept, Wilson had endorsed a plan proposed by his former dean of faculty, Henry Fine, whereby the federal government itself would define the courses, vet the content, and grade the examinations for university students in subjects pertinent to the war effort, such as medicine, engineering, and applied sciences.[71]

Far more important than the actual structure of the SATC was what it represented. Some, such as Geiger, have suggested that "in hindsight, it is difficult to imagine a regime more incongruous with the values and mores of the academy than that of the SATC."[72] Wilson would not have shared that assessment. If he had any misgivings about the effort, he did not express them at the time or in retrospect. Given his position as commander-in-chief, Wilson was the one academic leader who actually could have minimized the SATC's reach. He did not. Instead, he fully supported and promoted the initiative. Some might rationalize this as a symptom of war fever. But I would argue that the Wilson administration did not undertake this single largest government intersection with higher education out of simple zeal. Rather, Wilson "drafted" the nation's universities because he saw them as already constituting the intellectual underpinning and institutional apparatus that defined and extended the new American state.[73] In this context, the SATC does not represent a flawed experiment mercifully cut short. Instead, it stands as yet another of Wilson's bold initiatives that was frustrated by timing and circumstances beyond his control.

Does this analysis suggest that Wilson was simply an orator and innovator who planned and provoked but left no lasting imprint due to an inability to execute? Absolutely not. It simply suggests a new approach for considering his legacy, one that builds upon theories of state-building and political development to emphasize the intellectual and rhetorical foundations of institutions and their authority. For no matter how operational Wilson's academic and political activity remains at Princeton or in Washington today, his ideas about the link between universities and the American state remain vibrant. One hundred years after Wilson spoke at Princeton's 150th anniversary, Cornell president Frank H. T. Rhodes saw fit to use Wilson as his guide in responding to critics who believed that American higher education had lost its public purpose.[74] Having lost a few institutional battles, Wilson won the ultimate intellectual war. His model of and ambitions for the university-state nexus remains the talisman by which the modern American state still builds and our leading universities still perform.

NOTES

1. Mark R. Nemec, *Ivory Towers and Nationalist Minds: Universities, Leadership, and the Development of the American State* (Ann Arbor: University of Michigan Press, 2006).

2. Ralph Waldo Emerson, "Self-Reliance" in *Self-Reliance and Other Essays* (New York: Dover, 1993), 26.

3. John Milton Cooper Jr., "Woodrow Wilson: The Academic Man," *Virginia Quarterly Review*, 58:1 (Winter 1982), 38–53.

4. James Axtell, *The Making of Princeton University: From Woodrow Wilson to the Present* (Princeton: Princeton University Press, 2006).

5. Ibid., 71.

6. Stephen Skowronek, *Building the New American State: The Expansion of National Administrative Capacities, 1877–1920* (New York: Cambridge University Press, 1982), 196.

7. Brian Cook, *Bureaucracy and Self-Government* (Baltimore: Johns Hopkins University Press, 1996), 97.

8. John R. Thelin, *A History of American Higher Education* (Baltimore: Johns Hopkins University Press, 2004), 188.

9. Eldon Eisenach, *The Lost Promise of Progressivism* (Lawrence: University Press of Kansas, 1994), 1–2.

10. *The Papers of Woodrow Wilson*, ed. Arthur S. Link et al., 69 vols. (Princeton: Princeton University Press, 1966–1994), 14:239 (Nov. 29, 1902) (hereafter *PWW*).

11. *PWW,* 1:608–21 (March 5, 1880).

12. *A Resolution: Minutes of the Faculty of Princeton University on the Resignation of Dr. Woodrow Wilson from the Presidency, PWW* 22:80 (Nov. 12, 1910).

13. Alfred Stepan, The *State and Society: Peru in a Comparative Perspective* (Princeton: Princeton University Press, 1978), xii.

14. Peter B. Evans, Dietrich Rueschemeyer, Theda Skocpol, "Toward a More Adequate Understanding of the State," in Evans, Rueschemeyer, and Skocpol, eds., *Bringing the State Back In* (New York: Cambridge University Press, 1985), 356.

15. Mary Douglas, *How Institutions Think* (Syracuse: Syracuse University Press, 1986), 45.

16. *PWW,* 19:638 (Dec. 28, 1909).

17. *PWW,* 9:131 (Jan. 26, 1895); 19:636 (Dec. 28, 1909).

18. Skowronek, *New American State,* 42.

19. Eisenach, *Lost Promise,* 7.

20. Raymond E. Wolfinger and Stephen J. Rosenstone, *Who Votes?* (New Haven: Yale University Press, 1980); Rachel Milstein Sondheimer and Donald P. Green, "Using Experiments to Estimate the Effects of Education on Voter Turnout." *American Journal of Political Science,* 54:1 (Jan. 2010), 174–89.

21. Frederick C. Mosher, *Democracy and the Public Service* (New York: Oxford University Press, 1968), 71.

22. *PWW,* 9:131 (Jan. 26, 1895).

23. Woodrow Wilson to James Burrill Angell, Nov. 15, 1887, Angell Papers, Bentley Library, University of Michigan, box 3, folder 97. The reference is to Thomas Carlyle's satire *Sartor Resartus: The Life and Opinions of Herr Teufelsdrockh,* in which the protagonist, Teufelsdrockh, is a quiet and self-contained philosopher.

24. Woodrow Wilson, "The Study of Administration," *Political Science Quarterly,* 2:2 (June 1887), 197–222.

25. *PWW,* 14:316 (Jan. 3, 1903).

26. *PWW,* 19:640–41 (Dec. 29, 1909).

27. *PWW,* 19:645 (Dec. 29, 1909).

28. Spurred initially by the desire for uniform recognition of Berkeley's degrees at foreign (primarily German) universities, University of California president Benjamin Ide Wheeler, joined by the presidents of Columbia University, the University of Chicago, Harvard University, and Johns Hopkins University, invited the Catholic University of America, Clark University, Cornell University, University of Michigan, University of Pennsylvania, Princeton University, Leland Stanford Junior University, University of Wisconsin, and Yale University. All accepted. By the time of Wilson's talk in 1910, the membership had been expanded to include the universities of Virginia (1904), Illinois, and Missouri (1908), and Iowa, Kansas, and Nebraska (1909). Nemec, *Ivory Towers,* 177.

29. Willard Thorp, Minor Myers Jr., Jeremiah Stanton Finch, and James Axtell, *The Princeton Graduate School: A History,* ed. Patricia H. Marks (Princeton: Association of Princeton Graduate Alumni, 2000), 104.

30. *PWW,* 19:7 (Jan. 5, 1910).

31. *PWW,* 19:716 (Jan. 5, 1910).

32. *PWW,* 19:718 (Jan. 5, 1910).

33. *PWW*, 17:533 (Nov. 29, 1907).

34. *PWW*, 19:722 (Jan. 5, 1910).

35. Dorothy Ross, "The Development of the Social Sciences," in James Farr and Raymond Seidelman, eds., *Discipline and History: Political Science in the United States* (Ann Arbor: University of Michigan Press, 1993), ch. 6.

36. *PWW*, 19:726 (Jan. 5, 1910).

37. *PWW*, 14:299 (Dec. 23, 1902).

38. *PWW*, 14:300 (Dec. 29, 1902).

39. *PWW*, 14:239 (Nov. 29, 1902).

40. Philadelphia *North American*, April 18, 1903, in *PWW*, 14:415–16 (April 18, 1903).

41. "Woodrow Wilson Attacks Paternalism," *New York Times*, Dec. 15, 1906, 1.

42. *Yearbook of the New York Southern Society, 1910–11* (New York, 1910), 5.

43. William Rainey Harper to Nicholas Murray Butler, Oct. 3, 1904, Columbia University, Butler Library, President's Papers. Harris would leave office two years later.

44. *PWW*, 17:544 (Nov. 29, 1907).

45. Skowronek, *New American State*.

46. WW, "Princeton in the Nation's Service" (Oct. 21, 1896), *PWW*, 10:11–31.

47. Axtell, *The Making of Princeton University*, 2.

48. WW, "Princeton for the Nation's Service" (Oct. 25, 1902), *PWW*, 14:170–85.

49. Ibid.

50. Ibid.

51. W. Barksdale Maynard, *Woodrow Wilson: Princeton to the Presidency* (New Haven: Yale University Press, 2008), 41.

52. "Woodrow Wilson on a University's Use," *New York Times*, Dec. 12, 1902, 8.

53. *PWW*, 14:412 (April 17, 1903).

54. "Would Reorganize American College," *New York Times*, July 2, 1909, 7.

55. Franklin Giddings to Walter Sawyer, June 23 1909; Angell Papers, Bentley Library, U. of Michigan, box 7, folder 244.

56. Footnote to communication between Pritchett and Wilson, *PWW*, 17:546n1 (Nov. 29, 1907).

57. Ibid.

58. *PWW*, 17:527 (Nov. 27, 1907).

59. Ibid.

60. John Milton Cooper Jr., *Woodrow Wilson: A Biography* (New York: Alfred A. Knopf, 2009), 108.

61. *PWW*, 30:146 (June 5, 1914).

62. Ibid.

63. Roger L. Geiger, *To Advance Knowledge: The Growth of American Research Universities, 1900–1940* (New York: Oxford University Press, 1986), 104.

64. "Yale Head Advocates Credit for Army Work," *New York Times*, Oct. 22, 1915, 3.

65. Geiger, *To Advance Knowledge*, 103.

66. Michael Bezilla, *Penn State: An Illustrated History* (University Park: Penn State University Press, 1985), 71.

67. Geiger, *To Advance Knowledge*, 103.

68. *PWW,* 51:168 (Oct. 1, 1918).

69. Ibid.

70. Geiger, *To Advance Knowledge,* 104.

71. *PWW* 49:243 (Aug. 13, 1918).

72. Geiger, *To Advance Knowledge,* 104.

73. This view of universities as more formal extensions of the state was best articulated by a writer identified only as a "University Professor Now in the Service of the United States" via a Sunday editorial in the *New York Times* entitled "Drafting Our Universities." The lengthy editorial stressed that, although begun as a war measure, such interconnectedness would become the norm. "The universities, after this war, will be recognized as schools of national efficiency," the professor wrote, and "a precedent has been established." Most radically, he suggested, "The universit[ies] will be nationalized as they are already. Their control will not be entirely in the hands of a self perpetuating Board of Trustees or an elected Board of Regents. The old private or purely State institution has gone forever. Harvard and the University of Arizona will be alike and in a peculiar sense—if they are fitted for the test—national universities, passed upon and approved by a national body. And their students will come to them . . . because they are sent there by a constituted national authority. Men and women, too, will be drafted into an education." The professor recognized that "there are a thousand details to the scheme, which experience will let us work out. But what a horde of educational difficulties which we once had will disappear." He ended emphatically, "It all looks like a Utopian scheme, but already we are doing it, and acquiring the habit." "Drafting our Universities," *New York Times,* Oct. 20, 1918. The author gave no hint as to his identity and as far as I know has never been identified.

74. Frank H. T. Rhodes, "The University and Its Critics," in William G. Bowen and Harold T. Shapiro, eds., *Universities and Their Leadership* (Princeton: Princeton University Press, 1998), 3–14.

# The Higher Education of Woodrow Wilson

## *Politics as Social Inquiry*

Trygve Throntveit

As a young man Woodrow Wilson dreamed of a political career, of living a life through which his generation, as he put it in 1889, would write "its political *autobiography*."[1] Years before Wilson wrote those words that life began to seem out of reach, and he turned to scholarship and education as a substitute. As historians appreciate to this day, that decision proved enormously significant to the development of American higher education, but it also had momentous consequences for the course of American politics. Wilson's political dream had always been to lead as both a student and educator of the body politic, to "read the experiences of the past into the practical life of the men of to-day" and then "communicate the thought to the minds of the great mass of the people," in order "to impel them to great political achievements." While reaching the top of the historical and political-science fields, Wilson sought consistently to share his ideas about the nature and workings of power with a wider public, and to refine those ideas in light of his society's changing character. Thus, when he did finally enter politics, Wilson had developed an ideal of political leadership defined almost exclusively in educative terms. In his first presidential inaugural he called on all public servants to approach their duties "in the spirit of those who question their own wisdom and seek counsel and knowledge." He promised that his administration would learn from "the need of our people" and reflect on "whether we be indeed their spokesmen and interpreters," even while explaining and promoting specific solutions to their problems.[2] The legal and institutional innovations of Wilson's extraordinarily active and ideologically fluid presidency are directly attributable to this effort to transform politics into a constant process of communal inquiry and mutual education.

Despite his achievements as a scholar and educator, Wilson is remembered mainly as a practitioner rather than a student of politics, even by those most critical of his statesmanship; and since the close of the First World War, the lessons scholars have drawn from his political career have often been lessons of warning. Though routinely castigated for attending too much to political ideas and too little to political practice, Wilson is also, ironically, attacked by some of his most dogged critics for launching a world-political crusade with a meager knowledge and feeble theory of his medium. Had he only examined national and international politics more carefully, say these "realists"—had he but studied the world as it really is—subsequent U.S. leaders would not have had to play global police officers to expiate their nation's failed and futile quest, under Wilson, to end all wars.[3]

But Wilson was, among other things, a historian, and the world historians study changes—it is a world of indefinite possibilities, often made realities by people dissatisfied with "the way it is." Decades ago that same historical sensibility led Arthur Link to argue that Wilson grasped reality better than the realists. Wilson, he wrote, was guided by a "higher realism" informed by a "progressive view of history." It was true, Link admitted, that Wilson did not approach politics as did the leaders of other powerful nations in his day. Instead, he adapted to the "ultimate reality" that the failure of their power politics and the catastrophe of World War I revealed. His prescience, Link argued, led him to pursue an internationalist course, one "more likely to win the long-run moral approval of societies professing allegiance to the common western, humane, Christian traditions" that Wilson himself held dear.[4]

Sharp as it was, Link's thrust at the realists exposed Wilson's flank. It *was* unrealistic to criticize a historian and statesman for thinking and acting as if human choices caused real change. But the same logic exposes any appeal to folly-prone humanity's ineluctable "progress" as historicist fantasy rather than historical wisdom.[5] Historians sympathetic to realism easily dismissed Wilson's allegedly "higher" version as a projection of the old, familiar American exceptionalism onto a world as unlikely bound for such glory as America itself, while others lambasted him for being as nationalistic, chauvinistic, and imperialistic in his thought and actions as his European counterparts.[6]

Still, these arguments suggest that, whatever their opinion of the man, Wilson scholars can agree that determining what he *thought* is crucial to evaluating what he *did*—and that what he thought and did matters for today. Ideas shape decisions as much as the options and constraints under which they are made, and thus shape outcomes, too. Moreover, there are many ways to apply an idea, some of which may work better in a given environment than others. Finally, the ideas driving decisions can change. Applying these insights to a figure as pivotal as Wilson—whose accomplishments and failures in politics were momentous, and whose goals themselves have seemed contradictory to many—yields three lessons for students of political history in search of a usable past. First, the final outcome of a series of decisions cannot be treated as predetermined. Second, an actor's or group of actors' core ideas and beliefs are better reflected in some decisions than in others. And third, past "success" or "failure" of ideas is no sure predictor of their future fate. Wilson, champion of the League of Nations, could never have imagined in 1916 or 1917 that he would later be the deciding voice preventing U.S. membership in that body. However, his decisions in 1919 and 1920 were not those of the healthy, idealistic, yet pragmatic reformer of a few years earlier, but of a stroke-ravaged, emotionally unstable invalid. As such, those decisions are hardly proof that his vision of an integrated international order was doomed to fail. In short, rather than consigning his ideas to the dustbin of history, Wilson's career should remind us that critical, even humble historical reflection, not ideological certainty nor easy analogies between past and present, must guide policymakers and citizens as they shape the world in important yet uncertain ways.

In fact, these very lessons constitute the higher education in politics that Wilson gained by his close study of its history and its forms. Similarly close attention to the sources of Wilson's political ideas, and to examples of their influence on his practice, is not just important for excising certain mistaken assumptions embedded in the scholarship.[7] Such fresh examination of Wilson's higher education—and his uneven applications of it—reinforces its lessons about history, contingency, and human agency in politics, and suggests a new look at Wilson's best ideas.

Wilson's thinking changed much over his life, but some of his most persistent ideas were his most important. Prime among these was the superior importance he accorded contingency over determinism in human affairs, and history over theory in explaining them—including theories about God's will and work in the world. The common view of Wilson as a rigidly moralistic theocrat is mistaken. This deeply religious man did not deny God's ultimate direction of human events. But neither did he ignore the unpredictability of history as humans experienced and made it nor dismiss the fallibility of human judgments about God's ends and means.

Wilson's fatalism entailed neither apathy nor certainty. His father, a Presbyterian minister, taught him to view life through the biblical prism of God's covenant with humanity, which demanded constant service to others and vigilance over oneself, lest God's blessings be repudiated. Perfection, he taught his son, was always the goal, though rarely, if ever, achieved. This fallibilist lens led Wilson, like his father, to see tolerance of religious diversity and respect for secular values as means of testing and strengthening faith, and to view humans' constant exploration of their changing world and search for their proper roles in it, as the solemnest of obligations. Faith was an ever-present backdrop throwing events and choices into relief, as well as a reminder that each day's challenges made unique demands on the moral imagination. As young Wilson wrote his fiancée, Ellen, in 1884, any faith that meant "letting things drift, in the assurance that they would drift to a happy result," contravened his view of "*how* all things work together for good—through the careful performance of our duty."[8] As he matured, Wilson came to view life as a series of interlocking covenants of this complex sort. In his student days he wrote several constitutions for campus groups, translating his basic covenantal ideas into practical guides for human relationships. Importantly, all were amendable, on the theory that relationships changed, even if their animating principles remained constant. While away at graduate school he even solicited Ellen's ratification of one such instrument: a two-member "inter-state Love League," permitting adoption of new "bylaws . . . as they become necessary."[9]

An early source of this concern to reconcile ideal order with experienced change was Wilson's reading of the *Federalist* essays. Marginalia in his law school edition of the *Federalist* indicate that, by 1880 or so, he reached a conclusion he would often restate as a scholar and statesman: the framers' genius lay in making *explicit* the dynamism *implicit* in all social organization, so as to lubricate the institutional modifications social change required. Wilson took special note of the following from *Federalist* 34, by Alexander Hamilton: "Constitutions of civil government are not to be framed upon a calculation of existing exigencies; but upon a combination of these with the probable exigencies of ages. . . . Nothing therefore can be more fallacious, than to infer the extent of any power proper to be lodged in the national government, from an estimate of its *immediate* necessities. There ought to be a CAPACITY to provide for future contingencies, as they may happen; and as these are *illimitable* in their nature, so it is impossible to safely limit that capacity."[10] Wilson never abandoned this Hamiltonian view of constitutional government's purpose and character. Nearly thirty years later, in his final academic work, he would claim that a genuinely "constitutional" government "was one whose powers have been adapted to the interests of its people," and that the American Constitution, especially, was designed to facilitate such adaptation over time—not "to hold the government back to the time of horses and wagons."[11]

Wilson's well-known admiration for Britain's unwritten constitution was consistent with the dynamic strain he admired in the Founders. The wisest of the Founders, he believed, had thought states were healthiest when policy and institutions were consciously and continuously shaped over time, through strenuous debate among representatives directly responsible to public opinion. Power in such states should be vested in leaders adept at interpreting public opinion, crystallizing it, and mobilizing support behind a program embodying it. But by the time he entered graduate school at Johns Hopkins in 1883, Wilson considered the British system of parliament and cabinet, not its American cousin, the paragon of such vigorous, efficient self-government. Indeed, Wilson believed that American government had become dangerously dysfunctional, ruled by a factional legislature that completely marginalized the most nationally representative branch, the executive.[12]

Wilson did not trace America's problems to the ideas of the *Federalist*. Rather, he blamed subsequent abstractions, and the simultaneously constrained yet untended growth of the Constitutional "tap-root" that resulted. His dissertation, published as *Congressional Government* in 1885, argued that Americans' fetish for the separation of powers and fear of centralization had, ironically, sequestered all "motive and . . . regulative power" in a splintered oligarchy of Congressional committees. It was natural, Wilson argued, that as the nation expanded, the government would gain control over matters too complex and broadly significant for any state or locality to manage efficiently or fairly. Yet instead of coordinated legislative programs thoroughly vetted by debate, policy was made piecemeal by committees behind closed doors. Nor did any other American institution act with the "responsibility" that would make it truly representative, simultaneously speaking the nation's will, shaping its conclusions, and superintending its common affairs. The average citizen was shrewd in "esteeming government at best but a haphazard affair, upon which his vote and all his influence can have but little effect."[13]

This critique of the American system made Wilson's name as a scholar, but it is of more than academic importance. It is crucial to understanding a major feature of his mature political thought: his belief that strong party government and a powerful executive were vital elements of the genuinely accountable leadership self-government demanded. Wilson's attraction to British politics emerged from his intense love of oratory and admiration for masters of the art such as Edmund Burke and William Ewart Gladstone, and he became convinced they had honed their gifts in debates reaching levels of sophistication and importance no longer seen in America.[14] The reason, as Wilson argued in a series of essays prefiguring his dissertation, was the structure of British government, in which the executive was drawn from the ranks of the legislature and the party in power could be deposed at any time. Under that system, unified party action was the only means of realizing legislative goals, and the only way to create such unity was to convince party members that the goals were achievable, valuable, and politically expedient. That convincing occurred in the course of open debate in Parliament, where opposing views demanded recognition, prompted compromise, and—most important—publicized the lawmaking process. These circumstances also helped ensure that the party in power pursued genuine legislative *programs* reconciling a broad range of interests through complementary measures—thus increasing the efficiency and democratic character of legislation.[15]

The contrast with the American system was striking. "Congress is a deliberative body in which there is little real deliberation; a legislature which legislates with no real discussion of its business," Wilson wrote four years before arriving at Hopkins. In *Congressional Government* he repeated the charge. Even as Congress developed "the habit of investigating and managing everything" through a proliferation of standing committees, strict separation of powers had prevented American Gladstones from rising among the nation's representatives, unifying them under a national program, and putting the whole people's will into action. Under these circumstances national parties under strong leaders were the only means of holding Congressmen accountable to anyone but themselves—yet the obvious means of consolidating and exercising such influence, the presidency, was rendered useless by the weakness of the office.[16]

In the British system, however, strong executive leadership, like strong party government, was simultaneously encouraged and shown to advantage. Because the British executive was a subset of the nation's legislators, it could introduce legislation representing the national policies of its party and remain involved at every stage with the laws' subsequent development. In America, such inter-branch cooperation would require that the heads of the executive departments hold seats in Congress—a radical restructuring of the Constitution. Extreme as it was, Wilson believed his "cabinet government" solution would end the executive's isolation from the lawmaking process and make that process more nationally representative, not merely because the president was nationally elected but because of the double-edged nature of power in a representative democracy. Giving an administration "opportunity and means for making its authority complete and convenient" would give the people a solid basis on which to judge its performance, assign responsibility for government's successes and failures, and hold government's mismanagers, in or out of the administration, accountable at the ballot box. "*Power and strict accountability for its use* are the essential constituents of good government," Wilson declared in *Congressional Government.* "The best rulers" were those entrusted with "great power" and conscious that they would be "abundantly honored and recompensed for a just and patriotic use of it" but would receive "full retribution for every abuse of it."[17] Though Wilson, contrary to popular belief, never considered himself a prophet, in hindsight these words seem an eerie portent of their author's future.

*Congressional Government* was a smash in the political-science world. Disappointingly, however, it offered nothing resembling the "well-considered expedients" for making "self-government . . . a straightforward thing of simple method, unstinted power, and clear responsibility," which its author called for in his conclusion.[18] One thing is clear, however: Wilson's loyalty to the Democratic Party—firmly established at the time he was formulating his critique of American government—did not entail sympathy with the strict constitutional construction its Gilded Age leadership embraced. Indeed, Wilson cared little for theories of government in general. He was far more interested in how they developed and what citizens ought to do about it, an attitude directly inspired by Walter Bagehot's evolutionary analysis of the British system in *The English Constitution* (1867).[19] But Wilson was also influenced by another political economist of an evolutionist bent who drew him farther down the left fork of the political road: Richard T. Ely, his young instructor at Hopkins.

Ely's emphasis on the interdependence of individuals and society encouraged in Wilson a sympathy with nonrevolutionary socialism that most historians overlook.[20] In 1887, after reading Ely's *The Labor Movement in America* (1886), Wilson drafted an essay arguing that democracy and socialism were essentially similar, in that both implied society's use of the state as a tool upon itself. In 1889 Wilson's second major book, *The State*, endorsed the major protective and regulatory reforms that would characterize Ely's "Wisconsin Idea" of progressivism, justifying such "socialism," as Wilson called it, by government's duty to see that "individual self-development" be made "to serve and to supplement social development."[21] Granted, Wilson disdained theoretical socialism, just as he disdained classical laissez-faire dogma.[22] Lecturing on comparative government in the late 1880s, he concluded that no stable state arose from mere reifications of political theories—not because ideas lacked power, but because they inhabited history. As he reiterated in *The State*, even absolutist states proceeded from the specific character and history of a region and its inhabitants, while all states changed with the problems and aims of the peoples they constrained. Like Lorenz von Stein, Johann Kaspar Bluntschli, and most of the other German authors he studied in preparing his lectures, Wilson was developing an organic theory of the state, but of a far less teleological and more historical nature than his syllabi might imply. It would inform his view of political institutions for the rest of his life, eventually leading to his vision of a League of Nations that would evolve in unforeseen ways amidst unforeseen changes in the world.[23]

At the same time Wilson was developing his organic theory of the state, he intensified two other intellectual commitments, both reflecting his deepening interest in the paradoxical power and limits of human agency in politics. The expansion of self-government, in its reach and meaning, was one. Though Wilson's fixation on self-government is familiar, the early and abiding importance of what is now termed "deliberative discourse" to his conception is less noted. Yet such discourse was as central to Wilson's ideal of political democracy as it was to the cultural ideal that William James and John Dewey, future exponents of philosophical pragmatism, were drawing from their insights into the social and provisional character of knowledge.[24] The "Democratic state," Wilson privately noted in 1888, was better placed than others to grow in "organic wholeness & all-round adjustment," and for one simple reason: "all interests will have representation & a voice." That meant the body politic need not "depend for its progress upon the eye or upon the limited knowledge of a 'Government,'" but could "itself direct, from many sides . . . its own course of conduct & development."[25] This deliberative, experimental path of development was not just the advantage but also the duty of the democratic state. As Wilson wrote in 1885, the perfection and spread of deliberative institutions helped fulfill God's covenant on earth. Public deliberation let the individual serve God and himself by freely serving the entire social organism, as "a *thinking member* of the body politic." This self-coordination of society's multitudinous organs was both autonomous and contingent: Securing the "benefits of political cooperation," Wilson explained, required that cooperative mechanisms be unbounded by "abstract theory" and "found by experiment, as everything else has been found out in politics."[26]

The success of such experiments depended on conditions of free and enlightened public discussion and active yet accountable government—government by "common counsel," as Wilson was fond of saying.[27] Wilson's interest in improving these conditions explains his reputation as a champion of efficient administration, a second intellectual commitment that deepened in the late 1880s. Some careless phrasing in his seminal piece on the subject, "The Study of Administration" (1887), has led many to see him as a naïve proponent of an apolitical technocracy. Not only did Wilson deny that administration could be insulated from politics—he insisted it should not be. In an efficient administration civil servants would implement policies on the basis of both science and politics. The public's opinion on "constitutional questions" would set goals, which in turn raised "administrative questions" of execution, requiring study and experiment. Given the impracticability of referenda on every task at all levels of government, administrators needed broad powers to make specific *policies* that reflected the general *politics* of the public. Finally, for both policies and politics to serve the common good, scientific administration must be accountable to a public that was, itself, as scientific as possible in formulating its goals. Such scientific integrity depended not on manipulation by experts but rather on institutions that reflected and fostered the American culture of deliberation, experimentation, and cooperation—institutions complementing the American nation's "interdependent" character.[28] Lecturing at Johns Hopkins in 1888, Wilson was even more explicit about the constructive, even expressive, functions a democracy could exercise through efficient administrative tools. "Government does not stop with the protection of life, liberty, and property," he insisted, but "goes on to serve every convenience of society. . . . Business*like* the administration of government should be—but it is not business. *It is organic life.*"[29]

Despite his avowed liberal purpose, Wilson's focus on efficient administration has led some to portray him as conservative, even reactionary. His fondness for Burke, who often praised the slow processes of legal and institutional development as the best responses to social change, has encouraged this view.[30] But Wilson admired Burke the pragmatist more than Burke the traditionalist. To Wilson, Burke was a political empiricist, his thought "always immersed in matter," his judgment "steadied" by contact with real life. He was "the apostle of the great English gospel of Expediency"—the same "expediency" Wilson endorsed in *The State* to justify the catalog of regulatory responsibilities he thought modern society demanded of government. As a historian Wilson applauded Burke's rejection of "speculative" for "practical politics," his effort to treat human affairs not "as they are supposed to be" but "as they are found at the moment of contact."[31]

As social and industrial conflict flared at Homestead, Pullman, and elsewhere in the 1890s, Wilson found in Burke's "practical politics" the essentials of the political leadership that could invigorate public administration while fortifying self-government, by helping Americans grow together rather than apart. This fundamentally anti-ideological leadership was both conservative and radical. Its task was to prepare the "major thought of the nation" for change while respecting the centripetal force of tradition, a task demanding insight into what stirred the masses, judgment as to their "firm" rather than "whimsical" desires, and persuasion to direct their energies constructively—without forgetting that leaders who leap ahead of the people risk severing themselves from society, leaving it "deformed" by the amputation. Leadership of this sort was an exercise in "interpretation," an active effort to discover the popular attitudes that should inform political goals and determine the manner of their pursuit. It was also an exercise of power. Though the leader was "sympathetic" to the people's ideals and desires, his was "a sympathy whose power is to command . . . by knowing its instrument." Still, Wilson insisted that strong leadership was fundamentally democratic. "The ear of the leader must ring with the voice of the people," he declared; the leader's genius was to command the people down courses they revealed.[32]

Such leadership needed fostering, and Burke also reinforced Wilson's conviction that parties, despite their evils, fostered it best. Again, it was Burke's emphasis on the expediency of parties that appealed to Wilson. Parties, in Burke's opinion, not only coordinated political action but also often checked corruption, as Wilson noted in the following passage from his copy of Burke's collected works: "Whilst men are linked together, they easily and speedily communicate the alarm of any evil design. They are enabled to fathom it with common counsel, and to oppose it with united strength. Whereas, when they lie dispersed, without concert, order, or discipline, communication is uncertain, counsel difficult, and resistance impracticable. Where men are not acquainted with each other's principles, nor experienced in each other's talents . . . it is evidently impossible that they can act a public part with uniformity, perseverance, or efficacy."[33]

The use of the phrase "common counsel" in this passage may have inspired Wilson's adoption of the term, which to the end of his career expressed his ideal of both party dynamics and political discourse generally. Not that either thinker denied the tendency of parties to adopt a "narrow, bigoted, and proscriptive spirit," as Burke put it. Rather, "party" was to their minds the best method yet devised for negotiating political values and achieving political goals. *"Party is a body of men united for promoting by their joint endeavors the national interest upon some particular principle in which they are all agreed,"* Wilson underlined in Burke's *Works,* marking the rest of the paragraph with a line along the margin. "For my part," Burke continued in this passage, "I find it impossible to conceive, that any one believes in his own politics, or thinks them to be of any weight, who refuses to adopt the means of having them reduced into practice. It is the business of the speculative philosopher to mark the proper ends of government. It is the business of the politician, who is the philosopher in action, to find out proper means towards those ends, and to employ them with effect."[34]

It was this message that turned Wilson to the author of *Reflections on the Revolution in France* (1790) as his own nation seethed with social discontent. Change would happen, and should be directed as much as possible toward achieving high ideals; but always with care that the means did not destroy the ideals they were meant to serve.[35]

Clearly, Wilson greatly admired the man he referred to at one point as "the Master."[36] But to make too much of this comment is to mistake the character of the "conservatism" Wilson frequently endorsed, which bears little relation to that of the Burke most historians know. For Wilson (and, in his view, Burke too), conservatism meant eschewing theory and taking experience—past and present, individual and social—as one's guide for responding to change. Moreover, Wilson indulged no illusions of Burke's infallibility. Though Burke's insight into the evolutionary nature of the state put "high purposes . . . ever in [his] view," Wilson thought his mistrust of the mass of Englishmen made it "impossible he should be followed so far." On the other hand, Burke "erred when he supposed that progress can in all its stages be made without changes which . . . go even to the substance."[37] In short, Burke often failed to practice the expediency he preached, and the failures Wilson identified—mistrust of the people, fear of radical change—would top the sin-lists of few conservatives in any era.

Nor should Wilson's commitment to party government obscure his commitment to popular democracy. For Wilson, the communal inquiry, cooperative action, and productively adversarial debate facilitated by parties (at their best) made secret subversion of government harder, and public experiments in government possible. It is thus ironic when historians interpret Wilson's loyalty to the Democratic Party, and occasional support for its conservative wing, as support for elite maintenance of the status quo. Political circumstances rather than ideological affinity explain Wilson's sometime common cause with conservatives. After the electoral failures of the 1890s and early 1900s, Wilson's disappointment with "radical theorists" in the party's Bryanite wing led him to censure campaigns for populist Utopias. True, in these years he frequently invoked the "spirit" of Thomas Jefferson, venerated by conservative Democrats as a laissez-faire individualist. Yet he also argued that Jefferson's extreme individualism and fear of government were outmoded. In an age of organization, the question was, How to cultivate organization among *citizens*? Wilson's answer in the early 1900s was to begin locally; but instead of invoking laissez-faire or states'-rights theory, he evoked the analyses of Tocqueville, which had impressed him in the 1880s. "It is easier to apply morals in limited communities than in vast states," Wilson wrote for a Jefferson Day address in 1906. Long training in this communal application of morals had developed the habits of self-government that Tocqueville—and Wilson—identified as the lifeblood of American democracy. But still it was *training* in which Wilson was interested; the conditioning necessary to sustain a larger, nobler movement toward unified national life among "the general mass of the people."[38]

Wilson believed that the progress of such mass movement was accelerated by strong party government under leaders committed to educating their constituents. As Wilson wrote in 1885, wise policies reflecting the common good emerged from careful study of past events and present circumstances, a process taking time that few citizens could consistently spare. Thus, although society, as an "organism," could not "develop by any cunning leadership of a single member," it was nevertheless "led at last into self-consciousness and self-command by those who best divine the laws of its growth."[39] From his own study of those laws, Wilson concluded that achieving such collective "self-command" required a citizenry whose "object is [the] service, not of private interests, but of the general development," and organized politics was a leader's best mechanism for instilling that principle in citizens and guiding them in applying it wisely. Still, even at the height of his anti-populism, Wilson never questioned the ultimate authority of the majority to establish the fundamental priorities of government, or the duty of leaders to align policy with public opinion. Rather, he asserted in 1906, he "would *turn again,* and turn with confidence, to the *common people* of the country," who "speak in their judgments the true and simple spirit of all just law." Wilson's educative ideal of statesmanship affirmed both the importance and inadequacy of individual citizens, whether in or out of leadership, to ensuring the health of a free political system. "I cannot make Democratic theory out of each of you," he once told a group of conservative Democrats, "but I could make a Democratic theory out of all of you."[40]

In Wilson's view, broad-based parties were crucial to formulating working democratic theories reflecting the present experience of citizens. He believed they were the best means yet devised for synthesizing the diversity of American needs and desires into practical policies to meet them. His legislative records as a governor and president would demonstrate the power of that belief, which spurred reforms that permanently altered the American political landscape. Only late in his life would he allow his belief in strong party government to submerge his parallel belief in the frequent necessity and value of compromise. Unfortunately, it would prove the undoing of a body devoted to promoting the latter, among nations with far less civil alternatives than party government.

Wilson's first opportunity to put his political ideas into practice came not in public office but as president of a storied private institution, Princeton University, beginning in 1902. Though Princeton was not a government,

Wilson consciously approached his presidency—at least in his best years, from 1902 to 1908—in the spirit of a "prime minister." Conceiving broad and bold programs to be vetted by faculty, he delegated responsibility for particular features to capable lieutenants. Wilson also believed deeply in the importance of institutions like Princeton to the civic life of the nation, whose "affairs [grew] more and more complex" with each day and thus required "efficient and enlightened men" to manage them. His plan for making Princeton a school for such leaders belies the apparent elitism of that remark—though he certainly had white male leaders alone in mind. Still, each of his reforms—from modernizing the curriculum, to encouraging seminar-style courses, to reorganizing the school's institutions and even its physical campus—was designed to make Princeton a more meritocratic, egalitarian, and tight-knit community of inquiry. If Princeton failed to become such a place, Wilson warned his comrades in orange, it would fail a nation likely to be called to lead the world through the century just dawning.[41]

Wilson's Princeton presidency, however, is less important for the insights it lends into his political thought than for the role it played in his political career. Despite a string of successes, 1910 saw Wilson's defeat in a highly publicized contest over the location of Princeton's new Graduate College. The affair culminated a series of bitter controversies, convincing Wilson to resign the role he had come to see as his calling. The demise of his presidency was due partly to happenstance, partly to vicious academic politics, and partly to his neglect of the collegial, deliberative form of leadership responsible for his past successes, and its memory elicited painful feelings of betrayal and failure for the rest of his life.[42] Nevertheless, Wilson's rise and fall at Princeton brought him an opportunity he had dreamed of as a young man, but treated as only a dream ever since: a political career. As if to make up for lost time, that career would begin with the governorship of New Jersey.

The opportunity was presented by two unlikely characters: George Harvey, conservative editor of *Harper's Weekly*, and former U.S. Senator James Smith, boss of the New Jersey Democratic machine. Harvey had long admired Wilson's oratory, and Wilson's disaffection from the populist wing of his party led Harvey and Smith to recruit him as a candidate for senator in 1906, with hopes he might challenge William Jennings Bryan for the 1908 presidential nomination. Wilson, apparently considering the plan half-baked, declined.[43] His defeats at Princeton, however, made him more receptive to outside opportunities. Furthermore, despite their reputations, his suitors seemed amenable to a high-profile academic reformer taking advantage of the rising tide of progressivism to win New Jersey back to the Democrats. Aware of the growing cross-party appeal of progressivism to voters nationwide, they perhaps decided it was better to have a moderately reformist Democrat in the governor's seat—and if all went well, the White House—than a Republican.[44]

Wilson's later falling out with his backers has encouraged the view that Wilson was initially quite comfortable with their conservative politics, and embraced progressivism belatedly and opportunistically.[45] It is possible that Harvey and Smith considered Wilson a conservative of their ilk, for he did not write much on politics in his first several years as president of Princeton. But they more likely thought they could manipulate a middle-aged academic with no political experience. Wilson had returned to political writing in the three years before he ran for governor, and his output displays total confidence in the rightness and expediency of strong government measures to restore the voice of a growing, changing people to policymaking—or, as he put it in his 1908 book *Constitutional Government*, to "bring the active and planning will of the government into accord with the prevailing popular thought and need."[46]

Wilson's intensifying commitment to a more radically experimental, democratic politics seems to have been influenced in part by the pragmatist ethics of Harvard psychologist-*cum*-philosopher William James. Wilson's 1905 revisions of a speech first delivered in 1895 suggest he read James's bombshell essay, "The Will to Believe," sometime during that ten-year interval—possibly anticipating or responding to a meeting at Princeton's 1896 Sesquicentennial, where James received an honorary degree. Unlike Wilson's original speech, the revised version addresses the same conflict between religion and science examined in "The Will to Believe," and mounts a defense of religious faith that echoes James's. In fact, Wilson titled the later version "The Profit of Belief," and in explaining humans' power to shape their personal and social realities, he even used the phrase "wills to believe."[47]

Whatever the force of this influence, by late 1907 Wilson had written a treatise on government exhibiting a striking affinity for the pragmatist progressivism of John Dewey, Jane Addams, and other admirers of James who argued for more participatory, plastic, and powerful government.[48] In *Constitutional Government*, Wilson argued that individual liberty was both supreme and dependent on "common counsel" to socialize it, a paradox he resolved by affirming the basic premise of pragmatist ethics: the contingency of values. "The ideals of liberty cannot be fixed from generation to generation," he wrote; "fixed" liberty was "no liberty at all." Like the pragmatists, Wilson invoked Darwinian science to explain the evolution of values and the policies embodying them. Again like the pragmatists, his political Darwinism was prescriptive as well as descriptive. "Living Constitutions," he explained, "must be Darwinian in structure *and* in practice." Rather than laissez faire, this insight obliged experimentation in government, on grounds that human actions shape human constructs, and conscious action might shape them to our liking.[49]

The latent radicalism of this updated organicism justified, in *Constitutional Government*, what became the major themes of Wilson's political career: the legitimacy of interventionist government and the necessity of an activist executive, directly responsible to the people, to direct it. Though Wilson worried about "a mere act of will on the part of the [federal] government" usurping powers not implied by the Constitution, he saw nothing wrong with the states granting new powers, through the amendment process, if circumstances required. Categorically prohibiting such grants was to hew to an "old theory of sovereignty" which had "lost its vitality."[50] The nation, Wilson argued, was an indivisible whole; to focus its diffuse interests into political will and action required a center of power responsible to the mass. In the years since *Congressional Government* was written in 1885, the state's "natural evolution" had selected an unlikely coordinating organ: the president. Mass communications and the increasing importance of foreign affairs had given the president a reach and authority that made his office almost entirely distinct from the one Wilson dismissed as a young dissertator. "His is the only national voice in affairs," Wilson now wrote of the president. "If he rightly interpret the national thought and boldly insist upon it, he is irresistible." By performing an epistemological function analogous to that in James's scheme of human psychology, the president could truly be the head of government, registering, interpreting, and acting upon public opinion to facilitate informed and efficient collective action. Like a central nervous system that both directed and took direction from the body and its activities, constitutional government in the United States seemed ever more capable of making government a process of "synthesis, not antagonism"—and increasingly in need of such synthesis.[51]

If oversimplified, of course, this view of the president's link to the people can distract from the more mundane politicking that clears paths for big ideas. Such oversimplification and distraction marked the last years of Wilson's own presidency. Still, it is appropriate that in his last major work before assuming public office, this professor of politics once again argued that a hale body politic needed brains at the top.

It was not till Wilson was in his mid-fifties, when he won the governorship of New Jersey, that he began what most would consider his political education. He had held no previous political office. Yet in some ways Wilson was well prepared to serve as chief executive of an American state and, later, the American nation. He had devoted his adult life to studying, interpreting, and in some degree shaping America's political culture. In the process, he developed an ideal of politics and a conception of self-government reflecting that running dialogue. For Wilson, the ideal end of politics was to reconcile individual freedom and social growth, while maintaining a level of social order permitting both. Self-government, in turn, signified the power and responsibility of communities to adapt cooperatively to change, in order to achieve that ideal. Wilson often used "self-government" to express both of these mutually constitutive ideas, but another favorite shorthand for the pair was simply "democracy."

It is safe to say that every major policy Wilson pursued as governor and president was aimed, in his view, at infusing or enhancing democracy wherever he thought it lacking or weak. One major area was the realm of industrial relations. In his earliest political statement as a gubernatorial prospect, he asserted it was not only "legitimate" but in fact "absolutely necessary" that "Labor should organize . . . to secure justice from organized Capital." He went on to express "hearty support" for accident insurance, just wages, and "reasonable" working hours. Upon winning the nomination, he gave a clue as to the reason he took that stance: Americans were living in a "day of re-adjustment" that, more than ever, demanded "consultation" among diverse interests pledging "to yield to the general view" of the common good. The overweening power of certain interests impeded that process of adjustment through common counsel, and not only by stifling the voice of organized labor. Wilson thought most citizens had too little say in their government, either because making a living left no time or energy to participate meaningfully in it, or because others had bought the ear of their representatives. He thus called for expanded public education, increased oversight of corporations and utilities, an extended employer liability act, an eight-hour day for government employees, civil service reform, and direct primaries for state offices, while demanding that corporations bear a larger share of the state's tax burden.[52] Nor were these empty campaign promises. Within ninety days of his inauguration, bills on electoral reform, corrupt practices, utility regulation, and workers' compensation were enacted under his initiative, and more of the same would follow.[53]

Wilson's presidency began similarly. In the 1912 campaign he sketched out a "New Freedom" program embodying the experimental but accountable administration he first sketched in 1887. In a complex, dynamic economy, he told voters, it was government's job to correct distortions, curtail competition-stifling practices, ensure the availability of credit at fair terms, and in short restore prosperity to the mass of Americans. This would give them the time, the means, and the energy to participate in public life and to ensure by that participation that government continued to promote conditions fostering "a common understanding and a free action all together."[54] During the marathon sixty-third Congress of 1913–14, Wilson pushed his program through, rationalizing the tariff, reining in the trusts, and establishing the Federal Reserve. True to his belief that even successful experiments in government were time-bound, he also created commissions with constructive powers to interpret the new laws in future contexts, and thus keep "practices adjusted to the facts of the case."[55]

Wilson's policy *making* reflected his higher education in politics as much as his policy goals did. During the 1912 campaign, Wilson formulated the type of coordinated yet anti-ideological agenda he had extolled since *Congressional Government,* confronting each issue on its own terms and devising policies with a practical rather than rigidly ideological coherence. The common view that Wilson began as a "big-is-bad" trustbuster and ended as a Rooseveltian statist in sheep's clothing is mistaken. He never fit either profile. Rather, the pressure to apply his principles to real problems honed Wilson's thinking to a keen, pragmatic edge that, by the end of his campaign, cut absolutist arguments on all sides to pieces. "Big business," it was clear to Wilson, was "necessary and natural" in modern civilization; fair competition and productive cooperation were expressions and motors of economic, cultural, and social growth. Trusts, however, were "artificially created" constraints on these "natural processes," imposed by "the deliberate planning" of men seeking "to make their power secure against competition."[56] Therefore, clearly anticompetitive practices must be restricted by updated antitrust laws and revised tariff schedules. Yet mechanisms for evaluating new practices in new contexts were also needed, to ensure that good businesses of all sizes—and individuals in all legitimate occupations—continued to thrive. Thus, as noted, the Federal Reserve, the Federal Trade Commission, and the Federal Tariff Commission were established, to enforce and, if necessary, counterbalance statutory restraints of economic power.[57]

Wilson's attitude toward his subordinates also reflected the lessons of his academic career. Like the model president he described in *Constitutional Government,* Wilson coordinated his administrations without imperializing them. Biographer Arthur S. Link put it best when he wrote that Wilson acted as "prime minister" in New Jersey, initiating measures and shepherding them through the legislature.[58] Yet Wilson's presidency was also prime-ministerial and in some ways more collegial. Despite his reputation for high-handedness, Wilson, more than most presidents, treated his cabinet members as if they had a purpose: namely, to run their respective departments and advise him in their respective policy realms. He discussed with the group the basic philosophy and aims of policy and then, except for major affairs of state, let his lieutenants apply and pursue them. (The exception was his second secretary of state, the abrasive and, in Wilson's opinion, weak-minded Robert Lansing.) This style was not always fortunate, as he was no great judge of administrative talent. But it left Wilson time to reflect deeply on the most important matters before him.[59]

On those matters, Wilson was often boldly decisive, especially when he thought the people had made their needs clear—or were being prevented from doing so. He began his New Jersey governorship, for example, by ramming his direct primaries bill through the legislature, ignoring all precedent by personally addressing a legislative caucus, and convincing the shocked assemblymen to support the bill as a party measure.[60] Two years later, Wilson pulled a similar stunt in Congress, appearing before both houses on April 8, 1913, to introduce his agenda—the first such appearance since 1801. He informed his new associates that he was "not a mere department of the Government" but "a human being, trying to cooperate with other human beings, in a common service."[61] Wilson meant what he said. But men on both sides of the aisle soon realized that "common service," in Wilson's view, meant adversarial politics and party discipline as often as cooperation and negotiation. Wilson insisted he was elected to achieve the goals he campaigned on, not those of the opposition or factions in his own party. In the opinion of many on Capitol Hill, and the memoirs of some in his cabinet, he was a my-way-or-the-highway president.[62] But that perception, while true in some cases, also suggests ignorance of Wilson's efforts to consider divergent views seriously, without sacrificing goals to the gods of empty compromise. Certainly, he wrote a recalcitrant Democratic senator in 1915, there were times when "personal convictions should have full play" in making policy. But deliberation must be punctuated with action, and he could see "[no] surrender either of personal dignity or of individual conviction in yielding to the determinations of a decisive majority."[63] Wilson spoke here of intraparty dynamics, but this Burkean statement encapsulated the view of all democratic communities and institutions he had held since his twenties.

Nevertheless, Wilson did more than apply old political ideas to new political tasks. The red thread in his thinking was always that ideas needed refining as circumstances changed. His 1912 collaboration with Louis Brandeis, a major architect of his New Freedom policies, exemplified that attitude—and encouraged it. Brandeis, the "People's Attorney," had pioneered the use of economic and sociological data to convince courts that statute and precedent were frequently inadequate to the disposition of justice. Drawing on the empiricist, experimental logic of these "Brandeis Briefs," he helped Wilson articulate the notion that it was not trustbusting, tariff revision, or any single goal that defined the New Freedom. Rather, the goal was to build the general habit of learning from experience, and the means of acting on it, into government.[64] Once the New Freedom was largely achieved, Wilson demonstrated his commitment to that idea. Convinced that economic reforms could not alone restore equality to America, he initiated a cascade of social justice measures. Rural credits, child-labor restrictions, government workers' compensation, and a redistributive income tax were all passed or in passage before the Democrats unveiled their 1916 platform—which pledged to fulfill every remaining social justice promise of the 1912 Progressive platform. Wilson soon was urging the states to grant women suffrage and eventually supported a national suffrage amendment—a belated but happy change from his previous indifference to the matter and impatience with militant suffragists.[65]

One tragic omission from the list of struggling Americans Wilson empowered was African Americans, who never earned his sympathy the way laborers, immigrants, and women eventually did. Determining why is not as easy as might be assumed. Wilson was not the hideous racist most historians think he was. His Southern background had limited influence on his racial views, perhaps because he was the son of a Northerner and an immigrant. Like most whites, North and South, he considered radical Reconstruction a fiasco; and yet he always maintained that the Civil War was "an inestimable blessing" and abolition "a lasting benefit" for the region.[66] Still, he doubted, again like most other white Americans, that a people so recently enslaved had developed the cultural resources required for self-government, much less for governing whites, as they had during Reconstruction. He also assumed that the distinct historical and social experiences of blacks and whites created cultural barriers between them that few on either side desired to cross, and thus took segregationist arguments seriously. But he did not adhere to the white-supremacist argument that blacks were innately inferior. (Contrary to popular belief, he never compared D. W. Griffith's film *The Birth of a Nation* to "writing history with lightning"; indeed, he described it privately as a "very unfortunate production.")[67]

Wilson sometimes exhibited racial prejudice, and sometimes, unforgivably, he acted upon it—as when he acquiesced in schemes for segregating federal offices, swallowing (and then parroting) his subordinates' rationale that employees of both races preferred it.[68] He also sometimes expressed empathy for blacks, and sometimes acted upon that as well—as when, in 1915, he urged businesses, local governments, and private citizens to support a national exhibition commemorating "the achievements of the negro race"; or when, during the war, he vehemently condemned lynching and personally congratulated an African American minister with twelve sons honoring the family "in the service of our country." (Wilson failed to mention that the men served in a segregated army.)[69] Either way, he left few clues to his mind, except that it was generally elsewhere. From the scattered thoughts he did record, it seems that part of him knew he had failed black Americans, while a larger part of him blamed circumstances. At the start of his presidency he needed southern Democrats supporting his New Freedom; during the war he needed southern military men to mobilize an army. "I have never had an opportunity actually to do what I promised them I would seek an opportunity to do," he whined, privately, in 1918.[70]

Yet Wilson had made a career of finding opportunities where few presented themselves. That it took a wave of murders to prompt his public condemnation of racial violence shows just how remote the everyday injustice and terror facing blacks in America was to him. When he thought about it, the worst of those injustices and terrors troubled Wilson and in incremental degrees changed his thinking. But like the majority of white Americans at the time—and before, and long after—he rarely did think about it. It was not real to him.

It was in Wilson's thinking on foreign affairs that his experience of practicing rather than simply studying politics spurred the greatest changes. Wilson's early imperialism is taken for granted by scholars, and indeed, at century's turn, he emphasized America's duty to train other peoples in efficiency—the habits of self-mastery that enabled self-government—before bestowing democracy upon them. One reason was that his organic theory of political development proscribed the transplant of institutions to soils unlike those that had nourished them.[71] Another, somewhat inconsistent, reason was that his student Frederick J. Turner's thesis of dialectical expansion and democratization in American history fed his belief that the nation, as it grew and thrived, had acquired the capacity and duty to draw non-Western cultures into the West's liberal project.[72] Finally, Wilson's streak of cultural chauvinism, revealed most clearly in his 1902 *History of the American People,* suggests confidence in both the advanced political development of Anglo-Saxons and the privileges it earned them. It is no coincidence that the central aim of his early, blundering policy in Latin America was to teach the region's peoples to "elect good men"—men, that is, who thought as he did.[73]

Not long into his presidency, however, Wilson's policy shifted in a decisively anti-imperialist direction. Three factors account for this, all demonstrating his higher education in action. One was his deepening commitment to increasingly radical reform at home. In 1915, reflecting on the internecine violence that had ravaged Mexico for the past five years, he noted that the democratic "failures" prompting its descent into chaos were analogous to America's own, stemming from the depredations of an "educated, privileged, and propertied class, who are, as with us, owning and running everything. . . . Hence the wedge in our own domestic politics."[74] This equation of a failed state and poor, largely nonwhite nation with his own country contrasts starkly with Wilson's earlier paternalism. It suggests a growing conviction that self-government must in many cases *precede* self-mastery, a conviction affecting not only Wilson's domestic views, but his international outlook as well.

That outlook had already begun to change owing to a second factor: the Mexican Revolution itself. An ill-conceived American intervention in the spring of 1914 entailed a loss of life Wilson had not expected and that pained him deeply. Moreover, the outrage it sparked among Mexicans—even those opposed to Porfirio Díaz, the brutal new dictator Wilson sought to undermine—forced him to take a new perspective. He realized the Mexicans were not, as he once assumed, political children wanting a teacher. Indeed, he privately remarked in August 1914, "There were no conceivable circumstances" justifying any outside attempt to direct "a revolution as profound as that which occurred in France." He maintained that attitude for the rest of his presidency, even when revolutionary violence spilled across the border to threaten Americans and his presidency.[75]

From mid-1914 on, in fact, Wilson's lessons in Mexico informed all his policies toward peoples struggling for self-government. Subsequent interventions were ordered only when Wilson thought—wrongly at times, but genuinely—that it was necessary to prevent more damaging interference from other quarters. His 1916 intervention in the Dominican civil war is the biggest potential exception to this rule. But it is worth noting that Wilson inherited responsibility for Dominican customs receipts from his predecessors, under whom the United States had assumed the Republic's massive foreign debts to prevent intervention by European creditor nations. Moreover, the previous year Wilson had sent troops to neighboring Haiti out of genuine fear that Germany might invade that conflict-torn nation and establish a naval presence in the Western Atlantic. While these Caribbean interventions were mistakes that rightly left Haitians and Dominicans bitter, they did not reflect a fundamentally imperialist mindset.[76] More revealing of Wilson's evolving thought was his push for a Pan-American body that could assess regional crises collectively and respond with greater legitimacy than any lone state.[77]

The final factor in Wilson's embrace of internationalism was the First World War, including the response of the day's leading pragmatist progressives to it. John Dewey, Herbert Croly, and especially Walter Lippmann were most important in this process. Self-conscious pragmatists and vocal proponents of numerous progressive causes, they saw the war as a chance to reconstruct *all* human relationships on a social rather than self-regarding basis, through egalitarian institutions facilitating constructive cooperation. From mid-1916 on their strain of internationalism dovetailed ever more tightly with Wilson's and began to shape his policies. Wilson was an early and regular reader of *The New Republic,* and he frequently clipped and saved articles from the journal. Croly and Lippmann also conferred frequently with Wilson's friend and adviser, Edward M. House, and his secretary of war, Newton Baker. By the time Wilson asked Congress to declare war on Germany in April 1917, three shifts in his thinking had deepened its congruence with the *New Republic* pragmatists'. First, he accepted that strict neutrality was both "hypocritical" and "timid," favoring British trade yet ducking moral distinctions between "violator" and "victim." Second, he adopted *The New Republic*'s view of preparedness legislation as a "Trojan Horse" that could sneak a more socialized democracy into the fortress of laissez-faire America.[78]

Finally, Croly and Lippmann shaped Wilson's vision for the postwar world and America's role in it. Crucially, the *New Republic* pragmatists sketched a League of Nations embodying Wilson's ideal of a strong, adaptive, accountable state. They insisted that any league must "exercise a very sharp supervision over the foreign policy of its members," and argued that a league without provision for "organic alteration in the world's structure" was doomed.[79] Then in April 1916, Lippmann issued an "Appeal to the President," articulating what became the crux of Wilson's internationalism: the sanctity of deliberative discourse among nations. He urged the world to define the "aggressor" as "the nation that will not submit its quarrel to international inquiry" or "pursues its quarrel after the world has decided against it." To establish that "all nations" must cooperate to punish aggressors was paramount—as noted by Wilson on the copy of the "Appeal" he saved.[80]

Days before the "Appeal" saw print, Lippmann aired his views to Wilson in a private meeting at the White House. Early the next month, in a colloquy with prominent antimilitarists, Wilson deployed Lippmann's heaviest-caliber arguments for guaranteeing the integrity of deliberative processes by force. Less than three weeks later he made his first public commitment to a league of nations.[81] Then, in late December, Wilson found a phrase on the front page of *The New Republic* that captured his larger postwar vision: "Peace without Victory." The editorial inside, he told Croly, "served to clarify and strengthen [his] thought not a little" as he wrote the address invoking that famous phrase in January 1917.[82] Nations, Wilson told Congress, must reject the "balance of power" for "a community of power," upholding the principle of government by consent. Only a "peace between equals" could sustain these relations of equality and solidarity within and among states. It is telling that less than three months later, when Wilson called for war on grounds that the world "must be made safe for democracy," he did not charge America alone with the task: the nation was "but one of the champions of the rights of mankind."[83]

Despite their influence, the pragmatists could not control Wilson's pursuit of the ideals they shared—nor could Wilson control the world's response. Nowhere is this clearer than in the story of the Fourteen Points, timed to respond to the Bolshevik peace program of late 1917. The Points eschewed Lenin's rhetoric of national self-determination and emphasized "autonomous development," a synonym for Wilson's ideal of deliberative self-government amidst diversity. The Bolsheviks' rhetoric also clashed with the views of the man who drafted most of the Points, Walter Lippmann, who emphasized that lasting peace required cooperative responses to change. Wilson followed this logic in his address, and the result was a series of situation-specific, provisional solutions to territorial disputes, united by the idea that deliberative discourse within and among nations could best guarantee justice and order. As Wilson later explained en route to the Paris Peace Conference, the League he envisioned "implied [not only] political independence and territorial integrity," but "alteration of terms if . . . injustice had been done or . . . conditions had changed."[84]

But from February 1918 to June 1919, Wilson refused to discuss the specifics of a settlement that, he insisted, must reflect actual rather than assumed conditions at war's end. The world was left to make of his plan what it would, and "national self-determination" was the idea seized upon. Wilson never stated publicly that he had been misunderstood.[85] Meanwhile, he abandoned not just open diplomacy but also many of the democratic methods and principles that had attracted the pragmatists and made him a successful reformer at home. He supported the Espionage and Sedition Acts, acquiesced in the postmaster general's censorship campaign and the Justice Department's crackdown on radicals, and largely ignored antiradical, anti-German, and antiblack vigilantism.[86] These failures fractured the progressive coalition he needed to support his internationalist version of the League against that of powerful senators, leery of foreign entanglements and jealous of national sovereignty. Indeed, Croly, Lippmann, and Dewey advocated *rejection* of a League Covenant whose painful evolution at Paris they had not witnessed and did not understand. Yet it was Wilson's stubborn insistence that Senate Democrats vote *against* membership with reservations that ultimately derailed the movement toward engagement, a movement that might have set a course for true internationalism.[87]

What was he thinking? Some historians blame Wilson's alleged messiah complex for his actions. Far more convincing are those who blame the multiple strokes that left him physically frail, emotionally unstable, and "literally incapable of compromise."[88] But whatever their psychological or pathological origins, Wilson's thoughts in 1918–20 count, and clearly some of those thoughts differed from those of prior months and years. Most important was his newfound conviction that the perfect must never be sacrificed to the good; though as his painful concessions at Paris attest—concessions that were reasoned if not always "right"—this conviction was not always controlling.

What, then, can be learned from Wilson's higher education? Not surprisingly, the lessons are historical. Specifically, Wilson's work and career remind us that the past is best viewed as a metaphor rather than analogy of the present. Analogies are quickly and easily drawn, but they are far too imprecise to use, as they tempt us to use them; for, as Wilson asserted in an 1895 essay "On the Writing of History," historical truth "is abstract not concrete." Metaphors, too, are imprecise, but do not pretend otherwise. They suggest unexpected connections, expanding the imagination in the same way that the myriad possibilities disclosed by history should. "An infinite variety plays through all history," Wilson wrote. "Every scene has its own air and singularity." Historical truths, he continued, emerge not when events are treated as "tools," but as "objects of vision." As such, a historian needs "imagination" before "scholarship" can bear its full fruit—and readers need the same. "Histories are written in order that the bulk of men may read and realize"; they would be useless if nothing relevant to the present could be learned from them. And yet, "In no case can you do more than convey an impression, so various and complex is the matter."[89]

Regrettably, too many scholars draw clear but false analogies between the Wilsonian moment and their own, and miss the more impressionistic, more instructive connections. Given the remarkable materialization of a League of Nations and America's near membership in it, the veering off course of one internationalist, however powerful, is hardly proof of the whole project's perfidy. Nor, of course, is it proof that Wilson's ideas were right and all other approaches to foreign policy are wrong. Still, the near success of America's abandoned experiment in internationalism should prompt serious challenges to the conventional, realist wisdom of our own day. For that matter, twentieth-century America's impressive but still inadequate gains for social justice, achieved by the activist state he helped establish, should encourage a healthier balance of optimism and skepticism toward government's potential to improve people's lives. True, as a scholar Wilson argued that ideas should be judged by their effects, and the legacies of progressivism and internationalism are decidedly mixed. But he also argued that circumstances change and that we should not bind our judgments to the past. Moreover, as a statesman, Wilson demonstrated the constructive power of ideas as clearly as the fallibility of their originators, and we should not confuse the two.

In short, Wilson's higher education is relevant to Americans today, even if most fail to find it so. Rather than seeking in history a set of templates for action in the present, it suggests that Americans should try something simpler and simultaneously more audacious: namely, promoting a culture that nurtures historical wisdom in political practitioners before they become practitioners—and nurtures that wisdom in everyone else, too. Such a cultural commitment might check Americans' habit of seizing only on those facts from the past that most easily fit their theories of the present. Indeed, perhaps those theories themselves will increasingly recognize the degree to which the present, like the past, varies with the perceptions of each interpreter, even as it depends on the actions of all participants.

## NOTES

1. Woodrow Wilson (hereafter WW), journal entry, Dec. 28, 1889, in *The Papers of Woodrow Wilson,* ed. Arthur S. Link et al., 69 vols. (Princeton: Princeton University Press, 1966–1994), 6:463 (hereafter *PWW*).

2. WW to Ellen Axson, Feb. 24, 1885, *PWW,* 4:287; Inaugural Address, March 4, 1913, 27:151.

3. Edward Hallett Carr, *The Twenty Years' Crisis, 1919–1939: An Introduction to the Study of International Relations* (London: Macmillan, 1939), is seminal in this regard. Early but persistently influential examples from the post–World War II period are George F. Kennan, *American Diplomacy* (Chicago: University of Chicago Press, 1951); Robert E. Osgood, *Ideals and Self-Interest in America's Foreign Policy: The Great Transformation of the Twentieth Century* (Chicago: University of Chicago Press, 1953); and Roland N. Stromberg, *Collective Security and American Foreign Policy: From the League of Nations to NATO* (New York: Praeger, 1963). For rebuttals of the realist tradition's critique of Wilson, see Thomas J. Knock, "Kennan vs. Wilson," in John Milton Cooper Jr. and Charles E. Neu, eds., *The Wilson Era: Essays in Honor of Arthur S. Link* (Arlington Heights, Ill.: Harlan Davidson,

1991), 302–26, and more recently, Steven J. Bucklin, *Realism and American Foreign Policy: Wilsonians and the Kennan-Morgenthau Thesis* (Westport, Conn.: Praeger, 2001).

4. Arthur S. Link, *The Higher Realism of Woodrow Wilson* (Nashville: Vanderbilt University Press, 1971), 130.

5. Here I use the term "historicist" in the teleological sense coined by Karl Popper rather than the sense typically used by American intellectual historians, which, oppositely, implies appreciation of the contingency of experience. See Karl R. Popper, *The Poverty of Historicism* (London: Routledge and Kegan Paul, 1961) and James T. Kloppenberg, "Objectivity and Historicism: A Century of American Historical Writing," *American Historical Review,* 94 (Oct. 1989), 1011–30.

6. Lloyd E. Ambrosius is the most important historian of recent decades to criticize Wilson's foreign policy from a realist perspective: see especially *Wilsonian Statecraft: Theory and Practice of Liberal Internationalism during World War I* (Wilmington, Del.: SR Books, 1991). Critics of Wilson's racism and chauvinism at home and abroad abound. Important examples include Stephen Skowronek, "The Reassociation of Ideas and Purposes: Racism, Liberalism, and the American Political Tradition," *American Political Science Review,* 100 (Aug. 2006), 385–401; David Steigerwald, *Wilsonian Idealism in America* (Ithaca: Cornell University Press, 1994); Mark T. Gilderhus, "Revolution, War, and Expansion: Woodrow Wilson in Latin America," in John Milton Cooper Jr., ed., *Reconsidering Woodrow Wilson: Progressivism, Internationalism, War, and Peace* (Washington, D.C., and Baltimore: Woodrow Wilson Center Press/Johns Hopkins University Press, 2008), 165–88; and Lloyd E. Ambrosius, "Democracy, Peace, and World Order," in Cooper Jr., ed., *Reconsidering Woodrow Wilson,* 225–52. A measured but critical assessment of Wilson's domestic and international records in the context of the "racial nationalism" dominant in his day is Gary Gerstle, "Race and Nation in the Thought and Politics of Woodrow Wilson," ibid., 93–123.

7. In recent years scholars have begun to reconstruct a more complex, historically contextualized Wilson, through painstaking analysis of his papers and those of his circle and through original research into the larger cultural contexts he inhabited. See especially the new (and now standard) biography by John Milton Cooper Jr., *Woodrow Wilson: A Biography* (New York: Alfred A. Knopf, 2009); Erez Manela, *The Wilsonian Moment: Self-Determination and the International Origins of Anticolonial Nationalism* (New York: Oxford University Press, 2007); Thomas J. Knock, *To End All Wars: Woodrow Wilson and the Quest for a New World Order* (New York: Oxford University Press, 1992); and Trygve Throntveit, "Related States: Pragmatism, Progressivism, and Internationalism in American Thought and Politics, 1880–1920" (Ph.D. diss., Dept. of History, Harvard University, May 2008).

8. WW to Ellen Louise Axson (hereafter ELA), May 25, 1884, *PWW,* 3:191–92. The most thorough analysis of Joseph Ruggles Wilson's influence on his son is John M. Mulder, *Woodrow Wilson: The Years of Preparation* (Princeton: Princeton University Press, 1978), ch. 1; but see also John Milton Cooper Jr., *The Warrior and the Priest: Woodrow Wilson and Theodore Roosevelt* (Cambridge, Mass.: Belknap Press of Harvard University Press, 1983), 17–19, for Wilson's comparatively liberal outlook.

9. WW to ELA, July 15, 1884, *PWW* 3:248. See also Mulder, *WW: Years of Preparation,* xiii, 7–8, 82–83, 102, on Wilson's penchant for covenanting.

10. Alexander Hamilton, James Madison, and John Jay, *The Federalist, on the New Con-*

*stitution, Written in 1788* (Hallowell, Maine: Masters, Smith, 1852), 147, copy preserved in the Woodrow Wilson Library, Rare Books Reading Room, Library of Congress (hereafter cited as WL LC). The passage above is marked by two vertical pencil lines in the margins; underlined text represents Wilson's own underscoring. Dates inscribed on the inside front cover and other internal markings indicate Wilson first read the book in 1880 while a law student at the University of Virginia.

11. WW, *Constitutional Government in the United States* (New York: Columbia University Press, 1908), 2, 169.

12. On Wilson's earliest thinking along these lines, see Cooper, *Wilson,* 28, 30–32.

13. WW, *Congressional Government: A Study in American Politics,* 15th ed. (Boston: Houghton, Mifflin, [1885] 1901), 9, 11, 280–81, 331–32. It should be noted that although Wilson did not criticize the *Federalist* essays directly, he thought an absolutist attitude toward separation of powers had exerted a powerful influence on the Constitutional Convention, in which the authors of the essays participated.

14. For an excellent study of Wilson's lifelong love of oratory, his particular oratorical style and gifts, and the larger context of American oratory in the nineteenth and early twentieth centuries, see Robert A. Kraig, *Woodrow Wilson and the Lost World of the Oratorical Statesman* (College Station: Texas A&M University Press, 2004).

15. For Wilson's early formulations of the ideas summarized above, see especially WW, "Cabinet Government in the United States" (1879), *PWW,* 1:493–510, published in *The International Review,* 6 (Aug. 1879), 146–63, by then-editor and future Wilson nemesis Henry Cabot Lodge.

16. WW, "Cabinet Government," *PWW,* 1:495; WW, *Congressional Government,* 46, and chs. 2, 5.

17. WW, *Congressional Government,* 284. Oddly, Wilson did not explicitly suggest the remedy of cabinet government in his book, despite having again proposed that rather drastic measure in an article published in *Overland Monthly,* "Committee or Cabinet Government?" in January 1884—the same month he began writing *Congressional Government.* The article is reprinted in *PWW,* 2:614–40; for Wilson's embarkation upon his dissertation, see his letter to ELA, Jan. 1, 1884, 2:641.

18. WW, *Congressional Government,* 332–33. For discussions of the response to *Congressional Government* and its merits as a work of political science, see Arthur S. Link, *Wilson: The Road to the White House* (Princeton: Princeton University Press, 1947), 12–19; Henry W. Bragdon, *Woodrow Wilson: The Academic Years* (Cambridge, Mass.: Belknap Press of Harvard University Press, 1967), 124–40; and Cooper, *Warrior and the Priest,* 49–51.

19. "His book has inspired my whole study of our government," Wilson wrote Ellen on Jan. 1, 1884 (*PWW,* 2:641). This debt preceded Wilson's studies at Johns Hopkins. He first read *The English Constitution* in 1878 and listed it as evidence of preparation "to be examined upon the machinery of the English Government" in his application for postgraduate work at the university, dated Sept. 19, 1883 (2:430).

20. A notable exception is Knock, *To End All Wars,* chs. 1–2. Although he does not discuss Ely's influence, Martin J. Sklar emphasizes the socialistic strains in Wilson's thinking in *The Corporate Reconstruction of American Capitalism, 1890–1916: The Market, the Law, and Politics* (New York: Cambridge University Press, 1988), ch. 6.

21. WW, "Socialism and Democracy," ca. Aug. 22, 1887, *PWW*, 5:559–62 (for the timing of the essay's composition, see the editorial note following its transcription in 5:563); Wilson, *The State: Elements of Historical and Practical Politics* (1889; Boston: D. C. Heath, 1909), 631–32. For a comprehensive picture of Ely's political thought and reform activities, see Richard T. Ely, *Ground under Our Feet: An Autobiography* (New York: Macmillan, 1938). On the origins of the "Wisconsin Idea," see J. David Hoeveler Jr., "The University and the Social Gospel: The Intellectual Origins of the 'Wisconsin Idea,'" *Wisconsin Magazine of History*, 59 (Summer 1976), 282–98; and John Milton Cooper Jr., "Why Wisconsin? The Badger State in the Progressive Era," *Wisconsin Magazine of History*, 87 (Spring 2004), 14–25. On Ely's nonrevolutionary socialism and its place in the broad context of American and European reformism, see James T. Kloppenberg, *Uncertain Victory: Social Democracy and Progressivism in European and American Thought, 1870–1920* (New York: Oxford University Press, 1986).

22. For Wilson's early turn away from Ricardian economics, see his draft contribution to Ely's unpublished project on *The History of Political Economy in the United States*, reproduced at ca. May 25, 1885 in *PWW*, 4:631–63.

23. WW, *The State*, 574–76. The study of continental, and especially German, political thought and institutions were more important to Wilson's thinking than often recognized by scholars. A brief and useful study is Robert D. Miewald, "The Origins of Wilson's Thought: The German Tradition and the Organic State," in Jack Rabin and James S. Bowman, eds., *Politics and Administration: Woodrow Wilson and American Public Administration* (New York: Dekker, 1984), 17–30. Wilson was also still under the sway of British evolutionary/organicist thought of various stripes; in *The State* he listed Bagehot, Darwin, Huxley, Maine, and Spencer, among others, as sources (610–11).

24. The best account of James's and Dewey's early work in psychology and its role in the development of philosophical pragmatism is Kloppenberg, *Uncertain Victory*, Part I.

25. WW, "Note on the Democratic State," ca. Aug. 1, 1888, *PWW*, 5:758.

26. WW, "The Modern Democratic State," ca. Dec. 1-Dec. 20, 1885, *PWW*, 5:90–92; the reference to the citizen of the modern democratic state as a "*thinking member* of the body politic" is from WW, "Memoranda for 'The Modern Democratic State,'" c. Dec. 1-Dec. 20, 1885, 5:60.

27. WW, "Modern Democratic State," *PWW*, 5:90–91.

28. WW, "The Study of Administration," *Political Science Quarterly*, 2 (July 1887), 197–222, in *PWW*, 5:359–80, esp. 371–72, 376, 379.

29. WW, "The Functions of Government," ca. Feb. 17, 1888, quoted in Cooper, *Wilson*, 60.

30. Particularly vehement in arguing for the fundamental conservatism of Wilson's political science is Vincent Ostrom, *The Intellectual Crisis in American Public Administration* (University: University of Alabama Press, 1974). Ostrom claims that Wilson's "theory of administration was no less than a counter-revolutionary doctrine" (133). For a more nuanced, but still overstated argument for Wilson's alleged concern to enhance state power at the expense of popular political participation, see Niels Aage Thorsen, *The Political Thought of Woodrow Wilson, 1875–1910* (Princeton: Princeton University Press, 1988), esp. 218, 233. For Wilson's interest in Burke's thoughts on law as an agent of rational change, see

his detailed lecture notes for July 2–10, 1894, *PWW,* 8:597–99; and his notes for lectures on public law from ca. Sept. 22, 1894-Jan. 20, 1895, 9:5–106.

31. WW, "Edmund Burke: The Man and His Times," ca. Aug. 31, 1893, *PWW,* 8:333, 342: see also WW, *The State,* esp. 614–15.

32. WW, *Leaders of Men,* ed. T. H. Vail Motter (Princeton: Princeton University Press, 1952), 23–24, 41–45.

33. Marked by Wilson in Edmund Burke, *The Works of the Right Honorable Edmund Burke,* 12 vols., 7th ed. (Boston: Little, Brown, 1881), 1:525–26, WL LC.

34. Ibid., 1:527, 530.

35. For a similar perspective on Wilson's reading of Burke in the early 1890s, including a more detailed reconstruction than can be provided here, see the long editorial note in *PWW,* 8:313–18.

36. WW, *Leaders of Men,* 45.

37. Ibid., 28–29; WW, "Burke: The Man and His Times," *PWW,* 8:340.

38. WW, news release of a speech on Thomas Jefferson, April 13, 1906, *PWW,* 16:362; speech of Feb. 12, 1909, 19:41. In Wilson's copy of *Democracy in America* the following is marked: "When the members of a community are forced to attend to public affairs, they are necessarily drawn from the circle of their own interests, and snatched at times from self-observation. As soon as a man begins to treat of public affairs in public, he begins to perceive that he is not so independent of his fellow-men as he had at first imagined, and that, in order to obtain their support, he must often lend them his co-operation." Alexis de Tocqueville, *Democracy in America,* trans. Henry Reeve, 2 vols. (London: Longmans, Green, 1875), 2:94, WL LC.

39. WW, "The Modern Democratic State" (1885), *PWW,* 5:65–66.

40. WW news release, *PWW,* 16:360–61, 362 (emphasis mine); address on Thomas Jefferson, April 16, 1906, 16:366–67.

41. See Wilson's inaugural address, "Princeton for the Nation's Service," Oct. 25, 1902, *PWW,* 14:170–85, for an encapsulation of his vision for the university; for the "prime minister" reference, see WW to ELA, July 19, 1902, 14:27. Bragdon's *Woodrow Wilson: The Academic Years,* 269–384, was long the standard account of Wilson's Princeton presidency, but his characterizations of Wilson as generally intransigent and philosophically antimodernist are overdrawn and bizarre, respectively. A more balanced evaluation of Wilson's reforms and leadership is Cooper, *Wilson,* chs. 4–5.

42. Cooper, *Wilson,* ch. 5; James Axtell, "The Bad Dream: Woodrow Wilson on Princeton—After Princeton," *Princeton University Library Chronicle,* 69:3 (Spring 2008), 401–36.

43. A detailed account of the events described in this paragraph is Link, *Road to the White House,* 97–106.

44. See the selection from William O. Inglis, "Helping to Make a President," in David W. Hirst, ed., *Woodrow Wilson, Reform Governor: A Documentary Narrative* (Princeton: Van Norstrand University Press, 1965), 7–9. Inglis was hired by Harvey to publicize Wilson's candidacy; his account appeared during Wilson's second presidential campaign in three issues of *Collier's Weekly* in Oct. 1916. For Wilson's impressions, which corroborate Inglis's

account, see his letters to David B. Jones and Edward W. Sheldon on June 27 and July 11, 1910, *PWW,* 20:543–45, 572–73.

45. On Wilson's falling out with Harvey see Cooper, *Woodrow Wilson,* 148–49, and the more detailed account in Link, *Road to the White House,* 360–69, who also explains Wilson's assertion of independence from and ultimate break with Smith (esp. 188, 209–12, 218–37). In his early work Link also argued that Wilson was an opportunistic progressive; see *Road to the White House* and *Woodrow Wilson and the Progressive Era* (New York: Harper, 1954).

46. WW, *Constitutional Government,* 23.

47. A News Report of a Religious Address in Trenton, April 17, 1905, *PWW,* 16:63–64. Compare Wilson's notes for a "Chapel Talk," Jan. 13, 1895, 9:121, which the editors of Wilson's papers have determined were the same as Wilson used in 1905, yet contain none of the "Jamesian" features of the later address. James's "Will to Believe" was first published in the *New World,* 5 (June 1896), 327–47. On Princeton's Sesquicentennial Celebration, see the newspaper reports of the event reprinted in *PWW,* 10:9–11; regarding James's honorary degree, see 14:95, editorial note 3. There is also an extensive collection of archival materials relating to the event in the Seeley G. Mudd Manuscript Library at Princeton University. Along with "The Will to Believe," Wilson could very well have read James's *The Varieties of Religious Experience* (1902) before 1905. Another recipient of a sesquicentennial honorary degree, Edward Dowden, mentioned James's book to Wilson in a letter congratulating him on acceding to the presidency of Princeton. "Today I have another link with Princeton—for the book I have had for hours in my hand—Professor James's Gifford Lectures, reminds me of the conferring of Degrees at the celebration." He added, "A most interesting book it is." See Edward Dowden to WW, Dec. 16, 1902, *PWW,* 14:295.

48. On Dewey, Addams, and other early-twentieth-century proponents of pragmatist politics, see Jonathan M. Hansen, *The Lost Promise of Patriotism: Debating American Identity, 1890–1920* (Chicago: University of Chicago Press, 2003).

49. WW, *Constitutional Government,* 4, 57.

50. Ibid., 170, 178.

51. Ibid. 54, 59, 68, 106.

52. WW to Edgar Williamson, Aug. 23, 1910, *PWW,* 21:59–61; WW acceptance speech, Sept. 15, 1910, 21:91–94, esp. 91–92.

53. Wilson's governorship is succinctly surveyed and assessed in Cooper, *Woodrow Wilson,* ch. 6; see also Hirst, *Reform Governor*; and Link, *Road to the White House,* chs. 7–9.

54. WW, "To the Voters of America," Oct. 19, 1912, *PWW,* 25:434. Still useful for appreciating the development and thrust of Wilson's thinking during the 1912 campaign is Woodrow Wilson, *The New Freedom: A Call for the Emancipation of the Generous Energies of a People,* ed. William Bayard Hale (New York: Doubleday, Page, 1913). A brief but detailed intellectual history of Wilson's campaign is Trygve Throntveit, " 'Common Counsel': Woodrow Wilson's Pragmatic Progressivism," in Cooper, ed., *Reconsidering Woodrow Wilson,* 25–56, esp. 38–43.

55. WW, *New Freedom,* ed. Hale, 34. Detailed accounts of Wilson's major New Freedom initiatives—the Underwood-Simmons Tariff Act of 1913, the Clayton Antitrust Act of 1913, the Federal Reserve Act of 1913, and the Federal Trade Commission Act of 1914—are found

in Arthur S. Link, *Wilson: The New Freedom* (Princeton: Princeton University Press, 1956), chs. 6–7, 13. An excellent summary and analysis is W. Elliot Brownlee, "Wilson's Reform of Economic Structure: Progressive Liberalism and the Corporation," in Cooper, ed., *Reconsidering Woodrow Wilson,* 57–89.

56. WW, *New Freedom,* ed. Hale, 166.

57. As Martin Sklar points out, Wilson also renounced his party's opposition to the Supreme Court's "Rule of Reason" decisions of 1911, affirming not only the necessity of elastic policy but also the general principle of judicial review as a check on potentially bad or outdated laws. Sklar, *Corporate Reconstruction,* 418.

58. Link, *Road to the White House,* 249.

59. Cooper has persuasively argued this point in several places, e.g., Cooper, *Warrior and the Priest,* 239–43; Cooper, *Wilson,* 204–12, 396–97. Albert Sidney Burleson, Wilson's postmaster general, considered Wilson "a wonderful executive," whose virtue lay in his ability to be "prompt in his decisions, always sure of himself, always definite," combined with "his refusal, once a general policy was clearly understood, to interfere with the details. He made sure of his man and then trusted him." Quoted in Ray Stannard Baker, interview with Albert Sidney Burleson, ca. March 17–19, 1927, Ray Stannard Baker Papers, Library of Congress (hereafter Baker Papers), reel 72, microfilm edition.

60. WW, inaugural address, Jan. 17, 1911, *PWW,* 21:346; Link, *Road to the White House,* 252–54. For a contemporary assessment of the move's impact, see the account of Assemblyman Burton J. Hendrick, "Woodrow Wilson: Political Leader," *McClure's Magazine,* Dec. 1911, 230.

61. *Washington Post,* April 9, 1913, 1; WW, address to a joint session of Congress, April 8, 1913, *PWW,* 27:269–70.

62. This was not universally true. In the wake of an August 1919 meeting between anti-League senators and Wilson, as the League fight was heating up, Albert Fall of New Mexico praised Wilson for being "frank and open and manly in his treatment of the Senators." In the cabinet, too, Wilson's leadership style was admired by some: Navy Secretary Josephus Daniels, for instance, described Wilson as "the moderator" in cabinet meetings, who guided discussion but was interested in distilling the general "sense" of the cabinet on a given issue. Albert S. Burleson insisted it was "a mistake to say that Wilson did not take counsel. He took counsel with many men"; nevertheless, "when Wilson made up his mind, it was Wilson's mind that was made up." Fall quoted in *Congressional Record,* 66th Cong., 1st sess. (Aug. 20, 1919), 4027; Josephus Daniels, *The Wilson Era: Years of Peace, 1910–1917* (Chapel Hill: University of North Carolina Press, 1944), 136–37; Burleson quoted in interview with Baker, ca. March 17–19, 1927, Baker Papers, reel 72.

63. WW to Georgia senator Thomas W. Hardwick, March 15, 1915, *PWW,* 32:375–76.

64. See Throntveit, " 'Common Counsel,' " in Cooper, ed., *Reconsidering Woodrow Wilson,* 40–41; contrast Cooper, *Warrior and the Priest,* 194–95, and Kendrick A. Clements, *Woodrow Wilson: World Statesman,* rev. ed. (Chicago: I. R. Dee, 1999 [1987]), 81–82, 85. On Brandeis's life and thought, see the magisterial biography by Melvin I. Urofsky, *Louis D. Brandeis: A Life* (New York: Pantheon, 2009); for an interpretation particularly emphasizing Brandeis's experimentalism, see Philippa Strum, *Brandeis: Beyond Progressivism* (Lawrence: University Press of Kansas, 1993). An excellent short review and analysis of Brandeis's

reform activities and legacy is David W. Levy, "Brandeis, the Reformer," *Brandeis Law Journal,* 45 (Summer 2007), 711–31.

65. Cooper, *Wilson,* 307–33; WW, "Draft of the National Democratic Party Platform of 1916," ca. June 16, 1916, *PWW,* 37:190–201 (Wilson's text on social justice measures was adopted almost verbatim at the national convention in St. Louis). Wilson's role in the suffrage movement is best elucidated in Christine Lunardini and Thomas J. Knock, "Woodrow Wilson and Woman Suffrage: A New Look," *Political Science Quarterly,* 95 (Winter 1980–81), 655–71. A fine overview and analysis of Wilson's changing attitudes toward gender is Victoria Bissell Brown, "Did Woodrow Wilson's Gender Politics Matter?" in Cooper, ed., *Reconsidering Woodrow Wilson,* 125–62.

66. On Wilson's upbringing and early racial views, see Cooper, *Wilson,* ch. 1, esp. 24–25. For Wilson's view of the Civil War and its importance in modernizing the South and consolidating the nation, see esp. Woodrow Wilson, *Division and Reunion, 1829–1889* (New York: Longmans, Green, 1893), parts 4–5; and *A History of the American People,* 5 vols. (New York: Harper, 1902), 4:chs. 4–5, and 5:ch. 1. A brief, useful analysis of these views is Thorsen, *Political Thought of Woodrow Wilson,* 152–55. A critical analysis emphasizing the racism of Wilson's writings on the Civil War and Reconstruction is Gerstle, "Race and Nation," in Cooper, ed., *Reconsidering Woodrow Wilson,* 102–5. W.E.B. Du Bois, *Black Reconstruction: An Essay Toward a History of the Part Which Black Folk Played in the Attempt to Reconstruct Democracy in America, 1860–1880* (New York: Harcourt, Brace, 1935). Chap. 17 is an early, devastating, and still illuminating critique of the view of Reconstruction, which dominated American scholarship and memory from the 1890s to the 1950s.

67. WW to Joseph P. Tumulty, ca. April 22, 1918, *PWW,* 47:388n2; see also WW to Tumulty, April 28, 1915, 33:86. Neither Thomas W. Dixon—author of *The Clansman* (1905) upon which D. W. Griffith based the movie—nor a guest of the showing interviewed by the *PWW* editors in 1977, recalled Wilson uttering the "lightning" quotation. Indeed, in May 1915 Dixon told Wilson's personal secretary that he had purposely withheld the movie's subject matter from Wilson when requesting the White House showing, describing the film instead as an example of a new art form destined to become "the mightiest engine for moulding [*sic*] public opinion in the history of the world." *PWW,* 32:142n1, 267n1.

68. The move to segregate federal offices was initiated by Postmaster General Albert S. Burleson, with support from Attorney General Thomas W. Gregory. Burleson claimed to have consulted with "prominent negroes" who supported the plan, and he said that he personally wanted "what was best for the negro and best for the [Postal] Service." Wilson neither endorsed nor objected to the plan but declared he had promised "to do [blacks] justice" and did not want positions taken away from them. See Josephus Daniels diary, April 11, 1913, *PWW,* 27:290–91. For Wilson's later defense of federal segregation efforts, see WW to Oswald Garrison Villard, Aug. 29, 1913, 28:245–46; and William G. McAdoo to Villard, Sept. 18, 1913, 28:453–55. A comparatively recent interpretation presenting Wilson as philosophically committed to segregation is Gerstle, "Race and Nation," in Cooper, ed., *Reconsidering Woodrow Wilson,* 108–10, esp. 109. More detailed treatments include Kathleen L. Woglemuth, "Woodrow Wilson and Federal Segregation," *Journal of Negro History,* 48 (April 1959), 158–73; Morton Sosna, "The South in the Saddle: Racial Politics during the Wilson Years," *Wisconsin Magazine of History,* 54 (Autumn 1970), 30–49; and Kenneth

O'Reilly, "The Jim Crow Policies of Woodrow Wilson," *Journal of Blacks in Higher Education*, 17 (Autumn 1997), 117–19.

69. WW, proclamation, July 2, 1915, *PWW*, 33:464 (the exhibition was being planned by the Negro Historical and Industrial Association); WW, public statement, July 26, 1918, 49:97–98; WW to R. H. Windsor, Aug. 30, 1918, 49:391. On segregation in the armed forces during World War I, see William Jordan, " 'The Damnable Dilemma': African-American Accommodation and Protests during World War I," *Journal of American History*, 81 (March 1995), 1562–83; and Jonathan Rosenberg, "For Democracy, not Hypocrisy: World War and Race Relations in the United States, 1914–1919," *International History Review*, 21 (Sept. 1999), 592–625.

70. WW to George Creel, June 18, 1918, *PWW*, 48:346. For other expressions of Wilson's pity for victimized blacks, on the one hand, and contentment to wait for an "opportunity" to act against injustice, on the other, see WW to Joseph P. Tumulty, Aug. 1, 1917, 43:343; and WW to Robert R. Moton, June 18, 1918, 48:346 (quoted).

71. For Wilson's turn-of-the-twentieth-century imperialism, see Throntveit, "Related States," 101–7; and Thorsen, *Political Thought of Woodrow Wilson*, 163–65, 174–81.

72. See esp. WW, "The Ideals of America," *Atlantic Monthly*, 90 (Dec. 1902), 721–34, in *PWW*, 12:208–27. On Wilson and Turner, see Thorsen, *Political Thought of Woodrow Wilson*, 146–53.

73. WW quoted in Burton J. Hendrick, *The Life and Letters of Walter Hines Page*, 3 vols. (Garden City, N.Y.: Doubleday, Page, 1924–26), 1:204. For Wilson's chauvinistic remarks about "new immigrant" communities in the Gilded Age, see WW, *History of the American People*, 5:212. On Wilson's early policy in Latin America, see Lars Schoultz, *Beneath the United States: A History of U.S. Policy toward Latin America* (Cambridge, Mass.: Harvard University Press, 1998), ch. 12.

74. WW to Edith Bolling Galt, Aug. 18, 1915, *PWW*, 34:242.

75. WW to Lindley M. Garrison, Aug. 8, 1914, *PWW*, 30:362. The standard English-language treatment of Wilson's 1914 intervention is Robert E. Quirk, *An Affair of Honor: Woodrow Wilson and the Occupation of Veracruz* (Lexington: University of Kentucky Press, 1962). On the effect of the incident on Wilson's thinking and policy, see Kendrick R. Clements, "Woodrow Wilson's Mexican Policy, 1913–15," *Diplomatic History*, 4 (Spring 1980), 113–36; Lloyd C. Gardner, "Woodrow Wilson and the Mexican Revolution," in Arthur S. Link, ed., *Woodrow Wilson and a Revolutionary World, 1913–1921* (Chapel Hill: University of North Carolina Press, 1984), 3–48; Cooper, *Warrior and the Priest*, 268–71; Cooper, *Wilson*, 242–47; and Knock, *To End All Wars*, 27–28.

76. Major accounts of the Dominican and Haitian interventions include Bruce J. Calder, *The Impact of Intervention: The Dominican Republic during the U.S. Occupation of 1916–1924* (Austin: University of Texas Press, 1984); Frederick S. Calhoun, *Uses of Force and Wilsonian Foreign Policy* (Kent, Ohio: Kent State University Press, 1993), ch. 4; and Brenda Gayle Plummer, *Haiti and the United States: The Psychological Moment* (Athens: University of Georgia Press, 1992).

77. For the development of Wilson's Pan-American plans, presented to the governments of Argentina, Brazil, and Chile on Feb. 1, 1915, see Edward M. House diary, Dec. 16, 1914, *PWW*, 31:470; Wilson's draft of a Pan-American Treaty, Dec. 16, 1914, 31:471–72, 473n1; and

WW to William Jennings Bryan, Jan. 28, 1915, and Jan. 29, 1915 (with enclosure), 32:146, 159–60. For interpretations of Wilson's Pan-American plans that stress its internationalist thrust, see Throntveit, "Related States," 254–61; and Knock, *To End All Wars*, 39–44. Contrast the alternative interpretations, presenting the administration's Pan-Americanism in a more economic-imperialist light, offered in Mark T. Gilderhus, "Pan-American Initiatives: The Wilson Presidency and 'Regional Integration,' 1914–17," *Diplomatic History*, 4 (Oct. 1980), 409–24; and Mark T. Gilderhus, *Pan-American Visions: Woodrow Wilson in the Western Hemisphere, 1913*-1921 (Tucson: University of Arizona Press, 1986).

78. Throntveit, "Related States," chs. 4–7, is the only full treatment of the pragmatist progressives' influence on Wilson's thought and policy. For Wilson's reading of *The New Republic* (hereafter *NR*), see Ray Stannard Baker to Walter Lippmann, Oct. 25, 1928, Baker Papers, reel 79. For the *NR*'s stance on neutrality, see "Hypocritical Neutrality," *NR*, May 13, 1916, 28–29; "Timid Neutrality," Nov. 7, 1914, 7–8; and "An Appeal to the President," April 22, 1916, 303–305, esp. 304 ("violator and his victim"). On preparedness, see esp. "Preparedness—A Trojan Horse," *NR*, Nov. 6, 1915, 6–7.

79. "Security for Neutrals," *NR*, Jan. 2, 1915, 7–8; "A League of Peace," March 20, 1915, 168 (quoted).

80. Walter Lippmann, "Appeal to the President" (supra note 74), 303–5, copy in WL LC, reel 513, microfilm edition. Though unsigned, Lippmann was undoubtedly the primary author of this last piece. He had laid out its argument in a personal letter two months before its publication. See Lippmann to Graham Wallas, Feb. 21, 1916, Walter Lippmann Papers, Sterling Memorial Library, Yale University, reel 32, microfilm edition (hereafter Lippmann Papers). On p. 304 of his copy, Wilson made two dark vertical lines in the margin next to the passage cited, his typical marker of interest and approval. (After Wilson's graduate-school years written marginalia disappear almost entirely from his preserved reading material.)

81. Lippmann to Wallas, April 21, 1916, Lippmann Papers, reel 32; WW, in colloquy with antipreparedness leaders, May 8, 1916, *PWW* 36:641–46, esp. 645; WW, address to the League to Enforce Peace, May 27, 1916, 37:113–16. Lippmann later recalled drafting the memorandum upon which Wilson based his address, but this cannot be verified. See "The Reminiscences of Walter Lippmann," Columbia University Oral History Collection, pt. 2, no. 118, pp. 89–90 (recorded April 4, 1950).

82. WW to Croly, Jan. 25 1917, *PWW*, 41:13. Scholars have questioned the degree to which the ideas, as opposed to the mere language, of Wilson's speech were inspired by his reading of *The New Republic*, but the evidence of the journal's influence on his thinking is substantial. See Throntveit, "Related States," 418n102, 422n110.

83. WW, address to the Senate, Jan. 22, 1917, *PWW*, 40:533–39, esp. 536; address to a joint session of Congress, April 2, 1917, 41:525.

84. Wilson's Fourteen Points address is printed at Jan. 8, 1918, *PWW*, 5:534–39. Wilson's articulation of his adaptive vision of the League is quoted in a memorandum by peace delegate Isaiah Bowman, printed at Dec. 10, 1918, *PWW*, 53:354. For an account of Lippmann's role in the intellectual origins of the Fourteen Points and analysis of the final address's pragmatic internationalism, see Throntveit, "Related States," 491–505.

85. Throntveit, "Related States," 526–30. The peacemaking efforts and other activities

that distracted Wilson from his duty to educate the public are thoroughly recounted in John Milton Cooper Jr., *Breaking the Heart of the World: Woodrow Wilson and the Fight for the League of Nations* (New York: Cambridge University Press, 2001), chs. 1–3.

86. An accessible, masterful overview of these dark realms of the home front is David M. Kennedy, *Over Here: The First World War and American Society,* 25th Anniversary Edition (New York: Oxford University Press, 2004), chs. 1, 5. A detailed account and analysis of postwar repression and hysteria is Ann Hagedorn, *Savage Peace: Hope and Fear in America, 1919* (New York: Simon and Schuster, 2007).

87. Knock, *To End All Wars,* ch. 9; Throntveit, "Related States," 530–35, 548–60; Cooper, *Breaking the Heart of the World,* ch. 8.

88. Cooper, *Breaking the Heart of the World,* 423; see 414–23 for a careful analysis of the scholarship on Wilson's psychology and physical health, and the role of each in the outcome of the League fight.

89. WW, "On the Writing of History," June 17, 1895, *PWW,* 9:293–305, esp. 295, 301, 302, 305. See also WW, "The Unity and Variety of History," Sept. 20, 1904, 15:472–91, esp. 487: "I daresay . . . synthesis in our studies must come by means of literary art and conceiving imagination. . . . Not the inventing imagination, but the conceiving imagination. . . . [T]he historian must be in thought and comprehension the contemporary of the men and affairs he writes of. He must also, it is true, be something more: if he would have the full power to interpret, he must have . . . perspective, the knowledge of subsequent events which will furnish him with multiplied standards of judgment. . . . But he will be but a poor interpreter if he have alien sympathies, the temperament of one age when writing of another, [which] may be contrasted with his own in every point of preference and belief."

# Afterword

Stanley N. Katz

My task in writing the afterword to this fascinating volume is to comment briefly on how Woodrow Wilson's educational vision has stood up on his own campus over the course of the century that has passed since his presidency. The task is daunting since, although I teach in the school of public policy named for Wilson and the university uses a version of his most famous phrase as its public slogan, it is not at all clear how Wilsonian my university remains. Take the two specific references that persist. First, the Woodrow Wilson School is surely a unit that President Wilson would not have endorsed, since it violates some of his most deeply held beliefs: that Princeton should focus on undergraduates, that it should have a single faculty, that it should not provide vocational education, that there should be no separate financial endowments within the university, to name only a few contradictions. Second, the transformation of his phrase "Princeton in the Nation's Service" to "Princeton in the Nation's Service and in the Service of All Nations." Wilson did not intend "service" to be the active verb implied in President Harold Shapiro's reformulation of the slogan (as in "social service" or "community service") but he rather referred to the much larger and broader mission of the college in the development of the national ethos. It is tempting to say that we current Princetonians use Wilson's words rather than his ideas. Or, worse, we use Wilson casually and irreverently. The students in my school refer to our eponym as "Woody Woo," and they style themselves "Wooers." The Old Boy is probably not smiling.

As Jim Axtell has noted in his introduction, Princeton's current president, Shirley Tilghman, told our conference attendees that she "particularly admired Wilson's emphases on making Princeton a serious intellectual place, renowned for preprofessional liberal arts and sciences, and 'vertically integrated' from freshman to president, partly through the use of residential campus housing, including four-year colleges or 'quads' envisioned by Wilson." President Tilghman clearly and explicitly sees herself as the inheritor of President Wilson's educational legacy, and she is proud of the extent to which she has helped to sustain that tradition. And so she should be.

But the question I want to ask is: how much of Princeton would Woodrow Wilson recognize should he chance to walk through the FitzRandolph Gate onto the campus today?[1] There are many buildings he would not recognize, of course. But some of the new structures would represent the fulfillment of his most profound dream for the college—six residential colleges, three of them four-year colleges (with another in the plans). The sight of these colleges (the newest and some of the oldest in his beloved Collegiate Gothic style) would surely please him, but I am not so sure he would approve of the extent to which Princeton's campus has been built-out. He would find a tremendous extension of the Engineering School on the west side of Olden Street (on the western edge of the campus) and an ongoing attempt to erect large new buildings on most of the vacant land on the east side. As he walked down campus he would find an arc of large and bulky dormitories on what used to be athletic fields—and the elegant "pagoda" tennis courts were demolished to provide a site for the newest residential college, Whitman, a badly oversized retro Collegiate Gothic structure. As he walked down Washington Road (which bisects the campus), he would be dazzled by the new metal and glass Frank Gehry science library (apparently magically transported from Bilbao) and daunted by a series of imposing natural science laboratories on both sides of the road, with yet another under construction. He would surely be amazed by the plethora of large, elaborate athletic fields and other physical facilities. On the central campus he would encounter Firestone Library, replacing the much smaller library he knew in East Pyne, now transformed into a humanities center.

In short, the former president would be puzzled by the size and complexity of the modern structure that characterizes today's Princeton University. It is not the scale of the architecture that has changed. We do not have massive buildings, but I think that we are creating a rather closed-in feeling. We have lost so many of the great vistas on the campus. The new E-Quad (with the Friend Center and Sherrerd Hall) has closed in a wonderful open space, and the proposed Andlinger Center will be much worse—it is going to take up the entire parking lot that has kept the space behind the main E building open and airy. Bowen Hall was the first recent incursion into that open space, but now the whole area will be covered with buildings. The best long view in the university, in my judgment, was from Washington Road down to the beautiful new stadium, with the great Richard Serra sculpture clearly visible from Washington Road. And now the Gehry science library on the road totally obscures the long view.

Would Woodrow Wilson be pleased? It is hard to say, of course, but let me venture a guess. He was, among other things, an architectural traditionalist, and he (like many of our alumni) would be troubled by the plethora of modern architectural styles now represented on our campus.[2] But I suspect that he would be even more uncomfortable with the extent and density of the present physical university; for one thing, we now have 180 buildings on the 500-acre central campus. Circumstances were very different, but his vision was of a modest-sized, highly controlled environment for education. This is one of the reasons he favored the Quadrangle Plan. All but three of the present residential colleges are cobbled together out of formerly unrelated dormitory buildings; they are colleges rather than "quads." As one walks through the residential quadrant of the campus it is not really clear which structures are colleges and which simply dormitories. I think he would also be deeply disappointed to see that Princeton's planners have adopted a "neighborhood" model for the campus. We are now segregating the campus with "big science" on either side of lower Washington Road, with social science to the east and the humanities to the west of Washington. We are also planning an "arts neighborhood" down campus near the commuter railroad station (which will be moved farther from campus to accommodate it). Wilson's watchword for the campus was "organic" integration, and I feel pretty sure that he would feel that our planning has rejected that model in favor of specialization. Architecture is destiny, after all, and Princeton is gradually reorienting its physical self-image to that of a much larger, more standard research university.

To what extent is that what Woodrow Wilson aspired to? Clearly, as many of the essays in this volume make clear, Wilson was one of the leading visionaries of the transformation of the traditional American religious college into a modern university. He was deeply committed to the professionalization of scientific knowledge and to the promotion of teaching and research across the full range of the fields of knowledge. He was committed to the recruitment of faculty on the basis of professional competence and to the maintenance of the most rigorous standards of research and teaching. Wilson would therefore be delighted by the range, expertise, and eminence of the current Princeton faculty, which ranks very high both nationally and internationally. He would love the fact that Princeton is one of the best-known educational "brands" around the world. When you mention "Princeton" in China or South Africa or Germany, people recognize that it is one of the great universities. He would be impressed by the extent to which our faculty produce cutting-edge research and yet continue to take their undergraduate teaching responsibilities seriously. And he would feel justly proud that he had begun the process that has led to such educational success, even though many of our current departments represent fields of knowledge that did not even exist in his day.

Of course Wilson would be completely bemused by our current demography. Other chapters in this book have remarked on the extent to which Woodrow Wilson was completely a figure of his own day with respect to his views on race, religion, and gender. Confronted with a college that was half female and substantially nonwhite, he would surely have been dismayed. He would have been completely flummoxed by the sight of undergraduate women in *hijab* striding across Cannon Green. Wilson could hardly have anticipated that a college catering to well-to-do white, Protestant young men primarily from the Middle Atlantic States and the South has been transformed into an infinitely more inclusive college as to gender, class, religion, and even nationality. He would, of course, be even more surprised by the sheer number of people on the campus. We now have some 5,200 undergraduate students (an increase of 500 fairly recently), nearly 2,500 graduate students, and 1,200 (including part-time and visiting) faculty members. In addition, the university employs 5,700 staff members to do everything from mowing the grass to managing our finances. It is now a substantial and growing educational operation whose scale (and $1.3 billion annual budget) is steadily overshadowing the much more modest, nuanced, and controlled university that Wilson set out to create.

He would also be troubled by the fact that our desire to be a more broad-based and internationally competitive research university has created a new emphasis on the training of graduate and postdoctoral students. Princeton, consistent with our scientific building spree over the past decade, seems increasingly a science-dominated institution. This trend is in contrast to Princeton's pride in its adherence to Wilson's vision of selective, self-denying excellence and small scale, which was manifest even as recently as 1978, when I joined the faculty. I am in Wilson's camp on this point, but I fear that we are both on the losing side of the history of higher education. But Princeton still retains many of the virtues it inherited from our great President—emphasis on supervised student research, faculty involvement with undergraduates, the Honor Code, and much more. Where Wilson's spirit has especially won out, however, is in our unwillingness to provide for professional education—with the minor exception of the professional public-policy school named for him, a small school of architecture, and a multipurpose engineering school. Wilson would also surely be pleased that our university is still fundamentally a college surrounded by doctoral programs, all of them anchored in the arts and sciences.

I would be particularly interested to know what Wilson would think of how Princeton is governed, though here I have to be cautious. My original impression was that Wilson had a very strong conception of academic leadership, as exemplified by his attitude toward the quad plan and his stance toward the graduate school. Wilson was a leader with few doubts and considerable confidence in his own judgment. But, as Jim Axtell has pointed out in his history of the university, President Wilson was adept in working out his curricular reform program *with* the faculty, displaying little of the high-handedness that characterized his behavior at the end of his life. As a current faculty member, I have to say that I would welcome more of this form of Wilsonianism, since shared governance regarding the larger issues is now little more than a slogan at Princeton. We do not have anything remotely resembling a faculty senate, and reform is typically suggested to us rather than emerging through a process of faculty deliberation. This works at Princeton, I think, because our top administrators all come from the faculty, and the university follows through on Wilson's strategy of treating the faculty well in exchange for their deference to his policy judgment.

But it may well be that what would please Woodrow Wilson most if he could return to the college would be our continued adherence to the spirit and often substance of his curricular and pedagogical ideas. Princeton has retained his commitment to a broad liberal arts education based upon rigorous faculty pursuit of advanced research. We struggle with notable success to insist that the entire faculty teach undergraduates and that they take their teaching seriously. We maintain a low student-faculty ratio (5 to 1 at the moment), require every senior in the humanities and social sciences to write a substantial thesis, enable most undergraduates to have individual faculty supervision of their research (though increasingly we use lecturers and postdocs), and insist upon high levels of student achievement. In this, I think we have maintained the leadership role among elite universities that Woodrow Wilson sought and achieved.

We also continue to adhere to Wilson's highly structured notion of academic and curricular organization. He was the one who reorganized the faculty along disciplinary departmental lines and empowered their chairmen to exercise considerable authority. We are still organized in the same manner, much more rigorously than our peer institutions. At least in the humanities and social sciences, we still refuse to accord departmental status to interdisciplinary units, such as women's studies and African American studies, even when they are commonly organized as full departments in other universities. This accords with Wilson's notion of the "pure" arts and sciences and is entirely (though completely unconsciously) Wilsonian. I think that most of the curricular emphases that Jim Axtell notes in his chapter still constitute the basis for academic thinking and planning at Princeton. This includes, by the way, Wilson's respect for science as an integral part of the liberal arts, as well as his passionate advocacy of the humanities. What is at issue these days is what I perceive as our "tilt" toward the sciences.

I think we are also fulfilling a version of Woodrow Wilson's commitment to the idea of Princeton "in" and "for" the nation's service. Here national ideas and trends in higher education have moved decisively in Wilson's direction. We are increasingly committed to experiential education (Community-Based Learning Initiative), community service (such as the Pace Center for civic engagement, the Bridge Program for community action in foreign lands between high school and college, the preschool year Urban Action program), international engagement (study abroad, Institute for International and Regional Studies, the Woodrow Wilson School) and other forms of active community, national, and international engagement. In these areas, however, it is fair to say that Wilsonian expansionism comes into conflict with Wilsonian traditionalism. We have done far less than many peer institutions with service learning, for instance, since we adhere to a rigorous (and, I think, overly narrow) notion of what counts as academic "learning." But Wilson himself was not without contradictions.

Many things in the educational surround have changed, of course, making it difficult or impossible to be purely Wilsonian at Princeton. Our current preceptorials are not really the system that Wilson created; they are in all honesty very little different from the small sections of lecture courses offered at peer institutions. Precepts these days are infrequently taught by regular faculty members; more often they are taught by lecturers, postdocs, or graduate students. When I first came to Princeton, for instance, the preceptors in my large lecture course on American legal history were five or six regular History Department assistant, associate, and full professors. Very few faculty precept in colleagues' courses these days. This is a shame, but it is an inevitable consequence of our increasing expectations for faculty research output. There are still only twenty-four hours in a professor's day. Other traditional Wilsonian programs are under tension. We retain his Honor System, largely student run, but my impression is that it is more and more difficult to convince undergraduates that the second half of the honor commitment (not to cheat and *to report others who cheat*) deserves their respect. After all, our students are very different from those a century ago in almost every respect. What is remarkable at Princeton is the extent to which the education with which we provide them has remained pretty consistent.

I confess that I had not given much thought to Woodrow Wilson's educational ideas before attending the conference that preceded this volume. I had in fact read through the early volumes of my colleague Arthur Link's magnificent edition of the Wilson papers, but I had not appreciated the far-reaching (and I would now say breathtaking) innovative quality of his ideas taken in the context of his time. But having read through this collection of essays and having thought about the matter for nearly a year, I have come to recognize not only Wilson's originality and greatness as an educational thinker and leader but also the profound impact he has had on the educational character of "my" Princeton. Much of what I find most admirable in the undergraduate education we provide I now realize can be attributed to President Wilson. For the most part I regret those areas in which we have abandoned his commitments. After a century this is quite remarkable, and I doubt that any other twentieth-century university president has left such an enduring and admirable mark.

NOTES

1. In the first chapter of his *The Making of Princeton University: From Woodrow Wilson to the Present* (Princeton: Princeton University Press, 2006), Jim Axtell asks and answers a similar question. My take updates and differs somewhat from his.

2. See Dale Cotton, *Princeton Modern: Highlights of Campus Architecture from the 1960s to the Present* (Princeton: Princeton University, Office of Communications, 2010).

# Suggested Reading

WOODROW WILSON


Axson, Stockton. *"Brother Woodrow": A Memoir of Woodrow Wilson*, ed. Arthur S. Link. Princeton: Princeton University Press, 1993.

Axtell, James. "The Bad Dream: Woodrow Wilson on Princeton—After Princeton," *Princeton University Library Chronicle*, 69:3 (Spring 2008), 400–36.

———. *The Making of Princeton University: From Woodrow Wilson to the Present.* Princeton: Princeton University Press, 2006.

Baker, Ray Stannard. *Woodrow Wilson: Life and Letters.* 8 vols. Garden City, N.Y.: Doubleday, Page, 1927.

Bragdon, Henry Wilkinson. *Woodrow Wilson: The Academic Years.* Cambridge, Mass.: Belknap Press of Harvard University Press, 1967.

Bundy, McGeorge. *An Atmosphere to Breathe: Woodrow Wilson and the Life of the American University College.* New York: Woodrow Wilson Foundation, 1959; also in *Education in the Nation's Service*, intro. August Heckscher. New York: Frederick A. Praeger, 1960.

Carroll, James Robert. *The Real Woodrow Wilson: An Interview with Arthur S. Link, Editor of the Wilson Papers.* Bennington, Vt.: Images from the Past, 2001.

Cooper, John Milton, Jr. "Woodrow Wilson: The Academic Man," *Virginia Quarterly Review*, 58:1 (Winter 1982), 38–53.

———. *The Warrior and the Priest: Woodrow Wilson and Theodore Roosevelt.* Cambridge, Mass.: Belknap Press of Harvard University Press, 1983.

———, ed. *Reconsidering Woodrow Wilson: Progressivism, Internationalism, War, and Peace.* Washington, D.C.: Woodrow Wilson Center Press and Baltimore: Johns Hopkins University Press, 2008.

———. *Woodrow Wilson: A Biography.* New York: Alfred A. Knopf, 2009.

Craig, Hardin. *Woodrow Wilson at Princeton.* Norman: University of Oklahoma Press, 1960.

Daniels, Winthrop M. *Recollections of Woodrow Wilson.* New Haven: Privately printed, 1944.

Dodds, Harold W. "Woodrow Wilson's Impact on Higher Education in the United States." In *Woodrow Wilson in Retrospect*, ed. Raymond F. Pisney. Verona, Va.: McClure Press, 1978.

Elliott, Margaret Axson. *My Aunt Louisa and Woodrow Wilson.* Chapel Hill: University of North Carolina Press, 1944.

Frankie, Richard J. "Woodrow Wilson: Blueprint for Radical Change," *Journal of Education* [Boston University], 153:2 (December 1970), 16–25.

Frye, Roland Mushat. "Woodrow Wilson and the Nurture of Mind," *Emory University Quarterly,* 11:4 (December 1955), 208–20.

Garraty, John A. "The Training of Woodrow Wilson," *American Heritage,* 7:5 (August 1956), 24–27, 94.

Heckscher, August. *Woodrow Wilson.* New York: Charles Scribner's Sons, 1991.

Kraig, Robert Alexander. *Woodrow Wilson and the Lost World of the Oratorical Statesman.* College Station: Texas A&M University Press, 2004.

Lewis, McMillan. *Woodrow Wilson of Princeton.* Narberth, Pa.: Livingston Publishing, 1952.

Link, Arthur S. *Wilson: The Road to the White House.* Princeton: Princeton University Press, 1947.

——— et al., eds. *The Papers of Woodrow Wilson.* 69 vols. Princeton: Princeton University Press, 1966–94.

———. "Woodrow Wilson," *Princeton History,* 7 (1988), 11–29.

Maynard, W. Barksdale. *Woodrow Wilson: Princeton to the Presidency.* New Haven: Yale University Press, 2008.

McAdoo, Eleanor Wilson. *The Woodrow Wilsons.* New York: Macmillan, 1937.

———, ed. *The Priceless Gift: The Love Letters of Woodrow Wilson and Ellen Axson Wilson.* New York: McGraw-Hill, 1962.

McCleery, William. *Wit and Wisdom of Woodrow Wilson, Teacher. Selections by William McCleery from "The Papers of Woodrow Wilson."* Princeton: Princeton University Office of Communications and Publications, 1996.

Medina, Harold R. "The Influence of Woodrow Wilson on the Princeton Undergraduate, 1902–1910," *Princeton Alumni Weekly,* June 1, 1956, 3–8.

Mulder, John M. *Woodrow Wilson: The Years of Preparation.* Princeton: Princeton University Press, 1978.

Mulder, John M., Ernest M. White, and Ethel S. White. *Woodrow Wilson: A Bibliography.* Westport, Conn.: Greenwood Press, 1997.

Myers, William Starr, ed. *Woodrow Wilson: Some Princeton Memories.* Princeton: Princeton University Press, 1946.

Osborn, George C. *Woodrow Wilson: The Early Years.* Baton Rouge: Louisiana State University Press, 1968.

Osgood, Charles Grosvenor. "Woodrow Wilson [1856–1924]." In *The Lives of Eighteen from Princeton,* ed. Willard Thorp. Princeton: Princeton University Press, 1946.

Pisney, Raymond F., ed. *Woodrow Wilson in Retrospect.* Verona, Va.: McClure Press, 1978.

Reid, Edith Gittings. *Woodrow Wilson: The Caricature, the Myth, and the Man.* New York: Oxford University Press, 1934.

Saunders, Frances Wright. *Ellen Axson Wilson: First Lady between Two Worlds.* Chapel Hill: University of North Carolina Press, 1985.

Taggart, Robert J. "Woodrow Wilson and Curriculum Reform," *New Jersey History,* 93:3–4 (Autumn–Winter 1975), 99–114.

Thorsen, Niels Aage. *The Political Thought of Woodrow Wilson, 1875–1910*. Princeton: Princeton University Press, 1988.
Veysey, Laurence R. "The Academic Mind of Woodrow Wilson," *Mississippi Valley Historical Review*, 49:4 (March 1963), 613–34.
Weinstein, Edwin A. *Woodrow Wilson: A Medical and Psychological Biography*. Princeton: Princeton University Press, 1981.
Wertenbaker, Thomas Jefferson. "Woodrow Wilson—Educational Leader," in *Lectures and Seminar at the University of Chicago, January 30–February 3, 1956, in Celebration of the Centennial of Woodrow Wilson, 1856–1956*. Chicago: University of Chicago in cooperation with the Woodrow Wilson Foundation, 1956.
———. "Woodrow Wilson and His Program at Princeton" [1956]. In *Woodrow Wilson in Retrospect*, ed. Raymond F. Pisney. Verona, Va.: McClure Press, 1978.
White, William Allen. *Woodrow Wilson: The Man, His Times, and His Task*. Boston: Houghton Mifflin, 1924.
Wilson, Edmund. "Woodrow Wilson at Princeton" [1927], in *The Shores of Light: A Literary Chronicle of the Twenties and Thirties*. New York: Farrar, Straus and Young, 1952.
Ziolkowski, Theodore J. "Princeton in *Whose* Service?" *Princeton Alumni Weekly*, January 23, 1991, 10–16.

PRINCETON

Axtell, James. *The Making of Princeton University: From Woodrow Wilson to the Present*. Princeton: Princeton University Press, 2006.
———. "The Dilettante Dean and the Origins of the Princeton Graduate School," *Princeton University Library Chronicle*, 62:2 (Winter 2001), 239–61.
———. "The Making of the Princeton University Library, 1873–2003," *Princeton University Library Chronicle*, 64:3 (Spring 2003), 504–56.
Breese, Gerald. *Princeton University Land, 1752–1984*. Princeton: Trustees of Princeton University, 1986.
Brown, J. Douglas. *The Liberal University: An Institutional Analysis*. New York: McGraw-Hill, 1969.
———. "The American Liberal University," *Princeton Alumni Weekly*, May 6, 1955, 8–9.
Collins, Varnum Lansing. *Princeton*. American College and University Series. New York: Oxford University Press, 1914.
———. *Princeton: Past and Present*. Princeton: Princeton University Press, 1931.
Condit, Kenneth W. *History of the Engineering School of Princeton University, 1875–1955*. Princeton: Princeton University Press, 1962.
Cotton, Dale. *Princeton Modern: Highlights of Campus Architecture from the 1960s to the Present*. Princeton: Princeton University Office of Communications, 2010.
*Daily Princetonian*. *The Orange & Black in Black & White: A Century of Princeton through the Eyes of the "Daily Princetonian."* Princeton: Daily Princetonian Publishing, 1992.
Egbert, Donald Drew. *Princeton Portraits*. Princeton: Princeton University Press, 1947.
Evans, William K. *Princeton: A Picture Postcard History of Princeton and Princeton University*. Lanham, Md.: Taylor Trade Publishing, 2009.
Fosdick, Raymond B. *Chronicle of a Generation: An Autobiography*. New York: Harper & Brothers, 1958.

Gambee, Richard. *Princeton Impressions.* New York: W. W. Norton, 2011.

Gellman, Barton, and Beth English. *In the Nation's Service: Seventy-Five Years at the Woodrow Wilson School.* Princeton: Woodrow Wilson School of Public and International Affairs, 2005.

Grafton, Anthony. "The Precept System: Myth and Reality of a Princeton Institution," *Princeton University Library Chronicle,* 64:3 (Spring 2003), 467–503.

Greiff, Constance M., Mary W. Gibbons, and Elizabeth G. C. Menzies. *Princeton Architecture: A Pictorial History of Town and Campus.* Princeton: Princeton University Press, 1967.

Hoeveler, J. David, Jr. *James McCosh and the Scottish Intellectual Tradition: From Glasgow to Princeton.* Princeton: Princeton University Press, 1981.

Karabel, Jerome. *The Chosen: The Hidden History of Admission and Exclusion at Harvard, Yale, and Princeton.* Boston: Houghton Mifflin, 2005.

Kemeny, P. C. *Princeton in the Nation's Service: Religious Ideals and Educational Practice, 1868–1928.* New York: Oxford University Press, 1998.

Lane, Wheaton J. *Pictorial History of Princeton.* Princeton: Princeton University Press, 1947.

Leitch, Alexander. *A Princeton Companion.* Princeton: Princeton University Press, 1978.

Leslie, W. Bruce. *Gentlemen and Scholars: College and Community in the "Age of the University," 1865–1917.* University Park: Penn State University Press, 1992; New Brunswick, N.J.: Transaction Books, 2005.

Looney, J. Jefferson. *Nurseries of Letters and Republicanism: A Brief History of the American Whig-Cliosophic Society and Its Predecessors, 1765–1941.* Princeton: American Whig-Cliosophic Society, 1996.

McCleery, William. *Conversations on the Character of Princeton.* Princeton: Princeton University Office of Communications and Publications, 1987.

Merritt, J. I., ed. *The Best of PAW: 100 Years of the "Princeton Alumni Magazine."* Princeton: Princeton Alumni Weekly, 2000.

Murrin, John M. "Rise of Domination: Princeton, the Big Three, and the Rise of Intercollegiate Athletics," *Princeton University Library Chronicle,* 62:2 (Winter 2001), 161–206.

Norris, Edwin M. *The Story of Princeton.* Boston: Little, Brown, 1917.

Oberdorfer, Don. *Princeton University: The First 250 Years.* Princeton: Trustees of Princeton University, 1995. (Pictorial history).

Osgood, Charles G. *Lights in Nassau Hall: A Book of Bicentennial Princeton.* Princeton: Princeton University Press, 1951.

Perry, Bliss. *And Gladly Teach: Reminiscences.* Boston and New York: Houghton Mifflin, 1935.

Princeton Tiger. *Roaring at One Hundred: The "Princeton Tiger Magazine" Centennial Album.* Princeton: Princeton Tiger, 1983.

*Princeton University Press, 1905–2005: Whitney Darrow, "The Founding of Princeton University Press" (1951), Herbert S. Bailey Jr., "A Brief History of Princeton University Press" (1981), Walter H. Lippincott, "Reflections on the Occasion of the Centenary" (2005).* Princeton: Princeton University Press, 2005.

Rhinehart, Raymond P. *Princeton University.* Campus Guide Series. New York: Princeton Architectural Press, 1999.

Rolston, Brown. "'The Good Old Days': Student Life and Customs in the Wilson Era," *Princeton Alumni Weekly,* January 15, 1960, 6–9.

Savage, Henry Lyttleton. *Nassau Hall, 1756–1956.* Princeton: Princeton University Press, 1956.

Schmitt, Judy Piper, ed. *The "Prince" Remembers: One Hundred Years of the "Daily Princetonian"* [1876–1976]. Princeton: Daily Princetonian Publishing, 1976.

Scott, William Berryman. *Some Memories of a Palaeontologist.* Princeton: Princeton University Press, 1939.

Selden, William K. *Woodrow Wilson School of Public and International Affairs, Princeton University: Conception and Early Development, 1930–1943.* Princeton: Woodrow Wilson School of Public and International Affairs, 1984.

———. *Nassau Hall: Princeton University's National Historic Landmark.* Princeton: Princeton University Office of Printing and Mailing, 1995; Canton, Mass.: Next Generation Press, 2006.

———. *Club Life at Princeton: An Historical Account of the Eating Clubs at Princeton University.* Princeton: Princeton Prospect Foundation, 1996.

———. *Prospect House at Princeton University: A National Historic Landmark.* Princeton: Princeton University Office of Printing and Mailing Services, 1999.

Slosson, Edwin E. *Great American Universities.* New York: Macmillan, 1910.

Smith, Richard D. *Princeton.* Images of America. Dover, NH: Arcadia Publishing, 1997. (Historical photographs).

———. *Princeton University.* The Campus History Series. Charleston, S.C.: Arcadia Publishing, 2005. (Historical photographs).

Synnott, Marcia Graham. *The Half-Opened Door: Discrimination and Admissions at Harvard, Yale, and Princeton, 1900–1970.* Westport, Conn.: Greenwood Press, 1979.

Tenner, Edward. "The Honor Code through Wilson's Spectacles," *Princeton University Library Chronicle,* 64:3 (Spring 2003), 425–44.

Thorp, Willard, ed. *The Lives of Eighteen from Princeton.* Princeton: Princeton University Press, 1946.

———Thorp, Willard, Minor Myers Jr., Jeremiah Stanton Finch, and James Axtell. *The Princeton Graduate School: A History,* ed. Patricia H. Marks. Princeton: Association of Princeton Graduate Alumni, 2000.

Van Zandt, Helen, with Jan Lilly. *The Princeton University Campus: A Guide.* Princeton: Princeton University Press, 1964, 1970.

Wertenbaker, Thomas Jefferson. *Princeton, 1746–1896.* Princeton: Princeton University Press, 1946.

West, Andrew Fleming. *Short Papers on American Liberal Education.* New York: Charles Scribner's Sons, 1907.

Williams, John Rogers. *The Handbook of Princeton.* With an Introduction by Woodrow Wilson. New York: Grafton Press, 1905.

Wilson, Edmund. *A Prelude: Landscapes, Characters, and Conversations from the Earlier Years of My Life.* New York: Farrar, Straus and Giroux, 1967.

# Contributors

JAMES AXTELL is Kenan Professor of Humanities Emeritus at the College of William & Mary. A graduate of Yale and Cambridge universities and a member of the American Academy of Arts and Sciences, he is the author or editor of seventeen books, including *The Making of Princeton University: From Woodrow Wilson to the Present* (2006) and *The Pleasures of Academe: A Celebration & Defense of Higher Education* (1998). He is now writing "The University in History: Paris to Princeton" for Princeton University Press.

VICTORIA BISSELL BROWN is L. F. Parker Professor of History at Grinnell College. Educated at the University of Wisconsin and UC–San Diego, she is an expert in women's history and especially on Jane Addams, whose autobiography, *Twenty Years at Hull-House,* she edited (1999) and whose life she probed in *The Education of Jane Addams* (2004). She also participated in the 2001 television production of "Woodrow Wilson" (*The American Experience*) and in the 2006 conference on "Wilson at 150" at the Woodrow Wilson Center in Washington.

JOHN MILTON COOPER JR. is E. Gordon Fox Professor of American Institutions Emeritus at the University of Wisconsin. He graduated from Princeton and Columbia Universities. He is the leading authority on the life of Woodrow Wilson, having published books on Wilson's fight for the League of Nations and on a comparison of Wilson and Theodore Roosevelt. He also edited *Reconsidering Woodrow Wilson: Progressivism, Internationalism, War, and Peace* (2008). His magnum opus, *Woodrow Wilson: A Biography,* was published in 2009.

STANLEY N. KATZ is Director of the Center for Arts and Cultural Policy Research at the Woodrow Wilson School at Princeton. After earning a B.A., M.A., and Ph.D. from Harvard, he taught at Harvard and the universities of Wisconsin, Chicago, and Pennsylvania before serving as president of the American Council of Learned Societies (1986–97). He is the author or editor of numerous books and articles and is a former staff blogger for the *Chronicle of Higher Education.*

W. BRUCE LESLIE is Professor of History at SUNY–Brockport. A graduate of Princeton and Johns Hopkins universities, he is the author of *Gentlemen and Scholars: College and Community in the "Age of the University," 1865–1917* (1992) and coauthor of *State University of New York at Brockport,* an illustrated history of SUNY–Brockport (2006). In 2010 he coedited *SUNY at Sixty: The Promise of the State University of New York.* He and a colleague at Brunel University, London, are writing a book comparing British and American higher education.

ADAM R. NELSON, a graduate of St. Olaf College and Brown University, is Professor of Educational Policy Studies and History at the University of Wisconsin. He is the prizewinning author of *The Elusive Ideal: Equal Educational Opportunity and the Federal Role in Boston's Public Schools, 1950–1985* (2005) and of *Education and Democracy: The Meaning of Alexander Meiklejohn, 1872–1964* (2001). He is at work on a book entitled "Nationalism, Internationalism, and the Origins of the American University."

MARK R. NEMEC, a graduate of Yale and the University of Michigan, taught at Davidson College before becoming Managing Director at Forrester Research in Cambridge, Massachusetts. He is the author of *Ivory Towers and Nationalist Minds: Universities, Leadership, and the Development of the American State* (2006).

JOHN R. THELIN is University Research Professor in the College of Education at the University of Kentucky. After graduating from Brown University and UC–Berkeley, he taught at the College of William & Mary and Indiana University. He is the author of innumerable articles and six books, including *Games Colleges Play: Scandal and Reform in Intercollegiate Athletics* (1994) and *A History of American Higher Education* (2004). He is writing a book on philanthropy and higher education.

TRYGVE THRONTVEIT, a three-degree graduate of Harvard University, is Lecturer and Assistant Director of Undergraduate Studies in History there. His paper for the "Wilson at 150" conference, " 'Common Counsel': Woodrow Wilson's Pragmatic Progressivism, 1885–1913," was published in *Reconsidering Woodrow Wilson,* edited by John Milton Cooper Jr. (2008).

# Index